Drama and Community

———

MEDIEVAL TEXTS AND CULTURES OF NORTHERN EUROPE

1

MEDIEVAL TEXTS AND CULTURES OF NORTHERN EUROPE

EDITORIAL BOARD UNDER THE AUSPICES OF THE

CENTRE FOR MEDIEVAL STUDIES
UNIVERSITY OF HULL

Wendy Scase, Chair (University of Birmingham)

Andrew Ayton (University of Hull)
David Bagchi (University of Hull)
Elaine C. Block (City University of New York)
Janet Coleman (London School of Economics)
Alan Deighton (University of Hull)
Olle Ferm (University of Stockholm)
Valerie Flint (University of Hull)
Barbara Hanawalt (Ohio State University)
Wim Hüsken (University of Auckland)
Brian J. Levy (University of Hull)
Henry Mayr-Harting (University of Oxford)
Bridget Morris (University of Hull)
Veronica O'Mara (University of Hull)
Istvan Petrovics (Jozsef Attila University, Szeged)
Oliver Pickering (University of Leeds)
Graham Runnalls (University of Edinburgh)
Brigitte Schluderman (University of Hull)
Helmut Tervooren (Gerhard Mercator University, Duisberg)
Kenneth Varty (University of Glasgow)
David Wallace (University of Pennsylvania)

EDITORIAL ASSISTANT
Glen Innes

Drama and Community:

People and Plays in Medieval Europe

Edited by

Alan Hindley

MEDIEVAL TEXTS AND CULTURES OF NORTHERN EUROPE

1

© 1999, Brepols Publishers n.v., Turnhout, Belgium

All rights reserved.
No part of this publication may be reproduced, stored in a retrieval system or transmitted, in any form or by any means, electronic, mechanical, photocopying, recording or otherwise, without the prior permission of the publisher.

D/1999/0095/46
ISBN 2-503-50767-0
Printed in the E.U. on acid-free paper

Contents

Acknowledgments

Introduction i
ALAN HINDLEY

European communities and medieval drama 1
LYNETTE MUIR

Drama and community in late medieval Paris 18
GRAHAM A. RUNNALLS

Community versus subject in late medieval
French confraternity drama and ritual 34
ROBERT L.A. CLARK

Community drama and community politics in
thirteenth-century Arras: Adam de la Halle's *Jeu de la Feuillée* 57
FREDERICK W. LANGLEY

Acting companies in late medieval France:
Triboulet and his troupe 78
ALAN HINDLEY

Processional theatre and the rituals of social unity in Lille 99
ALAN E. KNIGHT

Cornelis Everaert and the community of late medieval Bruges 110
WIM HÜSKEN

A tale of two cities:
drama and the community in the Low Countries 126
ELSA STRIETMAN

Drama and community in South Tyrol 148
JOHN TAILBY

Individual and social affiliation in the
Nuremberg Shrovetide Plays 161
KONRAD SCHOELL

Contents

Performing medieval Irish communities   179
    ALAN J. FLETCHER

Contemporary cultural models for the trial plays
in the York Cycle   200
    PAMELA M. KING

Festive drama and community politics
in late medieval Coventry   217
    CHRIS HUMPHREY

Prompting in full view of the audience:
a medieval staging convention   231
    PHILIP BUTTERWORTH

English community drama in crisis: 1535-80   248
    ALEXANDRA F. JOHNSTON

York Guilds' Mystery Plays 1998:
the rebuilding of dramatic community   270

Contributors   290

Acknowledgments

It has been a great honour to take responsibility for this, the first publication in the new series of *Medieval Texts and Cultures of Northern Europe*, published by Brepols in partnership with the Hull Centre for Medieval Studies. In its preparation I have incurred the debt of a number of people, not least the contributors themselves, whose prompt responses to editorial requests and deadlines have greatly facilitated my task. Particular thanks are due to the Faculty of Arts Research Executive and the Centre for Medieval Studies of the University of Hull for financial assistance in the preparation of this book during the academic session 1998/9. I am also indebted to Mr Glen Innes of The University of Hull Press for his help with the preparation of the text for publication, and to Dr Simon Forde, of Brepols Publishers, for his advice at all stages of the venture. I should like to record my gratitude to Dr Wendy Scase, Director of the Hull Centre for Medieval Studies, for her support and encouragement. To my colleague Dr Brian Levy go special thanks for his characteristically unstinting and good-natured help in putting together the volume at a difficult time.

ALAN HINDLEY

August 1999

York Guilds' Mystery Plays 1998. The Butchers' 'Death of Christ' at station five, played by actors from Howdenshire Live Arts. (Reproduced by courtesy of the York and County Press).

Introduction

ALAN HINDLEY

THIS VOLUME OF ESSAYS arose out of a Research Day on 'European Drama in the Middle Ages' held in April 1997 at the Graduate Research Institute in the University of Hull as one of a series of events designed to celebrate the newly-established Hull Centre for Medieval Studies. In all, seven papers were delivered at the colloquium: three on 'Narrative and Drama', and four on 'Drama and Community in the Middle Ages'. It was subsequently decided that the second of these two themes might provide an appropriate title in the new series of 'Medieval Texts and Cultures of Northern Europe', with the papers given by Wim Hüsken, Frederick Langley, Graham Runnalls and Lynette Muir forming the core chapters. To these have been added twelve further studies around the same theme, contributed by invited international scholars, all of them reflecting, in the spirit of this new series of publications, an aspect of the central theme as it relates to a variety of performance cultures across northern Europe. This is not to say that the contributors were required to adopt a precise 'party line'; rather their chapters are reflections on the chosen subject undertaken independently, the aim being to produce a set of variations on a theme rather than any convergence in the conclusions reached.

This variety is perhaps firstly reflected in the wide geographical range of the drama examined, from Ireland's performing communities at Europe's westernmost edge, via England, France, the Low Countries and Germany, to the South Tyrol, with a brief detour to the Spanish village of Trevelez in the Sierra Nevada. If England and France take pride of place this is because the number of available texts and the scholarly interest in them has in recent years tended to relate predominantly to these two cultures.[1] Yet other parts of medieval

---

[1] See Eckehard Simon (ed.), *The Theatre of Medieval Europe: New Research in Early Drama* (Cambridge: Cambridge University Press, 1991), p. xiv.

Europe bear witness to a variety of mimetic activities, many of them essential to the expression of community. Secondly, since the end of the Middle Ages by no means everywhere denoted the end of medieval drama, the contributions also cover a wide chronological span, though with an inevitable emphasis on the urban communities in which much of late medieval drama was nurtured. Earlier periods are certainly not neglected, however, as the studies of Clark, Fletcher and Langley show. Nor are discussions of evidence from the later sixteenth century, when the high days of community drama were beginning to wane, threatened by the increasing appeal of neo-classical aesthetics, by markets driven more by entertainment than celebration, and by curbs imposed by authorities at a time of religious upheaval. Many different types of specific dramatic activity are covered here too, from the para-theatricals of late medieval Coventry, a satirical review from thirteenth-century Arras, fourteenth-century confraternity dramas, mystery and miracle plays, French *sotties*, German carnival plays, processional drama, Dutch *esbatementen*, *tafelspelen* and *spelen van sinne*.

What in fact do we mean when we speak of 'community' in a dramatic context? Most obviously, perhaps, we think of what theorists such as Manfred Pfister have termed the 'multimediality' of theatre, i.e., the collective nature of its production, without which functions – author, performers, producer, set-designers etc. – the play could not exist.[2] Very often it is this external 'division of labour' that is particularly highlighted in those records of medieval performance that sometimes seem to detail practically everything about the actual production except the play text itself. However, in the case of medieval drama, perhaps because of its origin in religious celebration, there is a spatially close contact between performers and public which conditioned a style of performance in which the division between action and spectator was less clear-cut than on the later picture-frame stage. Under such circumstances, 'a realist or illusionist type of theatre was neither possible nor intended',[3] a characteristic that is implicit, if not explicit, in most of the studies printed here: Robert Clark, for example, notes the 'holistic importance' of medieval theatre as an event, whilst several other contributions also stress this closeness of performer and spectator, as well as drawing attention to the extensive involvement of the urban community in play performances.

---

[2] Manfred Pfister, *The Theory and Analysis of Drama*, transl. by John Halliday (Cambridge: Cambridge University Press, 1988), p. 11.

[3] Pfister, op cit., p. 12.

INTRODUCTION

Following Lynette Muir's introductory essay, the studies in this collection trace the theme of drama and community across different national and linguistic frontiers, beginning with five chapters (Runnalls, Clark, Langley, Knight, Hindley) on theatre in French, with its inevitable concentration on areas that we now know as north-eastern France and Belgium. These are followed by two pairs of papers, first on the Low Countries (Hüsken, Strietman), and then on aspects of drama in German (Tailby, Schoell). A chapter on dramatic communities in medieval Ireland (Fletcher) leads to a group of four on English medieval theatre (King, Humphrey, Butterworth, Johnston), the last of which serves as an appropriate conclusion, given its examination of the decline of community celebration in England after the 1530s. A Postface (Oakshott) brings us back to the twentieth century, with its account of the York 'Mystery Plays 98' to remind us that medieval drama can still prosper, and that there are still communities dedicated to its production and peformance.

Lynette Muir provides a valuable starting-point by presenting a pan-European perspective on play-performing groups and communities, focusing not just on players and audiences, but also on what she terms the 'originators', or leaders, of those communities who put on plays: the Italian *Disciplinati*, for instance, or the Dutch Chambers of Rhetoric with their elaborate competitions; *confréries* and trade guilds; the various processional plays, often held at Corpus Christi; the unique guild performances of late medieval York, or their French equivalents for which writers and directors were sometimes hired to attract paying audiences from far afield. As Muir happily puts it, much of late medieval society, and especially the urban third estate, was 'strongly clubbable', with communities of all kinds characterized mostly by unpaid amateurs financed by patronage, and 'founded to celebrate or to mourn, to play and to compete'. As surviving records show, economic considerations are increasingly crucial, and once profit-margins become a key consideration (as in the Valenciennes *Passion* of 1547) then it can reasonably be said that commercialism has taken over and that the days of true community drama are numbered.

Graham Runnalls's overview of some of the manifestations of the religious theatre in Paris and its interrelation with the city's social history draws attention to two factors that will appear frequently elsewhere in these studies. The first is the combination of play performances with other social activities, as in the case of the fourteenth-century Guild of Goldsmiths, whose small-scale miracle plays were staged indoors as the culmination of what we might term the guild's Annual General Meeting: a community event combining drama, procession, the celebration of Mass, banquet and the election of guild officers. The community value of more lavish productions is also examined here: that of the Paris Bowmen for instance who, in 1540, glorified the city's patron saint by performing a life of Saint Denis; or the even more elaborate *Mystère des Actes des Apôtres* of the following year, the extensive performance details of which remind us that we are dealing not so much with a literary genre as with a mixture of theatrical event, religious experience and commercial venture, the effect being to increase the sense of community of those urban groups that undertook productions, which often brought economic dividends by attracting large crowds over a long period.

The notion of drama's role in fostering community identity is, however, questioned by Robert Clark, who discusses the ritual plays of the late fourteenth-century Paris Goldsmiths' Guild in the light of anthropological models of ritual theory. He considers the plays' formal aspects in order to determine how they work to resolve conflict and create a sense of community. Recognizing the importance of this collective dimension, he also considers the reception of the plays by the subjects who made up their audience, drawing on historical knowledge of late medieval urban society and on theories of subjectivity. Analyzing selected *Miracles de Notre-Dame*, Clark takes up in particular issues of class and gender to establish a model of collective experience of the drama which makes room for conflicts among and within the subjects who watched it. The standard view that medieval drama was efficacious in cementing community identity, as well as the largely unexamined assumptions about the nature of the collective experience and the role of subjectivity, are thus usefully re-examined.

Community politics, and their association with satire in a French context, are the subject of Frederick Langley's re-examination of the social aspects of Adam de la Halle's *Le Jeu de la Feuillée*, performed in Arras in around 1276, and one of the earliest play texts to be studied in this volume. Eschewing the tendency to regard this idiosyncratic work as explicable only in terms of its author's personal situation, Langley reconsiders Adam's concern with the local and topical issues of his day: the contribution of the play to the continuing controversy of the *clercs bigames*, for instance; or the insights it offers into the power-struggles of the local oligarchy. Whilst resisting the extremes of Ungureanu's interpretation, who saw Adam almost as the focus of class revolt, Langley provides a timely reminder that Adam is not too narrowly introspective 'as to fail to turn his sardonic eye on his fellow citizens in order to berate their follies and vices'. True community drama, then, not just in its concern with local issues and

INTRODUCTION

personalities, but also in that several of the characters, not least the playwright himself, were real-life citizens of contemporary Arras.

My own study reviews some of the evidence for the emergence of professional and semi-professional troupes of actors in France at the end of the Middle Ages, not just accounts of the activities of celebrated individual performers such as Jean du Pontallais, but in particular the less familiar evidence provided by a group of *sotties* in the famous *Recueil Trepperel*, an analysis of which allows us some valuable insights into the preoccupations of an emergent professional company of the fifteenth century. From these unusually self-reflexive plays it is possible to glimpse something of the life of a 'micro-community' of French entertainers, with their *chef de troupe* who took the stage-name of Triboulet, as their performances touch on matters of organization, performance technique, stock roles and repertory of plays. The available evidence perhaps suggests that earlier views that professional companies are an exclusively sixteenth-century phenomenon should be treated with some caution.

The collective aspect of community participation is particularly apparent in the drama associated with the 'Grande Procession de Lille'. Alan Knight argues that from the fifteenth century such plays had the effect of uniting the urban community in an elaborate ritual of religious devotion and civic pride, sponsored as they were both by the municipality and the collegiate Church of St. Peter. With medieval cities often agglomerations of groups with conflicting interests, he contends that the plays reinforced the burghers' image of themselves as members of a community. Plays in Lille were often staged by neighbourhood youth groups, usually associated with a particular part of town, and given to organizing public festivities, entertainments and contests, an element of competition that sometimes led to civic disorder. Knight suggests that on the day of the procession, such popular culture took the form of a more orderly dramatic contest, however, when the festival transformed Lille 'from an aggregation of fiercely competing interest groups into a city of single purpose and vision'. A recently found collection of 72 of the Lille plays is currently being edited by Knight, and it would seem that they support his thesis in their treatment of urban community issues and in their presentation of a vision of social harmony.

An interlinking between community and drama can be seen in the activities of the *Rederijkerskamers*, the Chambers of Rhetoric, which dominated theatrical life in the Low Countries at the end of the Middle Ages, and which are the subject of chapters by Wim Hüsken and Elsa Strietman. The former studies one of the earliest Chambers to be established in the trading town of Bruges in the early fifteenth century by focusing on plays by Cornelis Everaert (1480-1556), one of its best known playwrights. The plays examined provide a glimpse of community life in a late medieval city, with themes relating frequently to the community in which Everaert lived, notably in terms of popular devotion, social and political preoccupations, even domestic relationships. In *Mary's Chaplet*, for instance, can be seen something of Roman Catholic unease in pre-Reformation times; whilst there is feeling for the socially deprived in *Unequal Coinage*, banned for its anti-government stance. A more uninhibited carnival atmosphere characterizes such farces as *The Play of the Cousin*, with its perennial theme of the dimwit husband tricked by his scheming wife. With its emphasis on educating the urban population, Everaert's dramatic output reveals extensive community involvement; and the occasional curbs on performances of his plays herald what was to become more common in later years, when authors increasingly faced the antagonism of both civic and religious authorities.

Similar brushes with the powers that be are discussed in Elsa Strietman's examination of the Chambers of Rhetoric in Ypres and Haarlem. In Ypres, as in Lille, religious procession and political commemoration had long been combined with drama in a festival that provided an occasion 'to make merry, to make money, and to make an impression', an annual celebration of social cohesion by a community that prided itself on its political and economic importance. Details of performance organization reveal the extent of all levels of the community in the dramatic activities of Ypres, but unfortunately none of the plays have come down to us. In the northern town of Haarlem, however, plays by Louris Jansz. do engage with a range of issues, though Jansz. seems to have been neither partisan to the Catholic Church nor to any of the new Protestant creeds, but rather to have expressed an Erasmian tolerance coupled with a deep personal faith. In setting Jansz. and his relatively little known plays in their historical context, Strietman shows how the *Retorikers* dramatized contemporary preoccupations, thereby influencing public opinion and provoking debate. Some of Jansz.'s plays also reveal a loosening of links between drama and community, the effects of the Counter-Reformation, with its suppression of the great festivals of the Church, bringing about a fragmentation of the community of believers.

In methodological terms, Tailby's survey of drama in the German-speaking South Tyrol adopts a similar approach to that of Strietman, in that it shows how both archival material and the evidence of surviving play texts can efficiently combine to identify on the macro-level relationships between texts and known dates of performance, and on the micro-level matching individual items of expenditure with the

INTRODUCTION

appropriate textual passages. Much detail is provided on aspects of religious play-productions between 1495 and 1580, performed both indoors and outside, with information about who took the female roles, who played Judas (always a difficult role to fill), which groups and guilds performed the various scenes, the frequency of performances, the painters' expenses for repairs to Satan's mask, including painting in the teeth. The secular plays of the early sixteenth-century Sterzing collection were probably staged by guilds associated with the local mining community, and the texts shed a different kind of light on the relationship between drama and community: they include, for instance, a *Dives and Lazarus* play, with contemporary advice on how widows should be treated following their husband's death.

With Konrad Schoell's study of individual and social affiliation in the Nuremberg *Fastnachtspiele*, we are perhaps on rather more familiar German territory. In fifteenth-century Nuremberg, where political order depended on socio-economic order, wealth certainly counted. Though the patrician classes took no part in the Shrovetide plays, they nevertheless sought to curb their potentially subversive elements. A number of social groupings are depicted in the plays, but there are few representatives of the city oligarchy or the upper classes. Pride of place tends to be given to the peasant: that comic intruder into the urban world, a familiar blend of naïvety and sophistication, his closeness to nature possibly envied by the burghers, for whom he also functioned as a scapegoat. The essential question posed here is whether such character-types can possibly have any individuality. In an analysis of selected plays Schoell suggests that some characters, whilst representing social types, can also achieve a degree of individual characterization in such features as their sometimes moralizing function in the play, their clearly defined personal ideas and desires, or their self-awareness. Perhaps we can see, he argues, in the entertainments of a prosperous community like Nuremberg at the turn of the fifteenth and sixteenth centuries, certain medieval conceptions of rigid social affiliation beginning to give way to the concept of the individual.

A different perspective on our theme is examined in Alan Fletcher's chapter on performing communities in Ireland, which focuses not just on those communities before whom plays were staged, but on those companies of players and performers who put on the plays, sometimes touring them from community to community. Fletcher's intentionally ambiguous title highlights the distinction between the communities that were 'performed' and those groups which did the performing. Three broad ethnic communities are examined: ancient Gaelic, post-

Norman invasion, and Anglo-Irish; each of which was celebrated and 'performed' by the entertainers they hosted, 'performances' that were a public acclamation of the social group's value system; and also the entertainers themselves, 'micro-societies' which toured in search of patronage. Reviewing evidence that is a useful indicator of practice elsewhere in medieval Europe, a glimpse is given of the performance skills of such entertainers as the *druith* and the *cainti*, not to mention those forerunners of the later 'pétomanes', the *braigetoin*, or 'farters'. Following the post-Norman invasion of 1169 it was the elite harpers who actively sought English sponsorship, turning their hand to any community, Gaelic or foreign, but having an allegiance above all to themselves. By the early fifteenth century imported English *harpeurs* and *piperes* came to be organized almost into guilds, their performances a means of articulating the identity of the English settlers in urban Ireland, notably Dublin, where companies of performers sustained the community interests of their patrons.

Sometimes the dramatic treatment of biblical narratives is very precisely located in a specific cultural community, revealing a contemporary mentality that is not just aesthetic, but also social, topical and political. This, in Pamela King's view, is what the so-called 'York realist' does in the trial scenes involving Christ before Annas, Caiaphas, Herod and Pilate. In these scenes, she argues, we see not so much psychological realism as the presentation of social forms – especially those relating to the law – which present the action in terms that were understandable to York's mercantile middle-classes. The universally popular 'courtroom drama' framework allows the depiction of various modes of legal proceedings, especially jury trial practices, that would have had a special resonance for such audiences. There may even have been a more specific link with York's brush with the legal system in the early fifteenth century, when the city supported its Archbishop Richard Scrope in its rebellion against Henry IV. There are certainly procedural details in the scenes that allow the playwright to enrich their potential meaning as historical events, and thus bring to life for the York community the difference between true and false justice.

Community politics in Coventry is the subject of the Chris Humphrey's study, which examines the importance of paratheatrical activity in the context of medieval drama, notably such ceremonies as the processions held at Corpus Christi. Whereas Knight argues that the plays associated with the 'Grande Procession de Lille' had the effect of fostering social unity, Humphrey rejects this 'safety-valve' model, suggesting instead that certain 'transgressive' local customs can be seen as encouraging community precisely by inverting, rather than

INTRODUCTION

idealizing, such norms. Taking the example of the gathering of vegetation from private land in summertime, he proposes a different approach to medieval 'misrule', showing how such a custom became involved in negotiating politics and social status in late medieval Coventry, where it played its part in modifying the balance of power within the urban community.

Philip Butterworth's contribution tackles a rather less obvious aspect of the theme of drama and community, taking as its subject the convention of prompting in full view of the audience – from late medieval France to twentieth-century Spain, by way of sixteenth-century Cornwall – and usefully brings aesthetic and staging considerations into our discussion by showing how the practice might have had its effect on performance conditions and audience communication. Bringing together the familiar evidence from Fouquet and Carew, he compares it with stage-practice in the hitherto little known *Representacion de Moros y Cristianos*, a dramatized battle of Christians and Moors that is performed every June in the village of Trevelez in modern-day Spain. This play's mock battles and mimed dances are directed by a 'maestro' who, having memorized the full text of the play, prompts throughout the performance, cueing the actors with the assistance of three other prompters in such a way that every line of text is given to the players. The description of the performance not only informs our understanding of the standard evidence; it also suggests that this convention, far from being an alien intrusion into the performance, can have a powerful significance in its encouragement of 'a sense of identification and ownership among the audience', uniting actors and audience in a communal experience of a community event in which notions of 'reality' and 'illusion' become largely irrelevant.

Alexandra Johnston's account of the gradual decline of the medieval dramatic tradition in England, from the first Henrican reforms to the suppression of the Coventry plays, provides an appropriate conclusion to our survey. Though religious plays continued to be done in parishes well into the 1570s, they are no longer really community based, but brought to town by travelling companies patronized by Protestant courtiers deliberately 'selling' the Elizabethan Settlement. Drawing on the extensive REED material, Johnston demonstrates how community celebration, a part of every English locality before the Reformation, begins to wane from the late 1530s, as more partisan expressions of religious polemic bring with them serious tensions. Mary's reign saw some renewed activity at parish level, perhaps, but after the Settlement there are many examples of plays promoting the Protestant cause staged under aristocratic patronage. In the 1570s there is a marked increase in named acting troupes staging plays with more classical themes, and little parish biblical drama survives after 1580. The REED evidence allows a more multifaceted picture of how the English Reformation irrevocably changed the character of English communities: before Henry's break with Rome, community celebrations certainly demanded co-operative energy; but after 1535 such activities become more closely associated with the country's Catholic past.

Philip Butterworth's account of a medieval-style entertainment in the Sierra Nevada evokes the excitement of 'community drama' in its more recent sense of a non-professional association of interested amateurs engaged in a community activity.[4] Such a definition might well describe – though doubtless without doing it full justice – the production in the summer of 1998 of eleven of the York mystery plays, each produced and performed for the first time since the sixteenth century by a separate York Guild or group, and presented on pageant-wagons moving in procession through the streets of the city. The plays' artistic director, Jane Oakshott, usefully rounds off this volume by discussing the involvement of York's seven modern-day Guilds in these productions, demonstrating how 'Mystery Plays 98' effectively revealed a real sense of community among both performers and spectators alike.

* * * * *

It will by now be clear that this book is in no way intended to provide anything like a definitive coverage of its subject; indeed given its genesis, this could never have been the case. It is to be hoped, however, that its variety, together with its many overlaps and contradictions, might encourage further investigation into the question of medieval drama and community and related questions. The different approaches adopted by the contributors usefully indicate the preoccupations and practices of modern scholars, offering a representative cross-section of work currently in progress. The question of the community involvement and community reception of medieval plays in both a medieval and modern context also reminds us – if we really needed reminding – that not only is such an understanding important to our appreciation of medieval drama as performance, but it is also a guide to its value as living theatre now, as

---

[4] See G. and P. Kernodle, *Invitation to the Theatre* (New York: Harcourt Brace Jovanovich, 1978), p. 338.

INTRODUCTION

medieval drama 'returned to audiences', to use Glyn Wickham's phrase.[5] If the essential 'theatricality' of medieval drama alerts us to the dangers of a desk-bound reading of the texts, it should not, however, cloud the importance of a re-examination of those texts, together with a re-interpretation of the archival material and historical records that survive their performance, as a number of the studies here have shown. As more of the REED[6] records become available, for example, so is it possible to paint a clearer and yet more nuanced picture of theatrical organization in England at the end of the Middle Ages.

Not least significant, finally, is the comparative perspective of the volume, a feature which should make us wary of the pitfalls of working exclusively within our narrow cultural boundaries. Learning to look over our 'national fences', as Eckehard Simon has recently reminded us,[7] will no doubt reveal interactions and connections between different European dramas that can only heighten our awareness of their important social implications as essentially a mass medium. It is our hope that such an 'esprit communautaire' at work in the present volume will have played its part in enhancing our understanding of at least some of the European communities of medieval drama.

---

[5] Glyn Wickham, 'Introduction: trends in international drama research', in *The Theatre of Medieval Europe*, ed. by Eckehard Simon, pp. 5-6.

[6] *Records of Early English Drama* provides 'the basis for the first accurate picture of the English theatre before 1642'; it is published in Canada by the University of Toronto Press. See the chapter by Alexandra F. Johnston below.

[7] op cit., p. xi.

European communities and medieval drama

LYNETTE MUIR

ALTHOUGH MUCH ATTENTION HAS been paid in recent years to the texts and staging of medieval plays there is still little work on the groups and communities who performed them. In this survey I want to look at some of the communities who produced plays and establish who they were and why they did so. Drama is a group activity, involving as a minimum 'the Player and the Audience. Take these apart and you can have no theatre'.[1] For much medieval drama, the necessary ensemble also includes the originators[2] of the performance, the leaders of the communities who did the plays. In this essay I specially want to look at the national and international variants, from Italian *disciplinati* or Dutch *Rederijkers* to the craft guilds of England and Germany or the French *Basoche*.

Because of the unwieldy nature of this huge body of material I shall ignore the drama of courts and castles, usually performed by a fixed group for a specific audience as part of an aristocratic celebration, so that the theatrical community is fixed and circumscribed.

In liturgical drama, despite changes and developments in the texts, the community of performers was always made up of religious – clergy, monastic or secular, male or female – and the audience was the congregation. A less limited community, involving both clerical and lay persons, is found in the use of drama in connection with preaching by the orders of friars both Franciscan and Dominican. They might be

---

[1] R. Southern, *The Mediaeval Theatre in the Round*, 2nd revised and expanded edn (London: Faber, 1975), p. 21.

[2] This usefully ambivalent word is borrowed from the French term *originateurs* used in the contract of the Valenciennes Passion printed in L. Petit de Julleville, *Histoire du théâtre en France. Les Mystères*, 2 vols (Paris: Hachette, 1880; repr. Slatkine: Geneva, 1969), II, pp. 145-52.

a whole village presenting the Via Crucis as at Perugia in 1448 or merely an ad hoc group from the local towns or villages enacting episodes from the Passion story during a series of Lenten sermons – as at Laval in 1507.[3]

The common element in these religious plays is their purpose: celebration of the feasts of the church, encouragement to devotion and penitence. An occasional relaxation of discipline can be allowed in times of carnival or foolery – as in the ceremonies of the Boy Bishop, or the prose of the ass – for a securely established faith can afford to laugh at itself, though it was quick to clamp down on excesses.

At first, smaller groups dominated the drama, some of them directly linking the laity and the Church, such as the *compagnons* who performed the Resurrection at Cambrai cathedral in 1376 and received 30 *sous pour gratification* (the account is in French, not Latin);[4] or the companions who came by boat from Datchet to St George's, Windsor in 1449 to do a play for the Dean and Canons.[5] The most distinctive development in the early period of joint lay and Church activity, however, is undoubtedly the uniquely Italian vernacular liturgical drama by the *disciplinati* or flagellants, groups of laymen, mostly from the craft guilds, who from the end of the thirteenth century onwards sang *laude* (praises) – vernacular versifications of the gospel of the day – outside the church to which they were attached, during their acts of penance.

From these first lyrical *laude* developed dialogued texts performed with costumes and properties which may truly be called drama.[6] Later, the small groups tended to unite into larger confraternities which staged more substantial plays, or *sacra rapprezentatione*. For nearly a century, between 1460-1550, the best known company in Rome, the *Gonfalonieri di Santa Lucia*, staged a Passion play in the Coliseum on Good Friday which became an integral part of Holy Week for pilgrims in Rome.[7] In Florence. the Medici family, together with the *signoria*,

---

[3] Perugia is translated in *The Staging of Religious Drama in Europe in the Later Middle Ages: Texts and Documents in English Translation*, ed. and trans. by P. Meredith and J. Tailby, EDAM monograph series, 4 (Kalamazoo: Western Michigan University, 1983), p. 248. For Laval, see *Mystères*, II, p. 203.

[4] *Mystères*, II, p. 5.

[5] The Datchet reference is from the Archives of St George's Chapel, Windsor XV.34.44. I am grateful to the archivist, Dr Scarff, for the reference.

[6] The earliest flagellant plays recorded are from the groups in Perugia. In 1426 one of them lent a number of costumes to another group who returned them in less than perfect condition. See *Staging*, pp. 139-40.

[7] See V. de Bartholomaeis, *Origini della poesia drammatica italiana*, Nuova

contributed towards the big-scale performances put on for civic occasions, such as the Ascension and Annunciation plays watched by Abramio of Sousdal during the ecumenical council of 1439.[8]

In several countries, communities were formed devoted to a particular saint whom they honoured by plays based on their patron's life and miracles. The oldest vernacular miracle play extant, the *Jeu de Saint Nicolas* by Jean Bodel of Arras, was composed *c.* 1200 for performance (according to the prologue) on the vigil of the popular saint.[9] The players were probably students, for (among his many other duties) Nicholas is the patron of students, which may also account for the many Latin St Nicolas plays from France and Germany.[10]

In 1290 and 1302, some bourgeois of Limoges performed the miracles of their patron, St Martial, near the cross in the cathedral cemetery.[11] In York a Paternoster guild was founded in 1388-9, to organize and control the performance of their play but although we know the organizers and the purpose we cannot be certain who actually performed the play.[12] The fourteenth-century play MS from the *Bibliothèque de Ste Geneviève* in Paris includes both biblical plays and a series of Miracles of St Genevieve and was almost certainly written for a Confrérie of the patron saint of Paris.[13] When the Confraternity of St Romain in Rouen wanted to perform a play of their patron saint in 1476, the chapter of Notre Dame decided that they could set themselves up in front of the church and in the graveyard but they would be held responsible for any damage done to the buildings or other things belonging to the church.[14] The coopers of Bordeaux

---

biblioteca italiana, 7 (Turin: Società Editrice Internazionale, 1958), pp. 365-73.

[8] For Abramio's descriptions see *Staging*, pp. 243-47.

[9] Jean Bodel, *Le Jeu de Saint Nicolas*, ed. by F.J. Warne (Oxford: Blackwell, 1968), p. 4.

[10] The St Nicholas plays are printed in K. Young. *The Drama of the Medieval Church*, 2 vols (Oxford: Clarendon Press, 1933), II, pp. 324-57. He was also the patron saint of Aberdeen which had a procession in which the burgesses, merchants and craftsmen were expected to take part. See A.J. Mill, *Medieval Plays in Scotland* (Edinburgh and London, 1927; repr. New York: Blom, 1969), p. 140.

[11] *Mystères*, II, p. 2.

[12] The Latin document is printed in REED York, pp. 6-7; the translation is on p. 693.

[13] The complete MS was published by A. Jubinal in *Mystères inédits du quinzième siècle* (Paris: Techener, 1837; repr. Slatkine: Geneva, 1977). For details of modern editions of individual plays see the bibliography in G.A. Runnalls, *Etudes sur les mystères* (Paris: Champion, 1998).

[14] The 'things' included vestments, regalia and tapestries and it was also agreed: 'to give to the brothers to perform the mystery the *Bête de la Gargouille* which was kept

(who are sometimes referred to as being from the parish of St Michael) staged a procession for St John the Baptist's day, with plays done on waggons, which is extremely rare in France.[15]

As the vernacular lay-drama became more independent of the church, during the fourteenth and fifteenth centuries, putting on plays involved more than a community of actors and audience: it needed money. The court and the church had no problems paying for their plays; lay groups and civic authorities sometimes did, with the result that much of the information on the plays is in the form of financial records which, however, are not always as explicit as we might wish, especially where the payments are made by civic authorities to local groups. For example, who are the *scolaribus* and *virginibus civitatis* (later called *bacheliers* and *junkfrouwen* when the accounts go vernacular) who, between 1340 and 1380, are recorded as receiving payments for plays in the account books of the Rhineland town of Deventer? And what sort of plays did they perform? The only clue is the date of the payments, which is usually early in January, suggesting some kind of Christmas or carnival plays.[16]

Two French references to *confréries de Saint-Jacques* are particularly interesting from the financial point of view: in the fonds Saint-Jacques-aux-pelerins among the *Archives de l'Assistance publique* for 1324-5 we learn that £43P were collected by the pilgrims 'qui firent le jeu au jour du siege' (who performed the play on the day of the assembly) and collected the money 'par les tables au diner' (from the tables during dinner).[17] In 1506 in the little village of Velay near Le Puy a confraternity of St Jacques indulged in a very special kind of semi-dramatic activity to raise money for the maintenance of the religious services of the *confrérie*. This was the custom known as the *reinage*. Each person paid so many pounds of wax into the

---

in the church [...] in the care of the master of the fabric'. *Mystères*, II, p. 39.

[15] Ch. Mazouer, *La Vie théâtrale à Bordeaux des origines à nos jours* (Paris: CNRS, 1985), I, p. 30. The same group performed a Passion play for Corpus Christi which is equally rare in France. It is tempting to see in these plays an influence of the English cycles which must have been known to the English merchants, who had occupied the city for so many years.

[16] For the Deventer records see B. Neumann, *Geistliches Schauspiel im Zeugnis der Zeit. Zur Aufführung mitteralterlicher Dramen im deutschen Sprachgebiet* (Munich and Zurich: Artemis, 1987), pp. 271-75.

[17] See R.L.A. Clark, *The "Miracles de Notre Dame par personnages" of the Cangé MS and the sociocultural function of confraternity drama* (UMI: Ann Arbor, 1994), p.136. Clark points out that the members of the guild referred to themselves as *pelerins* so the actors were probably guild members.

common fund to earn the right to represent a character in the Court they were creating: to be King of France cost 7lbs of wax, for the queen, 2½ lb, and so on from the Dauphin down to the Master of the Horse or minor official. Everything was done by contract and with full legal Latin terminology. The game of kings and queens was well known in the Middle Ages but this unusual impersonation of the contemporary French court was carried to an unusual degree of formalized absurdity.[18]

The religious confraternities were sometimes associated with the craft guilds: in the fourteenth century, the Paris goldsmiths celebrated their annual guild meeting with plays based on Miracles of Our Lady. It has generally been held that this meeting was on the feast day of their principal confrérie, that of St Eloy; however, Clark has put forward new evidence to suggest that these plays were actually performed at the meetings of another of the goldsmiths' associations, the Confrérie Notre-Dame-de-1'Annonciation founded in 1353.[19] The French play of St Venice (Veronica) was written for a guild which regularly invoked 'Saint Fiacre et Ste Venise' which Graham Runnalls has identified as the Confrérie des maîtres jardiniers de Paris.[20]

An interesting account of a Passion play in Avignon in 1400 is contained in a letter by a factor of the Italian merchant house of Datini: 'many of the craftsmen [*artieri*] of Avignon at their own expense put on a play on the three days of Whitsun, which was the Passion of Our Lord when he was crucified. (Three months ago they acted a play of the siege of Troy, like the one the duke of Anjou attended)'.[21] The fact that the performers are described as craftsmen but without any guild references suggests some kind of general group, perhaps linked by a religious confraternity such as the Confrérie de la Passion just about to be founded in Paris [1402] or more likely the flagellant groups.[22] A number of religious confraternities staged

---

[18] The contract was printed by Ch. Marty-Laveaux in *Revue des Sociétés Savantes*. Série 6. t.l. Paris, 1875. pp. 557-58.

[19] See Clark, pp. 110-14. St Eloi (Eligius) was the patron of all types of Smiths and between 1518-53 the Hammermen of Perth fitted St Eloi into their Corpus Christi Creation play. See Mill, pp. 271-74.

[20] *Le mystère de Sainte Venice*, ed. by G.A. Runnalls. (Exeter: University of Exeter, 1980), p. XVII.

[21] 'Mystères religieux et profane en Avignon à la fin du XIVe siècle', in G. Cohen, *Etudes d'histoire du théâtre* (Paris: Gallimard, 1956), pp. 164-65. In 1400, Provence was an independent county ruled by the dukes of Anjou. It was not linked to the French crown until 1483 after the death of Roi René, the last duke of Anjou.

[22] Avignon was papal property from 1348 until the Revolution. It contained many

presentations in England: Beverley had a guild of St Elene [Helen] which set forth the Finding of the Cross, and a Guild of St Mary with a Candlemass ceremony.[23] In Lincoln, there were Ascension (and, twice, Assumption) plays in the cathedral on St Anne's day between 1457-69, but in 1483 it was agreed that the *'Ludum sive serimonium'* be played in the St Anne's day procession, organized by the guild of St Anne and the city crafts.[24]

Mons has many records of saints' plays by different groups performed during the late fifteenth and early sixteenth centuries: some *compaignons* performed the *Vie Sainte-Catherine* in the market-place (1487); the Confrères de Saint-Georges and the Confrères Sainte-Barbe (August and September, 1491) and the Confrères de Saint-Jacques (1502) all similarly performed plays of their patron. Each group was given money by the canonesses of St Waudrue who seem to have been indefatigable theatregoers and supporters.[25] The *compaignons* who acted the play of St Catherine received 100s but the *confréries* each received 60s which may suggest the former were not an organized group with financial resources. In 1524-5, when the *Vie Mons. Saint Roch* was staged by the *Vieswariers* [second-hand clothes dealers or fripperers cf. Fr. *fripiers*] the canonesses gave them £4 towards the cost of the stage.[26]

In Artois and French-speaking towns in Flanders, parish and neighbourhood groups, united under a prince or other dignitary, performed small-scale plays. In St-Omer (Artois), these were often on a horsedrawn cart: in 1456, two groups were paid 'for having made many entertainments and delights through plays on carts and waggons [*cars et carios*] [...] for each carting [*carée*] 4s which in this period has amounted to 36 cartings, making £7 4s'.[27] The Lille (Flanders) neighbourhood groups also performed on waggons but mainly in the annual *Procession de Lille* held on the Sunday after Trinity.[28]

---

flagellant groups who might have been involved with the plays.

[23] Lancashire 377.

[24] Lancashire 864-66.

[25] Mons, like the rest of Hainault, was part of the Low Countries, under Burgundian and later Spanish rule. For Rhetoricians' plays in Mons, see below.

[26] £ s d was the usual money of account in western Europe at this period. In France the *livre tournois* (£T) was divided into 20 sous each worth 12 deniers. The rarely used *livre parisis* (£P) was worth 25 sous.

[27] J. de Pas, 'Mystères et jeux scéniques à Saint-Omer aux XVe et XVIe siècles', *Mémoires de la Société des Antiquaires de la Morinie* 31 (1912-13), 343-77.

[28] For the Lille *Grande Procession* see Knight, below. Béthune had a variety of groups and guilds; see p. 8.

In Dutch-speaking Flanders, as elsewhere in the Low Countries, the dramatic community was dominated by the *Rederijkerskamers* (Chambers of Rhetoric). First recorded early in the fifteenth century these Chambers combined two types of societies, a lay devotional confraternity and a literary society similar to the French *puy* which was already flourishing in the thirteenth century as in the *puy d'Arras* (Artois) satirised in the *Jeu de la Feuillée*. The early French *puys* seem to have been primarily concerned with poetry not drama unlike the later French groups of *Rhetoriciens*[29] such as that formed in Amiens, in 1393, under the title of Confrérie du Puy and described by an eighteenth-century historian: 'The members of this confrérie were almost all the rhetoricians of Amiens.[...] On the feast of the Purification [2 February], the confrérie's feast day and [...] the day assigned for the election of the Master for that year, the latter had a great feast at his house and during the dinner the Master had a *mystère* performed and gave a green hat and a copy of the *mystère* to each of those present.'[30]

The Rhetoricians' most distinctive dramatic creation in Dutch was the allegorical *spel van sinnen* (morality play) but members were also involved in religious drama. In French-speaking Hainault, they took part in the Passions at Mons and Valenciennes and in 1530 the *Compaignons de la Rethoricque d'icelle ville* [Mons][31] presented several *jeux*, while in 1537 the Valenciennes *Rhetoriciens* came to Mons to perform the *Capture of Tunis by Emperor Charles V*.[32] When Valenciennes was preparing to perform the Passion in 1547, the start of the play was in fact delayed for two days because the supervisors included the current *Prince de Plaisance* – head of the local Rhetoricians' groups – 'lequel fit son voyaige a Lilles et a Tournay devant notre jeu'.[33]

A form of dramatic activity peculiar to the Low Countries was the organization of big play contests in which different groups or Chambers either within one town or from a number of towns competed for prizes for best play, best decorated waggon and so forth.

---

[29] The term *rhetoriciens* has not survived into modern French.

[30] G.A. Runnalls 'Medieval trade guilds and the *Miracles de Notre Dame*', *Medium Aevum* 39 (1970), 271. It seems probable the *mystères* were acted by members of the group.

[31] The term *puy* does not seem to have been used in the French-speaking Low Countries.

[32] Mons p. xix.

[33] *Mystères*, II, p. 196.

In 1547 the Valenciennes groups held a contest among themselves at which prizes were awarded for the best decorated waggon and 'the best automaton'. The name of the prize winner is given but not, unfortunately, a description of the automaton.[34]

If a group entered for a play contest in another town and was successful, it might be given a donation of money or wine from the town council as in Saint-Omer in 1462: 'To Jehan Descamps, called Wastellet,[...] and others to the number of 24, who, for the honor of this town, have travelled to the town of Aire [...] to act there several plays, both moralities and *sotties*, to win certain prizes which were being given by those of the said town of Aire to the best actors. [...] and acquitted themselves so well that they obtained the principal prize and two others. For this and to help with their expenses in this matter: £12.'[35] These contests were sometimes multi-lingual: in 1498 the *Rhetoriciens* from Mons took part in the *esbattements* [entertainments] at Ghent where the Mons crossbowmen[36] took a prize.

For certain civic occasions a number of groups might combine on a less adversarial level. Royal or ducal entries were regularly celebrated with tableaux put on by various guilds and confraternities. Some idea of the variety of groups in a town in Flanders can be seen from the list of those recompensed by the council of Béthune for taking part in a royal entry into the town in 1483: 8s for two riders on hobby-horses; 12s each for three neighbourhood groups, six craft guilds (including the barbers and butchers), the Cordeliers, the companions of St Bertremieu's Church, the crossbowmen, and the *caritables* of St Nicolas; the *caritables*[37] of St Eloy, however, received 30s.

Royal Entries only involved tableaux and dumb shows; the actual plays for which guilds and confraternities united were mostly annual, processional and linked with a major religious occasion, such as Corpus Christi. In principle, such plays are their own justification, their own *why*? but there is an interesting variation on the *who*?

---

[34] H. D'Oultreman, *Histoire de Valenciennes* (Douai, 1639), p. 395.

[35] The following year they went to Béthune but did not win. Saint-Omer p. 362. Bruges had a Confraternity of the Holy Spirit who organized a contest p. 361.

[36] Mons p. xv. Originally formed as local defence guilds by the fortified towns, the archers or crossbowmen were always important in the dramatic activities of the Low Countries.

[37] The *caritables* of St Eloy still exist in Béthune. They were founded in the twelfth century during the plague to bury the dead (one of the Seven Corporal Acts of Mercy) and flourished throughout the Middle Ages. Today they provide free transport for coffins to the churchyard. The *caritables* of St Nicolas, also mentioned here, were presumably a similar charitable lay-group.

Many processional plays in the Low Countries were Marian, notably those from Leuven, Lille and Brussels. The Lille procession was unusual for it was organized by the Bishop of Fools [*l'evesque des fols*][38] who was elected annually from among the canons of St Peter's Church, whose relics of the Virgin provided the *raison d'être* of the procession. The neighbourhood groups involved were mostly made up of young unmarried men whose popular rites of tree-planting and often rowdy celebrations were thus channelled into a religious procession - with the additional bait of prizes. The Bishop's proclamation of 1463 gives many details: 'We, Prelate [*Prélat*] of Fools, intend to award, with God's help, the prizes listed below to groups formed in one neighbourhood with no outsiders, who come on the day of the procession on large or small waggons, wains, or portable scaffolds to present histories from the Bible, both Old and New Testaments, saints' lives approved by the church, or Roman histories from ancient chronicles, each containing at least 300 lines and at most as you will'. The waggons with tableaux on them decorated the processional route and the plays were performed afterwards.[39]

Brussels had an annual procession, recorded for about a century, of the Seven Joys [*Bliscapen*] of Mary, one play of the cycle being performed each year after the procession. It was organized by the local guild of archers but several different groups were involved including the Chamber of Rhetoric called the Cornflower who staged the Seventh Joy in 1559 and 1566.[40] Other presentations of a mixture of plays and walking groups are the Leuven *Ommegang* and the Bruges Holy Blood procession – both are civic organized. Aberdeen had a craft-guild Candlemas processional cycle.[41]

Löbau in Germany had a Holy Cross Day procession with plays, presented by a wide range of groups: in 1521 they did a full credal cycle from Creation to Judgement. Different groups or individuals are

---

[38] The burgess who presided over the Aberdeen 'haliblude play' was known as the Abbot of Bonaccord, sometimes helped by a 'Prior', (see Mill p. 116). Elsewhere such titles were usually reserved for more frivolous occasions.

[39] Alan E. Knight, 'The Bishop of Fools and His Feasts in Lille', in *Festive Drama*, ed. by Meg Twycross (Cambridge: D.S. Brewer, 1996), pp. 157-66. The recently discovered manuscript containing seventy-two of the Lille plays is being edited by Alan Knight. I am grateful to him for copies of his transcriptions of records and texts.

[40] E. Strietman, 'Drama in the Low Countries', in *Medieval Drama in Europe. Cambridge Guide to World Theatre* (Cambridge: Cambridge University Press, 1988), pp. 644-47.

[41] Mill, p. 116, gives details of the floats.

described in various terms as being responsible for presenting them: the *vorsteher* [heads, leaders] of two neighbourhood groups 'who do not have horses' will set forth [*vor schaffen*] Abraham and Isaac. The *Gardianus* [Guardian: head of the monastery] will organise [*preorinabit*] the Annunciation. While the Mocking and the Flagellation are the responsibility of the cloth-makers *[Denn tuchmachern stehet zu vorsorgenn]*.[42]

There were annual St John's Day processions and plays in Dresden and in Florence. The former is notable for the reference in 1502 to *1gr. vor stecknadel den juncfrauenn in spil* [one *gros* for pins for the young ladies in the play]; the term *jungfrauen* suggests they were actually females, not cross-dressed.[43] The latter, which was staged by the crafts [*Arte*] as well as religious groups, included a number of waggons on which the plays were performed at certain stations.[44]

The best known feast day plays, however, are those for Corpus Christi. The obligatory procession for the feast was established in 1320 by the Synod of Sens and by the fifteenth century plays associated with the religious procession are recorded from most parts of Europe, with the notable exception of France.

The only extant Corpus Christi processional cycle from Italy, that of Bologna, is a combination of waggon plays and marching groups. We do not know who performed it but if we compare the St John's Day processional plays from Florence, we can at least suggest that the Bologna plays were done by the flagellant groups and other religious confraternities.[45]

In Catalonia, by 1350, Vich and Valencia had tableaux and floats, and records of processions of tableaux survive from Barcelona in the fifteenth century. Valencia also had later play-texts and in the records for 1517 the actors included priests and laymen, some of whose crafts are mentioned.[46] In Castile in the fifteenth century, Seville and Toledo both had notable processional plays of a tableaux variety[47] and in the

---

[42] Neumann, pp. 433-36.

[43] Neumann, pp. 282. The players do not seem to belong to any special guilds or groups.

[44] See *Staging*, pp. 240-42. For a detailed study of the Florentine companies and their plays see N. Newbiggin, *Feste d'Oltrarno. Plays in Churches in Fifteenth-Century Florence* (Florence: Olschki, 1996).

[45] A. d'Ancona, *Origini del teatro Italiano* (Turin: Loescher, 1891, 2nd revised edn; repr. Rome: Bardi, 1966), I, p. 297.

[46] See N.D. Shergold, *A History of the Spanish Stage from Medieval Times until the End of the Seventeenth Century* (Oxford: Clarendon Press, 1967), pp. 73-74.

[47] Shergold, p. 91. The Toledo records are printed in C. Torroja Menendez and Pala

sixteenth century numerous Corpus Christi plays were mounted and presented in major Spanish cities by the craft guilds and religious confraternities but under the general organization of the Church who often chose the subjects to be presented. In these *autos sacramentales* a play might be staged on two waggons[48] and it was a feature also of the Spanish plays that they were competitive - prizes for the best play, best decorated waggon etc., were offered each year. By the end of the sixteenth century, the guilds were employing professionals to write and stage the play which they were obliged to provide for the procession. This splitting up of the organizers and the performers heralds the professional takeover of the theatre everywhere.[49]

There are references to Corpus Christi plays performed by local religious confraternities or simple groups of citizens from Draguignan in Provence (which was under the rule of the counts of Barcelona for many years). Unfortunately, though they go back to 1437, the later fifteenth-century records are lost. The surviving references from the mid-sixteenth century suggest a general civic effort with no specific groups being involved: [In 1553] 'it was ordered that the said play [...] would begin in the presence of the Blessed Sacrament, at five a.m. on the market place and from there they will set off and march as is customary [...] those who have been chosen to act must each be ready in their costumes at the house of the Dominicans to act and present their roles. [1555] The morality of the Old and New Testaments shall be played as usual on Corpus Christi day [...] and those who act must only go to the places they know are suitable, and in each place a scaffold shall be erected at the expense of the town for them to perform each in their turn'.[50]

In Oudenaarde, the Corpus Christi processional plays were produced by the friars minor,[51] while sixteenth-century Béthune presented a substantial cycle of plays done at first by neighbourhood groups but taken over by the craft guilds and religious confraternities. In 1548 they presented a cycle of scenes from the Annunciation to the

---

M. Rivas, *Teatro en Toledo* (Madrid: Real Academia Espanola, 1977). See also *Staging*, pp. 252-58.

[48] Shergold, pp. 93, 97.

[49] Shergold, pp. 100-03.

[50] *Mystères*, II, 208-10.

[51] J. Vandeer Mersch, *Kronyk der Rederykkammers van Audenaerde* (Belgisch Museum, 1843), 6: 380. See also B. Ramakers, *Spelen en figuren: toneelkunst en procesiecultuur in Oudenaarde hissen Middeleeuwen en Moderne Tijd* (Amsterdam: Amsterdam University Press, 1996).

Last Judgement including the Nativity and Three Kings (Tanners and Cordwainers: eleven people); the Last Supper and Emmaus (Confraternity of God and St James); Judas hanging himself and Christ before Caiphas and Herod (Butchers: sixteen people); and Descent from the Cross, (Fishmongers: eight people). There were twenty-eight scaffolds altogether.[52]

Corpus Christi celebrations in German-speaking Imperial territories varied: Künzelsau had a procession with play sequences; at Freiburg in Breisau there was a procession with tableaux and the Butchers' Passion play was performed every seven years. In Friedberg, a lay religious fraternity founded in 1465 was responsible for a procession with 'figures' which were performed in various locations.[53] The Zerbst procession included many scenes including a lengthy cortège of saints representing the Church Triumphant. The *Ordnung* lists who is responsible for each episode and they include neighbourhood groups; a number of craft guilds; and the heads [*vorstender*] of the hospital, several churches and the poor [*elender*]. This last is presumably a charitable group. Many of the episodes are tableaux with scrolls and titles but the Tanners and Cobblers [*gerwer und schuster*] have a scene to enact for the arrest of Jesus and the flight of the apostles; it is performed *vor dem sacrament* [before the sacrament].[54]

There is no precise continental equivalent of the York play and other English cycles, with their repeated performances of each episode by the same craft from year to year.

Sometimes a whole town would turn itself into a community of players. As early as 1333, members of the best families of Toulon gathered together to perform an apparently extensive play of the birth of Our Lady and the Nativity and Childhood of Jesus.[55] From the mid-fifteenth century onwards there are examples of non-guild civic communities performing plays, especially Passions, throughout western Europe. These plays were not undertaken by the craft guilds nor performed annually; they did not answer to an existing need to celebrate a major feast. These were plays to the glory of God and

---

[52] For the Béthune records see Champollion-Figeac, *Documents historiques inédits* (Paris: Didot, 1841-48), t. IV, pp. 329-37.

[53] N. Brooks 'Processional drama and dramatic procession in Germany in the late Middle Ages', *Journal of English and Germanic Philology* 32 (1933), 159.

[54] Neumann, pp. 784-87.

[55] Only the cast-list with names of the seventy characters and the performers has survived. *Mystères*, II, p. 3.

especially the honour of this city and (in France anyway) the financial advantage of the principal inhabitants.

There is no information extant on the membership of the French Confrérie de la Passion which, from 1402 until their final dissolution in 1686, dominated the Paris theatre. They were motivated, we are told, by devotion but also by fairly mundane concerns, as is clear from the royal charter by which they were established: 'We, [Charles VI] will and desire the welfare, profit, and advantage of the said *Confrérie* and the rights and revenues thereof to be increased and augmented with favours and privileges so that everyone as an act of devotion may and should join them'.

Several towns in the Loire valley did Passion plays notably Poitiers, Issoudun, Angers, Saumur and Bourges. In each case the organizers were townsfolk, though experienced directors and, most importantly, makers of special effects might be imported. These attracted large *paying* audiences from far beyond the confines of the town. As a visitor from Germany commented in 1535, 'the passion play at Issoudun could scarcely have been finished before it was known that the citizens there had done such good business that several thousand francs were left, over and above all expenses besides the praise which had also accrued to them.' As a result, he tells us, the people of Bourges, ten miles away, bigger and richer, decided they could do better. For 'not only they who were meeting the costs would benefit from it greatly but that all the citizenry would derive great profit from it'. They were unfortunately hampered by the outbreak of war and excessive spending especially on costumes, so that the result was a disaster not a profit.[56]

In other French towns, such as Romans (1509) and Châteaudun (1510) there were notable differences in their chain of command and the all-important financing. In Romans, in Dauphiné, the expenses throughout were shared meticulously between the local church and the town, half each. Châteaudun is more complex: the moving force here was the local overlord, the duc de Longueville, who, determined to have a play performed, wrote to the neighbouring town of Amboise for a text: 'since it is my intention to have the mystery performed in our town'.[57] The townsfolk, fairly meekly, did as they were bid but the head of the financial committee was the local abbot and one of the senior clergy was also director and trainer of the actors and actresses,

---

[56] *Staging*, pp. 39-40.

[57] M. Couturier and G.A. Runnalls (eds.), 'Châteaudun 1510: Compte du mystère de la Passion', *Société archéologique d'Eure-et-Loir* (1992), 69.

so here at least all three estates were involved. Nobles and princes were often involved as patrons of plays but de Longueville is unique as the actual originator of a civic performance.

There was no need for noble intervention in Lucerne where the city and the *Bruderschaft der Bekronung* organized and presented a three-day *Osterspiel* at intervals for more than a hundred years.[58] Competition for roles was keen and some had become almost hereditary in certain patrician families.[59] Although the *Bruderschaft* were the nominal originators, in practice the play was handled by the city fathers, and Renwart Cysat, the Town Clerk, produced the performances in 1583 and 1597; he died in 1614 having already begun the preparations for the 1616 performance which was to be the last. In contrast to this, the plays of the Tyrol, though done by the burgesses, were organized by local notables, such as Benedict Debs, a schoolmaster or Vigil Raber, a painter.[60]

There were many civic Passions in German towns. A group of citizens (*aliqui cives*, Mainz 1498) might apply to the city fathers for permission to do a Passion play. Generally this was allowed provided the text was vetted by local churchmen. Permission might be refused, however, as in Frankfurt in 1470. Reasons for the choice are not often given.[61] Passions were rare in the Low Countries except in Hainault, where they were performed by *compaignons* in Mons in 1455, 1484 and, outstandingly, in 1501.[62]

Though religious and moral themes dominated the repertory of the medieval drama groups, plays on secular themes were written and performed, including those of Adam de la Halle of Arras in the thirteenth century which may have been presented by the *Confrérie des bourgeois et jongleurs d'Arras*.[63] In Paris (and other major French cities) in the fifteenth century, numerous farces, allegorical moralities and *sotties* were performed by special groups: the *basochiens* and the

---

[58] M. Blakemore Evans, *The Passion Play of Lucerne: an Historical and Critical Introduction* (New York: MLA; London: Oxford University Press, 1943).

[59] In 1597 and 1616, the actors had to pay a fee to take a major role, thus reducing the heavy cost to the city, for Germany, unlike France did not charge admission to its plays.

[60] See John Tailby, 'Drama and Community in South Tyrol', below.

[61] For Mainz and Frankfurt see Neumann, pp. 174, 313.

[62] G. Cohen, (ed.), *Le livre de conduite du régisseur et le Mystère de la Passion joué à Mons, 1501*, (Paris: Les Belles Lettres, 1925), p. xiii.

[63] J. Dufournet, *Adam de la Halle à la recherche de lui-meme* (Paris: SEDES, 1974), p. 223. See also Langley, below.

Enfants-sans-Souci.[64] The *Basoche* was the name given to the association of law-clerks attached to one or other of the *Parlements*, the legal/administrative centres of Paris or any large town. The *Enfants-sans-Souci* (similar bodies or *sociétés joyeuses* existed in many other major towns) drew their membership mainly from the professional classes: many *basochiens* were also *sots*. These formally organized, recognized societies were ruled, in Paris, by the Prince des Sots and Mère Sotte and in Dijon by Mère Folle. Like the *basochiens*, they presented mainly farces, *sotties* or moralities but it seems probable that when the Confrérie de la Passion put on one of their really large plays in the early sixteenth century and sent out an appeal or *Cry* for actors: 'Come, city, town, university;[...] come men of valour, solemn censors, magistrates, politicians, take part in the play of truth, by performing the deeds of the apostles'[65] they will have taken in a very large number of *basochiens* and *sots*.

In the Low Countries in the fifteenth and sixteenth centuries, neighbourhood groups and Chambers of Rhetoric wrote and produced a wide range of plays - religious, secular, serious and comic. They also frequently met for competitions ranging from the prizes given to the group who presented the best history play for the Lille Procession[66] to the great *Landjuwelen* between the cities of Brabant: in Antwerp in 1496, twenty-eight towns took part.[67]

Medieval man, like medieval society as a whole, was strongly 'clubbable'. The urban Third Estate, constantly formed associations for moral or physical or artistic support. Craft guilds and religious confraternities, literary and professional societies gathered to celebrate or mourn, to play and to compete. The finance for these activities normally came from either patronage, both personal and civic, or the societies' compulsory subscriptions or fines; the performers remained unpaid amateurs, whose only rewards were a meal, a drink or a trophy.

Although most plays were put on by such societies there are examples of plays being staged by small, ad hoc groups. In 1542, in Athis-sur-Orge (a small town near Paris) the clerk of the church, the local innkeeper and merchant signed an agreement with a painter to furnish them with costumes and properties for a trio of plays

---

[64] In the *sottie* all the characters wore the long-eared fool's head-dress.

[65] *Mystères*, I, p. 417.

[66] Alan E. Knight, 'The Bishop of Fools and his feasts in Lille', in *Festive Drama*, ed. by Meg Twycross, p.160.

[67] 'Annales Antverpiensis', *Belgisch Museum*, 1, p. 150.

(including a morality) to be performed over eight days. This was probably intended as a money-making project, like the East Anglian villages which hired a 'property player' to organize and stage their play.[68]

But the supreme example of an ad hoc group is that recorded in the contract drawn up for the Passion staged in Valenciennes (Hainault) in 1547. This contract creates a temporary, but strictly regulated, dramatic society with many similarities to the Chambers of Rhetoric found in the Dutch-speaking regions of the Low Countries.[69] The players undertook to accept the role allotted, to rehearse when required and to be on time for performances. These rules may be compared to those of the Chamber of Rhetoric 'The Lilies' in Diest, for example, 'whoever is then sent a role by [...] the Factor and Deacons, will have to play that role or pay six shillings, of which the Chamber shall have three and whoever accepts the role will have the other three'. The members of 'The Lilies' also had to give technical assistance: 'Item, when an extensive play is to be performed then every member will have to come and help to build the scaffold and no one will be able to absent himself or send apologies, except the ones who perform in the play' (*ibid.* p. 126). Failure to do so meant a fine and a warning. The Valenciennes group included several players who also helped construct the '*secrets*'.[70]

Unique to Valenciennes, however, is the complicated financial sharing arrangement they make: 'Item: it is also to be noted that the said thirteen [supervisors] and all the players who undertook the business, together agreed to pay any expenses incurred, if by chance there should be some disaster (*mortalité*) or war so that they could not act or carry out the said enterprise. [...] Item. All the actor-companions given a role by the said supervisors shall be required to

---

[68] J. Coldewey, 'That enterprising property player: semi-professional drama in sixteenth-century England', *Theatre Notebook* 31 (1977), 5-12. A peculiarly English practice is the parish ale -- using plays or quasi-dramatic ceremonies for fund raising in villages. See A.F. Johnson and Wim Hüsken (eds.), *English Parish Drama*, (Amsterdam/Atlanta: Rodopi, 1996).

[69] The Rhetoricians in the French-speaking regions, including Hainault, were organized by *quartier* or town, not in Chambers.

[70] 'Historische oogslag op de Rederijkerskamers van Diest', *Vaderlandsch Museum* 3 (1840), 119. In New Romney in Kent, in 1555, a number of townsmen undertook roles in a Passion play and pledged £5 that they would 'learn their parts [...] and be ready then to play the same' and attend rehearsals; see G. Dawson (ed.), *Records of Plays and Players in Kent 1450-1642*, Collections of the Malone Society, 7 (London: Malone Society, 1965).

hand over each of them one gold *écu* or equivalent when they accept the first role as contribution to the expenses *if they wish to participate in the profits or losses* [*au bon et au maulvais*, my emphasis], [...] and at the end each one will get back what he contributed unless there is a loss. [...] Item. As for the gain and profit, if there is any, it shall be divided in two parts i.e. one half fairly and equally between all those who have contributed money: supervisors, actors, or administrators, [...] and the other half shall be divided among the actors and administrators only, by shares as ordained, according to their merits, by the said supervisors, and no actors or administrators shall [receive a share] without the agreement of at least seven of the said supervisors.'[71]

Here, perhaps for the first time, a group of townsmen are taking on a considerable financial burden without the support of a guild or confraternity, in the hope of a possible financial reward at the end. It is, therefore, interesting that they are the only known example of a big Passion play that *did* make a profit. Surely they should be considered, if only temporarily, professionals – a real 'cry of players' in a European community?

---

[71] The full contract is given in *Les Mystères*, pp. 145-52 (see above, note 2). The final account is on p. 152.

Drama and community in late medieval Paris

GRAHAM A. RUNNALLS

IN 1550 A GROUP of Parisians met in the house of one of their recently deceased friends and performed a small-scale mystery play.[1] They were all members of the same confraternity, the *Confrérie Notre Dame de Liesse*, and the subject of the play was one of the legends associated with the sanctuary of Notre Dame de Liesse. In a little over 1000 lines, the drama told how a knight and his wife go on a pilgrimage to this sanctuary. However, on their journey, they are attacked by brigands, who leave the knight for dead and tie his wife to a tree. Justice appears to be done when, firstly, the devil appears and carries off the two brigands to Hell, and secondly, a count and countess and their entourage pass by and rescue the lady. However, unexpected complications ensue. The countess, who is deeply unhappy and hates her husband, commits suicide, and the unfortunate wife of the knight, who still thinks her husband is dead, is now blamed for the death of the countess. She is condemned to death and is just about to die; but her fervent prayers to the Virgin provoke divine intervention. Notre Dame resuscitates the countess and the lady is proven innocent. Moreover, the knight is not dead, but found alive at the sanctuary chapel.

This naïve play, yet another example of the well-known theme of the unjustly accused woman, hardly seems to correspond to what is generally understood by the term mystery play, although that is the title the author gave to it. It required but a dozen actors, who almost certainly included some women. (There are very few examples of women actors in the Middle Ages.) It was in every sense an amateur dramatic production, performed on a small stage in a private

---

[1] Parts of this chapter have appeared in Graham A. Runnalls, *Études sur les mystères* (Paris: Champion, 1998), pp. 83-99. I am grateful to the publisher for permission to reproduce them here.

household. In so far as it is possible to identify the participants, they appear to have been modest Parisian citizens, people that we might now describe as lower middle-class. The author of the play was Jean Louvet, who was a *sergent à verge* at the Châtelet. This performance was not unique, however. In fact it was the twelfth in a series of similar plays, composed and acted annually at the same place, and by the same confraternity, between 1536 and 1550. The texts of these plays have been preserved in a manuscript in the Paris Bibliothèque Nationale,[2] and they testify to a type of 'medieval' dramatic activity manifestly flourishing well after what most historians tend to think of as the end of Middle Ages.

At roughly the same period, just ten years before, another Parisian confraternity was putting on a very different kind of play. A number of prominent citizens, including distinguished lawyers and churchmen, took part in the performance of a mystery play on the life of Saint Denis, one of the patron saints of Paris (in fact, the first bishop of Paris). They were members of the *Confrérie des Arquebusiers de Paris* (the Paris Bowmen). This version of the life of Saint Denis combined material from biblical, apocryphal and legendary sources. It began with the lives of the apostles Peter and Paul after the death of Christ, included the stoning of Stephen, the conversion of Denis, the death and assumption of the Virgin Mary (at which Denis was present!), the journey of Denis and others to proselytize France, and the life and martyrdom of Denis in Paris. One of the main aims of the play was to glorify Paris and to enhance the Christian significance of Denis himself.

The text[3] used at this performance, part of which has survived, was not an original composition, as were the plays written by Jean Louvet. It was a compilation built up over almost a century. A few passages of the *Mystère de Saint Denis* are found in a play preserved in an early fifteenth-century Parisian manuscript. However, some parts of it were much more recent. It even included an originally independent complete mystery play on the Assumption of Our Lady. This latter play, published around 1515 in a printed edition, was copied *en bloc* in about 1540 into the manuscript of the revised and expanded *Mystère de Saint Denis*. The stage directions and other information

---

[2] BNF n.a.f. 481; see L. Petit de Julleville, *Les Mystères* (Paris: Hachette, 1880), vol. II, pp. 608-13.

[3] G.A. Runnalls, 'The Theatre in Paris at the end of the Middle Ages: *Le Mystère de Saint Denis*', *Mélanges Jeanne Wathelet-Willem* (Liège: Cahiers de l'A.R.U., 1978-9), pp. 619-35; 'Un siècle dans la vie d'un mystère: *Le Mystère de saint Denis*', *Le Moyen Age* 97 (1991), 407-30.

provided by this manuscript enable us to reconstruct many aspects of the performance. The play was an enormous one, over 30,000 lines long; the performance extended over six days and required almost 200 actors, many of whom are named in the manuscript, apparently all male. There seems no doubt that this play was performed outdoors, in a large theatre in the round, that is in a specially built wooden construction, made up of a large circle of raised galleries, under which were built rows of raked benches. The playing area was in the centre of the circle; the spectators, probably numbering several thousand, sat in boxes or on the benches, depending on their social status.

These two contrasting plays, Jehan Louvet's short melodrama and the vast hagiographic *Mystère de Saint Denis*, testify to the rich variety of religious drama in Paris at the end of the Middle Ages. However, in fact, they represent the end point of a tradition of dramatic activity going back over at least two centuries. Indeed, almost exactly 200 years before, a performance in some ways very similar to that of Jean Louvet's play was taking place in another Parisian confraternity.

Early in December in 1353, the Paris Goldsmiths' Guild[4] held their regular annual meeting; at that time, guilds were only allowed one full assembly a year, because such meetings were seen by the King as a potential threat to public order. The members of the Guild, all men, walked in procession to the local church, where they had a chapel, and attended a High Mass, sung in honour of the Virgin Mary and of their patron saint, Eloi (Eligius). They then moved on to their Guildhall, where a banquet took place, after which was held the annual election of the six *gardes* who were to control the Guild during the next twelve months. Then, for a couple of hours, they watched the performance of a miracle play.[5]

The play was performed by a dozen actors, all male, on a simple stage in the main hall (*salle*) of the society, in front of the members and their families, perhaps less than a hundred people all told. It enacted the tragic story of a contemporary middle-class Parisian family. The wife, who has for many years unsuccessfully prayed to have a child, discovers that she is at last pregnant, much to her joy and apprehension. Her husband, a successful merchant who is frequently away from Paris on business, is absent when, later, a son is born. After the birth, which is shown on the stage, the lady falls

---

[4] G.A. Runnalls, 'Medieval Trade Guilds and the *Miracles de Nostre Dame par personnages*', *Medium Aevum* 39 (1970), 257-87.

[5] *Le Miracle de l'Enfant Ressuscité*, ed. by G.A. Runnalls (Geneva: Droz, *Textes Littéraires Français*, 1972).

asleep whilst bathing the child, which slips from her grasp and drowns. Still in the absence of her husband, the mother is tried and found guilty of murder by the judge, for whom the guilty verdict is a political necessity, if he is to keep his job. She is condemned to be burnt alive. Fortunately, being a miracle play, the story ends happily. The steadfast faith and impassioned prayers of the wife and her recently returned husband impel the Virgin Mary to intervene on their behalf. Just before the pyre is lit, the Virgin Mary resuscitates the child and the mother is released.

What the Parisian Goldsmiths did on that day in 1353 was not unique. Indeed, we know that in almost every year from 1339 until 1382, similar processions, masses, banquets, elections and play performances took place. The only times when no such events occurred were between 1356 and 1358, when normal life in Paris was disrupted by the middle-class tax revolts led by Etienne Marcel. Similar protests in 1382 almost certainly led to the ending of this annual series of play performances.

Two hundred years separate the Goldsmiths' plays from those of Jean Louvet. The similarities between these two groups of performances – the place, the length, the participants, the type of indoor theatre, and even the subject matter – are striking. The Jean Louvet plays prove that in Paris the tradition of simple religious confraternity plays continued with little change from the fourteenth to the sixteenth centuries. The *Mystère de Saint Denis*, on the other hand, testifies to a very different tendency in medieval French religious drama, also evidenced in Paris, as we shall see later, that is the evolution of large-scale mystery plays performed out-of-doors.

The existence and the survival until today of both the texts of these plays and information about their performances provide convincing proof of the importance of the theatre in the life of Paris throughout the late Middle Ages; and yet this is an aspect of social life that is rarely mentioned in standard histories. To get a full picture of everyday life in Paris – or indeed any part of western Europe – towards the end of the Middle Ages, attention needs to be paid to any activities that engaged the attention and efforts of large numbers of ordinary citizens. Drama was certainly one of these.

Drama is a very different literary genre from most others. A play is an event. It occurs in a particular place, at a particular time; it occupies an amount of space and requires the participation of a number of people. A performance of a play is ephemeral. It may last a couple of hours or several days. But after that, the performance is gone forever. It costs money to produce, and time and trouble to prepare. Almost none of these features apply to a poem or a novel.

Nowadays, of course, plays can be studied from books, as well as from live performances; when plays are read, drama becomes more like other literary genres. But in the Middle Ages, plays were either seen live, or else they did not exist. Play manuscripts were usually written out only in one, or at the very most, two complete copies; and there was no way that the medieval public at large could study plays at leisure by reading, at least until the early sixteenth century, when printed editions of mystery plays became widely available.

However, for this very reason, plays had a big advantage over the other literary genres. They did not require or presuppose a literate public. Drama was accessible to every man and woman in every European country during the Middle Ages, regardless of whether he or she could read. Not surprisingly, there was a great deal of drama performed throughout Europe from the twelfth to the sixteenth centuries; much of it has survived.

The earliest plays completely written in French come from the twelfth and thirteenth centuries and most owe their existence to the expansion of trade guilds and religious confraternities. As usual, the evolution of the theatre reflects social and economic change. The growth of towns during the thirteenth and fourteenth centuries, especially important ones like Arras and Paris, produced a middle class of merchants, traders and artisans, who joined together to form associations, like trade unions, to protect their personal and commercial interests. These societies usually chose a patron saint to protect them; the cult of this patron saint led in some cases to plays based on the life or miracles of the saint.

Although play performances of this type continued to occur throughout France during the fifteenth and early sixteenth centuries, new developments also took place. In the provinces, in particular, large-scale plays, usually called mystery plays or *mystères*, were mounted by whole towns. This was probably because the cost of organising a lengthy play, for example, one that lasted several days, was more than one or two private individuals or small confraternities could afford. Moreover, the performances were often loss-making. The famous mystery plays performed in Mons in 1501, in Romans in 1509 and in Châteaudun in 1510, all cost about £2000 to put on and lost about £500 each.[6] £2000 in sixteenth-century terms must have

---

[6] G. Cohen, *Le Livre de Conduite du Régisseur et le Compte des Dépenses pour le Mystère de la Passion joué à Mons en 1501* (Paris: Les Belles Lettres, 1925); M. Couturier and G.A. Runnalls, *Le Livre de Compte de la Passion de Châteaudun 1510*, (Chartres: Société archéologique d'Eure-et-Loir, 1991); M. Giraud, *Composition, mise en scène et représentation du Mystère des Trois Doms* (Lyon: Perrin, 1848).

been the equivalent of at least £400,000 today. However, they attracted so many people from the surrounding areas that they were considered financially worthwhile undertakings for the town as a whole. These examples underline the fact that a medieval play performance could serve at least three contrasting functions: it was a theatrical event, a religious experience and a commercial venture.

In Paris, however, there are no examples of plays organised and financed by the city as a whole. As we have already seen, smaller-scale plays were organised by trade or religious societies. The larger-scale plays were usually left to a special *Confrérie* whose only *raison d'être* was the performance of mystery plays.

Plays of the sort described above continued well into the second half of the sixteenth century. However, by the middle of the sixteenth century, miracle and mystery plays were beginning to incur the disapproval of their most influential supporters. The Church, formerly a defender and indeed historically the recreator of drama in the Middle Ages, now found many aspects of miracle and mystery plays distasteful and shocking. The plays no longer appeared to be in keeping with recent changes in theology, either Catholic or Protestant. Attitudes to the theatre itself were evolving, too. The kind of intellectuals, who had earlier been the authors of such plays, became more interested in Classical and humanist theatre, both in Latin and in French. It is true, also, that some performances of mystery plays left a lot to be desired in the quality of the text and of the acting, and in the behaviour of the actors. It was in Paris that the first formal decree forbidding the performance of mystery plays was pronounced, by the *Parlement de Paris* in 1548.[7] The Parliament:

> deffend auxdits suppliants de jouer le mystere de la Passion Nostre Sauveur, ne autres mysteres sacrez, sur peine d'amende arbitraire, leur permettant neantmoins de pouvoir jouer autres mysteres profanes, honnestes et licites, sans offencer ne injurier personne; et deffend a tous aultres de jouer ou representer doresnavant, tant en la ville, fauxbourgs que banlieue de Paris, sinon soubs le nom de ladicte confrerie et au profit d'icelle.

> [The *Parlement* forbids the supplicants from performing the *Mystère de la Passion Nostre Sauveur* or any other sacred mystery plays, on pain of an arbitrary fine; they are allowed nevertheless to perform other mystery plays which are secular, honest and lawful, as long as they do not offend or injure anyone; it also henceforth forbids any

---

[7] Full text quoted in Petit de Julleville, *Les Mystères* (Paris: Hachette, 1880), vol. I, p. 429.

other people from putting on such plays, both in the city of Paris and in its suburbs, unless authorized by, and for the profit of, the *Confrérie*.]

It has often been thought that this decree meant the end of mystery plays in Paris. But this was not completely true. The wording of the decree makes it clear that what the Parliament objected to was the public performance of large-scale biblical drama, performances that the public had to pay to attend. Other sorts of religious drama were not affected by the edict.

Similar decrees in provincial towns followed over the next decade, and although none of these decrees was immediately effective, they do reflect the decline of the mystery plays. However, it is worth remembering that for much of the second half of the sixteenth century, there were simultaneously in France two different theatrical cultures: the intellectuals' humanist theatre and the popular mystery and miracle plays, – medieval and Renaissance drama side by side.

It is perhaps surprising that the criticisms of mystery plays were not primarily religious or theological. One might have expected that, as in England, the religious drama, which was essentially Catholic in mentality, would have been attacked by the Protestants. But this does not seem to have been the case. It is the performances of plays that were the object of the critics' scorn, rather than the texts themselves. Certainly, there was no ban on printing mystery plays. Printed editions of mystery plays continued to be published until the early seventeenth century.[8]

All play performances require a space; most require a building.[9] Before going any further, it is worthwhile looking at the question of theatre buildings. There were no permanent theatres during the Middle Ages. Either an existing building had to be adapted, or else a completely new building had to be constructed and then taken down again afterwards. Of course, for liturgical drama, the church was the theatre; and in many respects, the church resembles a traditional medieval theatre: an enclosed area, with several specially significant areas (altar, cross, vestry, chapels, aisles, etc.) arranged in a set manner and visible at all times to the congregation; a small number of unusually dressed men (rarely women) moving from one area to

---

[8] G.A. Runnalls, *Les Mystères français imprimés* (Paris: Champion, 1999).

[9] For further information on theatre buildings, see E. Konigson, *L'Espace théâtral médiéval* (Paris: CNRS, 1975); H. Rey-Flaud, *Le Cercle magique* (Paris: Gallimard, 1973); and P. Meredith and J.Tailby, *The Staging of Religious Drama in Europe in the Later Middle Ages: Texts and Documents in English Translation*, EDAM Monograph series 4 (Kalamazoo: Medieval Institute Publications, 1983).

another, singing or speaking pre-written words; all this witnessed by a silent public. These features lie behind the essential characteristic of medieval stagecraft, i.e., the concept of simultaneous staging. Texts were not divided into scenes and acts by closing or dropping a curtain. All the main sets required by a play were present on stage, in view of the audience, from the beginning of the performance until the end. Often all the actors were simultaneously visible too, even when they did not have lines to speak. A theatre therefore had to include a playing area which permanently contained a number of elements which suggested or represented the places required by the action, as well as places where the non-active actors could wait their turn. Traditionally, these two elements are called in French *mansions* and *lieux*. These could be very varied in nature and complexity. A Passion Play might need sets representing the following: Heaven, Hell, Jerusalem, Golgotha, a cross, a garden, Nazareth, Pilate's house, Herod's house, a synagogue, Judas's house, etc., It thus becomes obvious that the text of a play could influence the size of a theatre, and, of course, vice versa. Another major difference was that what we now call the proscenium arch had not yet been invented; that is to say that there was no assumption that the play was performed on a stage placed in front of the public. This could be the case; if so, we would now call it a linear stage. But often the public sat in a large circle, with the play performed in the middle; this was the theatre in the round. Much detailed documentation (contracts, quantities of wood, measurements, descriptions) about medieval theatres has survived. The theatres in the round were solid constructions, and often took many weeks to build.

It is probable that the trade guilds performed their plays, which were not open to all the public, but just to members, inside their guild-halls, as was the case with the Paris Goldsmiths. This tended to limit the scope of their plays, probably to about six or seven sets, arranged on a linear stage at one end of their hall. But the larger-scale plays had to be performed out of doors. The kind of space needed for this type of theatre was either a large square in the town or a cemetery or cloister. There are attested examples of each of these spaces being transformed into theatres. When this was the case, there was in theory no limit to the length and scope of the plays.

Before beginning to look at some of the major theatrical events in late medieval Paris, it is necessary to go into some detail in order to explain exactly how a major mystery play was organized in France at this time. The decision to perform such a play was usually taken at a special public meeting of some of the most important local citizens. The reasons for putting on a play were various. In some cases, it was merely routine, as with the Goldsmiths. But in the case of special, one-off performances, other factors were invoked. Plays were put on for various reasons: rivalry between towns or guilds (the play is a way of demonstrating the superiority of one town over another); to ward off a natural disaster like the plague or a drought (the play has the same function as a collective prayer); to obey the wish of an important individual (the performance is a political necessity); to attract visitors to the town (the play is a commercial event, a loss-leader). Since such a play could cost between several hundred and a couple of thousand pounds (at a time when a master carpenter might only earn three shillings a day), a few wealthy individuals had to provide loans to finance the preparations for the play. An accountant was appointed to control the flow of money and to arrange a number of contracts with suppliers, tradesmen and other employees. An author, sometimes called the *fatiste*, was chosen; he composed the text, often a reworking of a pre-existing play. A number of scribes were also asked to copy up the manuscript and the actors' roles. The main manuscript contained a complete version of the text, including the names of all the speakers, and the full stage directions, covering movements, effects, sets, etc. Each actor, however, was given his own role, i.e., a narrow strip of paper, with just that actor's lines written on it, plus the vital cue words. Medieval plays were always written in rhyme, and usually the first line of one speech rhymed with the last of the preceding one; this was the so-called mnemonic rhyme, which acted as a cue to the actors, reminding them when exactly to start each of their speeches. The actors' roles were in effect scrolls, that were gradually unwound as the play proceeded. They were mainly used during rehearsals.

A decision had to be made about the place of the theatre. This needed the approval of the town council if it was a main square, or the religious authorities if it was a cloister or cemetery. The theatre area had to be measured, wood had to be ordered and delivered, and plans drawn up for the building and the sets. Other major appointments were the *peintre,* who designed and helped to build the sets and the stage effects, and the person who was to control the whole performance, known as the *meneur du jeu.* These specialists were often professionals; they sometimes came from far away, and stayed in the town for several months surveying the preparations. During the actual performance, the *meneur du jeu* held the main manuscript and in effect directed the performance, rather like an orchestral conductor.

The actors too were named several months in advance; they had to sign legally binding documents promising to turn up punctually at rehearsals and to accept the roles they were given. There was great competition over who got what role; and the local aristocracy often felt it desirable to be one of the actors. However, such people avoided the main roles, which were often extremely taxing; central characters like Jesus, the Virgin Mary or an important saint, might have several thousands of lines to learn. Actors were not normally paid, and they usually had to provide their own costumes, except in special circumstances. The costumes in mystery plays were therefore not historically accurate. Labourers and artisans like carpenters, joiners, painters, locksmiths, etc. were also employed for weeks on end. One of the most striking aspects of mystery plays were the stage effects: fire and flames, noise, sudden appearances and disappearances, tortures, executions, and, of course, in the Passion plays, crucifixions. Medieval stage technicians were well capable of creating all these effects. Two of the main sets in any mystery play performance were Heaven and Hell. Heaven was represented as a raised dwelling of great splendour, inhabited not only by God the Father and the saints and angels, but also by musicians playing heavenly music. Hell was a place of torture, pain, cacophonous noise, explosions, smoke and fireworks. Many stages had a network of underground tunnels and trap-doors. The stage managers in these plays were experts in many fields, including pyrotechnics and noise-production.

When everything was almost ready, the play was announced by the *monstre*, a long procession of all the actors in costume, accompanied by the transportable stage effects; at the head of the procession came Lucifer and the Devils, at the end God and the angels. For public performances (as distinct from private plays like those of the Goldsmiths) the audience had to pay. The typical medieval mystery play was long, and needed performances on several, at least three or four, days. The ordinary people sat on benches, paying for each session they attended; the wealthy could rent boxes (*loges*) for the whole performance. The separation between actors and audience was not as clear-cut as today. The actors were just as keen to see the play – or at least the sessions they were not engaged in – as anyone else. Moreover, the construction of the theatre in the round often led to the juxtaposition of the *loges* occupied by spectators and the sets required in the play. (A distant reflection of this situation is found in the terms now used for the uppermost parts of a modern theatre; we talk of 'sitting in the gods', or '*au paradis*' as the French sometimes say.)

After the performance was over, the theatre was taken down and, as far as possible, everything useful was sold off. The accounts were drawn up and presented to the organizers; the losses (more often than profits) were distributed amongst those responsible. It will be clear from this description that the organization of a mystery play had a major influence on the life of the town over a period of several months. It caused the circulation of large sums of money throughout all the social classes of the town; it disrupted everyday activities; but it also increased the sense of community. This demonstrates once again my initial contention that the theatre in medieval France was much more than a mere literary genre.

This brief glance at theatrical life in medieval France in general can provide the background to a closer look, in roughly chronological order, at some of the more important theatrical events in Paris itself between the early fourteenth and mid sixteenth centuries.

One of the most significant events in the history of Parisian theatre was the establishment of the famous *Confrérie de la Passion*. Charles VI, King of France at the very end of the fourteenth century, was known to be especially keen on the theatre and frequently attended performances put on in his own Paris mansions. These performances were put on by a number of enthusiastic amateur actors, to whom he later accorded special privileges. In 1402, he published letters patent creating the *Confrérie de la Passion*, a special *Confrérie*, whose sole activity was to put on religious mystery plays. Indeed, the *Confrères* appear to have had a kind of monopoly in Paris for certain sorts of plays, especially the biblical plays like Passion plays, Resurrection plays, Old Testament plays, etc. They were active from 1402 until 1548, when their large-scale performances were suppressed. They occupied several different buildings during their history; the last one, the Hôtel de Bourgogne, was still being used, for very different plays, in the seventeenth century. The existence of the *Confrérie de la Passion* does make Paris stand out from other parts of France. No other town had a dramatic society with special royal authority and backing; elsewhere plays were organized either by trade or religious societies or else by town councils.[10]

It is thus both frustrating and paradoxical that, in spite of this royal and civic support, not much is known about the activities of the *Confrérie de la Passion* after its foundation in 1402 and its well-documented last years in the 1540s. We are much better informed about provincial drama. Hitherto, little hard evidence has been published throwing light on the *Confrérie de la Passion*'s performances during most of the 150 years of its existence. By that, I mean there are no known texts, accounts or other archives that can unquestionably attest to the *Confrérie de la Passion* putting on plays during the fifteenth and early sixteenth centuries. It is virtually certain

---

[10] G.A. Runnalls, 'Sponsorship and Control in Medieval French Religious Drama, 1402-1548', *French Studies* 51 (1997) 258-66.

that they did do so; it is simply the case that no records have survived – or yet been found and published. For example, the confraternity must have possessed a repertory of plays and therefore a number of manuscript texts, but the only surviving example is the unpublished manuscript of the *Mystère de Saint Louis*, which, according to an inscription in the fly-leaf, belonged to the *Confrérie*.

My own recent research, however, has produced a few little-known documents illustrating mystery play performances in Paris, including some by the *Confrérie de la Passion*, during these years. Even so, they relate to the early sixteenth century, rather than the fifteenth. In the course of studying the *Registres des Délibérations du Bureau de l'Hôtel de Ville*[11] (which are in effect records of meetings and decisions taken by the Paris town council), I discovered references to a *Mystère de la Trinité*, which was put on by the *Confrérie*. The office of the Paris Provost recorded on 5 December 1530 that:

> Aux Maistres de la Passion, pour le Mistere de la Trinité: aux Maistres de la Passion a esté remonstree que messieurs de la ville veullent entendre quel mistere ilz veillent jouer, pour leur dire ce que bon leur semblera, lesquelz ont promis de rendre response lundy prochain.
>
> [To the Masters of the (Confraternity of) the Passion, for the *Mystère de la Trinité*: to the Masters of the (Confraternity of) the Passion it was pointed out that the city councillors wish to know what mystery play they are intending to perform, so that they can give them their opinion on it; the masters have promised to reply next Monday.]

The reference to the *Mystère de la Trinité* is useful in itself, even if no such play has survived. Equally interesting is the fact that the document demonstrates the extent to which the city fathers (*messieurs de la ville*) took an interest in the *Confrérie*'s activities; indeed, it almost gives the impression of the threat of censorship.

However, as we know, the *Confrérie de la Passion* was not the only group interested in performing religious dramas. There was no lack of smaller societies putting on plays in Paris in the fifteenth and sixteenth centuries, about which we have information.

The Paris Shoemakers (*Cordonniers*) put on a play on the lives of their twin saints Crespin and Crespinien in 1458, the text of which still survives.[12] The Paris Confraternity of Master Gardeners also put

---

[11] *Registres des Délibérations du Bureau de l'Hôtel de Ville de Paris*, vols. 1-19 (*Histoire Générale de Paris*), II pp. 80-81.

[12] G.A. Runnalls, 'Le Théâtre à Paris et dans les Provinces à la fin du Moyen-Age: *Le Mystère de Saint Crespin et de Saint Crespinien*', *Le Moyen Age*, 82 (1976), 517-38.

on two different small-scale mystery plays relating to their patron saints.[13] This curious society, which possessed a chapel in the Church of Saint-Nicolas-Des-Champs, focused on the cult of Saints Fiacre and Venice. Fiacre was a Scottish-Irish saint, whose legend included the miracle of digging a large amount of land in a very short time. One can see why the Gardeners would hold such a saint in high esteem. However, Venice – a variant of Veronica – has no obvious connection with gardening; and joining these two saints together seems inexplicable. Nevertheless, two mystery plays were commissioned by this society, each one dramatizing episodes from the life of one of their two patrons. The texts of these plays were printed twice in the first thirty years of the sixteenth century. The epilogue of one of the plays clearly shows the link between them and the Confraternity of the Master Gardeners.

Similarly, and also in the mid-sixteenth century, the members of a church of Saint Christopher, then very close to Notre-Dame cathedral, put on a play showing the life and, especially, the gruesome death, of their patron.[14] In this case, not only the text of the play has survived – it was printed at least twice – but we also have the contract made with the carpenters for the construction of a theatre (probably linear), to be built at the 'Hostel d'Orleans' in 1541.

The examples just mentioned are reasonably well-known. Two other examples of Paris performances which I have recently discovered can also be used to complete the picture of small-scale mystery play performances. Three *laboureurs* from the suburb of Villejuif decided in 1547 to put on a *Mystère de Saint Cyr*, and signed a contract to pay the considerable sum of 20 *livres tournois* to a *painctre* who was to design the sets and special effects required;[15] and in 1529 a Paris baker paid a lawyer the enormous sum of over 70 *livres tournois* for the manuscript of a *Mystère de Saint Jean Baptiste*,

---

[13] *Le Mystère de Sainte Venise*, ed. G.A. Runnalls, *Textes Littéraires* (Exeter: Exeter University, 1980). [Out of print: text now available on the internet: http://www.uhb.fr/alc/medieval/venice.htm].

[14] *Le Mystère de Saint Christofle*, ed. by G.A. Runnalls, *Textes Littéraires* (Exeter: Exeter University, 1973).

[15] *Recueil d'Actes Notariés relatifs à l'Histoire de Paris et de ses Environs*, ed. By E. Coyecque, vols. 1-2 (*Histoire Générale de Paris*), Paris, vol. II, 4470: 1547: 'Jehan Boyvin, painctre a Lynoys soubz Montlehery, promet a Guillaume Maucoustellier, Mathieu Jolys et Noel Cresté, tous laboureurs a Villejuifve, de faire tous et chascun les portraictz et fainctes qu'il conviendra de faire pour le Jeu et Mistere de la Vie Sainct Cyr, qu'ilz entendent jouer ou faire jouer [qu'ilz consentirent le jour d'hier a jouer] aud. lieu de Villejuifve et ce bien et deuement, comme il appartiendra, aux jours de dimenche ou aultres festes…20 livres tournois.'

the baker having already taken part in a performance of the play.[16]

These examples show how quite humble Parisians – labourers, bakers, carpenters, journeymen – were involved in organizing play performances, in spite of the considerable expense. Putting on mystery plays was not something that was initiated only by the élite.

The surviving documentation suggests that there developed a gradual divide in the types of religious drama performed in Paris. The numerous examples of plays put on by the *Confréries* and private citizens clearly show that one of the most popular types of religious drama in Paris was the small-scale, intimate *mystère*. These continued to be performed, with little fundamental change, for over 200 years; significantly, they tended to be regular, often annual, events. On the other hand, Passion plays and other biblical dramas tended to get longer and more complex; these were probably therefore one-off or infrequent affairs, performed out-of-doors, and much more expensive and complicated events than the small-scale religious *confrérie* plays. It is generally believed that most of the plays put on by the *Confrérie de la Passion* were much more like the *Mystère de Saint Denis* described at the beginning of this article, than those of the Goldsmiths or Jean Louvet.

In some ways, the most remarkable Parisian play performance was one of the very last. It seems that the *Confrérie de la Passion* went out with a bang. Although there are no surviving official accounts or archives, several contemporary chronicles tell us that in 1539, 1541 and 1542, the *Confrérie* mounted three large-scale performances of biblical mystery plays, respectively the *Passion*, the *Actes des Apôtres* and the *Viel Testament*. They were all organized in the same way. The second of these was apparently the most splendid – and controversial – of all.[17]

The *Mystère des Actes des Apôtres* was an enormous play of about 60,000 lines, which embraced the dramatized lives of all twelve apostles. A considerable amount of information about this performance has survived, as well as the complete text, which was printed immediately afterwards. It was a massive undertaking. To announce and publicise the play, there was a *cri*. On 16 December

---

[16] *op. cit.* vol. I 1097: 1529: 'Vente par Gilles Borel, praticien en court laye a Paris, a Guillaume Duchemin, boulanger a Paris, d'un mestayre par personnages servant a jouer la vie monseigneur Sainct Jehan Baptiste tels que led. acheteur les a veuz et desquelz il a joué par ci devant, moyennant dix escus d'or soleil une fois payés et une rente de 100 sols tournois rachetable en une fois pour 60 livres tournois, et partant sera tenu et promect led. Borel servir led. Duchemyn du jour d'huy dud. mestayre.'

[17] R. Lebègue, *Le Mystère des Actes des Apôtres* (Paris: Champion, 1929); see also G.A. Runnalls, 'Sponsorship and Control'.

1540, at 8 o'clock in the morning, the four leaders of the *Confrérie* met with the other members and went around the city, with the town crier, trumpeters and policemen, and at every crossroad announced the plan to put on the play, and invited any would-be actors to come to the auditions which were to be held on 26 December, when the roles were distributed. The *fatiste* was then appointed and he set to work revising the text, which had already been in existence for some decades. When it was completed, approval was sought from the Paris Parlement and the Sorbonne; an attempt was thus made to appease both political and religious authorities. The scribes then set to work copying out the actors' roles, so that rehearsals could begin.

The performance itself started on 8 May 1541 and continued, on Sundays and public holidays, until 25 September 1541. Contemporary records tell us that the play occupied thirty-five days. Each day's performance began about 1 p.m. and continued until about 5 p.m. The audience naturally had to pay to enter the theatre, but most seats could not be reserved, so the general public arrived early, often by about 8 or 9 a.m. We fortunately have a detailed description of the theatre and other aspects of the organization, in the account of the servant of a nobleman who attended one of these performances. The Duc de Clèves had lunch with a gentleman whose house was next to the theatre. We learn that:

> Behind the gentleman's house was a fine large theatre covered by a high canvas awning. The theatre was arranged in the round, in the ancient Roman style, so that the spectators were seated on a series of twenty benches, each one higher than the one in front. Above these benches were constructed three circular floors consisting of galleries and boxes. In this theatre, during the afternoon, they performed a fine play based on stories from the Acts of the Apostles, to which a number of agreeable ceremonies and processions were added.[18]

The theatre described is that of the Hôtel de Flandres, which was where the *Confrérie de la Passion* regularly mounted their plays until 1541.

The play was undoubtedly a great popular success. But this cut no ice with many more influential people, who criticized the play on various grounds. In particular the organizers were on the receiving

---

[18] The original document in Dutch, together with an English translation, appears in N. Brooks, 'Notes on Performances of French Mystery Plays', *Modern Language Notes* 39 (1924), 276; French translations can be found in Lebègue, *op. cit.*, p. 194, in Gustave Cohen, *La Mise en scène dans le théâtre religieux français du moyen âge* (Paris: Champion, 1951), p. XV, and in Rey-Flaud, *op. cit.*, p. 233.

end of a vicious attack from the *Procureur Général* of the Paris Parliament. Firstly he complained of the excessive duration of the play. Then he was furious that the public were failing to attend mass on Sunday mornings in order to get good seats, and that this had led many priests to cancel or abbreviate their services. Then there were clear signs of technical incompetence in the stage effects, which led to public mockery of holy events. For example, one of the expected highlights – both in terms of the spiritual lesson of the play and in terms of theatrical effects – was the descent of the Holy Spirit. Unfortunately, it did come down when it was supposed to. The public hooted in derision. Finally, the quality of the acting, in spite of the auditions, was poor. The actors, some only semi-literate, were not able to do justice to the learned and latinate lines; they often finished up by speaking nonsense, forgetting lines, pausing in the wrong place, etc. Again, the public reacted derisively.

The performance thus provoked criticism from the general public, which in principle enjoyed the plays, as well as from the religious and political authorities, who detested them. The Protestants in particular were shocked by the mixture of sacred and profane, the legendary and the true. And all agreed that the mystery plays led the public at times to mock the great mysteries of the Christian faith. It was just seven years later that the performance of large-scale religious mystery plays was forbidden in Paris.

As one might expect in a heavily centralized country like France, Paris has played an absolutely crucial role in the evolution of French drama. From the seventeenth century through to the early twentieth century, the capital totally dominated the provinces, to the extent that the story of French theatre was largely the story of Parisian theatre. But this was not true in the Middle Ages. Provincial theatre was extremely active and varied; moreover, it was – and still is – well-documented.[19] Yet, although much information about medieval theatrical activity in Paris seems to have been lost, enough remains for us to be sure that ordinary medieval Parisians loved the theatre as much as their modern counterparts, and that the kind of theatre enjoyed by its citizens was in essence like that in the rest of the medieval French-speaking world. After all, it was in Paris that was created the first – and only – French confraternity exclusively devoted to performing religious plays. But, less fortunately, it was also in Paris, rather than in the provinces, that mystery plays were first officially suppressed.

---

[19] A. Hindley, 'Histoires locales du théâtre français: Moyen Age et Renaissance', *Le Moyen Français* 35-36 (1998), 129-59.

Community versus subject in late medieval French confraternity drama and ritual

ROBERT L.A. CLARK

IT HAS BECOME A commonplace in the scholarship on medieval drama to speak of the latter as an activity which involved the broad participation of the community for which it was performed and to emphasize the collective aspect of this experience. The privileging of the text by traditional literary scholarship has given way to an interest in the dramatic event in all its complexities as collective experience. Similarly, the theatre historians' interest in the staging of medieval plays has been broadened to include questions of performance and reception, allowing play-production to be seen more in the light of the expectations that performers and spectators brought to the dramatic event. Since these expectations were of necessity conditioned by social experience, much of this recent scholarship has been an attempt to determine the socio-cultural significance of the medieval theatre for its producers and consumers alike. Despite substantial differences in approach and emphasis, critics such as Elie Konigson,[1] Henri Rey-Flaud[2] and Jean-Charles Payen,[3] in their work on the French medieval theatre, and Mervyn James, in his work on Corpus Christi,[4] have all argued that the medieval theatre was above all a collective undertaking through which urban social groups and the urban élites in particular gave expression to what may properly be termed a bourgeois ideology. There has been a tendency on the part of many

---

[1] 'Religious Drama and Urban Society in France at the End of the Middle Ages,' in *Drama and Society* 1 (Cambridge: Cambridge University Press, 1979), pp. 33-34.

[2] *Pour une dramaturgie du Moyen Age* (Paris: PUF, 1980), p. 1.

[3] 'Théâtre médiéval et culture urbaine', *Revue d'Histoire du Théâtre* 35 (1983), 246.

[4] Mervyn James, 'Ritual, Drama and Social Body in the Late Medieval English Town', *Past and Present* 98 (1983), 1-29.

critics, however, to assume that the drama was efficacious in cementing the identity of the communities in question as it advanced the ideology of the urban élites. More nuanced and conflicted models of interpretation have been largely lacking in much of the scholarship, caught as it has been in its largely unexamined assumptions about the nature of collective experience in the Middle Ages and the role of subjectivity in that experience. My goal in the first part of this essay is to articulate an approach to confraternity ritual and drama (the *Miracles de Nostre Dame par personnages*) which, in the first instance, looks to their formal aspects in order to determine precisely *how* these cultural forms worked to resolve conflict and create a sense of community. I will argue that the ritual and theatre of urban confraternities were dynamic forms which allowed for the systematic processing of experience and its articulation into symbolic systems of meaning, and the analysis of their fundamental structures will show that both ultimately served as vehicles for the self-definition and social promotion of the groups in question. Through the manipulation of these symbolic structures, they promoted their socio-ideological values, reconciled these values when they were in conflict, and ordered their world. While thus recognizing the importance of the collective dimension, I propose in the second part of the essay to explore issues of reception by the subjects who made up the plays' audience. In particular, issues of class and gender will be used to put forward a model of collective experience of the drama which makes room for conflicts among and within the subjects who experienced it.

The *Miracles de Nostre Dame par personnages* bear witness to a sustained interest in the staging of drama on the part of a wealthy Parisian confraternity, the Puy des orfèvres.[5] From approximately 1339 to 1382, this confraternity associated with the Parisian Goldsmiths' Guild performed Marian miracle plays, doubtless in conjunction with their annual banquet.[6] One may generally say that thematically a number of the Cangé miracle plays do express a certain bourgeois ideology insofar as they clearly seek to reconcile spiritual and material concerns. This is what one might reasonably expect to find in a collection of plays produced by a confraternity associated with a trade guild, for confraternities were themselves institutions which could not avoid being caught in a web of conflicting interests.

---

[5] *Miracles de Nostre Dame par personnages,* ed. by Gaston Paris and Ulysse Robert, 7 vols. (Paris: Société des Anciens Textes Français, 1876-83); vol. 8, *Glossaire et tables*, ed. by François Bonnardot (Paris: Firmin-Didot, 1893); hereafter referred to as *Miracles*.

[6] See G.A. Runnalls, 'Mediaeval Trade Guilds and *the Miracles de Nostre Dame par personnages*', *Medium Aevum* 39 (1970), 257-87.

That is, confraternities were charged with promoting the *spiritual* welfare of individuals who were notoriously jealous of their *social* standing in the community and whose very existence was posited on the successful pursuit of *material* prosperity. Spiritual, social, material: even this superficial profile of the concerns of confraternity members suggests the extremely complex cultural dynamics in which they participated and argues against a socially homogeneous audience and a uniform reception of the plays and rituals performed by these groups.

In order to gain a better understanding of the significance of these plays as cultural performances, we must first consider how the festive life of the confraternity, especially the banquet and its rituals, promoted the fraternal ideal (*communitas*). The high point of the life of the confraternity was the patron saint's or other designated feast day, for this was the only occasion, excepting religious services, when the whole group was authorized to assemble. Since the feast day served to reaffirm the social integrity of the group for itself and others, confraternity statutes usually stipulate mandatory attendance at the feast-day celebrations and fines for delinquent members. The patron's feast was, like the confraternity itself, characterized by the intermingling of sacred and secular preoccupations. The celebrations culminated in the banquet, where official business and good cheer shared the stage with the expression of cultural values essential to the group's identity. Within the protocol of the feast-day meeting of confraternities, the mechanics of institutional self-renewal were in some cases of an extremely practical nature: new officers were elected and new members initiated. To instruct new members and remind old ones of their responsibilities, the confraternity's statutes might be read at the banquet.[7] But beyond these mechanics of institutional self-renewal, confraternities engaged in various cultural and symbolic practices which served to promote a coherent set of shared values, the most important of which were processions, banquet ritual and the performance of poetry and theatre. These highly ritualized activities added to the social lustre of the group while working to renew its identity and integrity.

The statutes of some confraternities show that the exercise of charity could be integrated into the very ritual of the banquet. The Grande Confrérie Notre-Dame aux Prêtres et Bourgeois had four almoners whose job was to collect the left-over food and place it in

---

[7] Le Roux de Lincy, *Recherches sur la grande confrérie Notre-Dame aux prêtres et bourgeois de Paris* (Paris, 1844), p.98; Abbé L. Meister, *La Confrérie de Saint-Jean-l'Evangéliste établie en l'Eglise Saint-Pierre de Beauvais* (Paris, 1909), p.7.

fine vessels. The food included that which was served at the table reserved for confraternity members who had died during the course of the year.[8] Other confraternities fed paupers at their banquet in what was essentially a symbolic gesture through which a reversal or levelling of social statuses was achieved. The statutes of the Confrérie de Saint-Jean-l'Evangéliste of Beauvais stipulate that each new member provide a token (*méreau*) for one pauper, and these new members were furthermore required to wait table at the banquet. The Confrérie de la Madeleine, according to tradition founded in the Eglise Saint-Eustache in Paris by twenty-five *pauvres*, commemorated this event at their banquet by feeding the same number of poor men and women. The poor also played an important role at the mass celebrated the same day in the confraternity's chapel. All paupers could attend the mass, and twenty-five of them were to receive a *denier* each, at the confraternity's expense, to offer as alms, passing ahead of the members to make their offering.[9] In these actions we see clearly illustrated the role of the poor as intercessors. More significant for our purposes, though, are the mechanisms through which statuses were levelled and the fraternal bond reinforced. We shall see a similar dynamic at work in the miracle play form.

The survival of such a large body of dramatic texts as the *Miracles de Nostre Dame par personnages*, which can be situated chronologically, geographically and socially, offers a rare opportunity for the scholar interested in the socio-cultural interpretation of the medieval theatre; and the interest of such an interpretation is further enhanced by the fact that the texts in question form a generically coherent ensemble. The stability of this form for a period of over forty years is all the more remarkable when one considers that this was a period during which war, insurrection and a devastating epidemic were visited upon this same community.[10] One is led to wonder if

---

8 Le Roux de Lincy, pp. 99-100.

[9] *Ordonnances des Roys de France de la Troisième Race*, ed. Secousse, 23 vols. (Paris, 1729-1750) 19, pp.117-20. For further details on confraternity feast-day rituals, see Robert L. A. Clark, 'Charity and Drama: The Response of the Confraternity to the Problem of Urban Poverty in Fourteenth-Century France', *Fifteenth-Century Studies* 13 (1988), 359-69.

[10] Runnalls has argued that the manuscript reflects this background of social turmoil, noting that there are no plays for the years corresponding to the burgher revolt led by Etienne Marcel (1358-60) and that the last play was probably staged in 1382, a fact attributable to the severe but temporary suppression of guild activities by Charles VI following the uprising of the *maillotins*. Runnalls has further suggested that the erasing of all references to the Puy des orfèvres in the manuscript's rubrics may be the result of political considerations ('Mediaeval Trade Guilds').

some generic aspect of these plays held particular significance for the urban artisans who formed their audience. Generically based criticism has often been more of an impediment than a help in the interpretation of the medieval theatre, and this certainly holds true for much of the earlier scholarship on the Cangé *Miracles*, which was dominated by source studies and a concern for classifying the plays according to sub-genre.[11] Recent developments in literary theory and the social sciences, however, have contributed to a revitalization of genre in the study of medieval literature. Hans Robert Jauss and Maria Corti have both posited the necessity of a critical approach combining formalistic rigour and socio-historical enquiry.[12] In the field of French medieval theatre, such an approach has been used most notably by Henri Rey-Flaud and Elie Konigson. In addition, Anglo-American scholarship has been influenced by the use of anthropological models, particularly those to be found in the work of Victor Turner.[13] It is in the light of these developments that I offer a new approach to the genre of the dramatized Marian miracle and a new appreciation of the significance of this dramatic form for its public.

The already noted durability and stability of the genre of the Marian miracle *par personnages* make possible a synchronic approach to this form. Before proceeding with this analysis, I must stress that a diachronic perspective can, of course, be useful, for it can help determine the extent of structural and thematic shifting. A diachronic perspective reveals, for example, a shift in the use of sources in the Cangé collection which is particularly suggestive for a generically based analysis. Only nineteen of the forty plays have sources which were already Marian, while the others derive from a variety of earlier source types, including epic, romance, and hagiography.[14] If one

---

[11] See Alexandre Micha, 'La femme injustement accusée dans les *Miracles de Notre-Dame*', in *Mélanges d'histoire du théâtre du Moyen Age offerts à Gustave Cohen* (Paris: Nizet, 1950); Grace Frank, *The Medieval French Drama* (Oxford: Clarendon Press, 1954), p. 119, considers the *Miracles* to be 'essentially religious plays'.

[12] Hans Robert Jauss, 'Theory of Genres and Medieval Literature', in *Toward an Aesthetic of Reception*, transl. by Timothy Bahti (Minneapolis: University of Minnesota Press, 1982), pp. 100-01; Maria Corti, *An Introduction to Semiotics*, transl. by Margherita Bogat and Allen Mandelbaum (Bloomington: Indiana University Press, 1978), pp. 10-16.

[13] See, for example, Kathleen M. Ashley, 'An Anthropological Approach to the Cycle Drama: The Shepherds as Sacred Clowns', *Fifteenth-Century Studies* 13 (1988), 127-38; Richard L. Homan, 'Ritual Aspects of the York Cycle,' *Theatre Journal* 33 (1981), 303-15. For a critique of the wide-ranging use that has been made of Turner's model, see Clifford Geertz, 'Blurred Genres: The Refiguration of Social Thought,' *American Scholar* 49.2 (1980), 172-73.

[14] For the plays' sources, see Rudolf Glutz, *Miracles de Nostre Dame par*

arbitrarily divides the collection into two equal parts consisting of twenty plays each, one sees that of the first twenty plays, fifteen are of Marian inspiration, while only four of the last twenty are drawn from Marian sources. This shows that we are in fact dealing with a dynamic form, and one may reasonably interpret this thematic shifting away from specifically Marian material as variation and extension of the genre to meet, or perhaps encourage, the widening of the audience's horizon of expectations, to use Jauss's term. Such variation and extension can, however, lead to a breaking of the limits and subsequent transformation of the genre. There is in the Cangé collection what would seem to be a move in the direction of such a break, for one of the last plays in the manuscript, the incomplete *Miracle de saint Laurent* (no. 38), breaks off after more than 2000 lines without Notre-Dame and her train having made their appearance, although this is perhaps but an instance of the author playing on the expectations of his public.

It is, however, the synchronic analysis of the form of the miracle play which I wish to pursue here. One cannot, of course, define genre in terms of a single factor; rather, a certain combination or configuration of factors creates a kind of family resemblance among several works which allows us to consider them as constituting a literary genre. In the case of the *Miracles de Nostre Dame par personnages*, one might reasonably consider as the *sine qua non* of the genre the highly stylized Marian interventions in which Mary descends from heaven accompanied by her escort of saints and angels to the strains of musical *rondeaux*. The audience certainly expected these scenes, but as we have seen in the case of the *Miracle de saint Laurent*, one can arrive at the last scenes of a play without the mechanics of such an intervention. One could in fact make the argument for several of the plays that they would come off just as well, if not better, without Mary. Clearly, the very real coherence, or family resemblance, of the collection is due to more than the Marian set pieces. The Marian interventions should not, however, be considered superfluous features. They function, rather, as an outward, exemplary sign, replicating and confirming the fundamental structures of the plays. It is these fundamental structures, which I propose to analyze here, and not the Marian interventions which create the generic coherence of the collection.

At the beginning of a typical miracle play, there is a stable social

---

personnages: Kritische Bibliographie und neue Studien zu Text, Entstehungszeit und Herkunft (Berlin: Akademie, 1954), pp. 67-76; Alfred Jeanroy, 'Le théâtre religieux en français: Les quarante Miracles de Nostre Dame', in *Histoire littéraire de la France* 39 (1921; Paris: Imprimerie nationale, 1967), pp. 200-57.

situation. The setting may be monastic or clerical, aristocratic or bourgeois, but in each case the initial stability is shattered by a human agent. Frequently, this involves the breaking of a vow or the committing of a crime. Since the cohesion and stability of the initial community is no longer functional, redress must come from outside. The redressive machinery may be judicial or more specifically penitential. In any event, there is an appeal to, or the intervention of, an outside authority, and usually both human and divine authority are called into play. These two may be in accordance with each other or in outright conflict, as in certain saints' plays where the social breach is due to the Christian faith of the saint and the human redressive action is instigated by the pagan emperor, for example. The solution of the crisis results in the reintegration of the original community or in the establishment of a new community. Almost exactly half of the forty plays (twenty-one, to be precise) involve a return to the *status quo ante*, while the others conclude with the founding of new communities, usually monastic.

Having established the framework of the Marian miracle play, I now offer a systematic and rigorous analysis of one of the plays in order to draw out the specific mechanisms involved in the movement from stability through crisis to resolution. In his *Pour une dramaturgie du Moyen Age*, Henri Rey-Flaud has offered an analytical method based on his reconstruction of the staging of the *Jeu de saint Nicolas*. Rey-Flaud embraces in one space both play and public, and the play is not simply a text but a cultural performance. But while his conception of medieval theatre as a socio-cultural phenomenon of a reflexive nature provides a welcome departure from prevailing interpretive models, his reconstruction, however compelling, is highly speculative, based as it is upon evidence which bears no direct relationship to the play in question.[15] For this reason I have chosen to adapt an analytical method developed by Elie Konigson which he has applied to four other plays in the Cangé collection.[16] The basis of this method is a situational analysis of the play which seeks to identify its elementary structures as expressed through the dynamic relationships among the characters. I propose to bridge the gap between play and public by showing that the typical

---

[15] Rey-Flaud's proposed staging of the twelfth-century *Jeu de saint Nicolas* is largely based on Fouquet's fifteenth-century miniature of the martyrdom of St Apolline, a document whose reliability as a representation of medieval staging practice is problematic.

[16] Elie Konigson, 'Structures élémentaires de quelques fictions dramatiques dans les miracles par personnages du manuscrit Cangé', *Revue d'Histoire du Théâtre* 29 (1977), 105-27.

miracle play presents the same formal dynamic of reversal which we have seen to be operative in confraternity ritual.

The play I have chosen to analyze (in a much simplified version of Konigson's model) is the second play in the collection, the *Miracle de l'abbesse grosse*.[17] The analysis yields the following chief points regarding the structure of the play:

1) The action follows the pattern of (a) initial stability (here, within a female monastic community); (b) breach (the Abbess's breaking of her vow of chastity); (c) crisis (the threatened disgrace of the Abbess and dissolution of the community); (d) appeal to outside authority (both heavenly, in the person of Mary, and hierarchical, in the person of the bishop); and (e) resolution (the original community restored and the bishop's community strengthened by the addition of new members). Through its structure, the play expresses a profound concern for community integrity and an awareness of the fragility of the social bond, and, as a corollary, a concern for individual responsibility and individual integration into the community structures.

2) The action presents a series of reversals as the Abbess's authority is first subverted by the nuns who denounce her, then re-established by the bishop after her examination and confession. This is one of the principal mechanisms of the play's dynamic form.

3) The characters rarely act directly against each other. Other characters intrude, as in the case of the clerk, or are sought out as intercessors, either human or divine. The single Marian intervention, which is a reciprocal action in that it occurs in response to the Abbess's prayer, is structurally integrated into, and even subordinated within, a chain of human actions. Mary's is only the most visible and the most stylized intervention, and, as such, is invested with exemplary sign value, thematically and, above all, structurally. The role of intermediaries is thus a major dynamic principle of the form.

4) The Abbess's sexual indiscretion results not only in the breaking of her vow but also in the transfer of wealth away from the community. Although this is a secondary element which is not subsequently developed in the play, it shows a concern for the material foundation of social stability, a point which would presumably not have been lost on the play's predominantly bourgeois audience.

---

[17] *Miracles* 1, 58-100. It should be noted that this method is most effective in plays in which the action is dominated by crisis or conflict; the *Miracle de la Nativité Nostre Seigneur Jhesu Crist* (*Miracles* 1, 204-43) and the *Miracle de l'évêque à qui Nostre Dame s'apparut* (*Miracles* 2, 56-87), both of which present static situations, do not lend themselves well to this mode of analysis.

Situational analysis thus shows how the miracle play serves as a frame within which human crises proceed from eruption through crisis to resolution, and it is conformity to this frame that creates to a great extent the generic coherence of the collection. This form is, of course, hardly unique to the plays under examination. Many readers will recognize in my analysis the classic, three-stage model for rites of passage proposed by Arnold van Gennep: separation from the old state, transition and incorporation into the new state.[18] The three phases of van Gennep's model can apply to individual rites of passage of the life-crisis type, or to cyclical, collective passages in which a social group makes the transition from one season to the next.

The British anthropologist Victor Turner subsequently adapted van Gennep's model in his study of African tribal ritual as social process, using the term 'social drama' for the process through which groups resolve crisis.[19] It was Turner's contention that social dramas were 'the raw stuff out of which theatre comes to be created as societies develop in scale and complexity and out of which it is continually regenerated'.[20] The analysis of the *Miracle l'abbesse grosse* here proposed shows that the miracle play is indeed a processual form (to use Turner's term) for the resolution of crisis; and, in its fundamental preoccupation with social cohesion, the play functions as a perceptual frame allowing cultural reflexivity. Turner's work on social drama, it would seem, offers us an insightful and provocative model for the analysis of the Marian miracle play.

The aspect of Turner's work which has had the greatest impact in theatre studies, however, is the emphasis he placed on the transitional phase *(rites liminaires)* of van Gennep's model, a phase for which Turner used the term 'liminal'. In his field studies among the Ndembu tribe, Turner observed such anti-structural actions as 'ritual humiliation, stripping of signs and insignia of preliminal status, ritual leveling, and ordeals and tests of various kinds...'.[21] As the term 'preliminal' in the last quotation would indicate, the result of these actions is the creation of the 'liminal' state. Turner describes

---

[18] Arnold van Gennep, *Les rites de passage* (Paris: Nourry, 1909), pp. 13-15. To designate these three stages, van Gennep uses the terms *rites de séparation (préliminaires), rites de marge (liminaires), rites d'agrégation (postliminaires)*.

[19] Victor Turner, 'Social Dramas and Ritual Metaphors', in *Dramas, Fields, and Metaphors: Symbolic Action in Human Society* (Ithaca: Cornell University Press, 1974), pp. 37-42.

[20] Victor Turner, 'Liminality and the Performative Genres', in *Rite, Drama, Festival, Spectacle: Rehearsals Toward a Theory of Cultural Performance*, ed. by John J. MacAloon (Philadelphia: Institute for the Study of Human Issues, 1984), p. 24.

[21] Turner, 'Social Dramas', p. 53.

liminality as the unstructured spaces that occur between an individual's or a group's successive participations in structured social milieux. Liminality is thus a state of being betwixt and between, a space in which structures are negated or reversed by ritualistic actions and in which rites of passage occur and bonds of *communitas* are reinforced. In liminality, society's structures are temporarily suspended or reversed, often during circumscribed festive periods, after which there is a return to the *status quo ante*. In Turner's model, festivity and liminality serve to reaffirm the social order, although Turner lessened the functionalist aspect of his argument by stressing the ludic and aesthetic possibilities offered by liminality. In the final analysis, ritual is, for Turner, a perceptual frame which allows the members of a community *consciously* to assess their collective strivings and failings, to effect transitions and to resolve crises.[22]

The heuristic usefulness of the concept of liminality is immediately apparent in a text such as the *Pregnant Abbess*. The Abbess is the only character, with the exception of the new-born child, who comes into direct contact with the holy. In the chapel she prays to Mary to save her from the disgrace of her pregnancy, already known to the nuns. She dozes off during her oration, and while she is sleeping, Mary descends from Heaven and delivers the baby. The Abbess is in a liminal space at this point, suspended between consciousness and unconsciousness, prestige and disgrace, and indeed, life and death, if one considers the dangers of childbirth for medieval women. But the Abbess, once delivered of the child, is not yet out of danger, for her innocence must be publicly established by the bishop. Her contact with the agent of human authority is thus also marked by liminality, for she must undergo the humiliation of a physical examination at the hands of one of her own nuns and of a midwife, the negative image of Mary as *ventrière*. As already noted, these situations are marked by a series of reversals from which the Abbess will emerge to retake her place at the head of her community. There is yet another aspect of liminality in the play, though. The Abbess's son, born into that liminal

---

[22] For a powerful critique of Turner's conception of liminality, see C. Clifford Flanigan, 'Liminality, Carnival, and Social Structure: The Case of Late Medieval Biblical Drama', in Kathleen Ashley, ed., *Victor Turner and the Construction of Cultural Criticism: Between Literature and Anthropology* (Bloomington: Indiana University Press, 1990), pp. 42-63, esp. pp. 57-58. For other theories which address in different ways the relationship between social reality and ritual, see Maurice Bloch, 'Symbols, Song, Dance and Features of Articulation: Is Religion an Extreme Form of Traditional Authority?' in *Ritual, History and Power* (London and Atlantic Highlands: Athlone, 1989), pp.19-45; and Stanley Jeyaraja Tambiah, 'A Performative Approach to Ritual', in *Culture, Thought, and Social Action: An Anthropological Perspective* (Cambridge: Harvard University Press), pp. 123-66.

space, is truly a liminal figure, and one could consider his successful insertion and acceptance into another community as the most significant structural development of this play.

The miracle play and the banquet ritual thus share a similar dynamic of ritual reversal resulting in the levelling of statuses. In these stylized, symbolic actions one sees the clearest expression of the ideal of the confraternity, that of *communitas* in which all were joined by a single bond, expressed through a generous commensality which could be extended to embrace, in symbolic fashion, not only all the living, but the dead as well. Mechanisms of ritual reversal or levelling were an effective way to recreate the fraternal bond in a festive and liminal space in which were temporarily suspended the distinctions between work and play, high and low, rich and poor, living and dead.

The use of Turner's model in the study of medieval European culture does, of course, present certain methodological problems. Turner, after all, based his theory on first-hand observation in the field, benefiting as well from interviews with participants in the rituals he was studying. These 'informants' could *tell* him what the ritual meant to them, and this 'indigenous exegesis' was the point of departure for the anthropologist's exegesis of the ritual and its symbols.[23] In studying the confraternity ritual and theatre of medieval Europe, we are obviously at a tremendous remove from these practices and their participants. We must rely on sketchy documentary evidence, and, while these accounts may in some cases be fairly descriptive, they do not tell us how the participants *experienced* the ritual in social or psychological terms. Our distance thus involves not only a time factor but an even greater gap in *mentalité*. The experiences of the men and women of the Middle Ages must, to a very large extent, remain irrevocably foreign to us. What is more, the more obvious tools of interpretation that we do possess may be of only limited value. For example, in interpreting the reversal of social statuses so often included in confraternity ritual, we are of course reminded of standard Christian teaching: 'The last shall be first,' etc. But to interpret the ritual in terms of Church doctrine leaves us in the same position as the anthropologist who would accept at face value the account of a ritual participant: standing outside the ritual looking in. The traditional Christian interpretation may serve as a point of departure, like the informant's interpretation in a field study, but it does not explain to us the particular efficacy of the ritual as it may have been experienced by the participants. Nor can it explain why

---

[23] Victor Turner, *The Ritual Process* (1969; Ithaca: Cornell University Press, 1982), pp. 14-15.

certain ritual actions or mechanisms were used instead of others. In a historical approach to confraternity ritual, on the other hand, certain elements, such as the oath and drink, may be singled out as remnants from earlier pre-Christian practices.[24] But in this case the interpretation is not adequate because it fails to see how these aspects are actually and presently engaged in a dynamic with the other elements of the ritual. Turner's model can be usefully applied to the study of the ritual of the medieval confraternity precisely because it seeks to address the question of ritual efficacy from the inside, as it were – that is, by studying the various elements of ritual as they actually engage in a dynamic process.

The undeniable importance of the collective dimension of the ritual and theatre of medieval confraternities has, however, all but obscured the fact that the urban audiences were anything but unified. In concentrating on the collectivity, much of the recent scholarship has, as a result, largely ignored the issue of subjectivity in the reception of medieval plays. In and through their engagement in their collective rituals, medieval men and women were of course subjected to a whole range of institutional and economic constraints, just as they were in their day-to-day lives. We have seen, for example, that confraternity members were required to attend the annual banquet, pay the entrance fee (at least in some cases), and give alms. But at the same time, each of them brought to these ritual practices his or her own subjectivity, actively fashioning it by engaging in the collectivity's practices. Just as these medieval subjects were differentiated among themselves, it stands to reason that, even in such a shared experience, their participation in theatre and ritual must have been to a certain degree subjectively different. In the second part of this essay I therefore propose to explore the issue of subjectivity within the *Miracles de Nostre Dame par personnages* and to theorize the reception of the plays in such a way as to allow for a range of subject positions, including a resistant or antagonistic subject. The treatment of sexual and economic transgression in the plays will be read against the social context in which the plays were performed. Gender theory, in particular, will inform much of the discussion, for this is an area of critical theory in which the questioning of the status of the subject has been particularly acute. Before I address the medieval theatre and ritual from this perspective, it will be necessary to define more closely the notions of subject and subjectivity.[25]

---

[24] See, for example, Jeanne Deschamps, *Les Confréries au moyen âge* (Bordeaux: Bière, 1958), pp. 11-35.

[25] I would like to emphasize that this theorizing of subject positions is, of course, self-reflexive, grounded in a particular discursive and material – that is, historical –

A Dutch morality play of the mid-sixteenth century, *Man's Desire and Fleeting Beauty*, provides a textbook example of how a play may be perceived differently by different subject-spectators.[26] The Chamber of Rhetoric that produced the Dutch play was essentially the same type of urban, bourgeois institution as the literary *puy* that produced the earlier French miracle plays. In addition to putting on plays, both kinds of group also held poetry competitions. These factors justify the recourse to a text which may at first seem to be at too great a remove from the fourteenth-century miracle plays.

The Dutch text is remarkable in that the morality play proper is framed by opening and closing scenes in which members of the audience talk of the play which they have come to see. In the opening scene, we meet a woman from Leiden who has walked from her city to hear the 'rhetoricians' songs and poetry' and to see 'their grand parade'. Her enthusiasm is not shared by the good citizen who asks her: 'But won't your husband fuss each time you go? / Doesn't he wonder what you've gone to hear?' And he concludes:

Poetry's her love. To me, it's all a waste
Of time and trifling Rhetoricians' feelings.
I'd rather be out planning clever dealings
To bring in gold, I wouldn't mind it.[27]

Nonetheless, a fellow citizen convinces him to attend the performance, despite his protestations that he will surely be bored. Clearly, the potential spectators bring to this performance different sensitivities and expectations. Furthermore, gender and economics are not irrelevant in the construction of these attitudes: the burgher thinks that the woman's husband must surely wonder what she is up to, while for himself poetry is simply time lost for commerce. In an epilogue the two citizens, who were separated in the crowd, exchange their reactions to the play. Ironically, the initially reluctant spectator is full of enthusiasm. Indeed, he must explain the play to his friend, who was 'behind a man who was so tall, / Beside two chatterboxes, chattering'. The disgruntled spectator has in fact only the vaguest idea of what he has just seen: 'What was it they performed? I read the title—/ About a Fleeting Beauty, right?'[28] This humorous scene allows the

---

position, that of my own subjectivity.

[26] *Man's Desire and Fleeting Beauty*, transl. by Robert Potter and Elsa Strietman, *Dutch Crossing* 25 April, 1985; (Cambridge and Santa Barbara: Viterbo Press, 1984).

[27] *Man's Desire*, p. 42.

[28] *Man's Desire*, pp. 81-82.

playwright, of course, to recap the moral of his play for anyone who may have missed the point. But presumably one may 'miss the point' of a play for reasons other than having a bad seat. Many other factors may come into play and interfere with the 'proper' reception of a play: level of education, age, status and gender, to name only the most obvious.

We have seen that confraternity members, while encouraged in their rituals to set aside status and identity in deference to the collectivity, were people who could not avoid participation in complex, multiple dynamic fields, including economics, social status and gender. The company at confraternity banquets was, in fact, extremely heterogeneous, including both men and women, young and old, rich and poor, lay and clerical, bourgeois, noble, and even royal.[29] Can one assume that through their collective rituals confraternities succeeded in making a single fabric out of these many threads, what one could term the warp and woof of subjectivity?

Both confraternities and their secular counterparts, the guilds, were socially exclusive organizations. One of the primary functions of the guild was to limit the practice of a trade to recognized masters and their valets and apprentices so as to prevent intrusions into this privileged domain from outside or below. Membership in a guild represented very real economic advantages. Guild members in Paris automatically belonged to the confraternity associated with their trade while other confraternities were less strictly tied to the guilds. For the wealthy bourgeoisie, leadership in a powerful guild or confraternity was the mark of social prestige and power, but membership alone conferred a certain social distinction. The historical record shows that very real antagonisms existed between the urban bourgeois patrician class and the mass of more humble artisans, apprentices, journeymen, and even more marginalized groups. Occasionally, this latent hostility erupted within the guilds. At the time of the *Livre des métiers* (mid-thirteenth century), the drapers and the weavers of Paris formed one corporation in which the latter were in fact salaried workers of the former; after many years of uneasy cohabitation they split into two corporations.[30] Disputes between the masters of the trade and the simple valets, who usually belonged to the same confraternity, were

---

[29] All confraternities invited non-members to their banquet: spouses and other family members, clerics, members of religious orders, and even the king ('*Item. Le Roy nostre Seigneur doit avoir son mez entier*', statutes of the Parisian drapers' confraternity, *Ordonnances des Roys de France* 8, p. 584).

[30] Bronislaw Geremek, *Le Salariat dans l'artisanat parisien aux XIIIe-XVe siècles: Etude sur le marché de la main-d'oeuvre au Moyen Age*, transl. by Anna Posner and Christiane Klapisch-Zuber (Paris: Mouton, 1968), p. 117.

not uncommon.[31] In some cases, the valets of a trade formed their own confraternity to protect their interests against those of the masters.[32] In short, guilds and confraternities, although exclusive, were far from being harmonious organizations. They were in fact riven with cleavages along economic and social lines.

There were cleavages in these groups along gender lines as well. Although these were much less likely to result in open contention and thus be documented, they can still be detected in the historical record. Although women worked in all capacities in late medieval Paris, their participation in the organized sector of the economy, as represented by the guilds, was economically, socially and politically limited. Since the predominant unit of production was the family workshop, many wives and daughters of master artisans found employment there.[33] Wives could inherit the *maîtrise* from their husband, but records indicate that these independent mistresses were a tiny minority in their trade, except of course in those trades which were traditionally the preserve of women. Girls could be apprenticed in a number of trades, and at least six crafts had predominantly female membership, but the political power of women in these female crafts was severely limited. The position of salaried female workers was even more precarious, comparable to that of working children. At best, their wages were supplementary income for a household having more than one wage-earner; at worst, it was a sub-subsistence wage that drove many women to prostitution or crime.[34]

It is against this social backdrop that the ritual and theatre of medieval confraternities must be interpreted. In the case of the ritual reversals that have been described, it is hard to imagine that they could have successfully rendered the social hierarchy irrelevant, even temporarily. These reversals could be efficacious only insofar as they flew in the face of dominant social practices and hierarchies. The norm is, in fact, never absent but is clearly inscribed in the inversion effected by the ritual. Furthermore, the members were a privileged group, and it was precisely their privilege that allowed them to participate in such rituals to begin with. The collective charity practiced by confraternities thus served not only to promote the alleviation of poverty but also to define and delimit it. As such, charity also results in a validation of the social structure and of one's place in it. In Miri Rubin's eloquent formulation, the weaker members

---

[31] Geremek, pp. 102-10.

[32] Geremek, pp. 115-16.

[33] Geremek, p. 14.

[34] Geremek, p. 91.

of the community became others instead of brothers.[35] The ideal of *communitas* was, however, never meant to be all-embracing; inclusion serves also to define those to be excluded. I do not mean to suggest that the ritual of the confraternities was a cynical manipulation that allowed members to promote their interests behind a fraternal mask. But the ritual participants, who were certainly capable of maintaining a critical distance, did not forget their place in the scheme of things, nor what kept them in that place.[36]

Confraternities, as institutions very much engaged in the material and social life of the community, offered sites where social groups might engage in intense negotiations with others and, more importantly, among themselves, in an effort to reconcile the different claims which their social world made upon them collectively and individually. As such, confraternities must be seen as deeply engaged in the formation of a bourgeois ideology – if, that is, one may define ideology as the systematic processing of values that allows social groups and the subjects composing them to reconcile their own contradictions. The *Miracles de Nostre Dame par personnages* show extreme tensions between conflicting claims made upon individual characters, and in many of the plays in the collection these tensions play themselves out with what I would term striking ambiguity. I see this ambiguity as characteristic of the texts, and it is essential to my interpretation of them as well. For it is precisely the conflicted, ambiguous construction of the characters in the typical miracle play which allows one to posit a conflicted and ambiguous – that is, subjective – reception of the play by audience members. The plays are especially rich in depictions of behaviour which is transgressive of cultural, social, economic and sexual norms. This concern with transgressive behaviour certainly expresses a preoccupation with community stability and cohesion, as I have argued in my analysis of the *Miracle de l'abbesse grosse*. It also betrays, however, an equally great concern with the problematic of the subject, here expressed in extreme forms of subjectivity.

The fourth play in the collection, *La femme du roy du Portigal*, presents some of the more extreme moral transgressions to be found in the collection.[37] Critics have been hard-pressed, understandably

---

[35] Miri Rubin, *Charity and Community in Medieval Cambridge* (Cambridge: Cambridge University Press, 1987), p. 299.

[36] In Tambiah's analysis, for example, the very formalization of ritual creates in the participants a psychical and emotional distancing from the enactment; and in the resulting interplay between the subject and the enactment, the symbolic order may be either affirmed or subverted (pp. 132-33).

[37] *Miracles* 1, pp. 148-202.

perhaps, to reconcile the conventional religious message of this and other plays – that no sin is too great to be forgiven – with the obvious relish given to the representation of the most lurid moral transgressions. Much of the early criticism on the Cangé miracle plays, as already noted, took a narrow philological approach and simply classified them according to type, identified their sources and analogues, and compared the different versions. Thus, in his 1921 survey of the collection, Jeanroy grouped *La femme du roy du Portigal* among those plays drawing on romance or epic, as opposed to Marian or hagiographic, sources. Such a scheme of categorization underscores, albeit unwittingly, the tensions which characterize the collection, even as it allows the critic to sidestep the interpretative difficulties posed by these tensions. Earlier critics also tended to view the entire collection as marked by what was termed 'bourgeois realism'. Thus, in her 1926 study of the collection, Marguerite Stadler-Honegger distinguished between the plays she saw as characterized, on the one hand, by an *esprit religieux*; and those plays she considered to be marked, on the other hand, by an *esprit réaliste*. Naturally, Stadler-Honegger did not place the *La femme du roy du Portigal* among the former. In her view, a play like *La femme du roy du Portigal* is one in which social concerns, translated by a relatively more realistic style, have prevailed over religious or spiritual preoccupations.[38] One remains, however, rather sceptical regarding the application of the term 'realist' to such a play and senses in both Jeanroy's and Stadler-Honegger's approaches a certain discomfort with the play's easy marriage of the sensational and the spiritual. The unstated assumption is that the social and the religious properly belong to separate realms of experience. Such a treatment of human experience, be it noted, is not likely to advance our understanding of how subjects respond to what may indeed be contradictory claims upon their feelings or beliefs.

More recent critics who have worked on the Cangé *Miracles*, have used hermeneutical approaches that incorporate psychological or social frames of reference. In a 1950 article which marks something of a departure from the older criticism, Alexandre Micha studied seven of the plays in which the main character is an unjustly accused woman, stating that this subject, 'riche de pathétique immédiat [. . .] convient à merveille à ce genre de public friand de dénouements moraux et heureux où l'innocence méconnue finit par triompher'.[39]

---

[38] Marguerite Stadler-Honegger, *Etude sur les Miracles de Notre-Dame par personnages* (Paris, 1926; reprint, Geneva: Slatkine, 1975), pp. 129-30.

[39] Micha, p. 85.

Micha's study has the merit of recognizing the importance of audience expectations in the conception of these works, but he uses a traditional interpretative paradigm which, among other limitations, obliges him to leave *La femme du roy du Portigal* out of his survey. The heroine of this play is not 'unjustly accused': she herself recognizes that she has committed criminal acts. This is, however, virtually the only difference between her and the unjustly accused heroines in the plays that he discusses, most of whom suffer from unfounded accusations or actions of a sexual nature.

The shortsightedness of these various critical efforts is fortunately not shared by Jean-Charles Payen, who suggests what would seem to be the obvious: the audience and producers of the miracle plays were fascinated by criminal or deviant behaviour, most often involving sexuality, and this fascination seems to have been especially keen regarding female sexuality. Payen explains this aspect of the plays in psychological and social terms. He argues that, even as a play fulfilled its ostensible role of edification, it channelled, or manipulated, the spectators' secret desires through the representation of behaviour that they might wish to indulge in, if only for a moment. Such behaviour can be represented precisely because the audience knows that it is criminal: Hell awaits the Wife of the King of Portugal and her ilk unless, of course, they repent. Payen, who qualifies this manipulation of the audience as 'ambiguous', sees the ideological recuperation of the urban bourgeoisie as the plays' ultimate goal; in the reconciliation of moral and religious values, he discerns the promotion of social complacency.[40] Payen's reading thus offers an opening onto issues of reception and subjectivity, but the latter remains unexplored in his discussion which is dominated by a vision of the medieval theatre as collective social experience.

Elie Konigson also speaks of tension between morality and religion in the miracle plays. Despite the emphasis that he also places on the collective dimension of the medieval theatre, in his analysis he argues that disruptive moral transgressions show the emergence of a new type of hero, the individual, who separates himself from the collectivity through the exercise of the only kind of free agency open to him, that of criminality. Although Konigson does not use the term, this new hero represents, simply put, the bourgeois subject. In the miracle plays, this hero becomes the victim of social and religious constraints but is nonetheless seen by Konigson as the standard bearer of an urban bourgeoisie that was slowly undergoing social emancipation.[41]

---

[40] Payen, p. 243.

[41] Konigson, 'Religious Drama and Urban Society', pp. 26-28.

Payen, in his analysis of bourgeois conformity, and Konigson, with his rhetoric of the individual, both betray a marked ideological bias in their approach to the miracle plays, but despite the differences in approach and emphasis, both critics seek to grasp the plays in their social dimension and to interpret them as social experience and expression. However, neither of these critics has much to say about the importance of economics in the plays; nor do they express any interest in seeing how gender, as opposed to sexual morality, figures into the bourgeois identity that they postulate. In my view, many of the plays are very specifically about economics and/or gender, and any discussion that seeks to assess the extent to which they express a bourgeois mentality or posit a bourgeois subjectivity must study these two aspects and their interrelationship.

The very first play in the collection, *L'enfant donné au diable*, offers a striking example of how sexual and economic transgression may be combined.[42] In its convoluted plot it is virtually impossible to separate the sacred, the sexual, and the socio-economic; and these issues play themselves out with the ambiguity of which I have spoken. Indeed, the outcome of the play turns on a fine point of medieval economic law. At the beginning of the play, an older married couple make a vow of chastity to the Virgin Mary.[43] But the husband, incited by the devil, breaks the vow and forces his wife to have intercourse with him. She then vows that, should a child be born from their union, she will give it to the devil. After the son is born, the wife secures a series of delays of payment from the devil; but, eventually, the devil claims his due and the case comes before the heavenly tribunal for a final determination. In the courtroom scene, Notre Dame asks the devils to show her the lady's written agreement to the effect that she would give up her son after fifteen years. When the devils confidently oblige, Notre Dame simply tears up the contract, arguing to Christ, the Judge, that since the boy had commended himself to their care, the lady did not have the right to give away what belonged to Christ and herself. In his judgement, Christ then finds the loophole in the case. While commending his mother's *entencion*, he corrects her interpretation of contract law. The lady's fault was that she had acted as an economic free agent when she did not have this right. Her fault was in giving away something that belonged to both her *and* her husband without *his* consent. The sacred is thus translated into the terms governing trade and into the world in which the audience lived.

---

[42] *Miracles* 1, pp. 2-54.

[43] See the discussion of this play and other versions of the story in Dyan Elliott, *Spiritual Marriage: Sexual Abstinence in Medieval Wedlock* (Princeton: Princeton University Press, 1993), pp. 181-83.

The-cut-and-dried aspect of Christ's decision cannot, however, mask the many ambiguities presented by this text. Perhaps the most ambiguous figure in the play is Notre Dame herself, who is somewhat less than the exemplary figure that one would expect in a play performed in her honour. Like the lady who, in a fit of irrationality, gives her child to the devil, Notre Dame angrily tears up the contract. And, just as the lady's action is condemned, so is Notre Dame's action corrected. Both must ultimately submit to the rule of institutional authority (i.e. patriarchy), and the necessity of restraining female impulsiveness would seem to be one of the lessons meant to be drawn from the play. One may question, however, whether all of the play's spectators would necessarily have responded to the text in the same way, for there is enough ambiguity in the construction of the female characters to allow audience reactions in which gender and marital status could well have come into play. The lady is certainly wrong to give her child to the devil, but she does so only after being forced by her husband to break her vow and submit to his sexual demands. The moral fault is his; hers is more the result of her socially instituted weakness than of a breach in morality. One can argue that she is not entirely to be blamed, just as Notre Dame is perhaps not entirely to be praised. These two female characters seem to be cut from the same cloth, a cloth in which we see what I have termed the warp and woof of a subjectivity constructed in large part in sexual and socio-economic terms. The several instances of feminine resistance and the ambiguous resolution of these within the play must have played on conflicting sentiments in the flesh and blood subjects for whose entertainment and edification this play was performed and in whom these many tensions were ultimately played out.

Two other plays in the collection deal directly with economic transgression. The earlier of these two plays, the *Miracle de un marchant et un juif*, was probably produced in 1377; the later play, *Pierre le Changeur*, was staged the following year.[44] The subject matter of these plays was certainly topical for their audience, and these are perhaps the clearest examples from the collection of how performative genres, as Turner would have it, offer a frame that makes it possible for the participants to reflect upon their lives. I have already noted that the Cangé *Miracles* were performed by a confraternity affiliated with the Parisian goldsmiths, and I have argued elsewhere at length that the texts of the Cangé manuscript may well have some connection with a confraternity founded by goldsmiths, money-changers and other burghers of Paris, the Confrérie Notre

---

[44] *Miracles* 6, pp. 169-300.

Dame de l'Annonciation.[45] Consequently, in seeing *Pierre le Changeur*, the spectators were seeing a play about a man in whom they would have recognized, if not themselves, perhaps a *confrère*. This less than exemplary brother – the miser Pierre is ultimately saved from damnation because he once threw bread at a beggar – could also have been perceived as an unscrupulous rival, certainly by the money-changers in the audience, and even by the goldsmiths, for these two groups had a long-running rivalry over the right to change money.

In the play of the *Miracle de un marchant et un juif*, however, the brother has become the 'other', an 'other' who was, an important economic rival of both the goldsmiths and the money-changers. The Jew Mossé lends money to a ruined Christian merchant. The latter, who has become rich trading in distant lands, suddenly realizes that he must repay the Jew the next day. Not knowing what else to do, he places the matter in God's hands by throwing a chest of money into the sea. The chest miraculously makes its way to Mossé on time, but he hides the money in his house; and when the merchant returns, the Jew denies having received the money. The Christian appeals to the image of Jesus and his Mother which he had taken as guarantor of the original loan, and the image speaks to reveal the deceit of the Jew, who converts to Christianity at the end of the play.

This was already an old story in the fourteenth century, but the play would have had a particular resonance for its audience in the late 1370s. Jews had been expelled from the lands under the control of the French monarchy in 1305, allowed back and then expelled again in 1322. Their return to the kingdom was slow and gradual, but by the mid-1370s they were once again established in Paris in sufficient numbers to play an important economic role.[46] Jews were authorized by law to charge interest at rates condemned by the Church and thus theoretically prohibited to Christian money-lenders. The situation was surely exacerbated by the fact that Christian goldsmiths and money-lenders and their Jewish counterparts were not just rivals but also did business with each other, as court records testify.[47] In such an atmosphere, goldsmiths and money-changers would certainly not have been displeased to see a play about a Jew guilty of dishonest lending practices.

---

[45] Robert L.A. Clark, '*The* Miracles de Notre Dame par personnages *of the Cangé Manuscript and the Socio-cultural Function of Confraternity Drama*' (dissertation, Indiana University, 1994), pp. 80-115.

[46] Roger Kohn, 'Les juifs de la France du Nord à travers les archives du Parlement de Paris (1359?-1394)', *Revue des études juives* 141 (1982), 21-23.

[47] See the court case reported in Kohn, pp. 27-28.

FRENCH CONFRATERNITY DRAMA AND RITUAL

In the representation of transgression, there is, then, an uneasy alliance of Same and Other, the clearest indication of which is that the transgressor who at first seems beyond the pale is typically brought back into the fold: the wife of the King of Portugal is saved by Notre Dame; Pierre undergoes a radical conversion and devotes his life to charity; the Jew Mossé converts to Christianity. The last example, while it may appear a particularly insidious instance of recuperation, was doubtless all the more effective in that it was most jarring for notions of fixed socio-cultural categories. The return to the norm does not occur, however, until after the subjective content of such categories as 'wife' or 'merchant' has been explored and the societal norm transgressed. These resolutions of what seem to be irreversible situations, which include the erasure of social and cultural distinctions, are but the dramatic equivalent of the ritual levelling practised by the play's audience at their banquet, the dramatic enactment of *communitas*. And, just as social levelling ultimately serves to affirm the status quo, so does the representation of the abnormal serve to affirm the norm.[48] In the Marian miracle plays, the representation of transgression can thus be seen as serving to legitimize the economic hegemony of the closed and fiercely competitive guilds and confraternities of the late medieval city. And in the fourteenth century, this hegemony was gendered male and, of course, limited to Christians. The guilds and confraternities were dominated by men, as was the basic unit of production, the family workshop. The family workshop was also the unit where there was the most volatile mix of familial, sexual and economic ties and in which transgressive behaviour could do the most harm. The negative interpretation of transgression is that it served the purposes of repression in the interests of the collectivity.

It is also possible to see in the plays' probing of the content – including the gender content – of such social categories as spouse, merchant, monk or knight, a questioning of what it means to be the subject occupying one of these positions and an acknowledgment that participation in different dynamics, particularly the social and the sexual, may well be 'out of sync'. It is not assumed that it is an easy matter to fill any of the roles represented in the plays, even that of

---

[48] The *Miracles de Nostre Dame par personnages* present other instances of transgression which were equally jarring, if not more so, for the apparently fixed categories of gender. Two plays in the collection, the *Miracle de Théodore* and the *Miracle de la fille d'un roy*, present female characters who crossdress and live as males for much of the plays' action. See Robert L.A. Clark and Claire Sponsler, 'Queer Play: The Cultural Work of Crossdressing in Medieval Drama', *New Literary History* 28 (1997), 323-29.

Notre Dame. Furthermore, the representation of extreme forms of subjectivity cannot be said to entail a condemnation of subjectivity itself. Rather, such a representation can be read as giving a certain recognition, if not legitimacy, to conflicted, resistant, or antagonistic manifestations of subjectivity. It cannot be emphasized enough that the transgressive can never be completely contained by the mechanics of recuperation because, once represented, it is open to subjective interpretation. In short, the collective and subjective are always held in tension, and the corresponding interpretive models must not be considered mutually exclusive but deployed in tandem to achieve a balanced interpretive strategy.

At the beginning of this essay, I suggested that confraternity ritual and drama served as vehicles for the formulation and expression of the socio-ideological values of the urban bourgeoisie. The formal, synchronic analysis offered above has, it is hoped, shown the usefulness of these techniques for understanding the importance of the ritual and theatre of medieval confraternities for the promotion of commonly held values. These techniques are valuable – and valid – only to the extent that they allow us to grasp the importance of cultural practices within a specific socio-historical context. I have also explored the heuristic value of anthropological models in the study of the drama and ritual of a particular urban bourgeoisie of the late Middle Ages. In this perspective the medieval theatre becomes much more than a literary or aesthetic accomplishment, although it may possess these qualities. Like ritual, the cultural performance we call theatre creates a space in which the participants, through various mechanisms and manipulations of symbolic structures, give expression to their strongest beliefs and play out their deepest fears. But, as Clifford Geertz[49] has said of ritual and as I hope to have shown, 'the world as imagined and the world as is […] turn out to be the same world'.

---

[49] Clifford Geertz, 'Religion as a Cultural System', in *The Interpretation of Cultures* (New York: Basic, 1973), p. 112.

Community drama and community politics in thirteenth-century Arras: Adam de la Halle's *Jeu de la Feuillée*

FREDERICK W. LANGLEY

THE SINGULARITY OF ADAM de la Halle's *Jeu de la Feuillée* has, since its first printed edition,[1] embarrassed, intrigued and provoked critics. Whatever its other qualities may be, the piece, dating from 1276, is the most original and idiosyncratic dramatic work to have come down to us from the French Middle Ages. It is made up of so many apparently disparate elements that it has become in the last thirty or forty years a fascinating object of attention for interpretative critics. It has variously appeared as a simple comic and satirical revue, or as a public playing-out of the author's deepest anxieties, or as pre-Freudian representation of the father-son conflict, or as almost whatever one cares to make of it. It is not surprising that most twentieth-century criticism has focused on what could loosely be described as the psychological and philosophical aspects of the piece.[2] The *jeu* is seen as a playing-out of the author's deepest spiritual, philosophical and psychological preoccupations, it is a reflection of his inner turmoil and of his struggle to come to terms with, or change, his personal situation.[3]

---

[1] L.J.N. Monmerqué, '*Li Jus Adan ou de la Feuillée* par Adam de la Halle', *Mélanges publiés par la Société des bibliophiles français*, t.VI (Paris: Firmin Didot, 1826). Our references to the text of the *Feuillée* are to J. Dufournet, *Le Jeu de la Feuillée* (Paris: Flammarion, 1989).

[2] See, in particular, A. Adler, *Sens et composition du Jeu de la Feuillée* (Ann Arbor, University of Michigan Press, 1958); J. Dufournet, *Adam de la Halle à la recherche de lui-même ou le jeu dramatique de la Feuillée* (Paris: SEDES, 1974); C. Mauron, *Le Jeu de la Feuillée. Étude psychocritique* (Paris: J. Corti, 1973).

[3] For a concise summary of critical attitudes up to the 1960s see Normand Cartier, *Le Bossu désenchanté. Étude sur le Jeu de la Feuillée* (Genève: Droz, 1971), pp. 3-17.

Interestingly, nineteenth-century critics took a markedly different view. Less concerned with Adam de la Halle's self-revelation, they viewed the *Jeu de la Feuillée* in its wider social context. Unable to point to anything in the medieval French theatre which remotely resembled the *Jeu de la Feuillée,* early critics were pleased to draw comparisons with the comedies of Aristophanes.[4] One cannot deny that the *Jeu de la Feuillée* and the comedies of Aristophanes have certain elements in common. Magnin, the first critic to point out the similarities, suggested that these elements were: 'des personnalités acérées, des obscénités sans voile, et la création ou l'emploi du merveilleux le plus incroyable'[5] ['sharp-tongued personalities, unveiled obscenities, the creation or use of the most incredible supernatural elements'].

It would be pointless and unrewarding to pursue too far a comparison between the works of the two authors. There is, between them, such a gap, of time, of religion, of language and of culture, that there can be no possibility of the link somewhat fancifully imagined by critics in the nineteenth century. However, it is enlightening to bear in mind that the similarities between Aristophanes and his Athens and Adam and his Arras are not fortuitous: they spring from a similarity of social and political circumstances. Adam's *jeu*, like Aristophanes's comedies, is deeply rooted in the author's place of birth and abode, and it is this fact that provides us with the focus of the present essay. Bédier was right to point out that: 'Le *Jeu de la Feuillée* est, comme la comédie grecque, la création spontanée d'une démocratie vivace, agitée par de factions...[I]l vit, comme la comédie grecque, de la

---

See also, M. Zimmerman, 'Controversies on *le Jeu de la Feuillée*', *Studia Neophilologica* 39 (1967), 229-43.

[4] See C. Magnin, *Le Journal des Savants*, 31 (1846), 549-50 Review of: L.J.N. Monmerque and F. Michel, *Théâtre Français au moyen âge: publié d'après les manuscrits de la Bibliothèque du roi (XIe--XIVe siecles)* (Paris, 1839); the supposed similarities between the *Jeu de la Feuillée* and the Greek comedies were taken up with enthusiasm by L. Petit de Julleville, *La Comédie et les moeurs en France au moyen âge* (Paris: Le Cerf, 1886; Genève: Slatkine Repr., 1968), p. 19; and *Le Théâtre en France. Histoire de la littérature dramatique depuis ses origines jusqu'à nos jours.*) 6e éd., (Paris: Armand Colin, 1906) p. 9; and P. Paris, *Histoire littéraire de la France*, XX (Paris: Firmin Didot, 1842), p. 650; C. Aubertin, *Histoire de la langue et de la littérature française au moyen âge* (Paris: Belin, 1883), p. 609; W. Creizenach, *Geschichte des neueren Dramas. I. Mittelalter und Frührenaissance* (Halle: Max Niemayer, 1893), pp. 394-95; L. Clédat, *Le Théâtre en France au moyen âge* (Paris: Hachette, 1896), p. 89 and *Revue de Philologie Française* 9 (1885), 885-86.

[5] Magnin, p. 550.

satire des personnages principaux de cette démocratie'.[6] [The *Jeu de la Feuillée,* is, like the Greek comedy, the spontaneous creation of a durable, faction-ridden democracy...Like the Greek comedy, it lives on the satire of the principal figures of that democracy.]

The purpose of this essay is modest. It is not to propose an overall interpretation of the piece but rather to concentrate on one facet which has been somewhat neglected of late: the element of political and social satire whose presence demonstrates that the author was deeply concerned with the local and topical issues of his day.[7] The *Jeu de la Feuillée* is community drama not only because of its concern with local personalities and issues, but also because many of its *dramatis personae* are actual citizens of Arras, the most important of whom, in this context, is the author.

The *jeu* opens with the author himself addressing a number of his friends and fellow-citizens (including his father, Maître Henri and

---

[6] 'Les Commencemens (sic) du théâtre comique en France', *Revue des Deux Mondes*, 99 (15 juin 1890. 3ᵉ période), 886.

[7] The *jeu* has been much discussed and very variously interpreted. For full-scale studies see: H. Guy, *Essai sur le vie et les oeuvres littéraires du trouvère Adan de le Hale* (Paris: Hachette, 1898); A. Guesnon, 'La Satire à Arras au XIIIᵉ siècle', *Le Moyen Age* 12 (1899), 156-58, 248-68; 12 (1900), 1-34, 117-68; 'Adam de la Halle et le Jeu de la Feuillée', *Le Moyen Age* 28, (1915), 173-233; A. Adler, S*ens et composition du Jeu de la Feuillée* (Ann Arbor, University of Michigan Press, 1958); J. Dufournet, 'Sur *le Jeu de la Feuillée*', *Revue des Langues Romanes* 79 (1965), 7-18; J. Dufournet, 'Adam de la Halle et *le Jeu de la Feuillée*', *Romania* 86 (1965), 199-245; N.R. Cartier, *Le Bossu désenchanté. Étude sur le Jeu de la Feuillée* (Genève: Droz, 1971); C. Mauron, *Le Jeu de la Feuillée. Étude psychocritique* (Paris: J. Corti, 1973); J. Dufournet, *Adam de la Halle à la recherche de lui-même ou le jeu dramatique de la Feuillée* (Paris: SEDES, 1974); J. Dufournet, *Sur le Jeu de la Feuillée: Études complémentaires* (Paris: SEDES, 1977); G.D. McGregor, *Adam's Game. A Reading of the Jeu de la Feuillée* (Ann Arbor, University of Michigan Press, 1978); M.-L.-H. Raphalen, *Étude stylistique et thématique du Jeu de la Feuillée d'Adam de la Halle* (Ann Arbor, University of Michigan, 1978); P. Ménard, 'Le Sens du Jeu de la Feuillée', *Travaux de Linguistique et de Littérature publiés par le Centre de Philologie et de Littérature de Strasbourg* 16 (1978), 381-93; J. Dufournet, 'Note complémentaire sur le *Jeu de la Feuillée*', *Romania* 99 (1978), 98-108; K. Gallagher, 'L'entrelacement du réel et de l'irréel dans le *Jeu de la Feuillée*', *Chimères* 8 (1974), 59-69; A. Kay, 'Une Étude de la réalité du *Jeu de la Feuillée*', *Chimères* 13 (1979), 7-45; J.C. Payen, 'Typologie des genres et distanciation; Le double *Congé* d'Adam de la Halle. Réflexions sur le sens de l'écriture dramatique au XIIIᵉ siècle', *Kwartalnik-Neofililogoczny* 27 (1980), 115-32; J. Maillard, *Adam de la Halle: Monographie* (Paris: Champion, 1988); P. Homan, 'Structures et mouvement dans le *Jeu de la Feuillée*', *Chimères* 16 (1982), 13-25; G.D. McGregor, *The Broken Pot Restored: Le Jeu de la Feuillée of Adam de la Halle* (Lexington, Kentucky: French Forum, 1991); G. Mermier, *The Play of Madness* (New York: Lang, 1997).

others known to have lived in Arras in Adam's day). In solemn alexandrines, he announces that he is to return to his studies, which he had abandoned in order to marry the fair Maroie (lines 1-12). His friends and acquaintances greet the announcement with derision (lines 12-50). Adam is unmoved, and in a speech which demonstrates to the full his poetic talents (he was one of the most prolific and skilled lyric poets of his day) he talks of the illusions of love, of the woman whom love made appear beautiful and sweet in character, but who is in reality ugly and bad-tempered (lines 51-174).

Having had his say (directly, at least), Adam practically retires into the background for most of the rest of his play, which then embarks on an apparently aimless conversational voyage. It is a voyage which takes in, among other things, the questions of well-known shrewish women of Arras, Maître Henri's miserliness in refusing to help his son financially, the question of avarice as it affects several prominent local citizens, the affair of the *clercs bigames* (bigamous clerics), the topic of madness and its local manifestations, the depredations and rivalries of the ruling classes of Arras. All this is enlivened by the sardonic interventions of the participants in the conversation, by the presence of some comic 'types' (a 'Physician' who claims to cure avarice, a Monk parading false relics reputed to cure madness, a violent madman, the *Dervé*) and the fleeting visit of some figures from folklore and legend, most notably Morgan the fairy and her two companions (lines 175-875). The play ends in the tavern, where, in a scene reminiscent of a *fabliau* and of the extensive tavern scenes in those other dramatic works from Arras, Bodel's *Jeu de Saint Nicolas* and the anonymous *Courtois d'Arras*, the Monk is tricked into paying for the drink consumed by the assembled companions (lines 876-1099).

It is probably the apparent heterogeneity of this curious work which has given rise to so many widely divergent interpretations of what the *jeu* is 'about' and what Adam de la Halle's intentions were in writing it and having it performed. Depending on one's personal, intellectual and aesthetic preoccupations, it is possible to see almost anything in this apparently loosely knit piece. However, the *jeu* is not as loosely constructed as it may at first sight appear. There is a framework. The play opens and ends with the author and his intention to return to his studies in the schools of Paris. Within this framework, whatever the topic of conversation may be, there is a unity of approach: that of the author's satire of his fellow-citizens. Misers, gluttons, fools and madmen, bourgeois with literary pretensions, the higher clergy, powerful and prominent local worthies, a quack-doctor, a dishonest monk, shrewish women – Adam omits little and ignores few occasions to attack human frailties by criticizing the individuals who display them.

Any appraisal of the *Jeu de la Feuillée* must take into account its social context. The piece, perhaps more than any other dramatic work of the French Middle Ages, reflects a social reality, and it may be instructive briefly to situate it in its milieu.

In the first place, we must note the economic and commercial prosperity of Arras in the thirteenth century. This prosperity was founded mainly on the textile industry, for Arras produced woollen cloth of the very highest quality, dyed with the town's famous *garance*.[8] Arras was also renowned for the manufacture of fine tapestries (hence the town's name being synonymous, in English at one time, with tapestry).

The other great commercial activity of Arras was banking, and the wealthy cloth manufacturers and merchants swelled their already large profits by lending money at interest, particularly, it would seem, to the aristocracy. There had grown up what in effect amounted to a patrician order, which comprised the wealthy and consequently powerful merchant and banking families. The existence of this patrician class gave rise to a great deal of class conflict, with the patricians dominating, in one way or another, the middle classes (the artisans and small merchants) and the lower classes, who formed what in modern times would be called an urban proletariat. The domination by the patricians arose not only out of their economic power, but also out of their appropriation of municipal authority. Throughout the thirteenth century, the *échevins* (who formed the ruling body of the towns in Northern France and Flanders) were chosen (not elected) from the wealthy merchants and banking families and formed a self-perpetuating oligarchy, jealous of its powers and privileges.[9]

Adam de la Halle's low opinion of some of his wealthy and powerful fellow-citizens is demonstrated by the grounds on which he chooses to attack: their preoccupation with money. Avarice is a central theme of the *jeu* (note that 'avarice' in this context means 'rapacity, greed' as well as 'miserliness'). The suggestion, made by one of Adam's friends, that his father is too miserly to help him financially to return to his studies (line 186), gives rise to the elaboration of the topic after the timely arrival on the scene of a

---

[8] A dye extracted from the plant of the same name (*rubia tinctorium L.*, Dyer's madder). There was a street (*Le Waranche*) named after the dye in medieval Arras.

[9] There is an admirable study of the patricians of medieval Arras in J. Lestocquoy, *Patriciens du moyen âge. Les dynasties bourgeoises d'Arras du XIe au XVe siècle. (Mémoires de la commission départementale des monuments historiques du Pas-de-Calais. T. 5, fasc. 1)*, (Arras, 1945).

Fisiscien (a 'Physician', in reality a charlatan) who claims to be able to cure avarice. In the space of a few lines, having diagnosed Maître Henri's illness, the Physician claims that *avares* are numerous in Arras. Specifically, he mentions some prominent citizens who are renowned for their rapacity and greed. The individuals he singles out (Haloi, otherwise known as Pierre le Waisdier, Robert Cosiel, le Faveriel – who can be identified with Grars Faverel – Ermenfroi Crespin and Ermenfroi de Paris) (lines 210-27) were all bankers or merchants. There is an element of class hatred and jealousy in the criticism made of them: one of Adam's friends does not mince his words when he says of two of them: 'It would be no loss if they were dead and buried!' (lines 216-17). The people mentioned by name are not the only misers in Arras: the Physician claims that he has patients 'far and wide' (line 202) and that he has more than two thousand in Arras itself (line 210). This is no doubt an exaggeration on the author's part, but it serves to indicate some of the envy and hatred of the impecunious for the rich and privileged.

Why did Adam single out certain individuals for his attack on avarice? Did he think that they were by far the worst examples of the frantic desire to amass wealth, or can we suspect some prejudice and score-settling on his part?

It is possible that the poet chose as targets some of the bourgeois who had not patronized him as a poet. Certainly, the view that Haloi (Pierre le Waisdier) was a miser was not shared by Adam de la Halle's contemporary and fellow lyric poet Baude Fastoul. In his *Congé*,[10] Fastoul mentions with gratitude a person named Aloi, who was probably the same as the Haloi whom Adam attacks. Similarly, Fastoul mentions a Grars Faverel, surname *le boisteus* (i.e., 'lame', almost certainly the *bietu le Faveriel* mentioned by Adam in line 214)[11] who had been kind and generous to him.[12] Adam may not have been even-handed in his attacks on the rich; he may have been motivated by personal resentments, but there can be no doubting the seriousness of his criticisms. The violence of his accusations leaves no doubt on that score. Avarice can go no further than in the case of Haloi:

---

[10] P. Ruelle, *Les Congés d'Arras* (Bruxelles: Presses Universitaires de Bruxelles, 1965), st. 29, p. 116.

[11] But see also P. Ménard, '*Et ce Biecu le Faveriel:* Note sur un passage du *Jeu de la Feuillée*', ed. by B. Guidoux, *Études de langue et de littérature françaises offertes à André Lanly* (Nancy: Université de Nancy, 1980).

[12] P. Ruelle, *Les Congés,* st. 41, p. 120.

COMMUNITY DRAMA AND COMMUNITY POLITICS

> Car il est de lui omicides;
> S'il en muert, c'ert par s'ocoison,
> Car il acate mort pisson,
> C'est grans mervelle qu'il ne crieve. (lines 224-27)

[For he is killing himself; if he dies, it will be by his own doing, since he buys dead fish (i.e. dead when taken from the water), and it's a miracle that he doesn't drop down dead.]

It is not only the ruling classes, however, who are the butt of Adam's satirical attacks. Early in the *jeu*, when the poet's father, Maître Henri, advises his son to return immediately to his studies, the author's friend Gillot interjects: *Or li donnés dont de l'argent!* (line 186) [Give him some money, then!]. Maître Henri replies that all the money he has in the world is twenty-nine pounds. When another of the circle of acquaintances expresses disbelief at this, Maître Henri claims that he has '*tout mis en canebustin*' (line 191) ['It's all gone into my belly']. Again, later in the *jeu*, when asked to make a contribution to the costs of a law-suit in Rome, the poet's father pleads that he is a poor man, that he cannot afford it, and that in any case he would have nothing to gain. When Gillot insists that Maître Henri is salting his money away, Henri denies it (with a not very subtle play on the words *vin* 'wine' and *vent* 'wind'): *Non fai: tout emporte li vins.* (line 505) [No I'm not: it's all gone with the wine.]

This last remark probably reveals the true state of affairs. It could well be that Maître Henri was known to be something of a spendthrift, and that the idea that he was a miser salting his money away would be very amusing to the assembled company. To accuse of avarice a man who spends all of his money on wine and who has a large paunch (as we shall see) because of his taste for good cheer is an amusing concept. It is probable that the poet's father was known to be far from avaricious and that the accusations made by his acquaintances would make an audience laugh with its unexpectedness rather than nod their heads in agreement.

Having dealt with the *avares* of Arras, Adam, through his mouthpiece the Physician, turns his attention to the sin of gluttony. Here again, Maître Henri receives the first broadside. He asks the Physician's opinion on the cause of his large paunch, and after a cursory examination of the patient's urine, the quack pronounces that he has the *mal Saint Lïenart* (lines 233-35). St. Leonard was credited with freeing many prisoners, but was also thought to bring relief to women suffering in childbirth. The Physician's diagnosis is clearly a humorous reference to his patient's impressive abdomen. Maître Henri plays along with the joke by asking: *m'en estuet il gesir?* (line 236) [must I take to my bed/go into labour?], the verb *gesir* having the meanings 'go to bed, lie down' and 'be in labour, childbirth'.

The Physician reassures Maître Henri, that he is in the same situation as three other bourgeois of Arras: Jehan d'Autevile, Willaume Wagon and Adan li Anstier: *Chascuns est malades de chiaus/Par trop emplir lor bouchiaus,/Et por ch'as le ventre enflé si.* (lines 243-45) [Each of them is ill with filling their belly too much; and that's why your stomach is so swollen.] Quite simply, Maître Henri, like the other three, eats and drinks too much. We have seen that Adam's father admits himself that he is fond of eating and drinking. It is perhaps because his taste for wine was well known that Hane le Mercier, early in the play, asks Maître Henri if he is drunk (line 190).

The Physician is prevented from elaborating on the theme of gluttony by the arrival on the scene of Dame Douce, who, like Maître Henri, has a swollen abdomen (lines 245-51). Her 'illness' is rapidly diagnosed as pregnancy, and when her supposedly immoral conduct is unmasked she accuses Adam's friend Rikier of being the father of the child. Rikier hotly denies this. It seems probable, in fact, that this 'pregnancy' is merely a comic device. Dame Douce is no more pregnant than Maître Henri was. She simply is a stout old woman who pretends to go along with the Physician's diagnosis in order to make fun of Rikier. Dame Douce, whose name appears in contemporary documents,[13] has been the object of much discussion by critics. Guy regarded her simply as 'une courtisane vielle, fardée [...] querelleuse, batailleuse, grossière' [an old, painted [...] quarrelsome, combative, vulgar whore].[14] Other critics, notably Adler, who saw her as a terrifying mother figure,[15] have attributed greater importance to her rôle. Within the context of our discussion of local satire, however, she is important in that she opens the way to the naming of a number of prominent shrewish women of Arras. While denying the possibility that he is the father of Dame Douce's child, Rikier begs the assembled company to say nothing of the matter to his wife, who is of such an evil disposition that she is predisposed to believe anything of him, even if it is patently untrue (lines 290-91). Another friend of the poet

---

[13] She died in 1279. See R. Berger, *Le Nécrologe de la Confrérie des Jongleurs et des Bourgeois d'Arras (1194-1362). Texte et Tables. (Mémoires de la commission départementale des monuments historiques du Pas-de-Calais, t. XI^2)* (Arras, 1963) p. 153, col. 3; A. Guesnon, *Le Moyen Age* 18 (1916), 210.

[14] Guy, *Essai*, p. 345.

[15] Adler, *Sens*, p. 31.

adds that the women of the *Waranche*, a street in Arras, are of a nature to be feared (lines 292-95). Hane le Mercier then gets down to personalities. Mahieu l'Anstier's wife, the widow of Ernoul de le Porte, is redoubtable, for she is known to have attacked the Baillieu de Vermandois with her fingernails. Her husband very wisely holds his tongue in her presence (lines 296-302). Margot as Pumetes and Aelis au Dragon[16] are another two women not noted for their gentleness of character: the one constantly nags her husband (line 306) and the other is a chatterbox (line 307). At the mention of their names, Gillot cries: *A! vrais Dieux! Aporte une estoile:/Chis a nommé deus anemis* (lines 308-09); [Ah! God of Truth! Bring a stole: He has named two devils!][17]

Hane le Mercier claims that Adam's wife is a shrew, and the poet does not deny it, only advising Hane not to let her hear him say it (lines 310-11). In any case, says Adam, annoyed perhaps despite himself, there are others who are just as quarrelsome: the wife of Henri des Argans scratches and spits like a cat, and the wife of Thoumas de Darnestal is no better. Hane agrees, saying that these fearsome women are inhabited by a hundred demons. 'Indeed they are', says Adam, 'and so is your mother, Eve'. Hane, annoyed at this, again points the finger at Adam's wife, saying that she is not much better (lines 314-21). The last useful word has been said on the subject, and the Monk arrives to interrupt what could have been an acrimonious quarrel between Adam and his friend. Again, however, Adam has created the opportunity to make fun of the wives of a number of prominent local worthies. Most of the shrewish women named are known to have been contemporaries of the poet and all would have been well known to Adam's audience.

The Monk has a rôle similar to that of the Physician. He is used as a device to refer derisively to some of the *sots* (fools, madmen) of Arras. The Monk has come from Haspre[18] where there is a great shrine of St Acaire, who, throughout the Middle Ages and beyond, was credited with the power to cure insanity, particularly its more violent forms (*frenesie, derverie*). He claims to have brought with him some relics of the saint, which will drive out the demon, curing persons afflicted with *esvertin*.[19] There is no saint whose miracles are so

---

[16] The names *Pumetes* and *Dragon* were given to two neighbouring houses in the Place du Petit-Marché in Arras.

[17] In the rite of exorcism, the priest's stole is, at one point, laid on the head of the person being exorcized.

[18] A village 7 km. from Bouchain (Nord), near Cambrai. The monastery there was a dependency of the Abbey of Saint-Vaast in Arras.

[19] The term seems to have been applied to various forms of cerebral derangement in

efficacious as those of St Acaire, and many *ediotes* have gone away from Haspre completely cured of their illness (lines 326-34).

It seems that the Monk has come to the right place, for he receives a succession of offerings. Walet is the first to come forward, pressed by his companions. However, it would appear that Walet is not, in fact, a *sot*. When he asks for *pois pilés* (pureed peas, reputed to cure madness)[20] he is probably making a pun on his own surname,[21] and in his offer of a *bon froumage cras* (soft cheese, also associated with madness) he is perhaps making fun of the Monk and his relics, which are undoubtedly false.[22] The apparent stupidity of Walet's remarks (lines 354-57) does not prove that he is a *sot*. It is quite possible that because of his surname, *Pois Pilés,* Walet was generally treated as something of a fool and that it pleased him to play the part that was expected of him.

However, there are some genuine *sots* who need St Acaire's help. Dame Douce gives the Monk some money on behalf of Colart de Bailloel (a member of a prominent patrician family) and of Heuvin, who have great faith in the power of the saint. These two seem to have been votaries of Saint Acaire for some time, as the Monk says he has known them since childhood (lines 265-369), which says little for the curative powers of his relics. Walet brings an offering on behalf of Wautier a le Main, who is suffering from a *mal qui li tient ou chervel* (a illness of the brain), and the mention of this unfortunate's name provokes a burst of derision from the assembled company (lines 372-78). Maître Henri offers the Monk a measure of grain on behalf of Jehan le Keu, a fellow-employee of the *échevins*. His affliction has worsened and he has had to take to his bed, but Maître Henri hopes that he will recover sufficiently to come and honour the relics in person the next day (lines 386-89).

The *sots* must have been numerous in Arras, at least in Adam's opinion, for the Monk is surrounded by a great crowd of people soliciting St Acaire's help (lines 360-61). The *sots* mentioned by Adam are merely a representative selection. The satire of these persons is relatively innocuous, although Wautier a le Main is cruelly

---

the Middle Ages.

[20] In later years, the term *pois pilés* came to have a particular meaning in the theatre, as *sotties* were frequently known as *jeux de pois pilés*.

[21] A *Pois Pilés Valés* is mentioned in the *Nécrologe* in 1283. See Berger, *Nécrologe*, p. 155, col. 1.

[22] It is very unlikely that the protectors of the 'real' relics of St Acaire would have allowed them to be touted in public places in the way our Monk is doing. The Monk himself has so little respect for them that he leaves them as a pledge for a drinking debt later in the play (lines 1012-24).

jeered. On the whole, Adam merely mentions the *sots*: he does not hold them up to public ridicule to the same extent that he did, for example, the shrewish women.

The most important madman in the piece is, of course, the *Dervé*. He is brought to Arras by his long-suffering father, who apparently hopes that the relics of St Acaire will cure his violently mad son. The antics of the *Dervé* are a source of much of the verbal and visual comedy in the *Jeu de la Feuillée*, but he has a more important function within the context of Adam's satirical intentions. It is in connection with the *Dervé* that Robert Sommeillon is first mentioned,[23] and it is the *Dervé* who tells us of the literary pretensions of Thomas de Clari and Wautier as Paus.[24] However mad, the *Dervé* is not lacking in a certain malicious shrewdness, and we can perhaps see in him one of the earliest examples in the theatre of the supposed fool who speaks wisely and whose apparently idiotic chatter is able to touch upon a very sore spot. He is a remote ancestor to Lear's Fool.

Certainly, like Lear's Fool, the *Dervé* is a destroyer of self-esteem. Adam, announcing his return to the Schools of Paris, and proudly wearing his student's gown, does not impress the *Dervé*. When told that Adam is a *parisïen* (a student of the University of Paris), the *Dervé* casts doubt upon the poet's sanity (lines 422-24) and then pointedly cries: *S'il li sousvenoit des bigames,/Il en seroit mains orgueilleus* (lines 426-27) [If he remembered the bigamists he wouldn't be so proud].

This thorny question of the *clercs bigames* (the bigamous clerks) illustrates most clearly not only a preoccupation with money, but also a bitter hatred on the part of the 'have-nots' (or those who considered themselves as such) for the ruling classes and their ally the Church.

What was a 'bigamous clerk', a *clericus bigamus*? He was a man who had taken minor orders and who had legitimately married successive wives; who had a legitimate spouse, but who had one or more mistresses; who had married a widow; who had married a woman of notorious reputation; who continued to live with a wife whom he knew to be adulterous. The definition was much wider than the modern term 'bigamous'.[25]

In response to the *Dervé*, the poet denies that he is a *bigame*, but his father, who was married more than once (see lines 492-93), launches into an impassioned, violent and abusive tirade against the Pope who

---

[23] See below, pp. XXX.

[24] See below, pp. XXX.

[25] Hostiensis, in his *Summa aurea* (1250-1253), ed. (Cologne, 1612), cols. 214-15 defines *bigamia* in great detail.

had 'deposed' (as he puts it) so many good clerks simply because they are married when prelates continued to enjoy their privileges whilst living publicly in concubinage:

> Certes, li meffais fu trop grans,
> Et chascuns le pape encosa,
> Quant tant de bons clers desposa.
> Nepourquant n'ira mie ensi,
> Car aucun se sont aati,
> Des plus vaillans et des plus rikes,
> Qui ont trouvees raisons friques,
> Qu'il prouveront tout en apert
> Que nus clers par droit ne desert
> Pour mariages estre asservis;
> Ou mariages vaut trop pis
> Que demourer en soignantage.
> Comment ont prelat l'avantage
> D'avoir femes a remuier
> Sans leur previlege cangier,
> Et uns clers si pert se franquise
> Par espouser en sainte eglise
> Fame qui eut autre baron?
> Et li fil a putain laron,
> Ou nous devons prendre peuture,
> Mainent en pechié de luxure
> Et si göent de leur clergie!
> Romme a bien le tierche partie
> Des clers fais sers et amatis.   (lines 434-57)

[For sure, the evil deed was very great, and everyone accused the Pope when he 'deposed' so many good clerks. However, it won't go on like this, for some have boasted, – some of the worthiest and wealthiest, who have found fresh arguments – , that they will prove clearly that no clerk deserves rightly to be reduced to servitude because of marriage; otherwise, marriage is worse than living in concubinage. How do prelates have the advantage of having women a-plenty without changing their privileges, and a simple clerk loses his indemnity[26] for marrying in Holy Church a woman who had another husband? And the sons of whores, the thieves, from whom we should take our spiritual food, live in the sin of licentiousness and so enjoy their ecclesiastical estate! Rome has indeed abased and enslaved a third of all the clerks.]

---

[26] That is, from paying civil taxes.

This speech of Adam's father is notable not only for the violence of its tone but for its length. Apart from Adam's 'set piece' about Maroie at the beginning of the *jeu*, few of the speeches are more that four or five lines long.

Maître Henri announces that a number of prominent *bigames* in Arras will fight the papal decision to 'depose' the *clercs bigames* (i.e. remove their clerical privileges): some of their number will plead their cause at the Papal Court, and others will defray the expenses.

The discussion of the affair of the bigamous clerks occupies 92 lines of the text, a significant proportion of a piece of only 1098 lines. Why was the question so important to Adam de la Halle and to his fellow citizens? When the *Jeu de la Feuillée* was written/performed in 1276, the dispute over the status of the *bigames* was not new. Although in the play it is the Pope who is criticized, the identity of the real and more immediate enemies of the *bigames* is revealed by Maître Henri. When asked by one of the author's friends if he will make a contribution to the costs of the action on behalf of the *bigames*, he claims that he is too poor, that he has nothing to fear from the loss of clerical privilege, but that in any case, as an employee of the *échevins*, he dare not do anything to offend them (lines 506-09). It cannot be stated more clearly than this that it was the *échevins* who were the prime movers against the *bigames*.

After a series of disagreements between the clerks of Arras and the *échevins*, the Papal Court had decided, in a judgement delivered on 28 January 1254, that clerks who were *bigames*, money-lenders, tavern-keepers and those engaged in *inhonesta mercimonia* (unseemly occupations) should lose their clerical privileges, that is, most importantly, should no longer be exempt from payment of the *taille* (in this case, municipal taxes). Pope Innocent IV, in a letter of 11 March 1254 to the *échevins*, confirmed this decision.[27] Two years later, Pope Alexander IV entered the dispute on the side of the *échevins*. At the request of the latter, on 21 March 1256, he addressed a letter to the bishop of Arras forbidding him to support the *bigames* in their determination not to submit to the imposition of the *taille*.[28]

It was more recent action against the *bigames*, however, which provoked the outburst in the *Feuillée*. In a general council held in Lyon under the presidency of Pope Gregory X, it was decided, on 14 July 1274, that the *bigames* should be deprived of all ecclesiastical

---

[27] See A. Guesnon, *Inventaire chronologique des chartes de la ville d'Arras*, p. 31. This work was never sold publicly. A copy is deposited in the *Archives départementales du Pas-de-Calais*, Arras.

[28] See Guesnon, *Inventaire*, p. 33.

privilege, should be subject to secular justice, and should be forbidden, under pain of anathema, to wear the tonsure and clerical garb.[29]

We have seen that the term 'bigamy' had a much broader sense in the Middle Ages than it has today. The only type of bigamy mentioned specifically in the *Jeu de la Feuillée* is marriage with a widow. Maître Henri states (lines 456-57) that the Papal decision has reduced a third of all clerks to servitude and ruin. He may be exaggerating, but nevertheless the *bigames* seem to have been numerous, and it is unlikely that they were all married to widows. Why, then, were there so many indignant *bigames* in Arras?

The answer would seem to be that the status of 'bigamy' had become confused with the condition of being engaged in occupations which the Church thought incompatible with the clericature. The Bull which Pope Alexander IV addressed to the *échevins* of Arras in 1256 specifically mentions not only bigamous clerks but also those engaged in dishonourable occupations (*qui turpibus negociationibus se immiscent*) and singles out money-lending as being particularly unsuitable for a clerk. Another document, much closer in date to the *Jeu de la Feuillée* concerns certain occupations thought to be unsuitable for a clerk. The synodal statutes of Arras of *c.* 1275 list a number of occupations which were incompatible with the clericature: a clerk should not be a fuller, a weaver, a horse-coper, a waffle-seller, a masseur, a butcher, a dyer, a shoe-maker, a tanner, or exercise what the statutes call *vilia officia*.[30] It is significant that workers in the textile industry are singled out for special attention, suggesting that many clerks were involved in this industry in Arras. These strictures, it could be argued, have nothing to do with the question of the *clercs bigames*, but it is probable that there were in Arras in 1276 large numbers of men who were nominally clerks but who were leading an essentially secular life. It is almost certain that clerks engaged in 'unsuitable' occupations made common cause with the *bigames*.

The advantages of the clerk were many, but the most important was that he was free of secular jurisdiction and was consequently exempt from payment of municipal taxes. There was a great deal to be said for taking minor orders, for one could marry and engage in a secular profession or occupation, and indeed enjoy all the advantages of

---

[29] The relevant article from the constitutions of the Council is quoted in E. Langlois, *Le Jeu de la Feuillée (Classiques français du moyen âge, No. 6)* (Paris: Champion, 1917; 2ᵉ éd. 1923; réimp. 1951), p. X.

[30] Document quoted by J. Lestocquoy, '*Inhonesta mercimonia*', in *Mélanges d'histoire du moyen âge dédiés à Louis Halphen* (Paris: Presses Universitaires de France, 1951), p. 413 note 4.

secular life without the disadvantages, such as the *taille*. The violent anger of the *bigames* as expressed in the *Jeu de la Feuillée* is not, therefore, surprising.

The civil authorities of Arras viewed with disfavour the large numbers of clerks who were in were in no real sense ecclesiastics but who enjoyed ecclesiastical privileges. In particular, the *échevins* resented the clerk's exemption from the *taille*. On at least three occasions in the twenty-five years preceding the *Jeu de la Feuillée* action had been taken against the *bigames*, yet the *jeu* makes it clear that the conflict was no nearer a solution.[31]

How was it that the *bigames* and their allies, the other clerks who had officially forfeited their clerical status, contrived to continue to enjoy the best of both worlds? The method was simple: lawsuits and long drawn out appeals to Rome delayed the implementation of any decision. By dint of keeping the matter permanently *sub judice* the *bigames* were able to prevent the municipal authorities from imposing on them the taxes which were paid by other citizens. The institution of a lawsuit is precisely the stratagem which the *bigames* of the *Jeu de la Feuillée* proposed to adopt (lines 437-43, 458-513). On one occasion, Robert le Clerc, author of *Les Vers de la mort*, appeared in Rome on behalf of the *bigames* of Arras.[32] The *jeu* tells us that Gilles de Sains,[33] Colart Fousedame and Gilles de Bouvignies[34] will present the case, and Jehan Crespin[35] will finance the litigation.

The *Jeu de la Feuillée* leaves us in no doubt as to Adam de la Halle's opinions on the question of the bigamous clerks. The mere mention of the *bigames* provokes a searing and bitter attack on the Pope, who is seen as a compliant ally of the *échevins*. The discussion in the play brings out not only the determination of the *bigames* not to yield an inch to their political masters but also their resentment of the higher clergy who have more women than they know what to do with (line 447) and live lives of conspicuous debauchery while the poor

---

[31] On the whole question of the *bigames*, see Génestal, 'Le *'Privilegium fori'* en France, t. 1, pp. 62-80 (*Bibliothèque de l'Ecole des Hautes Études, Sciences Religieuses*, vol. 35, (Paris, 1921)).

[32] See *Les Vers de la mort*, par Helinant, moine de Froidmont; publ. d'après tous les manuscrits connus par Fr. Wulff et Em. Walberg (SATF, Paris: Firmin Didot, 1905), st. 149.

[33] Gilles held the position of *avocat* of the Chapter of Arras and is mentioned as such in a document of 18 January 1276: see Guesnon, *Le Moyen Âge*, 18 (1916), 201.

[34] Like Gilles de Sains, he had connections with the Chapter of Arras. See Guesnon, *Le Moyen Âge*, 18 (1916), 201-02.

[35] Brother of Ermenfroi Crespin, member of a powerful Arras family of bankers and merchants. See *Feuillée*, line 219.

clerk in minor orders is penalised for marrying a widow. It is not without significance that the only person in the play to express support for the Pope is the madman: *Et vés me chi pour l'apostoile/Faites le dont avant venir* (lines 517-18) [Here am I for the Pope. So bring him forward].

We can see, therefore, that the play not only reflects a controversy surrounding a question of social and political importance, but it in fact contributes to that controversy. One feels the author's commitment to the party of the *bigames*. Here, as elsewhere in the play, Adam de la Halle expresses a strongly articulated opposition to the dominant oligarchy of his native town.

The stark realities of political power and patrician rivalry are reflected in another episode of the play. Morgue (Morgan) the fairy and her companions Arsile and Magloire have come to Arras as is their custom, as one of the characters says, 'on this night' (lines 566-67). Morgan reveals that she is enamoured of a young man of the town, one Robert Sommeillon. During the fairies' visit the goddess Fortuna appears with her Wheel. One of the spectators asks Morgan to reveal the identity of two figures, depicted on the wheel, and who seem to be powerful and important (lines 782-83). Morgan, showing a discretion which is not usually characteristic of her, replies that it is not always a good idea to say everything and asks to be excused. Her companion Magloire, who is angry because she thinks that she has been slighted, tells all: the two men are Ermenfroi Crespin (already mentioned as an *avare* earlier in the *jeu*) and Jakemon Louchart. The brief reference to these two wealthy and powerful patricians offers a summary of the organization of political and economic power in thirteenth-century Arras. We are told that they enjoy the favour of the count (Robert II of Artois) to such an extent that they are 'lords of the town' (line 791). Such is their power that 'each in his own sphere is king' (line 793). What is more, their power will not end with them, for they have children who will succeed to their positions of influence (lines 798-99). Nothing could describe more baldly the way in which Arras was governed in the thirteenth century, when the *échevinage* was passed from one member of a family to another, perpetuating that family's power and prestige.

Another prominent citizen, one whose power and prestige have gone, is depicted as falling from Fortune's Wheel. Magloire identifies him as Thomas de Bouriane and tells us that he once enjoyed the favour of the Count. He had been a draper, but had been disgraced and had suffered great misfortune and his whole family with him. Magloire's remarks make it clear that he had suffered some injustice (lines 810-13). Adam de la Halle is certainly alluding here to a set of circumstances of which his audience would be well aware. There is documentary evidence that one Jakemon Pouchin, who seems to have been one of the most ruthless and corrupt *échevins* ever to have ruled Arras, motivated by jealousy of Thomas's wealth and prestige, judged over-harshly some supposed misdemeanour of Thomas and engineered his disgrace. In 1289, in the course of an enquiry into the running of municipal affairs since 1282, Jakemon was accused of dishonestly dealing with Thomas. The latter's friends appealed to the king, and after an enquiry it was ruled that Jakemon must repay the sum of 260 *livres parisis* to Thomas. The sum was repaid, but Jakemon took the money from the municipal coffers![36] We have no detailed knowledge of Jakemon's mismanagement of municipal affairs, but the reference to Thomas in the *Jeu de la Feuillée* can be taken as a brief glimpse of the struggles for power that were no doubt common amongst the ruling classes in his day. Jakemon Pouchin was involved on at least one other occasion in conflict with his fellow-patricians. Along with a certain Robert Doucet, he illegally prevented Robert Nazart and Philippe de la Vigne from taking part in the elections for new *échevins*.[37]

Adam de la Halle was clearly opposed to the system of hereditary oligarchy in Arras and the commonplace abuses of power. In that respect, he adopts a consciously anti-patrician stance.

While Jakemon Pouchin is singled out as a sinister figure, another prominent bourgeois becomes the object of Adam's satire, but this time he inspired the poet's ridicule rather than his spleen. Robert Sommeillon, who is the object of the fairy Morgan's affections, was a wealthy member of Arras society, and, if the picture painted of him in the *jeu* is accurate, something of a *bourgeois gentilhomme*. We are told that he is the new Prince of the Puy, Arras's famous literary society which numbered both poets and wealthy bourgeois among its members (line 405).[38] He is fond of jousting (lines 721-23), but on at least one occasion (lines 733-41) his knightly efforts end in humiliation, although this is due not to lack of skill or courage but to the intervention of the malicious 'other world' King Hellequin, who is his rival for Morgan's affections. Morgan, who is in love with Robert,

---

[36] See document published by Guesnon, *Le Moyen Âge*, 18 (1916), 228, §32; Lestocquoy, *Patriciens*, p. 135, §32.

[37] See Lestocquoy, *Patriciens*, p. 137.

[38] On the Puy of Arras, see Guy, *Essai*, pp. xxvii-lvi; L. Passy, *Fragments d'histoire littéraire à propos d'un nouveau manuscrit de chansons françaises. Bibliothèque de l'École des Chartes*, IVe série, t. V (Paris, 1859), pp. 491-502; A. Dinaux, *Le Puy d'Arras*, in *Archives historiques et littéraires du nord de la France et du midi de la Belgique*, 3e série, III (Valenciennes, 1852), pp. 454-65.

thinks him the most noble man in all the world (line 724), and believes him to be worthy and discreet (lines 743-44), despite the fact that he seems to have boasted of Morgan's affection for him (line 736). However, Morgan's high opinion of Robert is soon destroyed when he is shown to be the 'falsest and most deceitful man between the River Lys and the Somme' (lines 750-51).

Does Adam paint a true picture of this wealthy bourgeois, or are we not to take his accusations seriously? Obviously, there could be no love relationship between the real Robert and the supernatural Morgan. One would have expected Adam to show more respect for the Prince of the Puy, for the poet was certainly a member of that society. However, we cannot be certain that Robert was aware of the attack on him. Even if the *jeu* had been written and acted for the Puy (and this is far from certain), there is no reason to suppose that Robert could not have taken Adam's portrayal of him in good part. Robert is not shown to be ruthless and corrupt, as many of his fellow patricians were. His failings are not of a nature that causes great harm to others. The young[39] bourgeois is not to be classed with the Crespins and the Loucharts. In any case, it is not impossible that a member of the Puy should ridicule its Prince. If Robert was Prince of the Puy (and we have no evidence of this other than the *Feuillée*), we need not assume that Adam approved of his occupation of this high position. None of the lyric works of the Arrageois poets is attributed to Robert, nor is he mentioned in any of them. If Robert were the Prince, then it was because of his wealth and not because of any poetic talent. It is quite possible that Adam thought Robert unworthy of the position so brilliantly occupied formerly by the *trouvère*'s great friend and mentor, Jehan Bretel.

Some critics have expressed surprise that Adam should attack the Prince of the Puy and the society over which he presided.[40] Not only is Robert Sommeillon held up to public ridicule, it is argued, but two poets of Arras are mocked. We are told (lines 408-15) that Wautier as Paus and Thoumas de Clari should by rights perform their *chansons* at Robert's Puy. Master Wautier, we learn, can already *chanter parmi le cornet* (sing to the accompaniment of cornets). However, Maître Henri's contemptuous retort makes it quite clear what kind of cornet accompanies Wautier's and Thoumas's efforts. It is the *cornet à dés* (the dice-box), not the musical instrument: *Dont sera chou au ju des*

---

[39] He died some time between 1301 and 1311: see Guy, *Essai*, p. 440.

[40] See, M. Ungureanu, *La Bourgeoisie naissante. Société et littérature bourgeoises d'Arras aux XIIe et XIIIe siècles* (*Mémoires de la commission départementale des monuments historiques du Pas-de-Calais*, 8), (Arras, 1955), pp. 204-05.

dés/Quíl ne quierent autre deduit (lines 416-17) [It'll be at playing at dice, then, let them not look for any other pleasure.]

There is no suggestion in the text that Wautier and Thoumas were members of the Puy. It must not be forgotten that it is the *Dervé* who mentions their literary pretensions, and all that this unreliable witness says is that they would like to take part in the Puy's literary competitions. As Maître Henri says, their pretensions are ridiculous and their hopes of literary fame ill-founded. Adam was in no way attacking the Puy through them.

Our analysis of Adam de la Halle's satirical attacks must address itself to one final and crucial question. Before whom and in what precise circumstances was the *Jeu de la Feuillée* performed? Was it, in fact, performed in public at all? Were Adam's barbed remarks about local notables of a nature that precluded a public performance? As so often with this most puzzling piece, there are no easy answers.

Early critics[41] argued that the *jeu* was composed for the Puy and was performed at one of its assemblies. It was the frankness of Adam's remarks about some of his fellow-citizens that led to this belief: Adam would hardly have dared to attack in public figures who could have done him harm. In contrast, it was thought that the *jeu* could not have any connection with the Puy[42] because of the mockery of the Prince of the Puy, Robert Sommeillon, and of the literary pretensions of Wautier as Paus and Thoumas de Clari. However, as we have seen,[43] it is only the *Feuillée* that connects Robert to the Puy, and the other two were decidedly not members of it.

None of the arguments concerning a connection between our *jeu* and the Puy are at all conclusive. The play could well have been commissioned for the Puy, of which Adam was a very prominent member, but there is no evidence that establishes a link beyond doubt.

Another important Arras institution may have played its part in the performance of the *Jeu de la Feuillée*, the *Confrérie des jongleurs et des bourgeois d'Arras.*[44] This association, sometimes called the *Carité des ardents*, was instituted in 1105 to commemorate a miracle performed by Our Lady. In that year, Arras, like other parts of

---

[41] See Guy, *Essai*, p. 337, where there is a summary of the arguments for this hypothesis.

[42] For example, E. Lintilhac, *Histoire générale du théâtre en France, t. II*, (Paris: Flammarion, 1904), pp. 61-62; A. Guesnon, *Le Moyen Âge* 18 (1916), 197-98; E. Langlois, 2ᵉ éd. of *Feuillée*, p. xvi.

[43] See above.

[44] On this association, see R. Berger, *Nécrologe*, t. II, ch. 3, pp. 39-51; J. Dufournet, *Adam de la Halle*, pp. 222-24.

northern France, was beset by an epidemic of an illness called the *feu Saint-Antoine* or the *mal des ardents*, a form of ergotism. The Virgin appeared to two *jongleurs* and told them to advise the bishop of Arras to spend the night in prayer in his cathedral. The bishop did so, and the Virgin appeared to him, giving him a precious candle which would cure the *mal des ardents*: if drops of wax from the candle were placed in water which was then drunk by those suffering from the disease, the unfortunates would be miraculously cured.

A reliquary containing the miraculous candle was exhibited in the Place du Petit-Marché in Arras every Whitsuntide. It is in order to venerate this reliquary that the companions leave the tavern at the end of the *Jeu de la Feuillée* (lines 1077-80), and the play itself takes its name from an arbour of greenery in which the reliquary was habitually exposed. Dufournet states categorically[45] that the *jeu* was performed on 3 June 1276 under the patronage of the *Confrérie des jongleurs et des bourgeois d'Arras*. All of the real characters in the *jeu* (with the exception of Adam himself and Hane le Mercier) are entered in the *Nécrologe*, and were members of the *Confrérie*. It is plausible, if unprovable, that the *jeu* was performed publicly in the Place du Petit-Marché as part of the annual festivities of the Holy Candle. These festivities began on the Thursday after the Octave of Pentecost (4 June in 1276) and lasted for three days.[46] It is likely, therefore, that our play was performed on the eve of the festivities, 3 June 1276.[47]

If the play, as would seem likely, was performed publicly, we must draw some conclusions as to Adam's satirical intentions. One forcefully argued view was that the poet's satire was essentially political in nature. Ungureanu claims that '... le poète ne vise toujours qu'une seule cible: le patriciat [...] la satire de la *Feuillée* semble être en réalité surtout l'expression d'une opposition politique',[... the poet always aims at a single target: the patrician class [...] the satire in the *Feuillée* seems to be in fact and above all the expression of a political opposition].[48] For Ungureanu, Adam is the spokesman of an extreme left-wing opposition, of a party of outright revolt among what she calls the *communards*.[49]

It seems hardly necessary to point out that this is a drastic oversimplification, not to say distortion, of the facts. Adam has targets

---

[45] *Le Jeu de la Feuillée*, p. 9.

[46] See M. Ungureanu, *La Bourgeoisie*, pp. 85-86.

[47] For suggestions on the staging of the *jeu*, see T. Walton, 'Staging the *Jeu de la Feuillée*', *Modern Language Review* 36 (1941), 344-50.

[48] *La Bourgeoisie*, p. 204.

[49] *La Bourgeoisie*, p. 282.

other than the patricians: the quack Physician and the Monk with his fake relics are the butt of Adam's sarcasm and they are not patricians. There is no denying that there is a great deal of anti-patrician political satire in the *Feuillée*: that has been the burden of this article. It is true that Adam was not the only outspoken critic in his day. The collection of satirical and comic poems known as the *Chansons et dits artésiens*[50] bear witness to a well-articulated criticism of the powers-that-be in thirteenth-century Arras. However, to suggest that Adam was the spokesman of a more or less organized opposition movement is to read too much into the *Feuillée*, and to misunderstand the intellectual and political climate of the time.

Other critics[51] have preferred to see Adam's satire as essentially light-hearted. However, whilst it is true that Adam is sometimes poking gentle fun (the shrewish women, the *sots*), one should not underestimate the seriousness of some other aspects of his satire. The attacks on the ruling-classes are heartfelt, as is his condemnation of the Pope and the higher clergy. Similarly, the condemnation of the wrong done to Thomas de Bouriane is couched in unequivocal terms. It is clear that at times Adam often meant simply to provoke a wry smile. At other times, however, he meant to wound. There is ample evidence in the *Jeu de la Feuillée* of the *saeva indignatio* of the true satirist.

It is perhaps unfortunate that most criticism of the *Feuillée* in recent years has placed an overstated emphasis on the more personal aspects of Adam's play. Dufournet claims that the work retraces the moral and spiritual journey of a poet.[52] That is undeniably true, but that is not all. We should always bear in mind that Adam was deeply rooted in Arras, that he was intimately involved in the affairs of his native city, and that he was a man of strong opinions who did not hesitate to express them. The *Jeu de la Feuillée* is a dramatic work set in a community, acted out by members of that community and concerning itself deeply with the affairs of that community. However inward-looking the author may have been, he was not so preoccupied with his efforts to transform his personal situation that he forgot to turn his sardonic eye on his fellow-citizens in order to berate their follies and their vices.

---

[50] *Chansons et dits artésien du XIIIe siècle, éd. Par A. Jeanroy et H. Guy* (Bibliothèque des Universités du Midi, II) (Bordeaux: 1896; Genève: Slatkine Repr., 1976). See also A. Guesnon, *La Satire, passim.*

[51] For example, H. Roussel, 'Notes sur la littérature arrageoise au XIIIe siècle', *Revue des Sciences Humaines,* 87 (1957), 281.

[52] J. Dufournet, *Le Jeu de la Feuillée. Édité, traduit et annoté* (Gand: Editions Scientifiques E. Story-Scientia, 1977), p. 10.

Acting companies in late medieval France: Triboulet and his troupe

ALAN HINDLEY

THEORISTS OF DRAMA ARE clearly justified in pointing out the essentially collaborative nature of the theatrical art, especially its manifestation in medieval Europe, when it thrived under the auspices of both civic and Church authorities, and like the great cathedrals of the time, played its crucial part in unifying, fulfilling and democratising whole communities. Though some of these performances were often highly complex in terms of what we would call production values, we need sometimes to remind ourselves that the creation of drama depends on very few prerequisites: a play can exist without expensive costumes and stages, indeed without a script; but it cannot, presumably, exist without performers working together in what Robert Cohen terms 'self-contained production units'.[1] It is the emergence and development of such semi-professional and professional companies – essentially 'communities' of players – that constitutes the subject of this chapter. I shall concern myself not so much with the dramatic activities of amateur players who put on often elaborate civic performances of religious plays;[2] nor with the many *sociétés joyeuses*, the Basoche and student groups, on which much has survived and much remains to be discovered.[3] Rather, the first part of my study will attempt a brief review of some of the evidence of early troupes of actors in France at the end of the Middle Ages, players who banded together to present shows, often indoors and at night, of what

---

[1] Robert Cohen, *Theatre*, (London/Toronto: Mayfield Publishing Co., 1994), p. 12.

[2] See Lynette R. Muir, *The Biblical Drama of Medieval Europe* (Cambridge: Cambridge University Press, 1995).

[3] As the many local theatre histories published from the end of the last century suggest. On these, see A. Hindley, 'Histoire locale du théâtre français: Moyen Age et Renaissance', *Le Moyen Français* 35-36 (1996), 129-59.

Glynne Wickham has termed 'the theatre of social recreation'.[4] I shall then focus upon a particular company of performers, that of the *farceur* Triboulet, as revealed in a group of plays in the Trepperel Collection. From these unusually self-reflexive texts, it may be possible to glimpse something of the activities of a community of entertainers in plays that touch on questions of theatrical organization, technique and repertoire.

I

Precisely when entertainers started to band together into companies is one of the imponderable questions of the history of European theatre. Yet it is an important question because it is closely linked to the development of theatre itself. It is clear that from the early Christian era, the ability to mime and impersonate formed an essential part of the skills of those *histriones, mimi, scurrae, pantomimi,* and *joculatores* that attracted the wrath of the early Church fathers. The ninth-century epitaph of the mime Vitalis extols in particular his gift of mimicry: 'I assumed the looks, behaviour, and words of those speaking, so that you would believe that many individuals spoke out of one mouth', a skill similar to that attributed by Thomas de Chobham to those thirteenth-century *histriones* '...who follow the courts of great ones and say scandalous and disgraceful things about those who are not present, in order to please them'.[5] Mimicry came to be regarded as one of a variety of performance skills required of the successful entertainer; indeed the well-known fabliau *Du Vilain au buffet*, testifies to a range of performance skills, reminding us that it is a *group* of entertainers being described, each member contributing his own particular 'turn', with a particular emphasis on the comic monologue: '...One acts the drunkard, another the fool; some sing, others play; some recite "La Riote" ('The Big Boast', a kind of fanfaronnade?), others "La Genglerie" (the 'Conman's Spiel'), [...] another tells a "fabliau" (a smutty story), and another "L'Erberie" ('The Quack and his Cures')'.[6]

From the late fourteenth century, account books record payments to individual 'joueurs de farces', or 'joueurs de personnages', terms

---

[4] Glynne Wickham, *Early English Stages 1300-1660*: Vol. I 1300-1576 (London: Routedge and Kegan Paul, 1959), p. 186.

[5] Quoted by William Tydeman, *The Theatre in the Middle Ages* (Cambridge: Cambridge University Press, 1978), p. 186.

[6] *Nouveau recueil complet des fabliaux*, ed. by Willem Noomen and Nico van den Boogaard (Assen: Van Gorcum, 1990), vol V, no. 52 (lines 148-58).

which seem to refer to a jongleur's way of presenting his repertoire dramatically. At the turn of the fourteenth and fifteenth centuries, the dukes of Burgundy and of Orléans were generous in their support of such entertainers, for instance the Jean de Besceu described in the accounts of Charles VI in 1388 as a 'joueur de farces'.[7] To stage more formal plays, however, it was necessary for performers to band together into ensembles, as at the visit of Gilet Vilain, Hannequin Le Fevre, Jaquemart Le Fevre and Jehannin Esturion, who entertained the duke of Orléans in 1392 and 1393, the first recorded example of entertainers described specifically as 'joueurs de personnages'.[8] During the course of the fifteenth century many more troupes of this type came into existence. The growth of such companies is unfortunately unclear, but fragmentary evidence does point to an active core of performers who gained a substantial part of their livelihood in this way. One of these groups, as we shall see, was that of the actor Triboulet. Another of which evidence survives was that of Jasme Oliou, part of whose repertoire survives in the Biblioteca Medicea-Laurenziana in Florence,[9] in two manuscripts containing farces, part of a *sottie*, and a morality play. Little is known about Oliou, other than that his stage-name was 'Jaquemart bon compaignon', and that his troupe probably performed around Avignon at the close of the fifteenth century.[10]

Before proceeding further, we should perhaps clarify in this context the concepts of 'amateur' and 'professional'. There were many performers throughout the fifteenth century who, like Jasme Oliou, made the transition from occasional player to full-time semi-professional or professional, supplementing their income by the rewards gained through performances both in public and in private. Yet it is hard to pinpoint the emergence of professional acting with any clarity. Many performers were like the Jehan Descamps, 'dit Watelet', whose troupe, from 1440-1460, was frequently rewarded by the municipality of Saint-Omer and who, though probably a 'chef troupe' involved in organizing, performing and writing plays, is nevertheless described in the accounts as a 'barbier' and a 'messagier

---

[7] P. Sadron, 'Les plus anciens comédiens français connus', *Revue d'histoire du théâtre* 1 (1948-49), 33-43.

[8] See Le Comte de Laborde, *Les Ducs de Bourgogne* (Paris: Plon, 1849) III, 66-7, nos. 5546 and 5548.

[9] P. Aebischer, 'Jasme Oliou, versificateur et auteur dramatique avignonais du XVe siècle', in *Neuf Etudes sur le théâtre médiéval* (Geneva: Droz, 1972), pp. 37-65.

[10] Where he may have entertained René d'Anjou: see Graham A. Runnalls, 'René d'Anjou et le théâtre', *Annales de Bretagne et des Pays de l'Ouest* 18 (1988), 157-80, esp. 170-71.

de pié'. Similarly, the 'Peyt Jehan', who provided farces at banquets in fifteenth-century Avignon, is described as a cobbler by profession.[11]

The distinction between amateur and professional player in the sixteenth century is just as problematic, the so-called amateurs of the *Basoche* and *Enfants sans soucy* seemingly devoting much of their energies to performing plays. Jean Bouchet, for instance, writes of Basoche-trained actors: '...whose only profession is performing farces', and who 'often, for lack of money, [they] die in hospitals after leading a riotous life'.[12] The famous Jehan de l'Espine du Pontallais who makes a guest appearance in Pierre Gringore's *Sottie du Prince des Sotz* of 1511, probably cut a similar figure. His love of satire as a Basoche actor soon involved him in difficulties with François Ier, however, earning him in 1516 a spell in jail along with two other *farceurs* Jean Serre and Jacques le Basochien for their performance in Paris of farces suggesting 'that Mother Fool ruled at Court, and that she stripped, pillaged and stole everything; as a result of which, when informed of this fact, the King and Madame Regent [Louise de Savoie] were very angry'. Imprisoned in Blois, they escaped some three months later, and were subsequently pardoned.[13] After 1512, Pontallais has all the appearance of a fully professional entertainer: with the stage-name of Songecreux, and with companions Mal-me-Sert, Pou d'Acquest and Rien-ne-Vault, he toured the land occasionally working again with Pierre Gringore, as in 1524, when they were engaged by Duke Antoine of Lorraine to stage 'farces old and new' at the baptism of Prince Nicolas. Probably an author as well as a performer, Pontallais is portrayed in later life almost as an official 'farceur' of François I, who seems to have forgiven him his escapade of 1516: he was frequently rewarded for organizing and appearing in royal entries, that of Eleonore d'Autriche in 1530, for instance, at which, with the actor Maître André, he is described as being in the King's service, and rewarded for composing 'the most exquisite farces and morality plays'.[14]

---

[11] See J.de Pas, 'Mystères et jeu scéniques à St Omer', *Mémoires de la Société des Antiquaires de la Morinie* 31 (1913), 345-77 (p. 351, note 2); and P. Pansier, 'Les débuts du théâtre à Avignon', *Annales d'Avignon et du Comtat Venaissin* 6 (1919), 5-41 (p. 22).

[12] J. Bouchet, *Epistres famillieres du traverseur* (Poitiers: Bouchet & Marnef, 1545), no. XXIII; (French Renaissance Classics, S.R. Publishers Ltd., Johnson Reprint Corporation, Mouton, 1969).

[13] *Journal d'un Bourgeois de Paris sous le règne de François Ier*, ed. by L. Lalanne (Paris: Renouard, 1864), p. 44.

[14] For a more detailed study of this actor, see J. Frappier, 'Sur Jean du Pontallais', *Mélanges Gustave Cohen* (Paris: Nizet, 1950), pp. 133-46.

It would perhaps be an exaggeration to see Jean du Pontallais as enjoying quite the status that patronage accorded official 'players of interludes' in England at a similar period. Certainly François I was much less tolerant of satirical performances than his predecessor Louis XII: witness the entertainer described in the *Journal d'ung Bourgeois de Paris* as 'a priest calling himself Monsieur Cruche', evidently a player of some standing, who in October 1515 staged in the Place Maubert a 'sottye, sermon, moralité et farce' of which the morality play made mock of the king's love-life. Not amused, the King had Cruche arrested at the inn where he was staying, and after being forced to act out the offending play:

> He was stripped down to his underclothes, whipped mercilessly, and reduced to great distress. At the end of it all a sack was produced for him to be put in, thrown out of the window, and finally pitched into the river; all of which would have happened had it not been for the fact that the poor wretch protested loudly, pointing out to them the priest's tonsure on the top of his head.[15]

In the early part of the sixteenth century life for the itinerant player can have been no less easy: the purely amateur associations still outnumbered professional ensembles, and the income of such groups was probably at best sporadic. The Jean Serre who was arrested with Pontallais in 1516 drew little profit from his talents, it seems, earning 'reputation and credit, love and popular esteem far more than "écus"', according to Clément Marot.[16] Efficiency no doubt required troupes to be organized on a more permanent basis, able to perform before a paying public, and from the 1540s there survives more evidence of players legally binding themselves together in formal associations. Surviving legal documents are a particularly fruitful source of information on such early theatrical companies. One of the earliest is a contract signed in Paris in 1544, showing how apprentices were engaged just as in other trades and professions, in this case by one Jehan Anthoine, who took on for a year a certain Gregoire Bauffre:

> ...who will be required to perform in the said Anthoine's company, duly and carefully, as appropriate, both at the Court of His Majesty the King or elsewhere in the kingdom of France for a period of eight months [...] and that the said Bauffre will share any profits, as will the other members who will perform in the said troupe during that period.

---

[15] *Journal d'ung Bourgeois de Paris,* pp. 13-14.

[16] Cl. Marot, *Oeuvres poétiques,* ed. by G. Defaux (Paris: Bordas, 1990), I, 107-08.

Such contracts are often rich in detail. Another, signed in the same year by the same Jehan Anthoine and his troupe of five performers (Anthoine de Veronne, Christofle de Veronne, Angel de Veronne, Thomas Molynier and Guillaume Quatrece – clearly something of a family affair), deals specifically with matters of profit-sharing, concluding that: '...the parties are agreed that the wife of the said Master Jehan Anthoine may perform with them, as he should see fit, but without her having any share in the profits, unless the others agree to it'.[17]

Contracts of this kind indicate a profession that was beginning to take itself seriously, and a profession that was beginning to attract women as well as men. At Bourges in 1545, an actress called Marie Fillé was hired for a year by Anthoine de L'Esperonnyère, a 'joueur d'histoires', who agreed to:

> duly keep, feed and attend to the medical needs of the said Marie at his expense during the said period. And for the service provided by the said Marie, the said L'Esperonnyère has promised to pay her the sum of 12 livres tournois when the said period of service is over.[18]

Contracts sometimes provide an insight into how performances were financed, for example by having each member contribute an initial sum of money. On 11 March 1549, for instance, five players from Chartres signed with their leader Noel Olier an agreement for a period of three years to: 'travel to cities, towns, villages and other places to perform farces, morality plays and other entertainments as they see fit...', each member having

> handed over to the said Olier, who will act as leader and manager of the said company, the sum of one gold crown, which sum of five gold crowns, together with a further gold crown to be provided by the said Olier, will be used to purchase suitable costumes for the said farces and morality plays, as well as other things required for the said venture.[19]

One of them had special responsibility for the performance receipts, his task being to share out the profits on a monthly basis using a

---

[17] E. Coyecque, *Histoire générale de Paris: Recueil d'Actes notoriés* (Paris: Imprimerie Nationale, 1905), nos. 3160 and 3264.

[18] H. Boyer, 'Engagement d'une actrice à Bourges', *Mémoires de la Société historique du Cher*, 4 (1888), 285-93 (p. 287).

[19] M. Josselin, 'Formation d'une troupe de comédiens', *Bibliothèque de l'Ecole des Chartes*, 89 (1928), 456-58.

method similar to that adopted by the troupes of Valleran Le Conte and Adrien Talmy some fifty years later.[20]

Some legal documents reveal the importance of musicians in the composition of dramatic troupes at this time. From the mid-sixteenth century, it became the custom of those members of the Paris 'Communauté des joueurs d'instruments' who failed their apprenticeship to band together to perform plays professionally: in 1545 six 'compaignons' who had not managed to become 'maîtres' formed their own company in order to '...sing and perform farces, mystery plays and other items',[21] whilst a contract of 1571 relates to a group of eight instrumentalists who agreed to: 'travel together in and outside this city of Paris in order to perform histories, tragedies, comedies, morality plays and farces, with musical and instrumental accompaniment'. In addition to sharing the proceeds, they made all their own stage equipment.[22] One of the most interesting contracts of association concerning the employment of musician-actors is one signed at Château-Thierry (Aisne) in 1552 by a 'joueur d'istoires et moralités' called Laugerot from Troyes. On this occasion Laugerot hired three musicians: Crespin Rosel, Claude Bocher and Jacques Le Veu, the first two being paid 26 'livres tournois' per year for providing musical accompaniment; Le Veu, however, earned only £15 a year, even though his work promised to be more exacting: besides having to play during the performances, he was also required to '...teach music to [Laugerot's] children'.[23]

In addition to household accounts and legal documents, a further valuable source of information on emergent theatrical companies are municipal accounts, especially where matters of censorship and the vetting of performances are mentioned. Both amateur and professional performers were often subject to such curbs: as early as 1397 in Lille, it was decreed that a fine of 20 'sous' would be imposed upon all those found performing plays on 'carts, waggons, wains, or in any other ways',[24] interdictions that were probably prompted by the

---

[20] See S.W. Deierkauf-Holsboer, 'Le Partage de la recette par les Comédiens du Roy', *Revue d'histoire littéraire de la France*, 47 (1947), 348-54.

[21] See F. Lesure, 'La Communauté des joueurs d'instruments au XVIe siècle', *Revue historique de droit français et étranger*, 31 (1953), 79-109 (p. 101).

[22] Quoted by H.M. Brown, *Music in the French Secular Theater: 1400-1550* (Harvard University Press: Cambridge Mass., 1963), p. 77.

[23] M. Mireur, 'Textes relatifs à des représentations scéniques à Draguignan', *Revue des Sociétés savantes des départements*, 3 (1876), 461-77 (p. 476).

[24] De la Fons Mélicocq, 'Les sociétés dramatiques du Nord de la France', *Archives historiques et littéraires* 6 (1857), 5-38 (p. 15).

satirical nature of the plays involved. We have seen how Jehan du Pontallais incurred the wrath of François I by performing a farce depicting Louise de Savoie as Mère Sotte. Similarly, it was proclaimed in Lille in 1544 that: 'nobody shall indulge, either on carts or in any other way, in the performance of heretical, scandalous, infamous or dishonest plays having to do with the activities of princes, members of the aristocracy, or of the judiciary or other individuals'.[25] When Pierre Le Pardonneur visited Rouen in 1556 – his six-strong troupe was probably the first to perform there 'moyenant sallaire' – the plays were condemned on religious grounds: on the third day of their visit, the tennis court where they were staging a *Vie de Job* was invaded by police officers and the show suspended. Le Pardonneur protested vigorously to such treatment, pointing out the expense incurred for the purchase of 'silk cloth, hangings and other items for the decorations of the plays [...] which are not yet paid for, but which would have been, had we not been forbidden from performing'. It was finally decreed that a local Carmelite Friar and a Canon Penitentiary 'will examine the moralities and farces that the petitioners propose to perform', after which the company was allowed to present all its plays except for one of the farces. Returning to Rouen two years later Le Pardonneur was received even less warmly, possibly because of the increasing influence of the Calvinists: on 15 January 1558, he was informed that his plays were unacceptable: '...because such entertainments lead to unnecessary and pointless expense.'[26]

The town of Amiens has preserved valuable information on visits of itinerant troupes in the later Middle Ages. Towards the end of the fifteenth century, visiting companies travel from the neighbouring communities of Soissons, St Quentin and Laon, to take part in the 'Fête des rois des Brayes' ['The Feast of the King of the Britches'] though these were probably amateurs. In 1529 we see the first indication of a troupe organized along more professional lines when, on 18 June, to commemorate the signing of the Treaty of Cambrai, the town rewarded: 'Jacques Platel, Jacques Harlé and others who performed many morality plays and farces to entertain the people'.[27] From this date on, almost every year saw visits of troupes of actors, usually for the Fête des Brayes, though it is doubtful whether they were all fully professional. After 1540 curbs on visiting performers became more stringent. Even before this some troupes had been

---

[25] Idem, p. 19.

[26] See E. Gosselin, *Recherches sur l'histoire du théâtre à Rouen* (Rouen: Cagniard, 1868).

[27] G.Lecocq, *Histoire du théâtre en Picardie* (Paris: H.Menu, 1880), p. 138.

subject to a high degree of control: in 1520, for example, Jean Dupré, Mathieu Doderel and others had been allowed to act 'en chambre', with performance times decided by the Council; and in 1538 some local 'joueurs de farces' could perform so long as they acted after divine service 'but without performing at night or sounding the bass drum'.

It is not until 1538 that the first truly itinerant troupe of players comes to Amiens, under its leader François Savary, who with his twelve companions is granted permission to perform the *Vie de Monseigneur Saint Fremin* at Pentecost: 'provided that they submit the said play to the mayor and magistrates'. The troupe of Phillibert, paying a visit to Amiens in 1541, were permitted 'to perform on feast days and holidays […] so long as they do not perform by candlelight', that is, presumably, at night. In later years the authorities appear increasingly concerned about the type of plays presented: in 1547 some 'farceurs' were allowed to perform on feast days, provided that it was in the afternoon, and there were no 'lewd or insulting farces'. The magistrates seem increasingly to be imposing restrictions on grounds of taste. In 1558 Rolland Guibert and his company were instructed to present their plays in the council chamber for vetting, following which two of the magistrates felt that the plays should be suppressed 'given the King's recent demise'; however, it was later decided that they could perform '...so long as they informed the authorities the day before which plays they intended to perform, otherwise permission would be denied'.

Performances of farces, as opposed to *moralités*, understandably attract the most censure. In 1550 Jehan de la Campaignye and his two companions were allowed: '...to perform on Sundays and feast days, but not by candlelight, in the great hall of the Châtelet, the *Holy Acts of the Apostles of Our Lord Jesus Christ*, together with the *Apocalypse*, but not to stage any vile or insulting farces'. In 1556, Anthoine Sené and his troupe from Dauphiné could perform morality plays 'en chambre', 'so long as they contained no obscene material' and the texts were submitted for inspection; they were not permitted to use the drum to advertise their shows either, but they were allowed to 'put up notices at crossroads and on the door of the place they intended to stage the said moralities and farces'. When Jacques Macron and company asked to perform in 1562, the magistrates were divided, some of them insisting that they could present only plays that were already in print 'avec privilège du Roy'. Permission was finally granted on condition that the texts be submitted to 'Maistre Adam ou autre docteur', that they avoided Sundays and feast days, and that their visit lasted no more than one week.

ACTING COMPANIES IN LATE MEDIEVAL FRANCE

Not only were entertainers hampered by the attitude of the Church in a period of considerable religious upheaval; they were also no doubt subject to the whims of often biased authorities, who probably also resented being invaded by performers from out of town. Their increasing number in a sphere that had previously been restricted mainly to local amateurs, and the fact that admission charges were being made for performances that had previously been under local control, probably had the effect of making civic authorities circumspect. The refining taste of the Pléiade, as well as the spread of Calvinism in certain areas, doubtless also provoked the denunciation of many a lusty farce. Entertainers of all kinds probably had a hard time, and after all their preparations, might well have been rebuffed in the manner of Samuel Treslecat and his company by the magistrates at Amiens in 1567, who decided:

> ...not to permit the said players to perform their plays in this town at the present time, in order to avoid all the commotion and argument that often takes place in such gatherings, not to mention the illnesses that are caused by the present hot weather, and given the orders issued by the King, the rulings of the court, the cost of living, the poverty of the common people of this town, who could waste their time in such pursuits.[28]

It would be rash to draw too rigid conclusions from such fragmentary material, but the selection of evidence cited above reveals a drama that is essentially different from the contemporary religious theatre of worship and celebration, being connected more with secular entertainments and leisure pursuits. Its practitioners performed largely small-scale shows with a limited cast, a feature sometimes reflected in the titles of the companies they formed: 'compagnons joueurs de moralitez histoires, farces et violles', plays that may have been on occasion financed by a wealthy patron, but which were also capable of being toured from audience to audience in the immediate region and beyond, by companies whose activities can be seen as the embryo of the fully commercial theatre of the early seventeenth century. Nor should we underestimate the importance of the patrons of drama in this development – the dukes of Burgundy, René d'Anjou, the duke of Lorraine, for instance – the last of whom employed for a time two of France's earliest theatrical personalities: Pierre Gringore and Jean du Pontallais. Such patrons fostered drama and its exponents, recognizing

---

[28] Further detail on Amiens can be found in G. Durant, *Département de la Somme. Ville d'Amiens. Inventaire sommaire des archives antérieures à 1790, t.II, série BB, 1 à 38* (Amiens: Imprimerie de Piteux frères, 1894), p. 324 ss.

and rewarding skill not just in their occasional largess, but also sometimes in the court functions and titles bestowed: a certain Pierre de la Oultre, for instance, is described in the accounts of François I as 'maistre compositeur et joueur de farces et moralitez',[29] though nothing further is known about him. As the sixteenth century unfolds troupes of actors become more concerned with practical and financial matters, and there is an increasing regulation of performances by vigilant town councils. In making the gradual transition from amateur to professional status, these troupes prefigure some of the later sixteenth-century professionals such as Valleran le Conte, Adrien Talmy and Alexandre Hardy, heralding the emergence in France of the commercial theatre as a public institution.

II

It is now time to turn to the evidence provided by the plays from the *Recueil Trepperel* relating to the activities of a specific company of actors, whose leader took the stage-name of Triboulet. In 1435, a troupe of actors led by a certain Maître Mouche was rewarded by Philippe Le Bon, Duke of Burgundy for performing unspecified plays.[30] Little more is known about this company and its activities. In the accounts, they are described as, 'joueurs d'apertise' (probably signalling their skills as acrobats or conjurers) but like the Bolequarre and Perrin Boisquement, rewarded by Philippe Le Bon in Paris the previous year, they may well have performed plays, and in the opinion of Gustave Cohen, operated in the Paris region.[31] Further interest in this dynasty of entertainers was aroused in 1935, when Eugénie Droz published the *sotties* of the *Recueil Trepperel*, three of which –, *Les coppieurs et lardeurs*, *Les Sotz qui corrigent le Magnificat*, and *Les Vigilles de Triboulet* [32]– testify to the existence of a company of performers led by a 'farceur' called Triboulet, decribed with characteristic hyperbole as: 'Vostre chef, vostre conduiteur/ Vostre pere, vostre conservateur' (*Les Vigilles*, lines 109-10). There appears

---

[29] Léon de Laborde, *Comptes et bâtiments du Roy: 1528-71* (Paris: Société de l'histoire de l'art, 1877), II, p.270.

[30] De La Fons Mélicocq, 'Les Rois de la fève, les fous, les joueuers de farces', *Messagier des Sciences Historiques* (1857), 397.

[31] See G. Cohen, 'Les grands farceurs du XVe siècle', in *Le Théâtre en France au Moyen Age et à la Renaissance* (Paris: Gallimard, 1956), p. 253, and G. Cohen, 'Maître Mouche, farceur et chef de troupe', *Revue d'histoire du théâtre* 6 (1954), 146-49.

[32] E. Droz (ed.), *Le Recueil Trepperel I: Les Sotties* (Paris: Droz, 1935), nos. 8, 9, 10.

to have been a link between Triboulet's troupe and an earlier company whose leader had been called Maître Mouche, for Triboulet is described as Maître Mouche's 'lieutenant', as well as his 'mignonnet' (*Les Vigilles*, lines 131 and 242). However, the Triboulet of the Trepperel plays could hardly have been the partner of the same Maître Mouche who had performed before Philip the Good back in the 1430s; he was probably therefore one of a line of comic performers who adopted this famous name. Such a practice was not uncommon amongst early performers, as exemplified by the name Triboulet itself, which, as Heather Arden has pointed out,[33] was not only a name adopted by several famous court fools (those of Louis XI, Louis XII, François I and René d'Anjou, for instance), but also became a synonym for 'fool', as well as a name used by actors to designate a particular type of comic role.

Mention of René d'Anjou brings us to a more recent theory concerning the activities of a company whose leader called himself Triboulet. In 1980, Bruno Roy put forward the ingenious hypothesis that the Triboulet of the Trepperel plays, far from being a late fifteenth-century entertainer from the Ile de France, was in fact none other than the celebrated fool employed by King René in his court at Angers between 1447 and 1479.[34] Roy further argues that René's court fool Triboulet composed the *Farce de Pathelin* sometime in the 1450s, taking the draper's name from the well-known Franciscan Guillaume Josseaume, who was then superior of the nearby convent of La Baumette.[35] Roy's analysis of some of the Trepperel *sotties* is certainly fruitful and valuable, though it is not my intention here to enter into the debate over the attribution of *Pathelin* to René's court fool. My interest lies rather in the evidence revealed by the plays about Triboulet the 'chef de troupe' and his company, whether that company operated in mid fifteenth-century Anjou or in the late fifteenth-century Ile-de-France.

Triboulet appears to have been leader of a company of at least five actors, described in line 300 of *Les Coppieurs* as 'les sots de

---

[33] Heather Arden, *Fools Plays: a Study of Satire in the Sottie* (Cambridge: Cambridge University Press, 1980), p. 39.

[34] B. Roy, 'Triboulet, Josseaulme et *Pathelin* à la cour de René d'Anjou', *Le Moyen Français* 7 (1980), 7-56.

[35] Roy returned to the debate in a subsequent article: '*La Farce de Me Pathelin* et sa création à la cour de René d'Anjou', *Revue d'histoire du théâtre* 43 (1991), 43-52, in which he proposes a cast-list for the first performance of the farce with the author Triboulet playing the lead role, the draper dressed as a Franciscan to represent Josseaume, and the shepherd played as Thibaut Belin, one of Roi René's legal representatives.

Triboulet': *Les Vigilles* is in fact composed 'à quattre personnages' (Sotuart, Croquepie, Mère Sotie and Le Rossignol), though the other two, like *La Farce de Pathelin*, each have five characters: Malotru, Nyvelet, Teste Creuse, Sotin and the Ecumeur de Latin in *Les Coppeurs*; two of whom (Teste Creuse and Sotin) also appear in *Les Sotz qui corrigent* together with Roussignol (also in *Les Vigilles*), plus the stock types Dando Mareschal and Maître Aliborum.[36] All three plays have been dated by Droz from the last two decades of the fifteenth century, though reference to a performance in 1455 of a play entitled *Les Sotz qui corrigent le Magnificat*[37] lends support to Bruno Roy's theory, whilst at the same time alerting us to the uncertain datings of many of these texts. Similarly, the distorting mirror that the *sottie* holds up to the world, quite unlike the 'slice-of-life' of the more 'realistic' farces, should also warn us against the dangers of drawing from them too precise conclusions about the realities of late-medieval theatrical life. Even so, this trio of plays provides a valuable glimpse of the activities of an organized company of actors, whether itinerant or in the service of a royal patron.

The basic *sottie*, often a short skit performed by characters wearing the fools motley, and sometimes a curtain-raiser to a more serious play, had little plot, relying for its effect on elaborate word-play and the visual comedy afforded by costumes and props. *Les Vigilles* contains the most elaborate parody, and is typical of those plays whose action mimics serious public ceremonies, in this case the Office of the Dead, in which the figure being mourned is not some royal or noble personage, but Triboulet himself, his 'body' carried comically round the acting-space by the attendant fools,[38] who chant mock lessons extolling his famous 'exploits', no doubt playing on the spectators' knowledge of contemporary accounts of the obsequies of the rich and powerful. *Les Coppieurs,* its action moving swiftly between the market square, Malostru's bookshop, and Nyvelet's rôtisserie, has a typical two-part structure: Sottin and Teste Creuse are

---

[36] There are characters called Triboulet and Rossignol in the *Sottie du Roy des Sotz* (E. Picot, *Recueil général des sotties* (Paris: Firmin-Didot, 1902-12) vol. III, pp.205-31), a play which Picot dates from 1545.

[37] Cited by E.Philipot, *Six farces normandes* (Rennes: Plihon, 1939), p. 45, who does not, however, give precise details.

[38] The text refers specifically (lines 321-22) to 'la replicque du corps' ['replica of the corpse']. Droz suggests (p. 237) that the 'lamentations' of lines 183-84, 211, 233, and 245 should be addressed specifically to it, not least by Mère Sotie, who may have been played by Triboulet himself. On the religious parody here, see H.M.Brown, *Music in the French Secular Theater 1400-1550* (Cambridge, Mass: Harvard University Press, 1963), pp. 173-77.

first 'copied' and 'larded' (i.e. ridiculed) by Malostru and Nyvelet, but finally take their revenge following consultations with the 'Ecumeur de Latin', who suggests that they should 'farcer' Malostru and Nyvelet, a prank that involves blackening their faces to show that they have been tricked. Though the action here is sometimes hard to follow, the play effectively mixes physical action and verbal fantasy, its use of comic *annominatio* accompanied by tumbling and acrobatics. *Les Sots qui corrigent* uses another familiar *sottie* technique: that of giving concrete dramatic expression to an abstract saying, in this case 'corriger le Magnificat' ('foolishly to undertake pointless and impossible tasks'), and 'mettre le frain aux dents' ('to reduce to silence').[39] After their success in mocking the 'Ecumeur de Latin' in *Les Coppieurs* (line 38 *et ss* refer specifically to this play), the fools Teste Creuse and Sottin are criticized for their frivolous clothes by the two sententious pedants Dando Mareschal and Maître Aliborum, on whom they seek revenge first by unmasking them as fools (lines 320-23), and then by placing 'a bit between their teeth' (line 390), and gagging them into silence; this play's two-part structure, with the fools finally avenged, thus closely ressembles that of *Les Coppieurs*.[40]

If we return now to *Les Vigilles*, we can appreciate that the difficulty here for the theatre historian is that the image we have of Triboulet is presented via a particularly distorting mirror, his life as a 'farceur', comically transformed into that of a larger-than-life boozer, hence the importance of wine in the text (cf. lines 190-91), not to mention the fools' comic exit chanting the 'rouge letanie' (line 341). A certain piquancy was perhaps also provided in performance by having Triboulet play the part of Mère Sotie, the humour deriving from the fact that his demise has clearly been much exaggerated! But just what can we learn here about this early 'chef de troupe'?

---

[39] See E. Droz, *Le Recueil Trepperel*, I, 185, who refers to a *Jeu de corriger le Magnificat*, performed in Metz in 1488. On the technique of literalising a phrase or saying, also seen in the *Sottie des Rapporteurs* and the *Sottie des Trompeurs*, see the study by Joseph A. Dane, 'Linguistic Trumpery: Notes on a French *Sottie*', *Romanic Review* 71 (1980), 14-21. Props are sometimes used in this elaboration, as here, where Dando's occupation is described as 'ferrer les oies' (i.e. attempting the impossible); line 198 of the play suggests that Dando carried a toy goose throughout the play. On the significance of objects in the *sotties*, see Olga Anna Dull, *Folie et rhétorique dans la sottie* (Genève: Droz, 1994), pp. 181-202.

[40] See J-C. Aubailly, *Le Monologue, le dialogue et la sottie* (Paris: Champion, 1976), pp. 275-77, for whom these two *sotties*: 'semblent toutes les deux appartenir au même répertoire [...] sont de la même veine comique et appartiennent aux premiers exemples du genre' (p. 275).

One can detect in *Les Vigilles*, behind the eulogy of Triboulet the comic legend, renowned as a formidable eater and drinker (line 80), whose curative powers are little short of miraculous (line 138),[41] who inspires fear as he struts on his 'old nag' ('rousin', line 156), something of the reality of Triboulet the man and the actor. Not least of his qualities appears to have been his versatility, praised by his companion Sotin: 'For he was an authentic fool/Ready to perform or do anything at all/In both comic and serious vein'.[42] In other words, he was equally adept in both serious ('rhetorique') and comic ('lourdoys') styles; an intelligent critic who used the mask of folly to give vent to his powers of observation and shrewd wit in the form of satire. His boasting here is similar to that of the entertainer Verconus, whose varied talents enabled him to change dramatic style as he changed his costume.[43] Such versatility extends not just to Triboulet's performance skills, but also to his talents as a writer: he was a prolific composer of comic plays, his companions ascribing to him in their enthusiasm the composition of *sotties* (line 229), farces (line 479) and of some four hundred morality plays! (line 226). Such indeed was his fame in the capital that his services had been sought by the Parisian Law Clerks ('The Basoche') to make a guest appearance at their Epiphany celebrations.[44]

Just as this group of Trepperel plays seems to have constituted part of the repertoire of Triboulet's company, so do the texts themselves provide indications of the nature of that repertoire. Triboulet's celebrated versatility is best exemplified, he boasts, by his mastery of 'tresdivers langaiges' (line 220); moreover, he is as good at 'jargon' as François Villon himself (lines 224-25), making him an obvious choice to play Pathelin in the famous farce; indeed such is his reputation in this role that his companions have it in mind to bury him wrapped in a script of the play, 'cousue de corne de belin' (line 254), [sewn together with a ram's-horn].[45]

---

[41] His *marotte* ['bauble'] is particularly noted for its curative powers; cf. lines 148-50; 160-62.

[42] *Les Vigilles*, lines 311-15. On the question of 'lourdoys', see J-C. Aubailly, *Le Monologue, le dialogue et la sottie*, ch. IV.

[43] Quoted by L. Petit de Julleville, *Les Comédiens en France au moyen âge* (Paris: Cerf, 1885), pp. 332-33.

[44] If lines 167-68: 'Qui au palays royal est sailly/Quant la feste des roys estoit' can be so interpreted.

[45] It is this detail above all, specifying precisely the four languages used in *Pathelin*, that for Bruno Roy clinches the argument that Triboulet actually composed this farce; see 'Triboulet, Josseaume et *Pathelin*', p. 26.

Maître Pierre Pathelin is by no means the only farce in the varied programme apparently offered to the public by Triboulet and his troupe. In *Les Coppieurs*, when Teste Creuse suggests they put on 'quelque vieille farce' (line 140), Malostru, the copyist, reads off some of the titles on his bookshelves. What about *La Farce de Poitrasse* (line 172, now lost), he suggests? Or *Le Pauvre Jouhan* (line 172), a fine example of the genre, surviving as the seventh play of the *Recueil Trepperel*.[46] Both these and *Pathelin* are felt to be too passé; *La Fillerie* (line 179, also lost) is later rejected as too 'crude'; whilst *Les trois coquins* (no. VI of the Trepperel *sotties*, of which line 264, 'Mais revenons a noz moutons', alludes specifically to *Pathelin*) is regarded, curiously, as being too 'badin'. The bookseller's final suggestion is *La farce des oiseaux* (line 184), probably *La Farce de la Pipée*, in fact a mixture of farce, *sottie* and morality play, which Teste Creuse accepts.[47] *Pathelin* is the subject of further brief discussion in *Les Vigilles* (lines 253, 264), as is *Poitrasse* (line 264) and *La Fillerie* (line 267); *Les farces* (sic) *des amoureux* (line 266) is also mentioned, but it is difficult to relate this to a surviving play.

A further significant aspect of the titles proposed by the fools in these plays is their variety: not only does the company put on plays, but seemingly other types of entertainment too, evoking different performance skills on the part of its members. As he sings his leader's praises, Croquepie notes Triboulet's ability to recite 'on his own' despite being in his cups (line 272) *La belle dame sans mercy* (*Les Vigilles*, line 270), possibly a dramatized version of Alain Chartier's courtly poem, with its well-known satirical overtones. In *Les Coppieurs*, as well as comic plays, Malostru suggests titles such as *La Danse de Macabré par personnages* (line 152), *La Basse danse nouvelle* (line 162) and the *Rosty boully joyeulx* (line 163), recalling the importance of music, song and dance in play performances of the period. They also remind us of the imprecise distinction between narrative and drama at this time, with certain literary forms lending themselves readily to dramatic presentation 'par personnages'. It is interesting to note, for example, that Triboulet's troupe performed the Dance of Death dialogues 'as a play', a further confirmation of the close rapport between theatre and the *danse macabré* on which others have commented.[48]

---

[46] It has been edited separately by E. Droz and M. Roques, *La Farce du pauvre Jouhan, pièce comique du XVe siècle* (Genève-Paris: Droz-Minard, 1959).

[47] See the recent edition by A. Tissier, *Recueil de farces: 1450-1550* (Paris: Droz, 1998), vol. XII, pp. 205-348.

[48] See Jane H.M. Taylor, 'The dialogues of the Dance of Death and the limits of late-medieval theatre', *Fifteenth Century Studies*, 16 (1990), 215-32.

Other significant typological questions are raised in *Les Coppieurs*, where four categories of play are listed by Malostru. Since various farces have been rejected, what then shall we put on, he asks: a 'farce d'eschauffault' [scaffold play], a 'farce de nopces' [wedding play], a 'farce de colleiges' [school play] or a 'farce de bende' [company play]? It is not easy to decide what some of these categories signified. For Droz the first simply meant 'simple shows'; the second, plays performed at wedding celebrations; the third, 'in which students made fun of their teachers'; and the fourth, 'written for a company of actors'.[49] Perhaps the most problematic category is the 'farce de bende', which Arden interprets in terms of the subject matter of the play, suggesting for instance that a 'sottie de bande' is a play, like *Les Vigilles*, '...based on the idea of the *sot* as a fascinating person', where we laugh 'at the life of the *sot* and his foolish problems'.[50] It may however be preferable to regard these categorizations as being more organizational than thematic, relating not so much to their content, as to *where* or *how* the plays were staged: whether publicly (and outdoors) on the platform stages traditionally associated with such performances ('farce d'eschauffault'); or privately at a wedding feast or within a school or college community ('farce de nopces', 'de colleiges'); or by a company of entertainers such as that of Triboulet and his men ('farce de bende'), each member specializing in his particular stock role, and probably performing indoors for money. We should certainly always guard against too narrow an interpretation of such technical terms: even the simple word 'farce' probably denoted a wider range of play than we might realize. And as Arden reminds us,[51] it was indeed *a range* of plays that Triboulet's company performed: not just *sotties* and farces, but also *moralités*, as well as other entertainments 'par personnages'.[52] Though the Triboulet plays mention only farces, *sotties* and *moralités*, evidence from the sixteenth century catalogued by Raymond Lebègue shows performers increasingly broadening their repertoire to appeal to more refined tastes, with titles such as 'comédie', 'anticques', 'ystoires morales' and 'tragédies morales'.[53]

---

[49] *Le Recueil Trepperel*, p. 181.

[50] H. Arden, *Fools Plays*, p. 61.

[51] H. Arden, *Fools' Plays*, p 6.

[52] Perhaps *sermons joyeux*, too, as Triboulet was a celebrated 'precheur'. (See B. Roy, 'Triboulet, Josseaume et *Pathelin*', p. 18).

[53] R. Lebègue, 'Le Répertoire d'une troupe française', *Revue d'histoire du théâtre* I (1948-49), 9-24.

The category of play described by Malostru as 'farce de bande', with its possible emphasis on the players as a *group*, invites us to consider the nature of the roles played by the different actors. If we assume that the versatile Triboulet did not play the part of his own corpse in *Les Vigilles*, then which part did he actually play? The 'leading role' of Mère Sotie, as Droz suggests? And what of the other two plays? Did he, as a 'vray sot sotouart en sottoys' (*Les Vigilles*, line 276), play one of the ordinary, natural, fools? Or do his medical skills, comically vaunted by Roussignol (lines 149-51) perhaps evoke the pompous 'magisters', variously named 'Ecumeur de latin', Dando Mareschal, or Maître Aliborum, an arrangement which would certainly have given him, together with *Pathelin*, another opportunity to demonstrate his mastery of 'tresdivers langages'?[54] Though we have no clear indication of the costume of the 'magister' type, he has a distinctive physical appearance here, which may have characterized other 'Ecumeurs': Malostru describes him (lines 399-403) as having 'a pointed nose [...] a veined forehead [...] dark eyebrows [...] and grey-blue eyes'; but it is the mixture of French and Latin that really distinguishes him (lines 340-45), and which Teste Creuse has such difficulty in understanding.[55] Triboulet's troupe must have been rich in actors equipped to take on the related role of the mock pedant, for in *Les Sotz qui corrigent*, Maître Aliborum and Dando Mareschal make their joint appearance as pedants whose ignorance brings about their downfall at the hands of the fools. The function of these two roles, illustrated in the better-known Maître Aliborum, is essentially that of the dim-wit who poses comically as a scholar, insisting on giving advice where it is not wanted. He appears in other plays, too: in the *Farce des Queues troussées*, for instance, where a certain loucheness is also a feature of his character, seen in the inappropriate counsel he gives to two wives who are having problems with their husbands.[56] Though it is not clear from the text of *Les Sotz qui corrigent*, Maître Aliborum, like the fool and the *badin*, may well have had his own costume and attributes, probably a 'bonnet rond', inkwells, and voluminous scrolls of parchment.[57] What is certain is that as in other

---

[54] His combination of innocence and cunning suggested in some of the comic eulogies of Triboulet in *Les Vigilles* would also have made him an obvious choice for the role of the 'badin'.

[55] The 'Ecumeur' role is close to that of the pedant, and may have been the type on which Rabelais based his portrait of the scholar from Limousin. See also Olga Anna Dull, op. cit., pp. 136-39.

[56] G. Cohen (ed.) *Recueil de farces* (Cambridge, Mass.: Medieval Academy of America, no. 47, 1949), no. VI.

[57] According to the description in the *Moralité de Chascun*; (see E. Droz, op. cit., I,

plays of the period, he is comically undressed by the fools, as is Dando Mareschal, in some characteristic 'jeux de scène' involving costume-change leading to the unmasking of the fool beneath.

The only other significant reference in these plays to performance matters relates to the question of men playing women's roles. As the troupe discusses the casting arrangements for their performance of *La farce des oiseaux* Malostru characteristically mocks Teste Creuse:

> You'll play the woman's role well. You have a shapely figure, laughing eyes, and an attractive nose. You look as if you've got make-up on (lines 186-89).

He is probably thinking here of the part of Plaisante Folie in *La Pipée*, in which Sotin is suggested initially for the role of the young lover Jaune-Bec (line 192), with Nivelet pointing out that he could just as easily play Plaisante Folie, since his voice is 'as sweet as a virgin's' (line 194). When Teste Creuse protests that his voice is too low (line 196), Malostru and Nivelet turn on Teste Creuse and Sotin derisively, jeering at his feminine appearance (in the case of Teste Creuse) or at his skills as a dancer (in the case of Sotin), in exchanges that in performance would have been accompanied by some kind of physical daubing, an indignity that will result in their faces being blackened in return. Other common stock parts mentioned in *Les Coppieurs* include those of the lover (line 210) and the chambermaid (line 206); and Sotin's quip that his shoulders are too broad to play the maid's part may provide a clue to the humour, intentional or otherwise, that must often have arisen when female roles were played mostly by men, features that show actors exploiting comically the relationship between the 'real-live' performer, and the role being played.

Finally, lest the spirit of carnival that we see in the Triboulet *sotties* should give the impression of a totally carefree existence, untroubled by the pressures of censorship and control – far from the case, as we have seen from the evidence reviewed earlier – it should be pointed out that Triboulet's company, too, may have had occasion to be wary of the curbs imposed on itinerant entertainers. The fool's motley, surrounding which there is much stage-business in these plays, reminds us of the strongly satirical flavour of the *sotties*, the *sot* being just as much a virulent critic as he is an innocent clown. His 'marotte', referred to in line 148 of *Les Vigilles*, was thought precisely to

---

186). It is a pity that the portrait of Maître Aliborum, commissioned by Roi René in 1478 has not survived (cf. B. Roy, art. cit., p.49, n.54). For more on Maître Aliborum, see also P. Sadron, 'Un emploi du théâtre médiéval: Maître Aliborum', *Revue d'histoire du théâtre*, 12 (1961), 34-35.

symbolize the scourge of the fool's utterance, and the 'chapperon', with its asses' ears, may well have had similar connotations. There is perhaps just a hint of this fear in a brief exchange between *Les Sotz qui corrigent*: as they debate what to perform, Sotin appears to concede that there could be repercussions: 'Par Dieu, se vous en faictes guere/Ne (vous) doubtez qu'on vous pugnira' [lines 219-20: My goodness, if you make trouble, you can be sure you'll be punished]... But this is a *sottie*, and the cloud of doubt soon dissipates, as Dando Mareschal and Maître Aliborum come cavorting back into the action.

* * * * *

The performers whose activities we have been seeking to outline here merit their place in a study of the 'communities' of medieval drama for they were communities not so much in the sense of entertainers staging plays that externalize the concerns and preoccupations of a collectivity of which they were themselves an intrinsic part, but in the sense that they established their own production companies designed to transport their plays between different publics. As such they no doubt helped their audiences to define and redefine themselves, but they also constituted what subsequently developed into acting companies – 'communities' of actors – each with his role within that community, not just as actor within a play, but also within the economic and cultural unit that was the company. We have glimpsed the organization of such groups, the attitudes of the actors to their craft, and some of the practicalities of performance. We have also seen something of their repertoire and of their attitude to the kind of material they staged in their attempts to earn a living: which plays were most likely to succeed because of their novelty, for instance, or flop because they were seen as out-of-date.

The evidence we have tried to assemble is of course fragmentary, and the picture we have attempted to paint necessarily conjectural; and with much evidence requiring reassessment, as well as new information doubtless awaiting discovery in civic rolls, household accounts and legal records, it is to be regretted that there is no French equivalent of the impressive Records of Early English Drama systematically to catalogue such material; no late medieval Scarron either to provide us with a *Roman comique* on the adventures of an itinerant company of players. But in the entertainers whose existence we can detect sporadically in the material at our disposal, and in play-scripts that are often obscure, we can perceive something of the beginnings of professional troupes of actors as they emerged from their medieval communities to become the acting companies that shaped the early public theatre in France. Essentially in the same tradition as Molière's *Illustre Théâtre*, such 'communities' of players can legitimately be said to embody the essence of drama at a time when it was becoming increasingly significant as social recreation, its vitality and creativity clearly apparent long before 'theatre' came to denote the familiar purpose-built public playhouse of stone and mortar.

Processional theatre and the rituals of social unity in Lille

ALAN E. KNIGHT

IT WAS A COMMONPLACE of medieval thought to conceive of political entities and social institutions in terms of the human body. Ideally the head ruled the members and the various organs, which were perceived as having different degrees of importance; but just as disease could sicken and sometimes kill the body, so disharmony and rebellion could weaken and even destroy social and political institutions. Rulers, therefore, sought ways to minimize conflict among competing interests, while maintaining the distinction of the group's various parts. The metaphor of the human body was applied to every level of social organisation from empire to parish confraternity, so that a group seen as a member of the body at one level might be viewed in terms of the whole body at another level. Since our discussion here will focus on urban processional theatre, the town or city will be the political entity that most concerns us. It should be understood at the outset, however, that the medieval comparison of the city with the human body was far from being just a clarifying or mnemonic metaphor. As Mervyn James points out in his study of the Corpus Christi cult in late medieval England, 'the concept of body provided urban societies with a mythology and ritual in terms of which the opposites of social wholeness and social differentiation could be both affirmed, and also brought into a creative tension, one with the other'.[1] Although James appropriately links the concept of body with Corpus Christi, the principle applies to urban rituals of all kinds. Here we shall examine a case in which processional theatre played a role in maintaining that creative tension between social wholeness and social differentiation, which is to say, in fostering a sense of community.

---

[1] Mervyn James, 'Ritual, Drama and Social Body in the Late Medieval English Town', *Past and Present* 98 (Feb. 1983), 4.

ALAN E. KNIGHT

The city, then, might be thought of as a living organism in which the streets are vessels carrying the life-giving blood of commercial enterprise and social interchange to all its members. But the streets can also be put to organized and dedicated uses, one of the most important of which in the Middle Ages was the city-wide procession incorporating representatives from every institution of the community. In that event one might view the streets as vessels carrying the blood of unity and concord from the members back to the heart. This alternating rhythm of daily activity and public ritual was no doubt typical of towns throughout medieval Europe, but here we shall examine the processional activity of the city of Lille in Flanders, one of the industrial, cloth-making centres of the Burgundian Netherlands. The case is particularly instructive not only because the relationship between procession and drama can be well documented from Lille's rich store of archival records, but also because a number of the play texts have survived as well.

For more than five centuries one of the most important annual events for the citizens of Lille was the great procession and novena in honour of the Virgin Mary. Called simply La Procession de Lille, it was founded in 1270 by the countess Margaret of Flanders, and it took place each year on the octave of Trinity Sunday under the aegis of the collegiate church of St Peter. The countess, in addition to honouring the Virgin, was especially eager to finance the reconstruction of St Peter's by establishing a public ritual that would attract large numbers of pilgrims to the city during the nine days of the observance.[2] By the fifteenth century the procession had developed into a great civic and religious spectacle in which all social groups and institutions of the city took part. In this way it united the whole city in a magnificent ritual of devotion and civic pride, and continued to do so until all such religious manifestations were suppressed by the Revolution.

From the late fourteenth or early fifteenth century until 1565 neighbourhood youth groups staged mystery plays on the day of the procession; that evening and sometimes on the following days they staged farces. The plays that were judged to be the best were awarded prizes, most often by a personage called the Bishop of Fools. The latter was usually a canon of the collegiate church, one of whose functions was to organize entertainments at public ceremonial events. Each year, it would seem, he issued a proclamation in which he invited the youth groups to participate in the contest by staging plays

---

[2] E. Hautcoeur, *Histoire de l'église collégiale et du chapitre de Saint-Pierre de Lille*, 3 vols (Lille: L. Quarré, 1896–99), I, pp. 367–68. See also his *Cartulaire de l'église collégiale de Saint-Pierre de Lille*, 2 vols (Lille: L. Quarré, 1894), I, pp. 432–33.

newly written for the occasion. Though only one such proclamation survives, dated 1463, it is quite specific about the types of plays that could be associated with the procession. Each group had to enter two plays in the contest in order to be eligible for a prize: a mystery play to embellish the procession itself and a farce to entertain the crowds at a later time. The mystery plays were first mimed on wagons set up along the route of march as the procession moved through the streets on Sunday morning. Then in the afternoon the wagons were pulled into the main square, which was the heart of the city, where the same plays were performed 'en bonne et vraie retorique'. The proclamation states that the processional plays must be based on biblical stories, saints' lives, or scenes from Roman history.[3] Of the many hundreds of plays that must have been written for the Lille procession, seventy-two have survived in a single manuscript from the second half of the fifteenth century.[4] These plays conform very closely to the requirements of the Bishop's proclamation in that there are sixty-four biblical plays, three saint plays, broadly defined, and four plays derived from Roman history. Only the morality play of the Assumption fails to fit the prescribed categories, since it contains no human characters.

If a procession of this kind projects the image of a community whose different parts are united in a common enterprise, we must not forget that the medieval city was also an aggregation of political, social and economic groups of varying power and influence, among which there was often much competition and little communication. Lille, with a population approaching 20,000 by the end of the fifteenth century, was similarly divided into many units. In addition to the usual social groupings of the various institutions – political, ecclesiastical, commercial and military – there were the spatial partitions of the church parishes, some of which were marked by economic disparities because they were populated by the lower-paid workers of the cloth industry. The population of Lille, in fact, like that of most towns at the time, 'was divided into a great variety of collectivities, which were like scales covering the vast body of the city'.[5] Most relevant to our

---

[3] The full text of the proclamation may be found in Léon Lefebvre, *Histoire du théâtre de Lille de ses origines à nos jours*, 5 vols (Lille: Lefebvre-Ducrocq, 1901–07), I, p.9. For excerpts see Alan E. Knight, 'The Bishop of Fools and His Feasts in Lille', in *Festive Drama*, ed. by Meg Twycross (Cambridge: D. S. Brewer, 1996), pp. 157–66.

[4] Wolfenbüttel, Herzog August Bibliothek, Codex Guelf 9 Blankenburg.

[5] Robert Muchembled, *Popular Culture and Elite Culture in France: 1400–1750*, transl. by Lydia Cochrane (Baton Rouge: Louisiana State University Press, 1985), p. 114.

enquiry, however, are the divisions into neighbourhoods or quarters, which were not coextensive with the parishes. The archival documents refer to these quarters collectively as 'les rues et les places' because they were situated around prominent streets or city squares from which they took their names. Each such neighbourhood was home to a company of young men, most if not all unmarried, who claimed a certain social authority over the other inhabitants. Each company had an elected leader – a lord, prince, abbot, or pope – who organized public festivities, games, and contests within the neighbourhoods during holidays and seasons of merriment. Moreover, these youth groups, coexisting in a constant state of rivalry, set up matches and contests of various kinds among themselves, going so far as to engage in mock battles between the neighbourhoods. At these times the streets of Lille were not vessels bringing sustenance to all parts of the urban community, but cell walls dividing one neighbourhood from another.

It was this aspect of the city's popular culture that most concerned the municipal authorities, because such encounters resulted far too often in personal injuries and the destruction of property. They therefore issued a steady stream of ordinances prohibiting assemblies of the rival youth groups and forbidding the potentially violent contests that took place at such gatherings. One of the early results of these efforts to preserve order in the city would be to change the nature of the play contests from unsupervised encounters in the streets to organized dramatic competitions associated with the annual procession. In this way the authorities took a first step toward incorporating the youth groups into the life of the larger community. If, as we noted earlier, the health of a collective body required a creative tension between wholeness and differentiation, then the incorporation of the neighbourhood groups into the life of the community could be achieved only by preserving their separate identities, not by suppressing them. In order to understand how this came about in late medieval Lille, let us first look at the authorities and the youth groups and then examine the relations between them.

The municipal government of Lille was made up of a body of thirty-nine men known collectively as the *Loi* or the *Magistrat*. In addition to the largely ceremonial figure called the *Rewart*, there were twelve aldermen or *échevins*, one of whom was named mayor; twelve councillors; eight men who attended to financial matters, known appropriately as *les huit hommes*; and six permanent civil servants.[6]

---

[6]Albert Croquez, *Histoire de Lille*, 2 vols (Lille: Emile Raoust, 1935–39), I, pp.73–74.

Only those who had been granted Bourgeois status were eligible to hold these offices. Though the municipal ordinances were usually issued in the name of the *échevins, conseil et huit hommes*, the real power in urban affairs lay in the hands of the aldermen, most of whom were patrician merchants who had a vested interest in maintaining a peaceful and orderly community.

The neighbourhood groups were the urban counterparts of the *abbayes de jeunesse* or associations of unmarried male adolescents, one of which was found in each rural village.[7] The activities of the latter groups included festive folk customs, such as the *charivari* and other rites related to marriage. Cities, however, because of their size, were divided into neighbourhoods, each of which had its own association. Though the urban groups maintained some of the rural customs, such as planting May trees before the houses of marriageable young women, they developed other practices that involved contests and rivalries among the different neighbourhoods. Their membership changed in the course of the fifteenth and sixteenth centuries to include young married men and even older adults, who may have acted as a stabilizing influence. In the late fourteenth century, however, their activities were of grave concern to the aldermen.

The earliest surviving register of Lille's municipal ordinances begins in the year 1382, and one of the very first ordinances of the register is directed to the activities of the youth groups. It forbids them to play any play (*gieu de personnages*) whatsoever, to organize encounters of one group against another, or to plant May trees in the streets.[8] The 1382 ordinance is the first of four issued through 1428 prohibiting the playing of plays on wagons or in the streets anywhere in the city. One wonders if the plays were irreverent and disrespectful of authority, or if they were prohibited just because the assemblies led to disorder. In the 1480s the ordinances were directed against dances and other entertainments in the streets, at which events prizes were often awarded to those judged best in each activity. The most urgent prohibitions, however, were directed against the so-called baptisms or inaugurations of newly-elected leaders of the groups. The aldermen clearly felt that this form of initiation was a mockery of the sacrament of baptism and might well bring God's wrath down upon the city. As early as 1416 water jousting had been forbidden. A century later we find the youths tossing each other into the city fountains, and in 1558

---

[7] Both types of association are described by Muchembled in *Popular Culture and Elite Culture*. See especially chapters 2 and 3.

[8] Archives Municipales de Lille [A.M.L.], Registre aux Ordonnances du Magistrat, 373, fol. 3v.

they were having water fights in the town's rivers and waterways. It would seem that by 1513 the contests and rivalries among the city's neighbourhood groups had turned into genuine fights and conflicts, since at that time they were forbidden to attack one another. Five years later fights between national groups, such as French and Flemish, were also forbidden. In 1558 it came to the attention of the aldermen that many people, both youth groups and others, were holding assemblies to make attacks, as if to wage war, one parish against another and one band against another. It is hard to know whether the stronger language of the later ordinances reflects a real increase in violence or whether it signals only a growing intolerance on the part of the aldermen. In any case, the persistence of disruptive rivalries among the youth associations created situations that for at least two centuries each group of aldermen felt obliged to counteract.

One of the public rituals that helped hold urban divisiveness in check was the city-wide procession, during which the streets regained their function as vessels connecting all parts of the urban body. Even if there was the occasional squabble over places of honour in the march,[9] such processions provided the inhabitants of Lille with a vision of the ideal city as a unified and harmonious community. It is highly significant in this regard that the 1382 ordinance prohibiting the playing of plays made an exception for the Procession of Lille. One possible reason for the exception is that already in the late fourteenth century the aldermen had begun their efforts to control at least one aspect of the neighbourhood groups' activities by incorporating the staging of plays in the procession. Though it took some years to effect a complete change, they apparently had no need to repeat the prohibition after 1428. Indeed, only five years later we find the first clear evidence that a dramatic contest had been established to reward the best plays staged at the procession. Thus, with the introduction of the competition, the *échevins* extended their control not only over the content of the plays, but over the spirit of rivalry among the groups as well.

We may speculate that the plays the youth groups originally performed at their assemblies were folk plays or farces, perhaps even satirical pieces analogous to the *Jeu de la feuillée* from nearby Arras. If so, it is to the credit of the municipal authorities that from the beginning of the contest they provided categories for both the biblical plays and the farces. All competitors, moreover, were required to enter

---

[9] In 1420 the aldermen had to settle a dispute between the mercers and the cloth weavers as to which guild should take precedence in the procession (A.M.L., Comptes de la Ville de Lille, 16164, fol. 74v).

a play in each contest. We have already noted that each biblical or historical play was presented twice, once in mime along the route of march as the procession passed, and once in full spoken production in the main square. Since the farces were most likely not connected to the procession in subject matter, they were played in the evening or the next day. In the sixteenth century they were performed on the three days following the procession. Nevertheless, they were always staged in front of the town hall in the main square and were thus shared with the entire urban community. By requiring the companies to present, in addition to the mystery plays, the kinds of comic or satirical plays they presumably had always performed, the municipal authorities all the more effectively channelled the youths' energies into a constructive activity.

The success of these early dramatic contests must have encouraged the staging of plays at other ritual and ceremonial events in Lille. Apart from the annual Corpus Christi and Lille processions, there were three types of occasional or general processions in the city: entries of rulers and noble visitors, processions of thanksgiving for peace or for a royal birth, and processions of a penitential character in which God was petitioned to grant victory in battle or relief from the plague. Only in the last type was there no dramatic activity, presumably because plays, even those of a religious character, were perceived as being festive rather than penitential. All general or occasional processions, however, shared certain traits that fostered the unity of the city. Participation was mandatory for the inhabitants; therefore the shops closed and all work ceased. Those who lived along the route of march were required to clean the streets and decorate their houses. At princely entries, those not processing with the noble visitor would watch from the sidelines. Otherwise, everyone took part in the march; families were led by the head of the household and parishioners were led by their priests. An exception was made to the requirement of universal participation during periods of plague. At those times members of households where plague was present were required to shut their doors and windows and remain inside.

References to theatrical activity at processions other than the Procession of Lille begin to appear in the records around the middle of the fifteenth century. The earliest pattern for spectacles at princely entries was the placement of *tableaux vivants* along the route of march. Later we find references to plays being staged after the entry was completed. At processions of thanksgiving in the sixteenth century, the neighbourhood groups were urged to stage new plays on the theme of the procession – a peace treaty, for example – but they could also present morality plays and farces. Prizes were awarded for the two best plays in each of the three categories. For this type of procession the documents make clear that all plays must be staged in the main square of the city before being played elsewhere. This is the first indication that plays were ever performed again after their competition performance. Presumably attendance at the plays was not mandatory, as it was for the procession. Therefore the companies, on returning home with their pageant wagons, must have repeated the plays for their friends and neighbours. Still, the requirement that the plays be shared first with the whole community seems to point beyond the practical necessity of staging the plays in one place so the judges could determine the winners. It suggests that the municipal authorities were as insistent as ever on keeping theatrical activity in a city-wide perspective.

The aldermen of Lille had no doubt always found it difficult to maintain an equilibrium between the needs of the city as a whole and the conflicting needs of its constituent parts, but the threat to their vision of a united community became especially severe in the second quarter of the sixteenth century with the appearance of the first Lutherans in the city. The latter were viewed not as forming another member of the social body, but as a foreign element, a disease that had to be expelled or exterminated. Natalie Davis has shown how in sixteenth-century Lyon the Catholic and Protestant conceptions of urban space, time and community were so different as to form two 'languages' whose grammars were ultimately irreconcilable.[10] In Lille the Protestant movement never gained the foothold that it did in Lyon because the repressive measures taken by the authorities at all levels were quick and harsh. Here, too, the city's *échevins* played an important role in maintaining order by taking several decisive actions as soon as they perceived a serious threat to the community. In the political area they responded by wresting jurisdiction over the 'crime' of heresy in Lille from the bishop of Tournai,[11] while in the cultural area they suddenly took full control of the dramatic competition at the annual Procession of Lille.

Perhaps it was only coincidence, but it was in 1527 that the first measures were taken against the Lutherans and that the aldermen assumed control of the dramatic contest, a function that had long been exercised by the Bishop of Fools and his associates from the church of

---

[10] Natalie Zemon Davis, 'The Sacred and the Body Social in Sixteenth-Century Lyon', *Past and Present* 90 (Feb. 1981), 40–70.

[11] Alain Lottin, 'Lille sous Charles Quint: sociabilité et vie religieuse', in *Histoire de Lille de Charles Quint à la conquête française (1500–1715)*, ed. by Louis Trenard (Toulouse: Privat, 1981), pp. 91–92.

St Peter. Nothing about the contest seems to have changed immediately, but six years later there was another coincidence involving these two domains. An imperial edict of 1529 had prescribed the death penalty for convicted heretics, and in 1533 seven Lutherans were burned or beheaded in the main market square of Lille, the same square in which the plays were always performed. Five of the executions took place in May, a month before the procession, and a sixth took place on 14 June, the very eve of the procession itself.[12] Was it just by chance that the aldermen chose that year to expand the spectacular and dramatic elements of the procession by establishing a new contest? Since the early fifteenth century some of the trade guilds had staged *tableaux vivants* on wagons that accompanied the guild members marching in the procession. In 1533 the aldermen issued a proclamation inviting all guilds to stage *tableaux* on any subject – presumably biblical – provided it not be the Passion, a few scenes of which had traditionally been mimed on wagons by one of the neighbourhood groups. To encourage the guilds to participate, the aldermen offered each one a monetary subsidy to help defray the cost of the wagon and *tableau*. In addition, they set up prizes in gold coin for the two best *tableaux*.[13]

The following year, overturning a century-old tradition, the aldermen took control of the Passion *tableaux*, greatly expanded the spectacle, and assigned a scene to each of twenty-three guilds, thus presenting an elaborate mimed Passion play that moved with the procession. The Passion proper was preceded by the Creation and Fall of Man, the Annunciation, the Nativity, and other scenes from the childhood of Jesus. The sequence ended with the Descent into Hell. The other twenty-three guilds, if they wished to stage a *tableau*, were allowed to choose any other biblical subject.[14] The municipality paid for two prizes for each of the two groups and again provided a small subsidy for each guild that participated. Since forty-one subsidies were paid, we know that eighteen of the remaining twenty-three guilds staged a *tableau* and entered the contest. At the same time the neighbourhood groups, who continued to perform plays in the usual manner, were directed to dramatize scenes from the Old Testament.[15]

In 1535 the *échevins* imposed on the guilds yet another pattern of biblical exposition by reorganizing the *tableaux vivants* of the procession. They chose eighteen scenes from the New Testament

---

[12] Lottin, 'Lille sous Charles Quint', p. 92.

[13] A.M.L., Registre aux Ordonnances du Magistrat, 380, fol. 104r.

[14] A.M.L., Affaires Générales, 654, Pièce 3.

[15] A.M.L., Comptes de la Ville de Lille, 16268, fol. 137r.

accounts of the life of Jesus and paired each one with a prefiguring scene from the Old Testament. Each pair of scenes was then assigned to two guilds, and the whole sequence of *tableaux* was arranged according to the order of events in the life of Jesus. Thus the procession began with the porters' wagon, which showed Abraham sending his servant to seek a wife for Isaac. This was followed by the plasterers' wagon, which showed God sending Gabriel to announce the Incarnation to Mary. In the final prefiguration the weavers mimed Abraham's sacrifice of Isaac, followed by the mercers, who presented the Crucifixion. The mercers' wagon was followed by three unpaired scenes: the Descent into Hell, the Resurrection and the Last Judgement.[16] The aldermen were apparently satisfied with this way of presenting the Bible to the public, for the same guilds staged the same scenes until 1565, the last year in which plays and *tableaux* were presented at the procession.[17]

These interventions in the dramatic representations at Lille's principal procession suggest that the aldermen were concerned about far more than just devising a spectacle to attract more visitors to the city. The didactic nature of the programme coupled with the growing anxiety about the presence of Lutheranism in Lille leads us to think that the municipal authorities were using the procession and its dramatic components to stop the spread of that 'disease' in the urban social body. According to Natalie Davis, Catholic processions in Lyon served to 'unite the two parts of the city cut by the Saône' as well as to 'dramatize the city's identity and give protection to the body of the town'.[18] The processions in Lille served analogous functions, as we noted earlier; but if we take into account the added didacticism of the *tableaux*, it would seem that the aldermen were also trying to counteract the teachings of the Lutherans by staging scenes from the life of Jesus with their Old Testament antecedents. They hoped, perhaps, that such a spectacular presentation of traditional Catholic teaching would reunite the city in one faith.

It is also significant in this context that the number of general or occasional processions increased greatly in the course of the sixteenth century. Though the guilds did not stage their *tableaux* at these events, the neighbourhood groups were invited to stage plays at all processions of a festive nature. If one examines the municipal ordinance registers for the forty years between 1532 and 1572, one

---

[16] A.M.L., Affaires Générales, 654, Pièce 3.

[17] See Alan E. Knight, 'Faded Pageant: The End of the Mystery Plays in Lille', *The Journal of the Midwest Modern Language Association*, 29 (1996), 3–14.

[18] Davis, 'The Sacred and the Body Social', pp. 56, 57.

will find proclamations of seven general processions in the first decade, twelve in the second decade, twenty-four in the third decade, and thirty-three in the fourth decade. These numbers do not include the annual Lille and Corpus Christi processions, which would add twenty to each of the figures above. It should be noted that these general processions were often related to the world beyond Lille. The participants might petition God for the emperor's success in a battle against the Turks, give thanks for his safe return from a long voyage, or celebrate the return of peace to another part of the empire. But, as Alain Lottin notes, 'Ces cortèges contribuent à forger une conscience collective d'appartenance à la fois à l'empire et à la chrétienté'.[19] What is relevant to our enquiry is the collective nature of the citizens' sense of belonging to these larger entities. Just as the ritual of processing through the city streets had always fostered the concept of the wholeness of the social body, so the presentation of biblical plays and *tableaux vivants* at the processions reinforced the town's sense of its place and its participation in the broader Christian community both historically and geographically.

We saw in the beginning that the staging of plays was one of the youth group activities that the city fathers banned on several occasions in the late fourteenth and early fifteenth centuries. But since this prohibition does not recur in the records after 1428, we may surmise that the aldermen finally succeeded in transferring those dramatic activities from the disruptive neighbourhood assemblies to the unifying ritual of the procession. Moreover, the awarding of prizes for the best plays helped transform at least some of the explosive neighbourhood rivalries into a controlled town event that promoted civic pride. In the sixteenth century, the aldermen perceived Lutheranism to be an even more serious threat to social wholeness than neighbourhood rivalries. After the first executions of heretics in 1533, they added another form of dramatic spectacle to the Lille procession in an effort to counteract its divisive effects. They also made a noble attempt to convert the Lutherans by using the *tableaux* of the guilds to teach the traditional story of salvation. Although there would be more executions, this time of Calvinists in 1545, the neighbourhood groups continued to stage their plays and the trade guilds continued to represent the life and Passion of Jesus in moving *tableaux* until both were suppressed in 1565. Thus for almost two hundred years, drama and procession had been combined in Lille, mutually reinforcing each other's vision of the ideal community as a harmonious coexistence of differences.

---

[19] Lottin, 'Lille sous Charles Quint', p. 89.

Cornelis Everaert and the community of late medieval Bruges

WIM HÜSKEN

ON MAUNDY THURSDAY, 1428, thirteen distinguished citizens of the Flemish town of Bruges were sitting together in the home of Jan van Hulst when a white dove flew into the room. The men regarded this as a sign to found a brotherhood, which they named *tgheselschip sHelighs Gheest*, the Company of the Holy Spirit. A poem prominently positioned on the opening page of one of the Company's account books, dating back to 1640, relates this event as follows:

> Int jaer duyst vier honderdt by wysen engiene
> ende acht en twyntich, doe waeren versaemdt
> te Jan van Hulst int houeken zy derthiene,
> op eenen Wittendonderdagh (vreught wast te ziene!)
> als hier boven staen reyn ghenaemt.
> Daer was gheordonneerdt ende gheraemt
> tgheselschap sHelighs Gheest vol deughden,
> mids eender duue wit, ongheblaemt,
> die daer kam vlerckende: dies zy verheughden.
> Dies zeyde Jan van Hulst met vreughden:
> "O broeders, den Gheest wil hier beeten!
> Dies zullen wy sHelichs Gheest broeders heeten".[1]

[On Maundy Thursday of the year one thousand four hundred and twenty-eight, through wise ingenuity, there were gathered (twas joyful to behold!) in the garden at Jan van Hulst's, thirteen men, all of whom mentioned here above. There was established and ordained the

---

[1] The account book was begun on Twelfth Night, 1640, the poem probably transcribed from an older source which has not survived. See *Spelen van Cornelis Everaert*, ed. by J.W. Muller and L. Scharpé (Leiden: Brill, 1920), pp. V-VI.

company of the Holy Spirit, full of virtue, by a white impeccable dove who came fluttering in. Therefore they rejoiced and Jan van Hulst said with joy: "O brothers, the Spirit aims to perch here! This is why we shall henceforth be called the brotherhood of the Holy Spirit"].

What did the activities of this Company in its first years of existence consist of? Many Chambers of Rhetoric in the Low Countries had developed out of religious guilds or charitable institutions. This is what in all likelihood happened in Bruges.[2] Details of the way the Company functioned shortly after it had been founded in 1428 have not come down to us, and it is therefore impossible to determine whether it was meant to function as a Chamber of Rhetoric from the start. The Holy Spirit was admittedly regarded as the source of inspiration for those involved in the art of rhetoric, but the Company's somewhat enigmatic motto, *Myn werck es hemelick* ('My work is divine/secret'), may also indicate a charitable background. For throughout the Middle Ages in the Low Countries hospitals and tables of the poor operated under the auspices of the Holy Spirit.[3] The phrase used by the Bruges Company not only referred to the inspiration poets claimed to receive from the Holy Spirit but it may also be interpreted to allude to the work of the guild members themselves who, despite the fact that their names were known, would have undertaken their charitable tasks with a degree of anonymity. The wondrous story of the Holy Spirit's foundation was no doubt based on legend rather than on historical fact. Be that as it may, the brotherhood was the first cultural body in Bruges to involve itself, some time during the fifteenth century, in the staging of drama.

In 1474 a second Chamber was established, *De Drie Santinnen* (The Three Women Saints), with St Catherine, St Barbara and Mary Magdalen as its patron saints. Twenty years later the two Rhetoricians' Chambers fell out with one another on various matters related to their literary activities, the conflict reaching such proportions that they had to seek arbitration. Eventually the 'Company of the Holy Spirit' gained priority over 'The Three Women Saints' in virtually every respect. If, for example, plays were organized within the city walls, The Holy Spirit was allowed to stage its play first.

About a century after the founding of the Company of the Holy Spirit, one of its members, Cornelis Everaert (*c.* 1480-1556), composed some thirty-five plays. The collection[4] has been preserved

---

[2] See, for example, J.J. Mak, *De rederijkers* (Amsterdam: Van Kampen en Zoon, 1944), p. 10.

[3] See G. Marechal, 'Armen- en ziekenzorg in de Zuidelijke Nederlanden', *Algemene Geschiedenis der Nederlanden* (Haarlem, 1977-83), vol. II, pp. 268-80.

[4] Everaert's plays were edited by Muller and Scharpé, *op. cit.* A new edition is in

in a holographic manuscript, which the playwright probably started copying in 1527. The most recent play dates from 1538, which may be close to the year when the author completed his collection. The manuscript contains examples of most of the dramatic genres current between 1509 and 1538 when the author wrote his works. Nine are *esbatementen*,[5] short comic plays dealing with attempts to regain male domination in marital relationships, verbal misunderstanding, deception, adultery, and other motifs typical of the genre, similar to the French farce, to which genre these plays belong. A further category of plays consists of dramatic eulogies of the Virgin Mary who, in a highly allegorical way, is compared to the throne of Solomon, to a ship, to the city of Jerusalem, and to the abstract concept of clarity. These plays prove their point by having the characters rely, in a discursive manner, on various biblical sources. A third subdivision consists of plays written on social issues or to commemorate political events such as the conclusion of a peace treaty. In some cases, like *D'ongelijcke Munte* ('Unequal Coinage'), a play was banned, as Everaert recorded in his manuscript in relation to this play, 'om dat ic te veil de waerheijt in noopte' [because I was too much a searcher after the truth]. A fourth group of plays consisted of short discussions between two, three or four characters, and called *tafelspelen*, plays intended to entertain a company of diners. Finally there is a group of plays that stand alone, without falling into any of the above categories: *Maria Hoedeken* ('Mary's Chaplet'), for instance, is a play which stages the legend of the invention of the rosary. I will return to it later in this study.

Some of Everaert's plays allow us a glimpse of everyday life in a late medieval city such as Bruges. Although the literary and dramatic products of the later Middle Ages can only be used with very great caution as sources for our knowledge of urban human relations, Everaert did occasionally refer to situations which related to the community in which he lived. In this essay, I will attempt to outline what his plays offer us in this respect.

---

preparation by the author of the present essay.

[5] Everaert termed his play *Aerm inde Buerse* an 'esbatement' but it is certainly not a farce. Before the middle of the sixteenth century, the word 'esbatement' had a broader meaning than it had after the 1550s, denoting a play in general. For the way 'esbatement' is used in archival sources, see my 'Politics and Drama: The City of Bruges as Organizer of Drama Competitions', in *The Stage as Mirror: Civic Theatre in Late Medieval Europe*, ed. by Alan E. Knight (Cambridge: D.S. Brewer, 1997), pp. 165-87.

CORNELIS EVERAERT AND LATE MEDIEVAL BRUGES

Religion and Popular Devotion

By the time Everaert became active as a playwright the veneration of the Dominican rosary had reached its peak. Inaugurated in 1470 by Alanus de Rupe († 1475), this Marian cult had spread rapidly throughout the southern Low Countries during the last quarter of the fifteenth century. Once the Lutheran revolt had started in the early sixteenth century, the rosary would be used as one of the weapons in a counter-attack against reform trends in order to keep the hesitant faithful within the safe boundaries of the Roman Catholic Church. In his first play, *Maria Hoedeken* ('Mary's Chaplet'), Everaert treats the legend of how the rosary was 'discovered'.[6] That it played a role in the attempts to restore faith in wavering Catholics is unlikely since it was written in 1509, eight years before Luther started his revolt. However, it did reflect a growing concern amongst large groups of believers about the direction of the Church during the decades leading up to the Reformation. The play's content is as follows.

A young man called *Goed Gheselscip* (Good Company) has taken up the daily habit of making a chaplet of roses for the Virgin's statue in the church so as to obtain her protection against evil. One day he is invited to join a couple of merry drinkers in a local tavern. A woman, *Inwendighe Wroughynghe* (Internal Remorse), warns him not to accept their invitation but he turns a deaf ear to her advice. Before joining the men, named *Quaet Beleedt* (Ill Conduct) and *Sober Regiment* (Sober Regimen), *Goed Gheselscip* sees to it that the Virgin's statue is adorned with a fresh garland. Once at the mercy of the two revellers he loses all his possessions in a game of dice. Left behind in desolation, the same woman who urged him not to visit the tavern now takes him to the prior of a nearby monastery who advises him to become a monk. Inside the walls of his new home the young man continues to make garlands of roses for the Virgin Mary. One day, however, the fields are covered in snow so that he is unable to wreath his garland. *Duechdelic Onderwysen* (Virtuous Instruction), the prior of the monastery, suggests an alternative: recite forty Hail Marys and the Lord's Prayer after each decade and these will make a rosary as well. While doing so his words are miraculously transformed into an actual rose chaplet. Some time later, the two freeloaders, accompanied by the innkeeper, plan to rob the first person to cross their path. As it happens, it is the

---

[6] For a more detailed treatment of this play and a historical background of the veneration of the rosary, see my essay '"Van incommen en begheert men scat noch goet": Cornelis Everaert and the Rosary', in Martin Gosman and Rina Walthaus (eds.), *European Theatre, 1470-1600: Traditions and Transformations* (Groningen: Forsten, 1996), pp. 119-29.

young monk whom they encounter. Unaware of his plight, *Goed Ghescelscip* kneels down to beg the Virgin Mary's protection, and as usual his prayers turn into a rose garland which he places on the head of the Virgin who, for once, has come to earth in person to safeguard her protégé through his perilous adventures. Beholding this miracle, the three evil-minded men drop their malicious plan and immediately convert. Together with the young monk they offer a long prayer in honour of the Virgin, thus concluding the play.

Maria Hoedeken allows us a glimpse into two very different worlds: the safe environment of a monastery and the wicked world outside, the latter represented by its morally most threatening secular institution, the tavern. In a monologue in which he expresses his wish to see his tavern filled with merry drinkers, the innkeeper bemoans the fact that the season of Lent causes serious harm to his business: 'De Vastene vry/ heift my ghescaet wel' [Lent certainly has harmed me].[7] From this remark we may learn two things: the tavern is run by a professional whose job it is to house, feed, and entertain guests, itinerant or otherwise. Secondly, during Lent, inns appear to have been frequented by fewer customers than at other times of the year, or so Everaert wants us to believe.

The monastery in which *Goed Gheselscip* will eventually find a new home represented the type of refuge legal sources called *hospitium*, a place run by non-professionals where travellers might enjoy food, drink and lodging after a long journey. Religious orders were not the sole institutions who felt responsibility in this area, especially after 789, when Charlemagne issued the order to his subjects to practice charity by housing any *itinerantes* in need of a safe place for the night.[8] By opposing these two very different types of refuge, the inn and the monastery, the play presents an emblematic treatment of hospices – some good, others bad – thus commenting on society as a whole. Bad taverns abounded in Rhetoricians' plays and invariably functioned as a warning for the spectators to maintain a virtuous life and avoid places where one might be seduced by evil or become a victim of evil-doers.[9] Surprising in this context, however, is the

---

[7] Muller-Scharpé (eds.), *op. cit.*, p. 8, line 55.

[8] See: B.H.D. Hermesdorf, *De herberg in de Nederlanden: Een blik in de beschavingsgeschiedenis* (Assen: 1957), pp. 4-16.

[9] Other examples may be found in: *sMenschen Sin ende Verganckelijcke Schoonheit* (Robert Potter and Elsa Strietman (eds.), *Man's Desire and Fleeting Beauty*. (Leeds, 1994)); Robert Lawet's *Vanden Verlooren Zoone* (E.G.A. Galama, *Twee Zestiende-eeuwse Spelen van de Verlooren Zoone door Robert Lawet* (Utrecht-Nijmegen: Dekker & Van de Vegt, 1941)); Jan van den Berghe's *De Wellustige Mensch* (C. Kruyskamp (ed.), *Dichten en Spelen van Jan van den Berghe* ('s-Gravenhage: Nijhoff,

taverner's name, *Cleen Achterdyncken* or 'Little Suspicion', suggesting that he is naively unaware of what is happening in his own house. However, the word *achterdyncken* has a second meaning, namely that of *contrition*, fitting the man's criminal mind much better. Taken in this sense, the name 'Little Contrition' reflects the innkeeper's amoral behaviour inside the tavern and later on outside, when he plans to rob any innocent traveller. Everaert depicts in this character the worst type of innkeeper imaginable. The fact that the tavern seems to be located outside the city walls – it is during his daily task of picking flowers for the Virgin Mary 'jnt velt' [in the open] that his presence is noted by the two ruffians – makes his crime even worse: away from the safe enclosure that a town provided for its inhabitants, the least thing one expected to find in a tavern would be security.

Lent was certainly not the best time of the year for innkeepers. Generally speaking, the Church's calendar did have a considerable impact on society as can be seen in one of Everaert's other plays, a farce named *De vigelie* ('The Vigil'). At the start of the play we hear a woman complaining about her husband, a cabinet-maker by trade, who suffers from a lack of physical interest in his wife. On suggesting that she would like to enjoy his company that night, he pretends to be unable to comply with her wishes because the next day will be a Church festival. They will therefore have to 'abstain from the pleasures of the flesh' and hold a vigil. When the husband remains adamant in his refusal to pay her any attention she decides that a real feast day it certainly will be! Early in the morning she dresses in her Sunday best and sends her husband's servant away with his daily wages, telling him to celebrate a Church holiday. Surprised at seeing his wife in all her finery and noticing his servant's absence, the cabinet-maker knows that he cannot perform his professional duties. He clearly recognizes his fault now and promises his wife to obey her in the future by meeting her physical needs.

1950, pp. 95-144)); Caprijcke's contribution to the Ghent competition of 1539 (B.H. Erné and L.M. van Dis (eds.), *De Gentse Spelen van 1539* ('s-Gravenhage: Nijhoff, 1982, vol. II, pp. 435-68)); and in farces such as *tCalf van Wondere* and *Een Crijsman die eens Buermans Paert steelt* (Herman Meijling (ed.), *Esbatementen van de Rode Lelije te Brouwershaven* (Groningen: De Waal, 1946) pp. 25-75); *Hans Snapop* (C. Kruyskamp (ed.), 'De Klucht van Hans Snapop', *Jaarboek De Fonteine* 21-22 (1971-72), pp. 27-45); and Gerrit Hendricksz van Breughel's *Deen en D'ander: Twee Soldaten* (J.J. Mak (ed.), *Vier Excellente Cluchten* (Antwerp: Wereldbibliotheek, 1950), pp. 64-94). An example of a good tavern run by a decent couple is *De Stathouwer* (D.A. Poldermans (ed.), 'Het Spel van de Stathouwer', *Archief [van het] Zeeuwsch Genootschap der wetenschappen* (1930), pp. 1-118).

Meant as a farce in the first place – though with obvious moralistic undertones – this play also shows how the large number of annual Church festivals obstructed normal working conditions during certain periods of the year. In 1527, the number of religious festivals celebrated in Bruges was established at twenty-nine, Sundays not included, with normal life coming to a virtual standstill between Christmas and Epiphany.[10] The Reformation would put an end to this situation, but even for those who did not wholeheartedly go along with the new teachings of Luther or other Protestant leaders, this large number of feast-days evoked reactions varying from severe criticism to mild scorn, as can be seen in Everaert's farce, *De vigelie*.

One of Everaert's other farces, *tWesen* ('Nature'), includes yet another priest involved in a marital conflict. Here, however, his role is much more positive. A man decides to refrain from having intercourse with his wife because when she is pregnant her nature turns her into a shrew. The wife does not understand the change in her husband's sexual appetite, especially when earlier in their marriage they had enjoyed such a good relationship, and she suspects him of having an affair. Which is why she turns to her parish priest. The only thing the priest can do, having no power to force the husband to change, is to try to persuade him to revert to his former friendly attitude towards his wife. Moreover, the priest will have known that men do not have any sexual obligation towards their spouses, for in the formula pronounced at the wedding ceremony it is only the wife who has to promise 'to be gentle and obedient, *in bed* and at board'.[11] Unlike their spouses, men were not bound by any nuptial pledges when they were joined in wedlock. The priest had thus no means of changing the reluctant husband's disposition. Yet thanks to his mediation, the farce ends happily, and the couple are reunited once the woman has learnt the reason for her husband's unwillingness. Knowing now why he acted as he did, she humbly promises that she will henceforth remain gentle, even when she is pregnant.

Earlier in this study, I mentioned that Everaert wrote a handful of plays in which he makes comparisons between the Virgin Mary and various religious concepts. In *Maria gheleken byden throon van Salomon*, for example, he elaborates on the concept of the Virgin as

---

[10] See E. Gailliard, 'De "Processiën Generael" en de "Hallegeboden" te Brugge', *Verslagen en Mededeelingen van de Koninklijke Vlaamsche Academie*, (1912), p. 1067, quoting from the municipal ordinances or *Hallegeboden*, part II, fol. 518v.

[11] The text quoted here is adapted from the *Sarum Missal;* Emilie Amt (ed.), *Women's Lives in Medieval Europe: A Sourcebook* (New York-London: Routledge, 1993), p. 85.

sedex sapientiae or seat of wisdom, thus establishing a well-known typological relationship with Solomon's throne in the Old Testament. Shortly after the start of the play Mary is shown sitting on a throne in a *tableau vivant*, its richly decorated interior remaining visible almost until the end. Meanwhile allegorical characters explain the meaning of the throne's ornaments, most of which have a close relationship to the Virgin's virtues at the moment of the Annunciation. Solomon's throne is depicted in the play precisely as it is described in 1 Kings 10: 19-20: 'The throne had six steps, and the top of the throne was round behind; and there were stays on either side of the place of the seat, and two lions stood beside the stays. And twelve lions stood there on the one side and on the other upon the six steps'.[12] The six steps represent Mary's *solitudo, verecundia, prudentia, virginitas, humilitas* and *oboedientia* ; the round shape of the back of the throne represents eternity, while the two large lions beside the armrests, as Everaert saw them – different from all patristic sources relating to Solomon's throne – represent holy confirmation as the virtue of virtues and Mary's piety. The text of the play not only functions as proof of Everaert's deep knowledge of theology but also reflects an aspect of the popular devotion of his contemporaries who were still given to admire the wealth of the Church which they witnessed in the processions at religious feast days. The faithful would have taken delight in the priests' richly adorned robes and the gold and silver thuribles and monstrances, just as they would have gazed at the beautifully arranged *tableaux vivants*. From a theatrical point of view, though perhaps uninspiring to modern readers, this play and the five others on similar topics no doubt left a deep impression on late medieval spectators, strengthening their belief and reaffirming their personal relationship with the Church.

Social Relations

On two occasions Everaert's plays were banned by the authorities. Earlier in this article I mentioned that the staging of his play of 'Unequal Coinage' (*Tspel van Dongelijcke Munte*) was prohibited on Easter Saturday evening, 1530. The main reason for this was the fact that the author blamed the central government for too lax an attitude towards foreign speculators who managed to export good coins and

---

[12] For a discussion of the theological background of this play see my essay on 'Cornelis Everaert en de Troon van Salomon', *Ons Geestelijk Erf* 65 (1991), 244-64. Its use of *tableaux vivants* is dealt with in my 'Aspects of Staging Cornelis Everaert', in Sydney Higgins (ed.), *European Medieval Drama 1998*, (Turnhout: Brepols, 1999 forthcoming).

replace them by coins of a much lower quality.[13] The social aspects of Everaert's plays have been studied extensively in the older, secondary literature on Dutch Rhetoricians' drama.[14] Some scholars even regarded him as a communist *avant la lettre*. It needs to be stressed, however, that Everaert was certainly not the only man of letters at the time to show a genuine commitment to the poor. Dutch Rhetoricians' drama abounded in plays in which authors took an unambiguous stance in support of the deprived and the exploited. Some, like Jacob Celosse in his contribution to Haarlem's drama competition, held in 1606 on behalf of the poor, expressed their opinions in terms of the traditional Christian idea of *caritas*.[15] Others, like Everaert and Lauris Jansz. in his plays of *Meestal Verjaecht Neering* and *Werlts Versufte Maeltijt*, refrained from using the cloak of Christian compassion, and were consequently perceived as being more genuine and direct in their feelings.[16] However, the only distinction between the two groups is that they used different modes of expression. Social matters can indeed be dealt with in quite a few ways. I will illustrate this by briefly discussing two of Everaert's other socially inspired plays, one of which can be seen as somewhat militant, *Tspel van Groot Labeur en Sober Wasdom* ('The Play of Great Misery and Frugal Flowering'), and one which has been regarded as relatively moderate, *Tspel van den Wyngaert* ('The Play of the Vineyard').

Tspel van Groot Labeur en Sober Wasdom, written in 1530 in honour of the Cambrai Peace Treaty of 1529, as well as of the coronation in the subsequent year of Charles V as Emperor of the Holy Roman Empire, has six characters: a carpenter; a pedlar carrying a basket of sulphur-matches; a warrior; a sharp-tongued woman dressed in old-fashioned clothes; a miser; and a person called *Beleedt van*

---

[13] A more detailed treatment of the monetary aspects of this play will be found in my essay on 'Cornelis Everaert on Power and Authority', to be published in the Proceedings of a Colloquium on 'Power and Authority in the Middle Ages', held in Groningen, November 1997.

[14] See J.W. Muller, 'Cornelis Everaert en de Maatschappelijke Toestanden van zijn Tijd', *Verslagen en Mededeelingen der Koninklijke Vlaamsche Academie voor Taal- en Letterkunde* (1907), pp. 433-91 and 'Een Rederijker uit den Tijd onzer Hervorming', *Onze Eeuw* 8 (1908), 88-124.

[15] Cf. *Const-thoonende Ivweel*, Zwol, 1607, fols. A1r-D3r.

[16] For a positive judgement of Jansz. as a socially inspired author see Rena Pennink, 'De Rederijker Louris Jansz.', *Oud-Holland* 30 (1912), 200-14, esp. 207-10. A modern adaptation of *Meestal Verjaecht Neering* was edited by N. van der Laan in *Noordnederlandse Rederijkersspelen* (Amsterdam: Elsevier, 1941), pp. 73-114. For *Werlts Versufte Maeltijt* see W.N.M. Hüsken, B.A.M. Ramakers and F.A.M. Schaars (eds.), *Trou Moet Blijcken: Bronnenuitgave van de Boeken der Haarlemse Rederijkerskamer 'de Pellicanisten'*, vol. VI: *Boek F* (Assen: Quarto, 1996).

Wijsheden (Testimony of Wisdom). The play opens with a conversation between the carpenter and the pedlar, named *Groot Labuer* (Great Misery) and *Sober Wasdom* (Frugal Flowering) respectively, both of whom appear to be in love. It soon becomes evident, however, that the shared object of their affection is a girl named *Couver Handelynghe* (Plenitude of Affairs). They realize that the girl's parents, *Ghaerpennync* and *Splyttemytte* (Penny-Saver and Farthing-Cleaver), will not allow their daughter to start a relationship with anyone unless he is rolling in money. The men used to have such a good time with her; *Tyt van Nu* (Present Times) is certainly to be blamed for their recent misery. No sooner is he mentioned than *Tyt van Nu* appears on stage, dressed as a warrior, 'zeer wranc ziende ende spyttich sprekende', looking very unfriendly and speaking in a harsh voice. He advises them to sing a song under her window playing instruments named *Scalc Vondeken* (Shrewd Invention) and *Loos Aket* (False Ruse). In the next scene we witness the parents of Plenitude of Affairs confirming their intention to protect their daughter from any suitor's attempt to woo her. When *Groot Labuer* and *Sober Wasdom* try to play their instruments they are unable to get them in tune, and as an alternative they decide to plant a maypole under *Couver Handelynghe*'s window and to sing a song together. Their noisy act provokes *Ghaerpennync* and *Splyttemytte* to come out. Though the couple are sympathetic to the young men's cause, they make it clear that there is no hope for them. They give each of them a letter of the alphabet: an L to *Sober Wasdom* and a P to *Groot Labuer*, standing for 'Lyden' (suffering) and 'Paciencie' (patience) respectively. Annoyed and indignant at this, they are next approached by *Beleedt van Wijsheden* who advises them to reconsider their anger. The letters they were given mean other things as well: P also stands for 'Peynsen' (to think carefully) and for 'sheeren punicie' (the Lord's punishment); L refers to 'Liefde' (love and, in particular, love of God) and to being 'lydtsaeming' (patient). So they had better put their hope in God. *Beleedt van Wijsheden*'s words apparently convince them that he is speaking the truth; and as they contemplate a *tableau vivant* depicting Christ holding a banner with the words *Venite ad me omnes*, the three say a prayer by way of conclusion in honour of Hope (*spes*), Comfort (*consolatio*) and Wisdom (*sapientia*).

The allegorical technique used by Everaert in *Tspel van Groot Labeur en Sober Wasdom* is one of combining moral concepts, represented mainly in the characters' names and in the objects they carry, set against an easily recognizable 'intermediate pattern'[17] of the

---

[17] The term 'intermediate pattern' is used by Jackson Barry in his *Dramatic Structure:*

wooing of a girl. In other words, the story of two men in love functions as a sugared pill to make the healthy medicine of moral instruction go down. In *Tspel vanden Wyngaert*, too, Everaert uses allegory in order to put across his moral message. But here the 'intermediate pattern' is of an entirely biblical nature in that the play dramatizes the parable of the Labourers in the Vineyard (Matthew 20, 1-16). As in *Tspel van Groot Labeur en Sober Wasdom*, Everaert adds an allegorical layer to the narrative structure of his source. Whereas Christ merely speaks of a 'householder', 'his steward' and a number of 'labourers', Everaert gives them names: *dUpperste Mueghentheyt* (Supreme Power) and *Duechdelic Vermaen* (Virtuous Incitement) for the first two, *Voorgaende Bewys* (Testimony from the Past), the couple *Ziende Blende* and *Hoorende Doof* (Seeing Blind and Hearing Deaf), *Vroom Labeur* (Pious Labour), and *Ghewillich Volghen* (Following Willingly) for the labourers. The conclusions Everaert reaches in the two plays are very similar: in *Groot Labeur en Sober Wasdom* man is advised to be patient and to practise charity; in *Tspel vanden Wyngaert* the labourers are reminded that salvation is not assured: *Vele esser gheroupen maer lettel vercoren. Tes Gods woort ende ons spels conclusye* [For many be called, but few chosen, this is God's word and our play's conclusion]. Though both plays aimed at teaching comparable moral lessons, and despite the fact that both use allegorical concepts to put across their message, the former play is still regarded as more directly related to the contemporary social situation than the latter. However, in my opinion the difference between the two plays is merely a difference in choice of intermediate pattern.

Domestic Relations

To conclude my observations on Everaert and the community, I return once more to one of his farces, the sub-genre in which marital relationships reflecting on society as a whole are present almost by definition. Some farces present allegorical characters similar to those in *Maria Hoedeken*, thus introducing a discursive aspect to texts which appear to refer merely to domestic situations. *Scamel Ghemeente ende Trybulacie*, for example, is named after a husband and his wife: Poor Community and Tribulation, where Death teaches Poor Community to bear with his wife during times of ordeal. In other plays, such as *tWesen*, characters are simply indicated by the function they have in the play: Man, Wife, Companion, Servant, Priest, etc. This is also the case in *Tspel vander Nichte* ('The Play of the Cousin').

The Staging of Experience (Berkeley-London: University of California Press, 1970).

Here we have a man who thinks he can control his wife by beating her every now and then. To show his neighbours that he is the boss, he always concludes the beating by arrogantly lying down in the sash-window to sing a merry tune. Today, he tells the audience at the beginning of the play, he will go to church. But before doing so he commands his wife to have lunch prepared for his return. The moment he has left the house, the woman curses her husband. We then switch to a soliloquy by the woman's cousin. She knows that her relative has a cheerful, even libertine nature, and in order to protect her from gossiping neighbours, decides to pay her a visit. The woman tells a story that is quite different from what her cousin had expected to hear and complains about the way she is treated by her husband. The cousin thereupon advises her to wedge the man in the sash-window the moment he lies down in it. Back home from mass, the husband finds no lunch prepared; moreover, his spouse refuses to lay the table. Consequently, he deals her a couple of blows, which the wife returns with even bigger ones. The man decides to hold back for a moment, retreating into the open window. Making the most of her opportunity, the wife now brings her counter-attack into effect. Curious about the outcome of her relative's conjugal fight, the cousin visits the couple precisely at the moment the man is stuck in this most uncomfortable position, thus giving the wife the opportunity to extract a pledge from her husband that he will never again treat her the way he used to. To which demands the husband humbly complies.

According to the words of the wife in the epilogue, *Tspel vander Nichte* was the dramatization of an actual historical event: *De boerde es ghebuert binder Ghendtscher stede* [This comic anecdote took place in the city of Ghent].[18] Its narrative strength is beyond any doubt, yet the play does contain some discursive elements as well. This is what we have in the discussion between the two women prior to the cousin's invention of the trick with the sash-window. We have seen that the cousin does not entirely trust her relative's moral standards; she is afraid that her cousin will fall prey to friends who might seize the opportunity to abuse her outgoing nature and lack of chastity. It is for this reason that her first reaction to the woman's complaints is to advise her to show greater willingness to deal with her husband's marital needs. Eventually, however, she delivers a brief lecture on the subject in a speech which no longer seems to be addressed to her relative but to the audience, and in particular the female members of it (lines 124-33). In the epilogue it is once more the cousin who holds up a mirror to those men who beat their loyal wives, on whom she wishes

---

[18] Muller-Scharpé (eds.), *op. cit.*, p. 542, line. 363.

a similar fate as befell the man in the farce just performed. Of course, the play will have provoked quite a few laughs among the audience, but some useful lessons are not lacking either.

In farces women often dominate their spouses, who invariably seem unable to stand up to them. The theme was, and is, characteristic of the sub-genre in all western European dramatic traditions. Other motifs frequently occurring in farces are drunkenness, stupidity, lust and fraud. A common explanation of the topsy-turvy relationships between men and women is that plays of this type were written as a warning to men not to allow their wives to act as farce wives do. Is this to say, then, that situations like these were likely to occur in everyday domestic relations? Literary sources should be distrusted in this respect. Everaert's remark on the authenticity of the story related in *De nichte* ('De boerde es ghebuert binder Ghendtscher stede') is clear enough. It not only served as an attempt to convince the audience of its veracity, but it also implicitly suggests that such an event would be very exceptional. His observation reveals a certain topicality, too, since in a number of other farces there are similar declarations of the type: 'Had the Rhetoricians known this story they would have turned it into a farce.'[19] We might look for another explanation for the popularity of this theme and of the genre of farce in general. Could it perhaps be found in Carnival?

Characteristic of the Carnival period is the *mundus inversus*, the world turned upside down. In churches the lower clergy and choir boys assumed the roles of bishops and pope, belching during mass and singing in falsetto voices as they burned the soles of shoes as incense. Festivities like these took place all over the Christian world throughout the Middle Ages.[20] In Bruges, too, Carnival was celebrated, though precise information is difficult to come by. In 1494-95, one of the priests of St Donaes' Church, named Pieter van Zouburgh, received ten shillings 'thulpe van zynder feeste die hy hilt binnen den tydt dat hy eselpaeus was van der voors. kerke' [for his celebrations when he was pope in the *festa asinorum* in the aforementioned church].[21] Performances of plays during this period of the year, whether conducted in the streets or inside people's homes, were a stock

---

[19] See, for example, Gerbrand Adriaensz. Bredero in *De klucht van de koe*: 'Wistent de Rederijckers sy speelden daer af een klucht', in *G.A. Bredero's Kluchten*, ed. by Jo Daan (Culemborg: Tjeenk Willink-Noorduijn, 1971), p. 104, line 669.

[20] One of the most detailed treatments of Carnival traditions in the lower clergy is still that by E.K. Chambers, *The Mediaeval Stage* (Oxford: Oxford University Press, 1903), vol. I, pp. 274-419.

[21] L. Gilliodts van Severen, *Inventaire de la ville de Bruges* (Bruges: E. Gailliard, 1871-1885), vol. VI, p. 402, quoting from the town records of 1494-95, fol. 188v.

element of Carnival celebrations. Archival sources can only be helpful in this respect insofar as they include donations by civic authorities to itinerant youth companies or neighbourhood groups. Moreover, since these groups were as a rule not institutionalized they often escape our attention. Only in those cases where they seriously disrupted communal life do they emerge from the darkness in which they otherwise exist.

Compared to the situation in the Low Countries, Carnival drama seems to have been much better 'organized' in Germany, in towns such as Nuremberg and Lübeck in particular. Hans Folz, Hans Rosenplüt and Hans Sachs were but three of the many authors, most of whom remain unknown, who composed *Fastnachtspiele*, plays which took their name precisely from the period of the year during which they were performed. In France, England and the Low Countries drama was staged during the pre-Lenten season as well, but genre denominations were not as specific as they were in Germany. However, both in France and in the Low Countries the farce genre also came to be related to 'rituals' or, to use a less loaded expression, to 'traditions' of reversal. Farces were certainly not staged exclusively during Carnival – neither were *Fastnachtspiele* – but one can reasonably assume that the genre would have been very popular during this particular period.

A brief review of the French farce shows us that plays of this type shared their subject-matter and comic vein with the Dutch *cluchten* and *esbatementen*. Moreover, comic drama in the Low Countries and France had a comparable organizational background. In France, many farces were staged by the *Clercs de la Basoche* of the 'Parlement de Paris',[22] and in the Low Countries it was the Chambers of Rhetoric who provided popular entertainment in plays similar to the French farce. As in the French farces and German *Fastnachtspiele*, an element of reversal was also frequently present in the Dutch *esbatementen*. Perhaps the fact that farces would often be performed – both in France and the Low Countries – following a morality play or a mystery play, is also significant in this context. In some cases comic plays may even have been linked to the preceding serious play by 'reversing' their contents. Such may also have been true for the *sotternieën* and the *abele spelen* in the Van Hulthem manuscript (late fourteenth or early fifteenth century).[23] The order in which Everaert copied his plays in

---

[22] For the involvement of the *Basoche* in Carnival, see H.G. Harvey, *The Theater of the Basoche: The Contribution of the Law Societies to French Mediaeval Comedy* (Cambridge, Mass: Harvard University Press, 1941), pp. 17-27.

[23] Cf. Frank van Meurs, 'De Abele Spelen en de navolgende Sotternieën als Thematisch Tweeluik', *Literatuur* 5 (1988), 149-56.

his manuscript is equally significant in that the fourteen plays with which the collection opens show a consistent alternation of a serious text (*Tspel van* ...) and a farce (*Esbatement van* ...). The author thus appeared to prefer a thematic order of plays over an historical arrangement.

This leads us to the conclusion that reversals were important in both farce and Carnival, whether related to a Dutch, a French or a German context, to marital relations, or to the social order. It is indeed almost impossible to overlook the importance of the theme in the two different expressions of a pre-modern popular culture. Farce did function in a way comparable to Carnival and was perhaps even a distinct aspect of it. But when trying to establish a direct relationship between the two we are definitely still in the dark. Both phenomena may have been interrelated at the end of the Middle Ages, but from a literary point of view it remains hazardous to assess their precise relationship. Scholars of early modern popular culture such as Peter Burger may be inclined to stress the mutual influence of the literary and social orders in pre-modern times. But the fact remains that farce belongs to a highly stylized literary culture whereas the Carnival tradition consists mainly of rituals based on improvisation. Farce and Carnival thus represent two very different worlds. In accordance with Burger's observations, and following a dichotomy introduced by other scholars of folklore, I would therefore propose that late medieval farce belonged to the 'great tradition' of the educated classes, whereas Carnival belonged to the 'little tradition' of the folk.[24] The two were interrelated without necessarily belonging to the same cultural background.

* * *

Everaert's collection of plays reflects the many sub-genres current in his day but, more importantly, most of the thirty-five plays in the manuscript show a manifest involvement with the community. His contribution to sixteenth-century Dutch drama is remarkable yet not exceptional. For most Rhetoricians' plays, especially those written before the middle of the century, were intended for urban audiences, varying from the fast developing merchant classes to the large mass of less wealthy artisans, both groups however sharing a post-medieval, socially and religiously inspired, education. Man, so the Rhetoricians were agreed, had to be thoroughly instructed in the many new views

---

[24] Cf. Peter Burger, *Popular Culture in Early Modern Europe* (New York-London: Temple Smith, 1978), pp. 23-29.

that were conquering the modern world. And in that respect the stage played for many years a decisive role throughout western Europe. It did so even more than the authorities, both secular and religious, would accept. The banning of performances of two of Everaert's plays may be seen as a foretaste of what would become normal practice during later years. However, whereas the Bruges playwright saw himself as merely confronted with a secular opposition, later authors had to face the antagonism of the religious authorities as well. Eventually, the Dutch Calvinist clergy would deny the Rhetoricians their educating function and, on 26 January 1560, categorically outlaw their activities. By the beginning of the seventeenth century the educating role of the Rhetoricians had completely come to an end. But before that happened hundreds of plays had been composed by authors such as Cornelis Everaert in Bruges, the great majority of which reflected the religious and social preoccupations of the community. As such, they offer a unique source for a better understanding of one of the most interesting periods in the history of modern man.

A tale of two cities: drama and the community in the Low Countries.

ELSA STRIETMAN

A GREAT NUMBER OF towns in the Low Countries had one or more Chambers of Rhetoric in the late fifteenth and the sixteenth century. Many of these cities were important as market towns, for instance Dordrecht, Amsterdam, Haarlem, Bruges or Antwerp; while some derived their main importance from being centres of local government, such as The Hague, Mechelen and especially Brussels; others, for example, Antwerp, Bruges and Ghent were internationally important trading cities; or, like Ypres, were rapidly declining in population and as a centre of commerce but nevertheless had a flourishing theatrical culture. Leuven, the only university town, had a long-standing processional culture which, as in Oudenaarde and many other towns, became intertwined with theatrical activities.

Trade and commerce, local and national government, provided urban centres with specific characteristics, but seem in themselves not to have been necessary conditions for a lively drama culture. Utrecht, one of the oldest towns in the Low Countries, a centre of religious and secular authority from Carolingian times, does not seem to have had much of a share in Rhetoricians' culture, though some evidence of liturgical drama does exist.

The river towns in the eastern provinces, Deventer, Zutphen, Zwolle, Kampen on the IJssel, Nijmegen and Arnhem on the Rhine, Venlo and Roermond on the Meuse, which were natural and long-established centres for local trade and for commerce with the Rhine *hinterland* seem not to have enjoyed the same buoyant Rhetoricians' culture as many western cities. The available data does mention religious theatrical activities, but the strong civic impulse to dramatic activities which was so characteristic elsewhere did not exist.[1] That is not to say that there was a total absence of dramatic activities, but such town accounts as have been published give scant evidence. The activity most frequently referred to is that of Lenten plays, *vastenavondspelen*. German towns, further east, show similar high-profile evidence of such plays. In the absence of organized drama in the form of Chambers of Rhetoric, it is difficult to get a grip on the identity of producers, sponsors (other than town magistrates), or actors.[2]

Other groups, apart from Chambers of Rhetoric, were involved in drama too, in particular in street theatre or in theatrical aspects of processions. Theatrical entertainment often accompanied competitions of archers and it is not clear whether the producers and actors were partly drawn from the Archers' Guilds or whether they were recruited for the occasion. There is quite a lot of evidence of streets or quarters of a town taking it upon themselves to produce a play or a *tableau vivant* or *figuere*.

Indeed, in a town with a lively Rhetoricians' culture, such as for instance Lier in the duchy of Brabant, the Chambers did have some competition from craftguilds: on the occasion of the celebrations in 1496 for the wedding of Joanna of Aragon and Philip the Fair of Burgundy the *Beenhouders* [Butchers] gained the highest prize for *'tvieren* [celebrating], and on the occasion of the birth of their son, the later Charles V, guilds, Chambers and craftguilds celebrated and the Woolweavers received the first prize for *'tvieren*; in 1501 the peace between the French and the Burgundians was celebrated enthusiastically and this time too the *Beenhouders* won the first prize for *'tvieren* and the guild of the *handtbooch* [Longbow Archers] the second prize. This, however, was processional display, possibly with *figueren*: theatrical but not drama in the narrower sense.[3]

If a town wanted to impress its overlord, as in the case of royal entries or a royal wedding, many different groups were involved, for

---

[1] G. Nijsten, 'Feasts and Public Spectacles. Late Medieval Drama and Performance in the Low Countries', in *The Stage as Mirror; Civic Theatre in Late Medieval Europe*. Papers from the symposium held at the Pennsylvania State University, March 1993, ed. by Alan Knight (Cambridge: D.S. Brewer, 1997).

[2] J.M. Hollaar and E.W.F. van den Elzen, 'Het vroegste toneelleven in enkele Noordnederlandse plaatsen', *De Nieuwe Taalgids*, 73 (1980), 302-24 and J. M. Hollaar and E.W.F. van den Elzen, 'Toneelleven in Deventer in de vijftiende en zestiende eeuw', *De Nieuwe Taalgids*, 73 (1980), 412-25.

[3] 'Chronijk van Lier 762-1615', in *Vaderlandsch Museum voor Nederduitsche Letterkunde, Oudheid en Geschiedenis,* ed. by C.P. Serrure (Ghent: H. Hoste, 1861) IV, pp. 392-93.

instance, when Philip the Good entered Ghent in 1458 as a reconciliatory gesture signifying the end of a bitter armed conflict between ruler and town, Jan van Eyck's *The Lamb of God* was hoisted onto a wagon, and painting and real people together formed a *tableau vivant*. The court painter, the townspeople and the Rhetoricians all worked together on that occasion.[4]

In short, interaction between community and drama, the form of drama in the community, the influence of the community on drama and vice versa, the practical and financial aspects of drama in the community, the social, political and religious functions of theatrical activities, present a very varied spectacle. In what follows I will give some instances of theatrical activities in two towns in the Low Countries and some of the ways in which community and drama were intertwined.

The town of Haarlem will serve as an example from a northern province, Holland; the town of Ypres will serve as an example of a southern province, Flanders. In both these towns the Chambers of Rhetoric were part and parcel of the urban scene. Each community had their own peculiarities, their own circumstances, determined by a number of factors. They will form a very small picture, part of a very large panorama.

Ypres is the older town and evidence of its theatrical culture stems from an earlier period than that in Haarlem. The reason that I choose to begin with Ypres stems not from its *ancienneté*, but from the fact that the documents under discussion will build up a picture of a town preparing for a great celebration in which the thearical element was of great importance and in which the community as a whole was involved. In the case of Haarlem we will look at the work of one playwright in the context of his town and his time, a period in which the culture of the Chambers of Rhetoric, though still flourishing, was soon to be beset by a variety of difficulties which eventually would loosen the bond between communities and drama.

Ypres

Ypres's glory began early: in the twelfth and thirteenth century it was a very large and prosperous industrial and trading centre, one of the Members of Flanders, together with Ghent, Bruges and, in the course of the fourteenth century, the Freehold of Bruges. Its economy

---

[4] E. Dhanens, 'De Blijde Inkomst van Filips de Goede in 1458 en de plastische kunsten te Gent', *Mededelingen van de Koninklijke Akademie van Wetenschappen, Letteren, Schone Kunsten in België*, 48 (1987), pp. 53-89.

centred on the textile industry and its Cloth Hall was the envy of other towns and a symbol of its self-confidence.[5] Ypres' fortunes declined considerably in later centuries and its population suffered drastic reductions; it is estimated that the town housed some 40,000 people at the height of its economic power in the thirteenth century, whereas by the end of the fifteenth century the number had dwindled to roughly 8,000.[6]

A Corpus Christi procession was held early in comparison with other towns and there is evidence from the town accounts that a civic, as opposed to a church, procession existed as early as 1323.[7] A more distinctive feature was that Ypres boasted an annual procession and festival which commemorated the end of a siege in July 1383, when the town was beleaguered by English and Ghent troops. The procession became known as the *processie van den thuindach* [procession of the day of the rampart] since Our Lady, whose statue stood on the ramparts of the town, had been instrumental in the lifting of the siege. Ypres was a walled town and the *tuin* in question refers to the ramparts over which Our Lady exercised her special protection. Illustrations show her and the Christ-child floating protectively above the town in a construction of hazel or willow twigs like the fencing often seen in medieval illuminations of garden enclosures.

The nineteenth-century historian Alphonse Vandenpeereboom collected and published a wealth of documents about Ypres and they show how faithfully and exuberantly this commemoration was celebrated, and continued to be commemorated,[8] even into the twentieth century. The procession started the celebrations on the last day in July and was the main ceremony of thanksgiving, but from as early as 1409 there is evidence that the commemoration lasted for several days and that it was enhanced by a number of civic activities and by all that a medieval town could offer in the way of entertainment and moneymaking.[9]

---

[5] H. van der Wee, *The Low Countries in the Early Modern World* (Aldershot: Variorum, 1993), pp. 204-5, 221; *Geschiedenis van de Nederlanden*, ed. by J.C.H. Blom and E. Lamberts (Rijswijk: Nijgh & Van Ditmar, 1995), pp. 33-34, 55-56, 63-65.

[6] P. Stabel, *Dwarfs among Giants. The Flemish Urban Network in the Later Middle Ages* (Leuven/Apeldoorn: Garant N.V., 1997), p. 28.

[7] B.A.M. Ramakers, *Spelen en Figuren. Toneelkunst en processiecultuur in Oudenaarde tussen Middeleeuwen en Moderne Tijd* (Amsterdam: Amsterdam University Press, 1996), p. 24.

[8] Alphonse Vandenpeereboom, *Ypriana. Notices, études, notes et documents sur Ypres*, 7 vols (Bruges: Aimé de Zuttere, 1881) V, pp. 1-14.

[9] Vandenpeereboom, (1881), V, pp. 94-135.

The town accounts of 1433 record a payment of £12 to 'Jan Poetin to help him with his expenses of the great costs he incurred in making an enclosure in the market-square where the blind men the other day on *Thuindach* slew a swine which the aforesaid Jan donated'.[10] The magistrates who came and watched this event had to be made comfortable, therefore a payment of 24 shillings parisis was made to Jan Borey, guard of the artillery, for cleaning the cloth for Our Lady's *Thuindach*, or to have it cleaned, for Jan Poetin's, where the magistrates sat to see the swine slain in front of everybody. Vandenpeereboom, in 1881, ventured to hope that these blind men might only be blindfolded men, 'because it would be too inhuman to expose the unfortunate blind men to the ridicule of the spectators'.[11] Some hope...

The town's fortunes were in severe decline and the documents show that this annual commemoration was seized upon as an occasion to make merry, to make money, and to make an impression. The *Thuindach*, rather than the Corpus Christi celebration, was for Ypres the annual confirmation of religious protection and urban cohesion, of the sacred Body of Christ which also symbolized the unity of the secular community. At the same time the town laid claim to political importance, economic potential and well-founded civic pride.[12]

There are two closely linked aspects of the theatrical culture of Ypres that are particularly worthy of note. One of these concerns the proportion of the population in this community that seems to have been involved, in the broadest possible way, with theatrical and processional activities and the second concerns the variety of ways in which they were involved. Both the extent and the degree of involvement of the inhabitants can be assumed to have been broadly similar to those of a range of other medium-sized towns.[13]

At some point in the fifteenth century, Ypres seems to have had four Chambers of Rhetoric, which added their poetic and dramatic talent to the procession and the following festivities. Apart from the traditional competitions of the Archers' Guilds the Rhetoricians also mounted competitions. These could consist of individuals competing,

---

[10] Vandenpeereboom, (1881), V, p. 113, note 1.

[11] Vandenpeereboom, (1881), V, p. 112.

[12] Vandenpeereboom, (1881), V, pp. 46-53; 181-87. This is particularly striking in the descriptions of the jubilee festivities in 1483 and from the competitive festivities, such as archery, which the town organized and from which it derived considerable pride.

[13] Ramakers, (1996), pp. 5-41 and M. Vandecasteele, 'Een groots opgezet rederijkersfeest te Ieper in 1529', *Jaarboek 'De Fonteine'*, 26 (1989-90), 7-20.

with, for instance, poems in honour of Our Lady, of the town's Chambers competing against each other with poetry or plays, or grander events, when Chambers from other towns were invited to come and vie for substantial prizes and honours.[14]

In 1491 Ypres seems to have had barely 8000 inhabitants; in the sixteenth century the town prospered a little more but the population seems not to have grown much; the number of Chambers however increased to six.[15] Membership of Chambers varied greatly in number and nothing is known about those in Ypres. Members would be adolescent or adult males who could read and write, who possessed civic rights and could afford the membership fees, the expenses that conviviality inevitably brings and the clothes that were worn on ceremonial occasions. If we take all these factors into account, then a fair proportion of the male citizens of Ypres would have been members of Rhetoricians' Chambers. Add to this that the *Thuindach* procession included magistrates, church dignitaries, religious orders, lay-devotional brotherhoods, craftguilds, parish guilds and street guilds as well as the Rhetoricians and there can hardly have been an able-bodied male who was not involved in at least that part of the commemoration.[16]

It is hard to say when the festivities began to include drama, but there was at least one year in which the Rhetoricians and their plays were of paramount importance in the *Thuindach* festivities. Maurits Vandecasteele's discovery of a set of town accounts for 1529 shows that the town had planned a large-scale Rhetoricians' competition in that year.[17] The main impetus as well as most or all of the funding seems to have come from the town, not from the Chambers of Rhetoric, although for them this must have been a welcome opportunity to display their art. The magistrates clearly saw the theatrical event as a means towards boosting the ego, the morale and the finances of the town.[18]

---

[14] Vandecasteele, (1989-90), 13.

[15] A. van Elslander, 'Lijst van Nederlandse Rederijkerskamers uit de XVe en XVIe eeuw', *Jaarboek 'De Fonteine'*, 18 (1968), 29-60.

[16] Stabel, (1997), pp. 19-43 and M. Spufford, 'Literacy, trade and religion in the commercial centres of Europe', in *A Miracle Mirrored. The Dutch Republic in European Perspective,* ed. by K. Davids and J. Lucassen (Cambridge: Cambridge University Press, 1995), pp. 229-83.

[17] Vandecasteele, (1989-90).

[18] W. Blokmans and W. Prevenier, *The Burgundian Netherlands* (Cambridge: Cambridge University Press, 1986), pp. 227-50.

The Ypres' celebration lasted some five or six days, from 31 July to 4 August 1529,[19] and may have attracted fifteen competing Chambers. The size of the membership of Chambers varied considerably and naturally so did the number of players, helpers and fans able to go to a given festivity. But all in all, Ypres might have had to find accommodation for some five hundred people, as well as carts and horses. Clearly, this was good news for innkeepers.

The special interest of the documents which Vandecasteele found is that they show a town preparing for a big event of which a large part was formed by theatrical activities. The documents do not give any information about plays, but by implication, we learn much about the physical preparations and the sociological intricacies of the planned festivities and competitions.

For instance, much importance was obviously given to the judges and the judging of the competition. The judges consisted of five laymen and five clergy,[20] and they were provided with ample quantities of wine whilst 'overseeing and judging the plays' that is to say that they checked the texts for possible heretical or otherwise unacceptable opinions.[21] The judges were well looked after: messengers were sent to fetch them wine during the performances[22] and they drank at the expense of the town when they were sitting in a tavern to make up their minds about the plays performed after the day of the procession.[23]

The prizes for the various competitive events were another source of employment for craftsmen and an item of great expense to the town. In 1529 one goldsmith was given a commission to make two silver townshields to be attached to the leather holders in which the messengers carried the invitations to towns far and wide.[24] Another

---

[19] Vandecasteele, (1989-90), 8-9.

[20] Vandecasteele, (1989-90), 15-16, item 4.

[21] The expenses are booked between 5 and 8 August, but there is no indication how far in advance the censoring took place; sometimes this happened far in advance, as in Gouda in 1546, where the plays to be performed were copied and sent to Brussels to be checked by the censors at the court of the regent, Mary of Hungary: see E. Strietman and R. Potter, *Man's Desire and Fleeting Beauty/'sMenschen Sin ende Verganckelijcke Schoonheit*, (Leeds: Leeds University Press, 1994), pp. ix, xx, note 6. Sometimes the censoring was done as late as after the ceremonial entry into the host town, as happened in Bruges in 1536: see Vandecasteele, (1989-90), 10, note 15.

[22] Vandecasteele, (1989-90), 16, item 8.

[23] Vandecasteele, (1989-90), 16, item 7.

[24] Vandenpeereboom, (1881), V, pp. 100-02, mentions that in 1409 the prizes to be won were displayed before the competition started. See for the invitations Vandecasteele, (1989-90), 17, item 13.

craftsman was given a far greater brief: to deliver 38 ounces of silver to be used for making 'plates, beakers, and other prizes which would be exhibited to be awarded for the plays and *esbatementen* as planned in the programme of the organisation' [of the competition].[25] A second goldsmith made the 'plates, beakers and other prizes' with that quantity of silver as well as an English pound of silver.[26] The prizegiving ceremony in or in front of the house of the justice of the peace was enhanced by a group of shawm players [schalmeyers]; they were very well rewarded with £16.[27]

Plays were to be performed in the market square and it took eight people to build scaffolds, five days at a labour cost of 12 shillings a day and four days at 6 shillings a day, which cost the town a total of £4 and 7 shillings.[28] Plays organized by the parishes of St Martin and St Niclaas and that of the Guild of Our Lady were performed on wagons and those who led the wagons and helped to set them up were paid £3, which means it was an elaborate or lengthy task.[29]

Important members of the audience must have been given seats because a painter decorated benches and 'bailgen' which were placed in front of the house of the justice of the peace.[30] The Zuivelmarkt, the Dairy Market, was beautified with red, white and yellow cloth, lent by Daniel Homs 'on certain conditions'. This poses some, as yet unanswerable, questions. What could the 'conditions' have been? Was Homs a cloth merchant? Was it normal to hire out cloth?[31] Were plays performed on the Zuivelmarkt or was the decoration in honour of the procession? Other preparations for the procession and the ceremonial entry of the fifteen competing Chambers included the clearing of the streets of obstacles: that was the responsibility of two messengers of the Ypres' Chambers and of the town's messengers and other servants of the magistrates; the perks of this and other tasks were that one could quench one's thirst in one of the taverns at the town's expense.[32]

That Fools were important personages in the theatrical culture of the Rhetoricians is amply illustrated by the effort and cost of fitting

---

[25] Vandecasteele, (1989-90), 18, item 33.
[26] Vandecasteele, (1989-90), 18, item 34.
[27] Vandecasteele, (1989-90), 18, item 27.
[28] Vandecasteele, (1989-90), 14, item 1.
[29] Vandecasteele, (1989-90), 18, item 27.
[30] Vandecasteele, (1989-90), 17, item 15.
[31] Vandecasteele, (1989-90), 17, item 22.
[32] Vandecasteele, (1989-90), 18, item 26.

out Ghyselbrecht Hovyn, who was to play the Fool in 1529. Different pieces of cloth, presumably different colours, were ordered and a coat made up with matching stockings and other garments. Loys the embroiderer enhanced the coat with the arms of the town and Hovyn was also given two tailor-made pairs of shoes and £4 as payment.[33] A merchant procured leather and belts for two baubles which were made by the saddlemaker.[34]

Those who had no particular skills could also pick up some extra employment, such as the six men who, as ordered by the magistrates, made the rounds of the town five nights in succession, calling out: 'Guard your fires and candles well from causing fire' after the official firemen had already visited all the taverns and inns to check on fire precautions.[35]

There were those who had fingers in different pies and were rewarded accordingly: Ghyselbrecht van den Kerchove, the usher of the chamber of the aldermen, earned himself a commission on the purchase of a large quantity of wine from Auxerre 'to present wine for the recent *thundach* procession to diverse persons both religious and secular who had come to the procession'.[36] Van den Kerchove also procured the cloth for the Fool's cloak and no doubt got some change out of £14, 29s., 6d.[37] The Morissis family, Jan Morissis the Younger, painter, and Jaques Morissis, were very involved too. Jan had two painting commissions, totalling 22 shillings, but Jaques served on the judging panel, procured various materials such as wooden 'schachten' (poles), leather skins and other materials and fulfilled a number of unspecified services for the aldermen, which earned him £.6, 14s. and an ample quantity of alcoholic refreshment.[38]

All this shows not only that many and diverse individuals participated, but also that quite a few people were involved in multifarious ways. It would not be surprising, if we were in possession of the lists of members of the Chambers of Rhetoric or of other groups, to find the same names again, perhaps as actors, prompters or producers.

---

[33] Vandecasteele, (1989-90), 17, items 16, 17, 18, 19, 23.

[34] Vandecasteele, (1989-90), 18, items 24, 25; 19, item 37.

[35] Vandecasteele, (1989-90), 19, item 35.

[36] Vandecasteele, (1989-90), 19, item 37. The amounts, and the kinds, of presentation wines are revealing as evidence of the importance a town attached to a feast or a drama competition or to the visiting dignitaries or participants. See for this Ramakers (1996), pp. 44-46, 59-69, 82-84, 249-51.

[37] Vandecasteele, (1989-90), 17, item 16.

[38] Vandecasteele, (1989-90), 16, items 4, 10; 17, items 20, 21; 18, item 32.

A TALE OF TWO CITIES

There are many questions still to be asked and answered about the Ypres' documents, but the picture they, in particular those relating to 1529, conjure up, is that of a town where community and drama were intertwined, where plays were not something that other people did and which you went to see: there can hardly have been a functionary or a craft or a group that was not in some way involved in the preparations and the actual festivities.

This picture cannot be very dissimilar to that of other towns of the size of Ypres. Naturally, if we were to look at Antwerp or Ghent, with, incidentally, a smaller number of Chambers of Rhetoric and a population five to seven times larger, then community and drama might not have overlapped in the same way, though there is abundant evidence of the importance of drama in the larger towns as well.

Haarlem

Lauris Jansz. was the literary leader, the *factor*, of one of Haarlem's Chambers of Rhetoric, *'De Wijngaertrancken'*, The Vines. What we know of his work survived in the collection of plays which belonged, and belongs, to the older Haarlem Chamber *'De Pellicanisten"*, The Pelicanists, often referred to by their motto *'Trou moet blijcken'*, ('Loyalty has to be proven'). That collection, compiled around the year 1600, contains twenty-one plays which bear the signature 'Lauris Jansz. fecit'.[39]

All but one are *spelen van sinne*, that is to say moralities: some with biblical subject matter, *'Jesus onder de leraars'*, ('Jesus amongst the teachers'), *'Die geboorte Johannes Babtista'* ('The birth of John the Baptist'); some with titles which indicate their preoccupation with moral matters, *'Die Mensch veracht die Redelickheijt'* ('Mankind holds Reason in contempt'), *'Die Mensch wil die Werelt bevechten'* ('Mankind wants to fight the World'); some that indicate a preoccupation with contemporary issues: *'Meestal verjaecht Neering'* ('Most People chase out Commerce'), *'Meestal die om Paijs roepen'* ('Most People cry out for Peace').

The play that is best known, because it is available in an excellent modern edition, is *'Een spel van sinnen beroerende Het Cooren (1565)'* ('A morality concerning The Grain (1565)').[40] This is not

---

[39] *Trou moet blijcken: bronnenuitgave van de boeken der Haarlemse Rederijkerskamer ' De Pellicanisten'*, ed. by W.N.M. Hüsken, B.A.M. Ramakers, F.A.M. Schaars, (Assen: Quarto, 1993), Deel 4, Boek D; Deel 5, Boek E; Deel 6, Boek F; Deel 8, Boek I, K, L.

[40] *Een spel van sinnen beroerende Het Cooren (1565) van Lauris Jansz., factor van de Haarlemse rederijkerskamer 'De Wijngaertrancken'*, ed. by W.M.H. Hummelen

about the parable of the sower, it is a vehement attack on grain speculation which caused terrible famine and hardship in Haarlem, as in the rest of the Low Countries, in 1564-66 and which produced ructions at the highest levels of government in Brussels. The spectre of a spontaneous if the grain shortage was not solved very rapidly featured large in the correspondence of Margaretha of Parma and her advisors, who rightly also feared that in the reigning climate religious dissent, in particular that of the Calvinists, would feed upon the socio-economic misery and win ground.[41]

The grain shortage was indeed only one kind of misery with which the troubled Low Countries had to contend. All of Jansz.'s plays were written at a time that the many conflicts, religious, economic, socio-political, in which the Spanish rulers were embroiled with their subjects in these provinces, were coming to a head and would remain on the boil, so to speak, for many years to come. Jansz. died, it is surmised, in 1604. If that was so, than he will have seen, in his last years, something of the improbable miracle of the Republic, tiger economy and all. In 1565, things did not look hopeful.

At the time that Jansz. wrote '*Het Cooren*' Chambers of Rhetoric all over the Low Countries were in several respects in trouble because of their real or suspected association with religious dissidents and heretical ideas. Secondly, the literary and artistic climate was changing in a way that was not favourable for Rhetoricians. More and more their plays and poetry were criticized as outdated and unsophisticated, as untouched by all that was new and exciting, that is to say, untouched by the spirit of the rebirth of classical art and literature.[42]

It would not be true to say that the more modern minds did not have contact with the milieu of the Rhetoricians. Indeed, some of them had a foot in both camps: the Leiden Rhetorician Jan van Hout translated Janus Secundus's Neo-Latin *Batavia* (1533), an ode to the cultural contribution of the Low Countries to Europe, into Dutch in the 1570s, in collaboration with Janus Dousa, himself an ardent Neo-Latin poet.[43]

---

and G.R.W. Dibbets, (Zutphen: Thieme, 1985).

[41] Erich Kuttner, *Het hongerjaar 1566*, (Amsterdam, 1974), p. 192 ss.

[42] G.A. van Es, 'Het drama van de rederijkers' in *De letterkunde van de renaissance*. Geschiedenis van de Letterkunde van de Nederlanden III, ed. by G.S. Overdiep, ('s-Hertogenbosch/Brussel, 1944), pp. 276-305.

[43] C.L. Heesakkers, '25 Juli 1554: De ambassadeur van de Republiek der Letteren feliciteert het bruidspaar Prins Filips van Spanje en Koningin Mary van Engeland-De Europese horizon van de Nederlandse Neolatijnse literatuur', in *Nederlandse Literatuur, een geschiedenis*, ed. by M. Schenkeveld-van der Dussen et al.,

The accusations that the Rhetoricians were outmoded and outdated were in part justified from the perspective of some, although there are more than enough instances where the Rhetoricians demonstrate that they too can use classical material in innovating ways.[44]

An important aspect of their art that came under scrutiny was what they were most proud of: their skills in rhyme, in allegory, in imagery were increasingly dismissed as too convoluted by fellow poets who had drunk deep of the well of the ancients.[45] Amsterdam and Leiden, even in those days within easy reach from Haarlem, were bulwarks of the adherents to the *bonae literae*. All these factors together did not bode well and it is surprising to note just how many Rhetoricians' plays nevertheless seem to have been written in these years on a great variety of topics which often reflected contemporary issues.

With hindsight it is easy to see that the Low Countries in the second half of the sixteenth century were beset by a great many changes. To what extent Jansz. was well-informed, it is impossible to say. It is possible that he was a governor of one of the houses for the poor in the town; as such he would have been aware of fluctuations in the number of poor and the circumstances that had caused them to be, or kept them at, the edge of society.[46] As the literary leader of a Rhetoricians' Chamber he would have been in the circles of the literate and scholarly; he would also have met Rhetoricians from elsewhere and travelled with the members of his Chamber to other towns.

In '*Het Cooren*' he showed himself well informed about the real and the artificial causes for the grain shortages in 1565 and where he was mistaken he was so in elevated company: even some of the Regent's councillors in Brussels were prey to misconceptions.[47] For

---

(Groningen: Martinus Nijhoff, 1993), pp.147-51.

[44] 'Hue Mars en Venus tsaemen bueleerden', ed. by I. van de Wijer in *Uut goeder jonsten. Studies aangeboden aan L. Roose*, (Leuven, 1984), pp. 33-91; *Piramus en Thisbe. Twee rederijkersspelen uit de zestiende eeuw*, ed. by G.A. van Es (Zwolle, 1965); *Eneas en Dido, Twee amoureuze spelen uit de zestiende eeuw*, ed. by K. Iwema in *Jaarboek 'De Fonteine'* 25, (1982-83); many more plays with classical subject matter can be found in W.M.H. Hummelen, *Repertorium van het rederijkersdrama, 1500-c. 1620* (Assen, 1968).

[45] M. Spies, '1 Juli 1584: De Amsterdamse kamer "De eglentier" draagt de "Twespraeck vande Nederduitsche letterkunst" op aan het Amsterdamse stadsbestuur-Nieuwe opvattingen over literatuur', in *Nederlandse Literatuur, een geschiedenis*, ed. by M. Schenkeveld-van der Dussen et al., (Groningen: Martinus Nijhoff, 1993), pp. 177-81.

[46] Hummelen/Dibbets (1985), pp. 17-18.

[47] Hummelen/Dibbets (1985), p.7 and Geoffrey Parker, *The Dutch Revolt*, (Harmondsworth: Penguin Books Ltd., 1977), pp. 19-89; Sj. de Vries,

instance, in the play Jansz. has the greedy grain merchants implicated in the closure of the Sond, so that grain from the Baltic could not reach the hungry Low Countries. This belief was adhered to by, amongst others, William of Orange, though it has been proven to have been unlikely.[48]

Knowledge of war, and its consequences, came at first hand to Jansz.: the by now legendary siege of Haarlem which nearly wiped out the population in the winter of 1572 and the spring and summer of 1573, until July, when the town was finally defeated, had brought terrible hardship to its people and its commerce, in particular to the breweries which were its industrial mainstay. Jansz. returns time and again to the deprivations of war, and the allegorization of this scourge does nothing to distance the audience from the terrible reality. Fear must have been a dominant emotion; reports of other towns massacred after surrender were not infrequent. The Spanish troops in the Low Countries went unpaid for long periods of time and the mutinies that broke out had terrible consequences for the population.[49]

Taking into account the *realpolitik* of the time we must remember that this was a period in which Philip II, desperately trying to save parts of his empire from the incursions of the Ottoman rulers as well as being engaged in lengthy and costly warfare with France, also had to combat heresy and other difficulties in the Low Countries. As his father before him, Philip tried to weld the motley collection of provinces, regional rulers and autonomous towns into a centralized well-run entity which would not, at the drop of a hat, be able to withhold tax revenue which he badly needed.[50]

All these aspects are well known and I reiterate here some of them to try and build up a picture of how a playwright in a northern town might have been affected, and see his family and his fellow citizens affected, by the seemingly far off concerns of a distant king in a far-away land. There is every likelihood that authority, desperate to get a grip on an explosive and fragmenting country, impinged in various ways on the playwright and the audience for whom he wrote.

'Rederijkersspelen als historische dokumenten', *Tijdschrift voor Geschiedenis*, 57 (1942). pp. 185-98.

[48] De Vries (1942), p. 196.

[49] The sacking of Zutphen and Naarden in 1572 became proverbial for the atrocities committed by the Spanish troops: cf. Parker (1977), p.142. Ironically, the Spanish mutinies were devastating for the civilian population but from a military point of view were good news for the provinces: cf. Parker (1977), pp. 162-68.

[50] Geoffrey Parker, *Spain and the Netherlands 1559-1659. Ten Studies* (Glasgow, 1979), pp. 15-82.

A TALE OF TWO CITIES

What power has the playwright? What influence the message from the stage? In Jansz.'s case we can only try and infer this, at our peril, and lacking convenient documents, from the plays. Some are dated and show us how immediate Jansz.'s response to contemporary events could be. In one of these he reacts to the end of the war between Spain and France, concluded at Le Cateau-Cambrésis on 3 April 1559. Jansz.'s play too is dated 1559 and is not so much a celebration of peace as a graphic exposé of the miseries of war.[51]

Some aspects in particular deserve attention. Jansz. does not dwell on the historical causes of the war. Instead he dwells lengthily on the devastating effects on all trade, agriculture and industries such as the breweries and the textile industry which were the lifeblood of Haarlem; in a wider context he mentions for example the disastrous effect on the herring fishing caused by French privateering: no herring was landed for some years;[52] that too, as a staple food, would have had a severe effect on the food provisioning for Haarlem as for other towns.

The dramatic strategy which he then developed and which the allegorical form facilitated, was that of war as a scourge sent by God to show mankind how sinful their mode of living was. This exonerated him from the difficulty of tackling the main protagonists in the war, Henri II of France and Philip II of Spain. From the king of France he would not have had anything to fear, but the town authorities could not have let him get away with an attack on their rightful king. This was a time at which close scrutiny and censorship of Rhetoricians' plays was quite normal.[53]

---

[51] 'Meestal die om Pais roepen' , in *Trou moet blijcken.: bronnenuitgave van de boeken der Haarlemse Rederijkerskamer 'De Pellicanisten'*, ed. W.M.N. Hüsken, B. A.M. Ramakers and F.A.M. Schaars, (Assen: Quarto, 1994), Deel 5, Boek E, 139v-152v.

[52] Elsa Strietman, ' Pawns or prime movers? The Rhetoricians in the struggle for power in the Low Countries', in *European Medieval Drama 2 (1998) Papers from the Second international Conference on European Medieval Drama, Camerino , 4-6 July, 1997*, ed. by Sydney Higgins (Turnhout: Brepols, 1998), pp. 111-21.

[53] It is quite revealing to see how much of a threat plays, refrains, ballads and other forms of entertainment were deemed to be not only by the Spanish authorities, but also by William of Orange in the 1580s, when it was clear that support for the rebels, and thus also for the Prince of Orange, was strong in the circles of the Rhetoricians; the role of the refrains, ballads and other songs, as means of communication between, and propaganda for, the rebels and their supporters, cannot be underestimated. See for instance: Cornelis Cau, *Groot Placaet -Boeck, vervattende de Placaten, ordonnantien ende Edicten van de [...] Staten Generaal der vereenighde Nederlanden, Heeren Staaten van Hollandt en West-Vrieslandt, [...], Heeren Staaten van Zeelandt*, ('s-Gravenhage, 1658), Deel I, XXXVI-XXXVII, col. 357-88.

Jansz. did, however, put the king into his cast and created the character of a sympathetic ruler who is horrified by the ravages which war has inflicted on his subjects. The manner in which Jansz. created this character stands in a tradition which would continue long after in Dutch drama and which is to be found in many a historical document[54] too and which echoes in the *'Wilhelmus'*: it is not the king himself who inflicts misery on his subjects in the Low Countries, it is the fault of his councillors, who advise him wrongly.[55] This particular stage is omitted in this play, but it is profiled nevertheless because here the king, as soon as he realizes the reality of the destructive war, asks advice of decent councillors such as Love for the Wellbeing of Everyman and Loyal Care together with the messenger Goodwill. Peace claims to be the victim, ravaged and driven out by War. A trial will be held to investigate the claims of each of the parties.

War, when summoned, is unrepentant: he only carried out the orders from the king! 'From me' exclaims Philip, horrified. 'No' is the answer, 'from a greater king than you are, the King of Heaven'. This is a neat stratagem: it safeguards the playwright and his actors from any blame on the part of the authorities; it also enables the playwright to interweave the contemporary, all too real situation into a wider, metaphysical situation: mankind lives so sinfully that God resorted to send them war in order to teach them a lesson. In this context sin and punishment, atonement and forgiveness become cause and effect: war and misery, cessation of war and the advent of peace.

In the latter sequence, Philip is made the agent: the defender of the people, the king who, as he says, would rather conclude an unjust peace than continue a righteous war. This is a king image that would become part of the dramatic tradition of the Republic: Hooft and Vondel would use and reuse it and it would function simultaneously in the apologetic literature occasioned by the abjuration of Philip II and in the mass of writing that builds up a picture of the 'ideal' ruler.[56]

Jansz.'s play, in the interweaving of the historical and the metaphysical issues, is by no means seamless: the paradox that

---

[54] A.F. Mellink, *Texts relating to the revolt of the Netherlands* (Cambridge: Cambridge University Press, 1975), amongst others: documents 3, 4, 9, 14, 48, 49.

[55] A. den Besten, *Wilhelmus van Nassouwe. Het gedicht en zijn dichter* (Leiden: Martinus Nijhoff, 1983).

[56] I. Schöffer, ' The Batavian myth during the sixteenth and seventeenth centuries' , in *Geschiedschrijving in Nederland*, ed. by P.A.M. Geurts and A.E.M. Jansen, vol. 11, (The Hague, 1981), pp. 85-109; H. Duits, *Van Bartholomeusnacht tot Bataafse opstand. Studies over de relatie tussen politiek en toneel in het midden van de zeventiende eeuw*, (Hilversum: Verloren, 1990), pp. 232-72.

punishment is inflicted (by means of a trial) on the character War, who obstinately stands by his claim that he 'only carried out orders' from God, sits uneasily in the larger claims that mankind should pay heed to God's command. Moreover, if Jansz. indeed wrote the play after the peace of Le Cateau-Cambrésis had been concluded, then he did not know, or chose to ignore, that far from having abandoned a righteous war in favour of an unjust peace, the French had ceded all that Philip had wanted and Spain had come out of that particular hole rather well.

In fact, not to mince words, the end of the play is a bit of a cop out, however much the 'morality' here urged upon the audience is a customary part of Rhetoricians' drama. This is a recurrent situation in a number of Jansz.'s plays. Some base their argument on the notion that trade and industry are harmed by the continued unsettled situation in the Low Countries and that therefore the population and most of all the ordinary people suffer terrible hardships. Jansz. was an intelligent observer who saw that political causes have economic and therefore social effects. He did not go into specific contemporary detail as he had done in his play about the Le Cateau-Cambrésis Peace of 1559, but the situations he described are easily reconciled with what is known of the history of the period. All these plays seem to be framed in the same way: however 'man-made' in terms of politics or economy Jansz.'s settings are, they all have but one solution: mankind must repent, God's will be done and in the end salvation will arrive, if not on earth, then in heaven: Amen.

This is even the case in Jansz.'s justifiably praised and much quoted '*Het Cooren*', which is in almost all particulars an accurate reflection of the situation in the Low Countries in 1564-65: a terrible shortage of grain, in part artificially induced. Jansz. recreated for his audience the situation in Haarlem: because of the many breweries which employed so many people it was doubly affected by a shortage of raw material as well as of grain as a staple food. The manner in which he allegorized the villains of the piece, the greedy grain merchants, leaves very little room for conjecture: his audience would have known at whom he pointed a finger, they would have known who the rich merchants in the town were and what their warehouses might have contained.

Jansz. put his hope initially in a legal regulation of grain imports and exports which might have had the effect of curbing speculation, and these measures he expected to come from the central government in Brussels rather than from the town authorities where the interests of the merchant and the magistrate, as he implied, easily overlapped, and hindered a check on immoral or illegal practices.[57] Hummelen and Dibbets paid particular attention to its unique character: this is not, they state, a play which points out social evils to its audience only in order to convince them that they themselves are the root of all evil and that if only they would improve their ways, God would reward their obedience. They argue that, at least in *Het Cooren*, the playwright is exhorting the audience to active criticism and rebellion against those who are identifiably the villains of the piece.[58]

At the same time, however, Hummelen and Dibbets conclude that Jansz. in *Het Cooren* as in his other plays, knows that he is fighting enemies who will not be moved to any course of action or mode of thought other than the one portrayed. His advice to trust in God they interpret as satisfying to the audience because he has meanwhile managed to make them aware who their enemies are. Jansz.'s hope for practical help in the form of governmental regulation came to nothing but neither playwright nor audience could have known that at the time the play was written and performed.[59]

However, Jansz. adopted this same stratagem in his other plays, whenever he identified injustice and misery of one kind or another: the vehemence that he displays about the issues in question seems to evaporate before a very conventional, rather lame, exhortation to abolish sinful living and resign oneself to God's will. That does not seem to tally with his real, and in my view, non-conventional interest in socio-economic aspects. If indeed he was the same Jansz. as one of the governors of the St. Pietershof then not only would he have had plenty of material for that interest, but also have seen that those who were the victims of poverty were not the victims of sinful living, but of economic, social and political forces beyond their control.

That Jansz. did not lack courage is clear from *Het Cooren* and from the way in which he exposed religious and political enmities and advocated mutual tolerance and understanding. This is evident for instance in the prologue and epilogue of '*Een spel van sinnen van die geboorte Johannes baptista die voorloper christo*' (A morality about the birth of John the Baptist the precursor of Christ) where the character *Redelick Verstant* (Reasonable Mind) mediates in a heated debate between a supporter of the Protestants, *Geus,* and *Catolick* (Catholic).[60] Just as for his fellow citizen the humanist D.V.

---

[57] Hummelen/Dibbets, *Het Cooren*, lines 517-612.

[58] Hummelen/ Dibbets, pp. 14-20.

[59] Hummelen/Dibbets, p. 20.

[60] 'Geus', derived from the French 'gueux', or 'beggar', was the contemptuous term which Granvelle used to describe the nobles of the Low Countries when they handed

Coornhert, for Jansz. too religious or political party rhetoric and attitudes were abhorrent.[61]

The conclusion I feel myself forced to draw and hope to be able to disprove after further study of Jansz.'s work, has already in part been indicated for *Het Cooren* by Hummelen and Dibbets. It is a rather pessimistic view, namely that the playwright felt that he could not change anything in the prevailing injustice and that the parameters of his power allowed him no more than to try and console his audience with the thought that better days might yet come, God willing. They contrasted that, however, with their conviction that Jansz. tried to 'galvanize the audience into criticizing and rebelling against the corrupt grain merchants'. These two attitudes seem not easily reconcilable and the option of resignation, albeit resignation in the hope of divine intervention, seems to me to be far more emphatically advocated by Jansz. than that of rebellion.

The *Trou moet blijcken* volumes show a group of plays by Jansz. written in the late 1570s: *Lieft boven Al* (1579) ('Love most of all'), *De gebooren Blinde* (1579) ('The Person who was born blind'), *Menich Bedruct Hart aen een droege chysterne verleijt* (1577) ('Many an oppressed Heart is tempted to a dry well'), *Goetheijt, Lijefde en Eendracht* (1579) ('Goodness, Love and Unity'), *Die Geboorte Johannes Baptista* (1578) ('The birth of John the Baptist').[62] The cast-lists in themselves are indicative of the tone and subject of the plays: any militancy is a moral militancy, any religious fervour is that of a non-denominational believer, any hope of improvement lies in mankind taking responsibility for its moral wellbeing in adhering to God's Word as laid down in Scripture. Characters abound with names such as *Simpel Verstant* (Simple Mind), *Schriftuerlijcke Sin* (Scriptural Sense), *Redelick Gevoelen* (Reasonable Feeling), *Menich Goet Mensch* (Many a Good Person), and *Helsche Nijdicheyt* (Evil Envy).

---

their petition for more lenient religious and secular measures to the regent, Margaret of Parma, on 5 April, 1566. It was soon adopted by the rebels as an *epitheton ornans*. A facsimile and transcription into modern Dutch of *Die geboorte Johannes Babtista* is available in *Trou moet blijcken; bronnenuitgave van de boeken der Haarlemse rederijkerskamer 'De Pellicanisten'*, ed. by W.N.M. Hüsken, B.A.M. Ramakers, F.A.M. Schaars, (Assen: Quarto, 1994), Deel 5, Boek E, 94r-109v.

[61] H. Bonger et al., *Dirck Volckertszoon Coornhert. Dwars maar recht*, (Zutphen: Walburg Pers, 1989) gives extensive and recently updated information about Coornhert's work and life.

[62] *Trou moet blijcken*, (Assen: Quarto, 1994), Deel 4, Boek D, fols 35v-94r, fols 133v-150r, except for *Die geboorte Johannes Babtista*, which is in *Trou moet blijcken*, (Assen: Quarto, 1994), Deel 5, Boek E, fols 94r-109r.

It is interesting to note how frequently Jansz. creates allegorical characters who in one way or another reflect man's capacity to reason, to use cool and calm persuasion rather than passion and physical violence. In that too he resembles Coornhert as he does in his tolerant, all-encompassing religiosity. In this sense Jansz. seems far from unsophisticated and old-fashioned, a charge levelled at the Rhetoricians more and more as the sixteenth century drew to an end. Neither is he frightened to show the extent to which fanatic religiosity and narrow-mindedness can cause damage: even the character *Redelick Verstant* (Reasonable Feeling) loses his patience and all is lost.[63] In a climate where religious and political bigotry were the order of the day voices such as Jansz. and Coornhert were not often welcomed and Jansz., as the more prolific playwright, reached his Haarlem audience frequently and directly, from the stage.

In these years the troubles between the Spanish rulers and the Low Countries were intense though the very manner in which the provinces were forced into grouping themselves for greater strength in the Union of Utrecht and the Union of Arras in 1579 did indeed pay off in the long term.[64] That, however, cannot easily have been detected by the contemporaries. It is tempting to surmise that the tone of Jansz.'s works in these years reflected a general feeling of helplessness amongst ordinary citizens, a malaise that would last until, at least in the Northern provinces, the Republic became a fact.[65]

Very few of the dated plays were written after the 1570s, none of his plays other than that of 1559 *'Meestal die om Paijs roepen'* ('Most People cry out for Peace') or 1565 *'Het Cooren'* ('The Grain') display the same vehemence about recent or current contemporary issues although the topic of war which destroys normal life, trade and industry does recur.[66]

There is, however, a marked emphasis on all the human failings which are held responsible for the prevailing misery. There is a desperation in these plays, an impotence that prevents any real optimism and the endings seem to me frequently not in harmony with the message so often reiterated: trust in God and all shall be well. Even the Sinnekens, so often employed for the purposes of piercing satire and hilarious entertainment in many other Rhetoricians' plays,

---

[63] *Trou moet blijcken* (1994), Deel 5, Boek E, fols 94r-109r.

[64] See G. Parker, (1977), pp. 194-95.

[65] G. Parker, (1977), pp. 187-252.

[66] As, for instance, in *Meestal verjaecht Neering* and *Goetheijt, Lijefde en Eendracht* in *Trou moet blijcken*, (1994), Deel 4, Boek D and *Saul ende David* in *Trou moet blijcken* (1994), Deel 5, Boek E.

seem a dull bunch. Depressing is the word that comes most often to mind when reading Jansz.'s work and imagining it on the stage, notwithstanding the flashes of passion, or the fearless criticism that can also be found.

Jansz. is not representative of the Rhetoricians' drama of his time: he is but one of many. But he was prolific and since he wrote for his own Chamber there is a very good chance that his plays were performed. Moreover it would seem unlikely that he would have confronted his actors and fellow members with a play that was doomed not to succeed. Haarlem was not such a large town that the *Factor* of a Chamber would not have had some idea of what the audience could be expected to take. If all this can be surmised, then the crisis which the playwright portrayed must to some extent have been the crisis that the audience felt themselves to be living in. We know that better times did come, not for the majority, but for quite a few people. That the town they lived in would have a good share of the economic and cultural miracle of the Republic. That they would be subject to an authority which, however limited and faulty in our eyes, would somehow cause the citizens of the Republic to become the envy of travellers and of those foreigners who lived amongst them. What a pity Jansz. and his fellow citizens could not foretell the future.

With hindsight, this was a time when the links between drama and the community were about to be loosened and drama was about to become divided in itself. The culture of popular and educational entertainment that for most of the fifteenth and sixteenth century had been inextricably linked with the culture of the Low Countries would disappear. Its place would be taken by a popular theatrical culture and the development of an intellectual, literary, writing of plays which avidly strove to keep up with the latest interpretation of prescriptive ideas based on classical models.[67]

In the northern provinces which proclaimed themselves the Republic of the Seven United Netherlands in 1581, a national-historical drama would develop in which the popular and the literary sometimes combined. Chambers of Rhetoric would continue to exist but the great days of drama and the community were well and truly over. In the southern provinces too great changes took place from the

---

[67] Mieke B. Smits-Veldt, '24 september 1617: Inwijding van de Nederduytsche Academie-De opbloei van het Renaissance toneel in Amsterdam' in *Nederlandse Literatuur, een geschiedenis*, ed. by M. Schenkeveld-van der Dussen, (Groningen, 1993), pp. 196-201; Lia van Gemert, '3 januari 1638: De opening van de Amsterdamse Schouwburg-Vondel en de Gysbreght-traditie', in *Nederlandse Literatuur, een geschiedenis* , (1993), pp. 230-36.

last quarter of the sixteenth century onwards: the political and religious troubles which eventually resulted in the great exodus of many who were seen as undesirable in the eyes of the Spanish authorities and of the Catholic Church drained the provinces of many talented and questing minds. The Counter-Reformation instigated and facilitated great baroque painting and architecture but it gradually stifled the vernacular literature and drama which had been part of the splendour of the Burgundian and the Habsburg Low Countries.

And yet, how unpredictable is the course of history: in the north the notion of the Chambers of Rhetoric gradually became *gesunkenes Kulturgut*, its products and its members easy prey for ridicule and dismissal by those who considered themselves the *literati*. The Catholic traditions of the communal celebrations of the great feasts of the Church were suppressed. The community of believers which enabled rulers and prelates to use the same processional and theatrical ceremonial modes of expression became divided forever. Those Chambers which survived changed: *Trou moet blijcken* in Haarlem is still a society but no longer a creative one: it acts as the guardian of a treasure trove of plays and documents from which we, the descendants, gratefully and haltingly, try to piece together the lost jigsaw of the past. This extensive collection of plays, amongst which are many texts from the southern provinces, is now available to scholars in a facsimile edition with transcriptions in modern Dutch, and of the greatest importance for researchers and for performers.

In the south, however, in particular in the Dutch-speaking counties, the national revival in the nineteenth century that was in part inspired by political events, in part by the impetus of Romanticism, created a fervent interest in the past. The role of the Chambers of Rhetoric and of drama in all its manifestations was rightly perceived to have been crucially important. That perception gave us such monuments as the *Belgisch Museum* and the *Vaderlandsch Museum*, publications which have by no means been exhaustively investigated and which are often essential in following back the faint traces of the past.[68]

The Ghent Chamber *De Fonteine* no longer performs or commissions plays, but the eponymous periodical which it publishes is an indispensable tool for the study of the theatrical and dramatic culture of the past.[69] Until the late 1980s, Ypres still celebrated its

---

[68] *Belgisch Museum voor Nederduitsche tael- en letterkunde en de geschiedenis des vaderlands,* ed. by J.F. Willems (Ghent 1837-1846), 10 vols.; *Vaderlandsch Museum voor Nederduitsche Letterkunde, Oudheid en Geschiedenis,* ed. by C.P. Serrure (Ghent: H. Hoste, 1861), 7 vols.

[69] *Jaarboek van de Koninklijke Soevereine Hoofdkamer van Retorica 'De Fonteine'* (Ghent: 1943).

annual *Thundach* with a procession and a fair which involved a significant part of the community; and although, sadly, the procession no longer now exists, a 'foor', a great fair, is still held on the day of *Onze Lieve Vrouwe van den Thuin*.

Drama and community in South Tyrol

JOHN TAILBY

THE AREA SOUTH OF the Brenner Pass, today part of Italy, has always been German-speaking. Though on the very fringe of the German language area, it has always been on an important route across the Alps and in the early sixteenth century owed its wealth to silver mining.

The Passion Plays[1] from this area have been studied for over a century and were the subject of a substantial volume by Wackernell in 1897.[2] It is fashionable to deride his efforts in his edition to reconstruct the archetype of the Tyrolean Passion Play, but his understanding of the relationships between the surviving texts has not been bettered by any subsequent scholar. Criticism that essentially reproaches him for being a product of his age must not be allowed to detract from the value of his three hundred pages of introduction, which, for example, on the sociology of the plays and performers, has not been matched, let alone surpassed, since.[3]

These texts and the whole society in which they were performed have been the subject of regional scholarly interest throughout the nineteenth and twentieth centuries – even though little awareness of them has percolated through to the English-speaking world. Nevertheless we do not yet have satisfactory editions of all the texts in

---

[1] German scholars insist on the distinction between Easter Plays (*Osterspiele*), which begin with the resurrection, and Passion Plays (*Passionsspiele*), which deal with the events of Holy Week and possibly include earlier episodes: Christ's ministry, the nativity, and scenes from the Old Testament, especially such as may be thought of as having prefigurative significance. This distinction is not made consistently in medieval sources or in modern secondary literature from certain regions, notably Switzerland.

[2] J.E. Wackernell, *Altdeutsche Passionsspiele aus Tirol* (Graz: Styria, 1897).

[3] Thus also Max Siller, in *Literatur und Sprache in Tirol*, ed. by Michael Gebhart and Max Siller (Innsbruck: Universitatsverlag, 1996), p. 224.

the collection made by Vigil Raber in Sterzing in the period 1510-38. The edition of the religious plays by Lipphardt and Roloff got off to a disastrous start when the error-strewn first volume edited by Lipphardt was withdrawn shortly after its appearance (and Lipphardt's death) in the face of scholarly expressions of horror; its replacement and the other volumes of texts have now appeared but the promised sixth volume of Regie material remains outstanding.[4]

Before this project got under way the secular plays had been edited by W.M. Bauer,[5] building on Oswald Zingerle's work last century. Alongside the play texts, the other source of information is the archival record, largely noted by Wackernell but now also available with reference to the religious plays in Bernd Neumann's two-volumed collection.[6]

Perhaps the most striking point concerning the extant plays from Tyrol is that we owe the survival of them all to the same individuals. Whereas in most areas those who organize and perform religious plays are careful to keep their distance from secular plays,[7] there is no such reluctance on the part of Benedikt Debs and Vigil Raber.

---

[4] *Sterzinger Spiele: Die geistlichen Spiele des Sterzinger Spielarchivs*, ed. by Walther Lipphardt and Hans-Gert Roloff; Vol. 1 (revised edition, Berne and Frankfurt: Lang, 1986) contains the plays in the 'Debs Codex', see below; Vol. 2 (1988) contains 'Lienhard Pfarrkirchers Passion' of 1486 and the 1496 and 1503 versions of the Sterzing Passion Play; Vol. 3 (1997) contains the Passion Play copied by Raber in 1514 after that year's performance; the 'Passion von Hall' obtained for 1514; the fragment of a further version of a Passion Play; plus three shorter plays, *Ludus paschalis* (1520), *de nativitate domini* and a *planctus* with prophets; Vol. 4 (1990) contains two Palm Sunday plays, a Last Supper play, an Ascension Day play and a Pentecost play; Vol. 5 (1980) contains in much smaller font five previously unpublished plays, two related versions of a dramatization of St John's Gospel, both incomplete, a court scene entitled *Ain recht das Christus stirbt*, a dramatisation of the parable of the Rich Man and Lazarus, and a short David and Goliath play. Vol. 6.2 (1997) contains the commentary on the music; Vol. 6.1 is intended to present all relevant Regie material.

[5] *Sterzinger Spiele; die weltlichen Spiele des Sterzinger Spielarchivs nach den Originalhandschriften (1510-1535) von Vigil Raber und nach der Ausgabe Oswald Zingerles (1886)*, ed. by Werner M. Bauer (Vienna: Österreichischer Bundesverlag, 1982), Wiener Neudrücke, 6.

[6] Bernd Neumann, *Geistliches Schauspiel im Zeugnis der Zeit* (Munich and Zurich: Artemis, 1982), 2 vols. Entries are in an alphabetical list of places, then in date order with the date in bold, with the individual entry number in square brackets at the end, whether this is two lines or two pages later. Bibliographical information for each entry follows below the line.

[7] See, for example. the request for permission to perform made by citizens of Colmar (now in France) in 1534, Neumann item 1157, English translation as item F2 in the volume on medieval European theatre in the series *Theatre in Europe*, ed. by William Tydeman (Cambridge: Cambridge University Press, 1999).

Relatively little is known about the life of either of them; what we know about Debs derives almost totally from Raber. Debs came from Ingolstadt and in 1511 he became schoolmaster and consequently also choirmaster in Bozen. On his death in 1515 he bequeathed his collection of play texts to Raber, notably the *alte Scarteggen* ('old manuscript') on which volume 1 of the *Sterzinger Spiele* is based. Raber came from a Sterzing family of bakers and probably attended the local Latin school, despite his poor Latin shown in the manuscripts he copied. We do not know the date of his birth. From 1510 to 1522 we find him in Bozen, where he is employed in repairing works of art and painting altar panels alongside his dramatic activities, for which he receives payments (see below). From 1524 until his death early in December 1552 (he was buried on 14 December) he was based in Sterzing, though there are no records from there for the years 1527-33. Between 1533 and 1552 the town records show him active in all kinds of dramatic performance in Sterzing.

Whereas the archival records relate to specific towns, notably Sterzing (now officially in Italian Vipiteno), Bozen (Bolzano) and Meran (Merano), the situation regarding the play texts is more complicated. The collection today is known as *Sterzinger Spiele* (Sterzing Plays), as in the titles of the published volumes, even though several of the texts originate from Bozen.

The situation is indeed even more complicated because there are several strands of religious play texts; though the *Sterzinger Spiele* have been largely published, there are other religious plays from this area and date, the manuscripts of which are located elsewhere and regarding which the prospects for publication are even less good. Because it does not now constitute part of the 'Sterzing collection' the Bozen 1495 text has been edited separately.[8] Space available here allows only a sampling of the kinds of information revealed by these play texts. The performances in Bozen in 1495 make a convenient starting point. Immediately on reading the archive entries in Neumann, one is struck by the diversity of the plays. We have manuscripts and lists of actors and the roles they played for the Passion Play. The municipal archives contain the church provost's accounts, which record expenditure for an Ascension Day play – chiefly food and drink for the apostles on stage – and for a procession at Corpus Christi, for which stages had to be erected in several locations and for which St George's dragon had to be repaired and three men paid to carry it, presumably during the procession. Food and drink for twenty-three persons were paid for out of church funds at a cost of 1m £4 6gr.

---

[8] *Bozner Passion 1495*, ed. by Bruno Klammer (Berne, Frankfurt and New York: Lang, 1986). See also the article by Siller in note 3.

The provost's accounts continue with items relating to expenditure for the Passion Play, presumably performed several weeks earlier, making clear how the town was engaged simultaneously in different strands of play planning. Paper was purchased and then one Hainricus was sent to Sterzing to copy the text. Various purchases of cloth were paid for by the town, for devil costumes – a later entry records their being dyed black – , for Christ's robe (brown) and for Judas's coat (yellow). More intriguingly 11 ells of white cloth were purchased for Christ's purple robe and Hanns Walhabter tailor (*tuchscherer*) is paid £1 11gr for cutting 33 ells of cloth. At two points payments were made for wood for stage construction, including its transportation to the churchyard.[9]

Further information about the Ascension Day performances can be culled from the records for later years. The same set of accounts records in 1505, 1507 and 1509 payments for food and drink (*ain marend* which Götze's *Frühneuhochdeutsches Glossar* explains as 'Imbiss am Nachmittag', an afternoon snack) to the stonemasons who pulled up the image of Christ; happily the 1507 accounts refers to the image (*das pild*) and those for 1509 to the Saviour (*denn salvattor*); the 1509 record continues with the cost of the gold lamé/tinsel for the garland needed on Ascension Day for the hole in the top of the arched ceiling. This makes unambiguously clear that these performances did take place inside the church.

The cast-lists for the 1514 performance contain the first references from this area to female roles being played by women. The list quoted both by Neumann and in the *Sterzinger Spiele* has the Canaanite woman's daughter played by a girl (*Endl Kramerin tochter*, i.e. the daughter of trader Endl and his wife), though the Canaanite woman is played by a (young?) man Peter Pekin. The sisters Mary and Martha are also played by women, *Martha: Mullerin in der Hell*, i.e. 'the miller's wife in "hell"', the normal name for a certain spot in the town; *Magdalena: Jochm Goldsch[mid] gschb[ester]*, i.e the sister of Jochem the goldsmith.

The idea that this may well have been the first time that some women's roles were played by women is reinforced by another cast-list for the same year, in which the performers' names for earlier years are replaced by the new names. Here it is possible to see that the two maids *Prima ancilla, Secunda ancilla*, were previously played by men, – the first name is not completely legible but begins *Joh[annes?]*, the second was *Steffanus*. For 1514 however the new names were *Els an*

---

[9] One has to rely on Neumann's judgement that this entry does refer to expenditure for the play, since as he presents these small items individually this is not unambiguously clear.

der wag, i.e. Elsa or Elsie, and *Endl Furstn kellerin*, i.e probably Endl Furst's female cellarer. In the Easter Day part of the action, Day 4, *Mullerin in der Hell* had another part, this time of *Uxor medici*, i.e. the wife of the Unguentarius/Spice Merchant and was joined in this scene as *Puella medici* by *Plasy Paders tochter*, the daughter of the bathhouse keeper Plasy, i.e. Blasius, compare French Blaise.

It was notoriously difficult to get actors to play Judas Iscariot and the cast list shows that on this occasion Vigil Raber himself took on the role (*Räber pictor*, i.e. Raber the painter).

Shortly before the Bozen records break off, we have from the year 1543 the text of the Corpus Christi play, preceded by the following list of the groups responsible for the various scenes

> Parish church: Herald first, Margaret leads the dragon (*wurm*) in which are four bearers. Knight St George with six horses and a shieldbearer (He is followed by a boy who says his text, demonstrates the argument.)**[10]
> Shoemakers: the masters: the devil with the fruit, Adam and Eve, the angel with the sword
> Builders (*Pauleut*): St Urban, two who carry the grapes
> Blacksmiths: the six prophets or church fathers (they are to say their lines only on the stage)**
> Parish church: two bearers carrying Noah's ark
> Fraternity of St Anna: (is missing)** the ancestry of St Anna
> Fraternity of St James: the annunciation
> Joiners: Joseph and Mary together with the child in the cradle
> Saddlers: the shepherds
> Butchers: the first king with six horses
> Carpenters: the second king with six horses
> Tailors Cloth-cutters: the third Moorish king with six horses and several advisors (?*rätzen*) (these three kings say their lines on the stage)**
> Cobblers men: Our Lady on the donkey with Joseph
> Bakers: King Herod with the four men in armour on horseback who put the Innocents to the sword, Annas and Caiaphas
> (The sack makers (?*söckhler/seckhler*): the Jews school follows, the sackmakers do [it])**
> The builders from the *Predigern*/preachers =? : Christ on the donkey with the twelve disciples
> Stone masons or bricklayers do the Last Supper (now Christ says his lines as follows)**
> Builders in the parish [church]: the Mount of Olives with its appurtenances (Christ says his lines and the angel consoles him as

---

[10] This is the first of numerous additions in a different hand. I follow Neumann in including them in round brackets followed by **.

follows)** Judas and the devil (together with [word omitted] say their lines and do their actions as follows)**

Tailors: Scourging at the pillar (Christ says his lines likewise the Jews)** The presentation of Christ *ecce homo* (that is the crowning. The Jews do their actions and say their lines as do Pilate and the High Priest as follows)** and Pilate (Now follow the two thieves and the executioners say their lines, behind them follows Christ with the cross)**

Coopers: Christ carrying the cross together with the Jews (say their lines)** (with four boys [who] say their lines against them [or 'towards them'] as follows)** Mary Magdalene, Martha and Salome (follow behind him)**

Weavers: Christ's resurrection. (Christ goes from them to the women (? *get Cristus von inen den frauen*) [Mary Magdalene and Martha] and Mary Jacobe, Salome and Cleophe follow behind, Christ and the angels say their lines as follows)**

Fraternity of St Sebastian at the *Predigern*/preachers: the company of St Ursula with sixty virgins

Saint Sebastian's fraternity of the bowmen: St Michael with the scales St Sebastian with four boys

The shoemakers men: St Christopher with the child [Jesus]

Bathhousekeepers (*bader*): Magdalene with the tin [of ointment], St Gosman and Domian St John the Baptist, the Last Judgement with two angels who carry the [rain]bow.

End of the scenes. Thereafter start the banners, candles, poles (*stanngen*), schoolboys, *parfüeser, prediger, beneficiaten, geselbriester*, the sacrament, four bearing the baldachin, two angels for the *ecce panis*. After that, when the procession is over/past, the spoken texts begin.

The play text then follows in the manuscript.

Modern scholars were not the first to consult the Bozen church records; in 1749 the town council examined those for the period 1473-1500 when discussing the continuation of the Corpus Christi processions and plays. They concluded that the afternoon performances in the minster (*muster*) had taken place almost annually, some twenty plus times during this period, but it was not clear whether this necessarily included slaying the dragon. They concluded further that it had been an arbitrary decision of their forebears to put on these performances, not the result of an oath, the same situation as in other places, some of which at this point still continued with performances, though they had ceased elsewhere.

Other places in Tyrol from which there are sixteenth-century records include Brixen (Bressanone) and Bruneck/Pustertal (Brunico). From Brixen, like Bozen, we can note that the community put on various plays in the same year; beside references to Corpus Christi plays involving the familiar recurrent repairs to the dragon, there are also references to the 'other play' done at Easter, which according to a set of instructions to the church verger from about 1555 was indeed an Easter Play, performed after mattins.

From Bruneck we have references to a Passion Play (*der Passion*), for which the town council first gave authorization – without signs of financial support – in 1538; the 1542 and 1546 entries make clear that this performance was outdoors and that the municipality was now making financial contributions to the cost of erecting the stage. These three dates suggest an attempt at regular four-yearly performances.

The records from Sterzing that relate unambiguously to religious plays begin only in the last third of the fifteenth century. There is good reason to follow Wackernell's suggestion that the Passion Play performances took place at seven-year intervals, perhaps starting as early as 1455; certainly the reference to a mask for Our Lady in the church provost's accounts in 1469 cannot refer to an Easter Play. For 1476 the only reference is to paying for linen for the play; and for 1482 the accounts contain only a global reference to payment made by the Church of Our Lady for the play. Later records make it clear that the performances took place in this church. From the 1496 performance we have a list of roles and names of performers included with the text, but scant information about who paid the expenses.

In 1503 the same text was used, lists of performers again survive and we can see several prominent citizens again performing the same roles. Hans Pösterl and Conrat (*Chuenrat*) Gärtringer were again directors (*Regenten*, the term also used in Lucerne to describe this function); and Lienhart Pfarrkircher again spoke the prologues (*Precursor*). The surviving manuscript dated 1486 is referred to by Vigil Raber as *Lienharden Pfarrkirchers passion*, (see above note 4), so it seems this major performer also had a hand in recasting the text. The next date under which any Sterzing records survive is 1514, the date of the major performance in Bozen referred to above. Interestingly, the only reference here comes not from church accounts but from the Clerk of Works office (*Baumeisteramt*), and notes payment for erection and dismantling of the stage. Reference to dismantling the stage occurs again in the accounts for April 1533, this time being paid by the mayor's office, and noting dismantling of the stage from inside the church on Maundy Thursday. In June the same accounts note a payment to Vigil Raber for his efforts concerning the play at Whitsuntide. These puzzling references initiate another period of dramatic activity, with further performances in 1535, 1538, 1541 and 1543. For 1535 the mayor's office again made payments: to a carpenter for the erection of the stage, the costs of materials and feeding his workforce; to a saddler for repairing the belts (*girten*) on which the thieves hung on their crosses; to the *Stadtknecht* (beadle?) for flour which was smeared on the thieves, perhaps to give them a corpse-like appearance. The same source in 1538 paid for entertaining the players after the performance, which is explicitly stated to have been in the church.

In 1541 the church provost paid a man to put a lock on the door of the room in the church tower in which costumes, including devil costumes, were stored. In this year the town had considerable expenditure concerning hell and the devils,[11] including payments for cloth, wood for the rafters, nails, also those made to the tailor who sewed up (? or 'renewed' *übernaunt*) hell; the joiner who worked on it also delivered a scythe[12] and the devils' staffs. Raber, the joiner, the carpenter and the cooper (? *pinter = Fassbinder*?) were also paid for bread and wine while on the job; Raber was further paid for making devil masks, four front parts and one rear part, another old one was repainted, and five devil costumes had their colour renewed. The next group of references concerning the erection of the stage again make clear it is inside the church; and we find the carpenter and his assistants being given an extra payment, a tip, for working overtime on holidays (*in feirtagen*). The relevant 1543 records begin with payments to the same carpenter and assistants for constructing the stage, paid for by the Clerk of Works office. The church records show a series of payments to Vigil Raber: for a volume of four play texts and another from which the play has been directed (*ain register, darin das osterspiel gregiert ist worden*), for gilding the big angel's wings and writing out the texts of the Jews' songs; for renewing the picture of the resurrection (*das pild der urstent zu verneuern*), followed immediately by further expenditure on the picture which is put into the tomb (*das pild, so man ins grab legt*). Though I know of no textual evidence to support this, it would appear that in this performance an image of Christ was placed in the tomb at the burial.

The expenses of this performance were split three ways since the mayor's accounts also show payments to six named individuals who acted as the watch (*feuers halben* 'in case of fire') during the play performances in the Church of Our Lady on Easter Sunday and Monday; and the same fund paid for a meal on the Monday evening after the performances for the thirteen people chiefly involved in organization and performance.

---

[11] We know from elsewhere that such roles were unpopular and that those who took them on could expect to have their costumes and hand props provided, even where most performers were required to pay for their own.

[12] Presumably for Death and therefore presumably a singular, though the word-form could also be plural.

Next year, 1544, the church provost's funds paid for a meal for only four people after a performance which Neumann belives was not a play but a sung passion. It seems that in 1548 only an Ascension Day play was put on, and again afterwards a meal was provided, at the mayor's expense, for a total of sixteen adults including the singers (*cannttorei*) plus ten boys who were Mary and the angels. Four men were paid to act as watch and three others, *lanntt und perckhpottn*, were paid extra to help keep order. Payments were made from the church provost's account to the two who stood guard in the church, to Vigil Raber for a now lost list of items, to the locksmith who made three hooks and six rings required for the ascension of Christ and the angels, and to Lienhart Pfarrkircher for his Lucifer costume. Disaster struck a week later on Saturday 19 May, when the storage shed containing among other items all the wood from the stage burnt down.

In 1550 a Magi play was put on in the town hall on the eve or evening of 6 January (Epiphany) to honour an important visitor; this involved the purchase of paper and glue and payment for making the star. All these items were paid for from the mayor's funds.

The last references to religious plays in Sterzing relate to July 1580. Payment for the board on which Pilate's judgement appears makes clear this is a Passion Play which was done *umb Jacobi*, around St James's day, and referred to only as *di spil*, the plays.

The Sterzing collection also contains material relating to Hall/Tirol, just north of Innsbruck and therefore today in Austria. The archival records begin in 1430 but commentators disagree whether they refer to religious plays. Though Wackernell ascribed the references to a play to be performed at Eastertide, a Passion Play or Easter Play, Neumann queries his precise dating and gives convincing arguments for the view that these first three 1430 records indicate a Shrovetide performance for which a stage was constructed.

Since the 1434 reference is to erecting a stage in church on Easter Eve, it seems to refer to an Easter Play. The 1451 reference is to an Ascension Day play. The 1471 references are again clearly to an Easter Play. These all relate to payments being made from municipal funds for the erecting of stages. Most make clear that it is outdoors, in the 'town garden' (*in der stat garten*). Also from 1471 two references note payments made for wine on stage; payment was also made for Christ's robe and breeches (*pruch*) for the two thieves.

Payments made from town funds in 1479 and 1501 relate chiefly to stage construction, including repainting the three crosses and hell. Noteworthy is that after the latter performance the schoolmaster, who was most probably one Balthasar Zott, was paid a fee, an honorarium (*ain rate hat [ihn] geert*) 1m £5; his *darlegen des spils* appears to mean he was director, rather than just narrator.

DRAMA AND COMMUNITY IN SOUTH TYROL

In 1507 a Last Judgement play was performed at Pentecost, which involved the hasty construction of a stage on the eve and day of Whitsuntide and the same painter as previously, Lorentz Weissman, painted among other things the angels' wings and rainbow, the latter of which also required work by the joiner. We have the best set of details from Hall about the 1511 performance, and this is especially interesting since the 1514 Bozen performance text was based on one from Hall, presumably the Hall 1511 text. Therefore, though this text itself does not survive, we can reasonably assume that it was close to the surviving 1514 Bozen text.

Notably we have an entry in the contemporary chronicle of Franz Schweyger[13] concerning this performance:

> In the year of our Lord 1511 an excellent play was performed in Hall, namely the Passion of Christ, in which were many well known people and prominent individuals, who paid for much of the expenditure out of their own pockets. On Palm Sunday they did the gospels, which for the most part had been preached on during Lent, on Maundy Thursday [they did] the Last Supper together with the Capture at the Mount of Olives, on Good Friday the trial (?*fürfüerung*), scourging, crowning [with thorns], crucifixion, burial, with great solemnity and devotion. And on holy Easter Day the resurrection of Christ together with other happy scenes.

The town records again note payments for erecting and dismantling staging, for painting and repairing the crosses, hell, the shaft for the sponge [for the crucifixion scene] and also three shields with the town's coat of arms. A saddler was also paid for harnesses for the crucified thieves to hang in (*gehenng*) and a strap to go across the Saviour's chest, presumably also as added support during the crucifixion.[14] Hans Strauss the hatter played the part of Judas and was paid for his costume after the performance; earlier commentators have read the last part of this entry as *ain grossen hunt*, a large dog, but Neumann suggests that the word is to be read as "huot", – the man used his costume for a little self-advertisement, and indeed it would be unlikely for the town to take over the long term responsibility for a dog. The painter Gothard was paid for repairing Satan's mask, including painting in teeth, painting Longinus's spear silver, and painting Christ's bodystocking (*leibgewannt*) for the scourging and the resurrection. The town also paid for the costume of the boy who

---

[13] *Franz Schweger's Chronik der Stadt Hall 1303-1572*, ed. by David Schönherr (Innsbruck, 1867); this entry quoted by Neumann, item 1896.

[14] The word used is *krebsriem*; Lexer's *Mittelhochdeutsches Taschenwörterbuch* explains *krebs* as 'brustharnisch in plattenform'.

played the part of the Virgin Mary, and bought from Hanns Perl his Lucifer costume, once more an accommodation for someone who took on an unpopular part.

The last item of expenditure from this year recorded by Neumann is the construction in the attic of the town hall of a storeroom for equipment for the play. We can see from entries such as those cited above that the town now had a considerable stock of props in its ownership which it wanted to preserve for future performances.

The twenty-five surviving secular plays in the Sterzing collection were all copied by Vigil Raber between 1510 and 1535, the biggest concentration in 1510 and 1511, the great majority – twenty out of twenty-five – by 1520, and thereafter none until 1529. Relatively little has been written about them and we lack a reliable modern transcription of the archive entries concerning them to match Neumann's work for the religious drama. Without citing details Bauer[15] reports in his edition of the texts that from 1426 there are records of groups of performers drawn mainly from journeyman members of guilds, and especially because of their social importance in this area, from those associated with mining. It was their custom to appoint a leader responsible for obtaining texts, costumes and props and for organizing the whole performance. From 1527 onwards the Sterzing town records regularly refer to groups of performers made up of local guild members or members of the mining guilds or even peasants from neighbouring villages, who apply for permission to put on their plays. We can envisage Raber in the role of organizer of such a group and of provider of written texts for other groups.

A quite different light on the relationship between drama and community is shed by a consideration of the texts themselves. Raber's collection contains a most unusual play 937 lines long, based on the parable of the Rich Man and Lazarus (Dives and Lazarus). The text several times over tells us that it contains a contemporary warning about the way people behave, not only the rich but also those around them. The rich man's steward states categorically he is there to do his master's will, not what is right; the bailiff (? *ambtmann*) says further that because their master is rich, he knows what it is right to do or refrain from doing, and this extends to his refusing to help beggars like Lazarus. He is on the other hand generous to entertainers and musicians, encouraging one to drink up and have his cup refilled, with the prospect of 'all' getting drunk that evening. The porter notes the old proverb about the young courtier becoming an old beggar (*ain wars sprichwort [...] Junger hofman, allter pettler*) and fears he could end up like Lazarus. The messenger adds that he has never got more

---

[15] See note 5, p. 555.

than the minimum in ten years working for the rich man, who is good only to those who tell him what he wants to hear. When Lazarus dies he is taken by two angels to Abraham, to the chagrin of the devils.

If the above might be argued to be general comment on mankind, what follows seems closer to specific local experience. As soon as the rich man falls ill, before he is dead, the doctor advises the wife, unless she has a very good will in her favour, to look to her own interests because once he is dead his five brothers will be along and soon take everything away. The steward repeats this, telling her to grab what she can while she can and not to bother about her dying husband who is beyond saving. The chamberlain's further repetition ends with 'remember what has happened to other widows'. Other upper servants claim their share of what allegedly has been promised them before their master is dead. Before his death he acknowledges his multifarious sins, all based on selfishness and self-indulgence. Then follows the biblical scene of the rich man in hell imploring Abraham, ending here with the devils rattling chains and producing smoke.

When the brothers arrive to claim their inheritance, the upper servants' attempts to keep some for the widow and themselves lead to a swordfight. In the following scene they report their injuries and admit their guilt: the steward has lost an arm in trying to defend what was not rightfully his against the brothers as heirs and admits he was in the habit of lying to the master about debtors. The chamberlain admits he served his master's every whim and imagined himself better than he really was; the entertainer has lost a foot and admits he indulged himself with drink and caused hardship to others. After all the upper servants have spoken in these terms, the Herald (*Einschreier*) has a monologue in which we are told that the five brothers are now squandering their inheritance, gambling, drinking, cursing, swearing and womanizing. His final words make clear the local relevance:

> This scene is unfortunately seen daily, that is why it is shown here in public. In all wisdom it is acknowledged that such a lifestyle leads to a bad end.[16]

The Herald's final speech again exhorts the audience to take note of the action of this play to 'protect the poor, punish evil and reward good'. It is a message for a society in which there were enough prosperous citizens to whom this message applied, not a mere handful of lords in whose hands all wealth reposed.

---

[16] Though not relevant to the present topic, one must note that the final scene of this play involves four peasants who comment on the action. Though the biblical basis of this play is undeniable, we see here a clear connection to Shrovetide plays.

Lack of space in the present context prevents the citing of further examples from these areas. It is hoped that the above samples show how much there is to be learned from the surviving texts and records from South Tyrol and especially from putting the two together.

Individual and social affiliation in the Nuremberg Shrovetide Plays

KONRAD SCHOELL

IT HAS BECOME COMMONPLACE to maintain that research in the field of the fifteenth-century carnival plays has been set back for decades by nineteenth-century judgements that such plays are 'vulgar' or 'obscene'.[1] In spite of the early editorial achievement of Adalbert von Keller's collection of Shrovetide plays issued in the years 1853-58, comprising more than a hundred plays from Nuremberg (and, it must be said, not up to modern editorial standards),[2] critical interest had to wait almost until the second half of the twentieth century to produce a balanced, unprejudiced and uninhibited approach to the texts. In fact, it is only with the publication of Eckehard Catholy's important thesis of 1961[3] that literary research on carnival plays really got started. It will certainly not be my object here to trace the successes and the failures of subsequent research: its results and any controversies can be left open for further discussion. But without being at all exhaustive, it will be necessary to make a few points, in order to place this essay in its appropriate context and to set at the same time the limitations of its scope.

Many scholarly contributions, both older and more recent, have traced the origins and development of the carnival play in German-speaking countries, and especially in the Nuremberg of the fifteenth and sixteenth centuries. It is a well known and indisputable fact that the city of Nuremberg played a prominent role in this history because

---

[1] K. Goedeke, *Grundriß zur Geschichte der deutschen Dichtung* (Dresden: L. Ehlerman, 1859); see E. Catholy, *Fastnachtspiel* (Stuttgart: Metzler, 1966), p. 2.

[2] A. von Keller (ed.), *Fastnachtspiele aus dem 15. Jahrhundert*, Bd.1-3 u. Nachlese, (Reprint, Darmstadt: Wissenschaftliche Buchgesellschaft, 1965-66).

[3] Eckehard Catholy, *Das Fastnachtspiel des Spätmittelalters. Gestalt und Funktion* (Tübingen: Niemeyer, 1961).

of the number of extant plays and of the extent of this tradition. Although this may be partially due to there being more of a written tradition in the Meistersinger town, the fact is that Nuremberg's Shrovetide plays constitute as much as two thirds of the corpus of some 150 texts, whereas the different tradition in the Hanseatic town of Lübeck comprises only one text,[4] together with seventy-three titles of plays. Several other towns, some in the north, but most in the south of Germany, in Switzerland, and in Tyrol, can also boast a handful of plays.

There is no need to discuss hypothetically the origins of the genre here, a question that was particularly debated in the first half of this century.[5] It is perhaps worth noting, however, that from the Neidhart play tradition onwards (located mainly in the south) the genre was continued by the celebrated fifteenth-century authors Hans Rosenplüt and Hans Folz, leading to the Shrovetide plays of the *Meistersinger* Hans Sachs (the only author whose plays are still performed today, if mostly in amateur school productions) and finally to Jakob Ayrer at the end of the sixteenth century.

One of the main distinctions established by Catholy, and subsequently accepted by all specialists, is that between 'Reihenspiele' (reviews, or linear plays) and 'Handlungsspiele' (plays with action). The first group is based on series with an enumerative structure, whereas the second presents a more 'dramatically' organized plot, so that it is tempting to see in this shift the idea of there being two successive phases in the evolution. In the fifteenth century, both kinds of plays adopt essentially the same overall construction, beginning with a 'Praecursor', or herald, a kind of prologue figure, who enters, greets the assembled company and demands silence as well as free space for the performance; and ending with an 'Ausschreier', or epilogue, who asks for drink, invites the audience to dance, and apologizes for any bad language that may have offended the audience. Some plays by Hans Folz and especially Hans Sachs's later variation on the genre are characterized, finally, by the signature of the author in the very last verses of the Ausschreier: 'Dütz spricht Hans folz der barbierer' (*Die Bauernheirat*); 'Daß uns kein unrhat darauß wachß, / Wünscht uns zu Nürnberg H(ans) Sachs.' (*Der Eifersüchtige*).

---

[4] *Henselin oder Von der Rechtfertigkeit* (About Righteousness).

[5] Notably by Robert Stumpfl, who saw its origin in Germanic men's organizations; for a full discussion see the studies of E. Catholy and almost every book or article on the Shrovetide plays.

THE NUREMBERG SHROVETIDE PLAYS

Fifteenth-century plays of 200 lines' average length reveal no interior organization into scenes unless we take the term at its face value by regarding a character's entering and leaving the stage as a new scene (of which there are a great many, especially in the 'review' plays). By Hans Sachs's time, Shrovetide plays comprised more than 300 lines, but those of Hans Folz already could go up to over 400 lines in the case of an important subject such as that of King Solomon and Markolf.

As to style and form, the preoccupation with bodily functions, often crudely expressed, had been responsible for the long shadows cast over the genre, a linguistic obscenity which one may suppose also had its echo in the physical 'business' that would no doubt have accompanied the performance. However, there is no evidence, for instance, of actors wearing prominent fake *phalloi*, an item of costume well known in the history of comic theatre. Among the students of Shrovetide plays, Rüdiger Krohn has offered a most detailed analysis of their obscene nature, which he explains, as do other scholars, by stressing their function as a safety valve.[6] In fact little is known about how the plays were performed; the little we do know has been deduced from the texts themselves or else from ordinances and interdictions imposed by the city council.[7] It is obvious that the young men playing female parts used cross-dressing and disguise that probably exaggerated the female form. It may be, as some interdictions suggest, that the actors sometimes wore masks, and it is quite certain that all of them put on some sort of disguise according to their role. But even in this dressing-up function, they remained closely linked to their audience, among whom many people at that time of the year would also have been in disguise. One of Catholy's fundamental findings is that there was no essential difference between actors and public and that their mutual roles could easily be exchanged during the course of the evening.[8]

---

[6] Rüdiger Krohn, *Der unanständige Bürger. Untersuchungen zum Obszönen in den Nürnberger Fastnachtspielen des 15. Jahrhunderts* (Kronberg/Taunus: Scriptor, 1974).

[7] See A. Müller, 'Zensurpolitik der Reichsstadt Nürnberg', *Mitteilungen des Vereins für Geschichte der Stadt Nürnberg* 49 (1959), 66-169.

[8] A comprehensive general treatment of the social types in the Shrovetide plays is to be found in the study by Edelgard DuBruck, which also attempts an analysis, as far as possible given the lack of evidence from detailed reports or illustrations, of those elements that the semiotics of performance have taught us to distinguish. E. DuBruck, *Aspects of Fifteenth-Century Society in the German Carnival Comedies. Speculum Hominis* (Lewiston, NY; Lampeter: Mellen, 1993).

In contrast to the otherwise similar tradition of performing carnival plays in Lübeck, where young upper-class men, members of the 'Zirkelbrüderschaft', acted in the plays,[9] in Nuremberg references in the city council records reveal that there the organizers and performers of the plays were young middle-class artisans who had to request permission each time from the city council. During carnival time they frequented taverns and probably middle-class houses in order to perform in the hall among the guests, or to private groups already assembled for a drink and some other kind of entertainment. As in the case of the three best known authors of Nuremberg carnival plays, Hans Rosenplüt, Hans Folz, and Hans Sachs, the dramatists were both artisans and well-known poets whose literary activities ranged much more widely than Shrovetide plays. Hans Folz and, a century later, Hans Sachs, obtained most of their contemporary renown as 'Meistersinger' poets. There is some uncertainty and dispute amongst critics as to the question of the audience: whether people of all social ranks had access to the performances,[10] or whether the audience was more likely to be limited to the people and the middle classes and to exclude the patricians.[11]

For an historical appreciation it is indeed most important to be aware of the scope of the intention of the Nuremberg Shrovetide plays. In this context we exclude the serious plays, some of which even adopt a precise political position. In the tradition of carnival and the feast of fools, the Shrovetide play will certainly be a sign of a temporarily upside-down world which functions as a safety valve for oppression and grievances (Lenk, Krohn). Once a year allowance is made to give vent to critical feelings and especially to take into consideration some release for the suppressed sexuality of journeymen who had to wait many long years before they were admitted as masters and allowed to marry. On the other hand, Dietz-Rüdiger Moser argued in the 1970s that the carnival play was very closely and directly integrated into religious *praxis,* suggesting that even the animal character and the obscene are part of the divinely conceived

---

[9] On the Lübeck Shrovetide plays, see E.H. Fischer, *Lübecker Theater und Theaterleben in frühester Zeit bis zur Mitte des 18. Jahrhunderts* (Lübeck: Veröffentlichungen der Gesellschaft Lübecker Theaterfreunde, 2, 1932), and the article by Hansjürgen Linke, 'Mittelalterliche Fastnachspiele Lübecker Patrizier', *Lübeckische Blätter,* N.R. 88, Nr.3 (1952).

[10] Dieter Wuttke, 'Nachwort', in Dieter Wuttke (ed.), *Fastnachtspiele des 15.und 16. Jahrhunderts* (Stuttgart: Reclam, 1973), p.424.

[11] R. Krohn, op. cit., and W. Lenk, *Das Nürnberger Fastnachtspiel des 15. Jahrhunderts. Ein Beitrag zur Theorie und zur Interpretation des Fastnachtspiels als Dichtung* (Berlin: Akademie Verlag, 1966).

world, and even that the carnival play serves the moral teaching of the church *ex negativo*.[12] In this more 'medieval' view, then, as long as the Catholic faith was predominant, carnival and the carnival play function as a different kind of religious theatre, a role which changed only with the rise of Protestant austerity.

After this brief review of the generally accepted, and only occasionally controversial, positions about the Nuremberg Shrovetide plays, we are now ready to consider more closely the question of the relationship between community and individual, between integration into different social groups and the affirmation of individuality.

There are numerous documents on the city of Nuremberg, most of which have been exploited. From monographs and collections of essays like those published by G. Pfeiffer[13] and by Horst Brunner[14] it is easy for us to be informed about the size of the city (22,800 inhabitants in 1430), about the attraction of a city offering peace and security, about political and social structures, and especially about political power. In contrast to other large German cities, by the end of the fourteenth century guilds had lost their political power to the patricians. The city council is elected, but is in fact composed of patricians, members of the ruling families, with little opportunity for a social climber to enter its ranks. In this rich city, where wealth is founded on major and foreign commerce, the political order is strongly dependent on economic and social order.[15] To be admitted as citizens, people had to prove their wealth. Even if Nuremberg also had a prosperous cultural life, the education offered by a large number of schools was of interest not to the oligarchy, but rather to the upper middle classes. In spite of the widely known poetry clubs of the 'Meistersinger', literature was not an important consideration for most of the inhabitants, only perhaps as theatre, in the form of spiritual or carnival plays. As the different social ranks seem to have been rigidly separated, it is sensible to believe, however, that the leading class did

---

[12] Dietz-Rüdiger Moser, 'Fastnacht und Fastnachtspiel. Zur Säkularisierung geistlicher Volksschauspiele bei Hans Sachs und ihrer Vorgeschichte', in *Hans Sachs und Nürnberg: Bedingungen und Probleme*, ed. by Horst Brunner et al. (Nürnberg: Verein für Geschichte der Stadt Nürnberg, 1976); and *Fastnacht-Fasching-Karneval. Das Fest der verkehrten Welt* (Graz-Köln-Wien: Styria, 1986).

[13] G. Pfeiffer (ed.), *Nürnberg - Geschichte einer europäischen Stadt* (Munich: Beck, 1971).

[14] Horst Brunner (ed.), *Literatur in der Stadt. Begegnungen und Beispiele städtischer Literatur des 15. bis 17. Jahrhunderts* (Göppingen: Kümmerle, 1982).

[15] R. Endres, 'Sozial- und Bildungsstrukturen fränkischer Reichsstädte im Spätmittelalter und in der Frühen Neuzeit', in *Literatur in der Stadt*, ed. by H. Brunner, pp. 37-72.

not regularly take part in such artisans' amusement as the Shrovetide plays. What is known on the other hand is that, conscious of the subversive element in all popular amusements,[16] but without attempting to forbid them entirely, the city council continuously restricted carnival entertainments, and sought to keep an eye on those striving to put more critical elements into their performances (Krohn).

Approaching life in a late medieval city like Nuremberg from a twentieth-century point of view, we must bear in mind the fact that, though enclosed by ditches, walls and gates, offering security to its inhabitants, the city, though densely populated, was divided into quarters of closely-knit social communities, according to rank and wealth, and even into streets in which different trades were plied. What is even more important for a clear understanding of community and social conflicts is the fact that the difference between townspeople and village folk was not so pronounced. First of all, most citizens had their fields and earned some revenue from outside the city; also, many country people settled just outside the city walls in order to be near to the market and to try to gain admittance to live within the walls. In the light of this knowledge, the controversy between townsmen and peasants, often at the centre of interest in Shrovetide plays, as well as in many narrative tales (Schwänke), does not correspond to a total opposition between town and countryside.

All critics have noted that in the Nuremberg carnival plays, the social group most widely represented is that of the peasants.[17] In addition, there are servants and maids, craftsmen, doctors, judges, priests and monks, a few knights and representatives of the aristocracy, but hardly any recognizable patrician or other representative of the city oligarchy. It is true, however, that a great many of the characters cannot be easily attached to an identifiable social group, especially the women, who probably belonged either to the peasantry or to the town's artisan class, and represented a social group by themselves and with specific attitudes. Our interest here is not in statistics, but the small number of members of the upper classes and on the other hand the mass of peasants (and their wives, servants and maids) must be taken into consideration if we are to discover the intention of these plays.

---

[16] See Michael Bachtin, *Literatur und Karneval. Zur Romantheorie und Lachkultur*; transl. by A.Kämpfe, (Munich: Fischer Taschenbuch Verlag, 1969).

[17] See John E. Tailby, 'Peasants in 15th-Century Fastnachtspiele from Nuremberg', *Daphnis* 4 (1975), 172-78, and H. Ragotzky, 'Der Bauer in der Narrenrolle. Zur Funktion "verkehrter Welt" im frühen Nürnberger Fastnachtspiel', in *Typus und Individualität im Mittelalter*, ed. by H. Wenzel (Munich: Fink, 1983), pp. 77-101.

THE NUREMBERG SHROVETIDE PLAYS

First of all, let us recall that the Shrovetide play is an urban event, directly related to the season of liberty that is carnival, and as such regarded with suspicion by the authorities because the revolutionary element, present in each masquerade and inherent in each representation of the world turned upside-down, could be dangerous for the reigning authorities. It therefore sounds perfectly reasonable that authors and actors, aware of their precarious situation would, by adopting a kind of self-censorship, refrain from representing (in other words mocking) the urban upper classes. The same reasoning may account for the comparatively small representation of middle-class craftsmen in the plays, if we are agreed that the leading group of actors were journeymen who had still to display some level of conformity in order sooner or later to be accepted into full mastership. This would mean that even the carnival season was not free from oppression or at least from self-imposed restrictions. Following the same line of argument, it would seem easier in a Reichsstadt like Nuremberg, subject directly only to the Emperor, to feature time and again a knight who may be out of touch with more modern times, e.g. *Die verdient Ritterschaft* ('Merited Knighthood', Keller, no. 47). With such motifs, the carnival play demonstrates the continuation of a tradition which had begun with the Neidhart plays, showing the decay of courtly culture.[18] On the other hand, it would appear daring to have the peasant 'Markolf' outwit 'King Salomon', in whose rank the audience would certainly see an image of the Emperor himself.[19] Yet the subject was a traditional one in narrative literature to such a degree that the scandal would probably have been less perceptible. There was certainly much less risk, and much more fun, in putting on stage a quack doctor[20] – that stock figure of all comic literature representing the very embodiment of fake authority – or a corrupt, incompetent judge,[21] or a lascivious monk or priest[22], whose sins are apparent in the contrast between his profession and the actual life he leads. A similar idea may be the reason for the peasant's frequent presence on

---

[18] See B. Knühl, *Die Komik in Heinrich Wittenwilers 'Ring' im Vergleich zu den Fastnachtspielen des 15. Jahrhunderts* (Göppingen: Kümmerle, 1981), p. 170.

[19] See also *Ein Spil von einem Keiser und ein Apt* ('A Play about an Emperor and an Abbot', Keller, no. 22).

[20] e.g., *Ein Spil von einem Arzt und einem kranken Paur* ('A Play about a Doctor and a Sick Peasant', Keller no. 6, and many more).

[21] e.g., *Ein hubsch Vasnachtspil* ('A Pleasant Shrovetide Play', Keller no. 24, as *Das lustige Gerichtspiel* in Wuttke's edition, no. 4).

[22] e.g., *Vasnachtsspil vom Münch Berchtolt* ('Shrovetide play of the Monk Berchtolt', Keller no. 66).

the boards. For the audience in Nuremberg, in spite of his comparative proximity mentioned earlier, the countryman is a person from outside, someone who does not belong to the ruling classes, perceived as an intruder into the urban world. This would be especially true if the peasant-figure were invariably represented as the boorish rustic, the naïve and predestined victim of a practical joke in bad taste. He may indeed be simple-minded, as in many other forms of late medieval European literature, not least the theatre (from the *badin* of French farce to the Spanish *bobo*-figure),[23] but he will, at the same time, be identified with the fool, an ubiquitous character in late medieval and Renaissance literature. In this function he is certainly not merely naïve, but also clever in all practical issues, sometimes even outwitting his superiors. The aforementioned Markolf is certainly also a 'wise-fool' character. This is part of the subversive element of the Shrovetide play. In this respect, however, more often than not, the peasant-fool finds a master in his wife, a practical, domineering figure in some Shrovetide plays, in which both of them, at least by the time of Hans Sachs, are successfully cheated by the wandering scholar.[24]

There is much more to be said about the peasant in the Shrovetide plays. In his simple, rural life, as imagined by an urban public, he represents something of the old bucolic function, an escape into the ideal. In his case, however, the muses of music, dance and poetry, are little referred to, and similarly, perhaps, the idea of leisure, but rather he presents the image of an unrestricted, sensual life.[25] In this respect the peasant's life may well be a source of envy to the burghers who feel more controlled by civil and ecclesiastic authority. The Shrovetide peasant character thus becomes a figure for compensatory identification for the urban spectator. On the other hand, being a person from outside, he may also function as a scapegoat, in whom many prohibited instincts are represented and scorned. This function is certainly responsible for so many 'dirty' speeches uttered by peasants, especially their stressing of matters anal and their boasting about sexual matters. It would seem that the peasant is closer to nature in that he is allowed to live out (but also, mainly, to speak of) overeating, defecation, fornication, and even to set up a competition for such bodily functions.

---

[23] cf. Ch. Mazouer, *Le personnage du naïf dans le théâtre comique du moyen âge à Marivaux* (Paris: Klincksieck, 1979), and J. Brotherton, *The Pastor-bobo in the Spanish Theatre before the Time of Lope de Vega* (London: Tamesis, 1975).

[24] One of the best known examples is in the play *Der farendt Schuler im Paradeiß* ('The Wandering Scholar in Paradise'; see Hans Sachs, *Meistergesänge, Fastnachtspiele, Schwänke*, ed. by E. Geiger (Stuttgart: Reclam, 1969).

[25] Krohn, p.112.

THE NUREMBERG SHROVETIDE PLAYS

Obviously all representatives of social groups, who do not exist by themselves, peasants included, will have to be considered in opposition, and this is shown mostly in contrasting couples: peasants are opposed to burghers, to a doctor, to a knight, even to a king, to a priest, to a scholar and most often to other peasants, to their wives and to servants. Whereas the peasant figure, among many stereotypical examples, sometimes shows individual characteristics (e.g. Markolf), the country-women are very similar to each other. Among them, it seems to be difficult to distinguish individual traits. In fact their characteristics or failings are mainly those presupposed by age-old antifeminist attitudes: sensuality, a naïvety that borders on stupidity and stubbornness but, on the other hand, cunning and deceit. In general we may say that the peasant woman possesses the same traits as her husband, but to an even more prominent degree.

After these general remarks on the characters, we will now take a few examples for more detailed analysis, trying to find out to what degree the characters are representatives of a given social group, and when and where they have the opportunity to become individuals. Our first example will be *Der Bauer und der Bock* ('The Peasant and the Buck'),[26] attributed to Hans Rosenplüt. The particular importance of Rosenplüt's contribution is due not only to the fact that he is the first known author of Nuremberg Shrovetide plays, but that in this early period, as well as writing comic plays, he also composed serious Shrovetide plays with a political theme, plays such as *Des Türken Fastnachtspiel* ('The Shrovetide Play of the Turkish Emperor').[27] The comic play *Der Bauer und der Bock* consists of 176 lines of which sixteen at the beginning and twenty at the end are spoken by the intermediary character of the herald, whereas the rest forms an action play with three main characters. Even in the 'prologue', little is said about the audience, but at the end, in the herald's epilogue-like farewell addressed to 'herr der wirt' [mine host] there is the promise that they will be back: 'Und wollen euch ettebas neues machen, das ir

---

[26] The text is published in the editon by D. Wuttke, no. 3. In Keller's edition the old title reads: 'Gar ain hüpschs und aubenteirlichs Vasnachtspil von ainem Edelman seiner Frauen, die sich understuont ainen seiner Pauren zuo ainer Lügin pringen' no. 46.

[27] A general appreciation of Hans Rosenplüt's works is to be found in J. Reichel, 'Handwerkerleben und Handwerkerdichtung im spätmittelalterlichen Nürnberg: Hans Rosenplüt genannt Schnepper', in *Literatur in der Stadt*, ed. by H. Brunner pp. 115-42. *Des Türken Fastnachtspiel* is analyzed together with some other more serious Shrovetide plays, in Joël Lefebvre, *Les fols et la folie. Etude sur les genres du comique et la création littéraire en Allemagne pendant la Renaissance* (Paris: Klincksieck, 1968), p. 33 ss.

und alles euer haußgesinde must lachen.' [And we will present you something new, in order to make you and all your servants laugh]. It thus seems clear that in this case, where host and servants but not guests are expressly mentioned, the performance was meant to take place in a private house. The group of actors on the other hand, though probably close to the audience socially, is clearly distinguished by the same farewell speech of the herald which, as so often, begins with an excuse: 'ob wir es zu grob hetten gespunnen...' [if we have spun it too coarsely...], but continues with the confirmation that the troupe will go on learning more about the world's activity, in order to be able to present a new play. For this they will take lessons in two kinds of schools: first among the vagabond musicians near the townhall and then near the 'smelzhutten', probably an ill-famed haunt of drinking, gambling and cheating.[28] It is in any case certain that by mentioning these 'schools', the herald is stressing the real-life inspiration of their plays and the 'imago vitae' function of comic theatre, whilst also indicating the outsider role of musicians and other entertainers to whom he and his group at least temporarily belong.

At the beginning of the play the herald had given the exposition and a kind of shorthand synopsis of the play up to its climax: a woman (according to the title of Keller's edition, the knight's wife) tries to make a peasant, in this case an honest man who has never told a lie, commit perjury. The structure of the play, as so often, will then be that of a bet. As the wager is not set up directly between the woman and the peasant, but rather between the woman and the gentleman, there are three major characters in the play. Only the person of higher rank has a name: Jungkher Dietrich von Turnau, which does not add very much to his individuality. In the forty lines he has to speak, he never goes farther than his dominant role of a just and equal master, though his first 'scene' with the peasant has the function of exposing the special confidence the master has in his farmer. After this short dialogue leading to the special task for the peasant to undertake and to feed the master's favourite buck, the woman, who does not have a personal name either but is presented as an 'eynfeltig frau' ('a simple woman'), almost without any introduction, proposes a wager to the knight. She pretends to be able to make the peasant lie and thus be untrue to his reputation, wagering three bulls and four cows. This woman certainly must have special qualities, which are displayed by the way she is conscious and sure of her power. In metaphorical language she speaks of the net in which she will ensnare the peasant, and of the bonds with which she will bind him.

---

[28] cf. Wuttke's comment.

THE NUREMBERG SHROVETIDE PLAYS

After she has left to try out her power, four men refer the case to precedent, citing the traditional examples of Aristotle, Solomon and Samson, or speaking more generally of the power of sexuality to explain the tricks that women play successfully on men. These four male figures, 'herren' as the knight addresses them, have no social or individual traits. Even more than in many of the Reihenspiele ('reviews') with their sequence of peasants boasting or telling of their experiences, they are given the task of distributing the series of examples among the four of them, each of whom is allowed exactly eight verses. This bestows a kind of chorus function on them. Dramatically, of course, this interruption of the plot serves to leave some time for the woman's stratagem. Shortly afterwards, she returns to the gentleman, fully confident of her success. But the peasant, in what is the longest speech in the play (18 lines), explains his shame, thus in reality saving his honour. First directly, and then using conventional sexual metaphors, he confesses to having been lured and cheated by a lovely woman to whom he had to offer the buck as a present. In his sincere way he admits that the woman had suggested that he should tell his master the lie that a wolf had carried off the buck:

Sie lert mich, ich solt euch ein lugen sagen,
In hett ein wolff hinweck getragen.

[She taught me I should tell you a lie/ that a wolf had taken him away, lines 141-142]

Of course, the master has won the bet against the woman, and being a just person he not only excuses the peasant's human failing, but even offers him three years rent-free. It might seem that the peasant here represents the conventional image of the peasant in carnival plays: his comparatively long speech after the deed employs metaphors of sexuality, thus reinforcing the idea of the peasant reduced to the main bodily functions, this time, however, minus defecation. But there is more to his character than this. For the development of the action, his main characteristic has to be his honesty. We are told from the outset that he will never tell a lie, and that his master has every confidence in him – and our peasant indeed proves to be true to this quality. Being only human, however, he is prone to temptation, especially if it presents itself as a lovely woman. What is much more important for his evaluation as a complex and individualized character is the fact that he is entirely conscious of his strengths and his faults. In the first scene with his master, he apologises for being late paying the rent. He then explains that honesty is inborn in him. This is certainly one of the very rare Shrovetide plays in which a person speaks of his parents and of his moral heritage: *Mein vater und mutter kein lug nicht tetten* [My father and my mother never told lies, v. 44]. And after his fall, our peasant feels guilty and admits the stupidity of his action. He explains the result of the temptation in him as a kind of temporary loss of reason: *Das ich meiner synne nicht halber hett* [So that I had not half of my senses, v.134]. This belated but clear insight reveals a degree of self-reflection and self-criticism, faculties which lead me to interpret the character as a complex and individualized person.

I am certainly not much inclined to overdo this kind of interpretation, but I think I may be allowed to venture a second, more medieval interpretation. Beneath the comic surface of the play we may at the same time find an allegory of the way of the sinner. Humanity is portrayed in the peasant who is subject to a just master, in whom we may see God. The scheming woman is an Eve figure, perhaps an allegory of Temptation defeating Man who is inclined to overestimate his strength and self-control. But through consciousness of his fault, through confession and contrition, he will find forgiveness and grace, even an unmerited indulgence from the Almighty. According to this view, this comic Shrovetide play offers many features in common with a morality play.

I have taken the opportunity elsewhere, as have other critics, to mention one of the most frequently discussed carnival plays of the second great master of the genre, Hans Folz, namely *König Salomon und Markolff*.[29] A further discussion of this play would by far exceed the limits of this essay. Instead, I have chosen another of Hans Folz's plays, *Die Bauernheirat* ('The Peasant's Marriage'),[30] in order to explain the characters and their opposition. This text gives a good idea of the typical Shrovetide play themes of the fifteenth century. As usual, the Praecursor, or 'Ausschreyer', starts by greeting the audience and then pretends to have been invited to make peace between quarrelling parties. However, his main interest seems to be in

---

[29] See K. Schoell, *La Farce du quinzième siècle* (Tübingen: Narr, 1992), chapter I 'Les origines et les intentions du théâtre profane du XVe siècle en France et en Allemagne'. There is thus no need to return to it here, other than to repeat that, as prominent and as individualized as he may seem, the character of the peasant Markolf is certainly meant to signify the fool. The most extensive analyses of this play are to be found in Catholy's book of 1961 and several articles by W. Lenk, especially: 'Salomon und Markolf. Die dichterische Gestaltung gegensätzlicher Existenzweisen des Menschen in der Klassengesellschaft', in *Grundpositionen der deutschen Literatur im 16. Jahrhundert* (Berlin-Weimar: Aufbau-Verlag, 1972), pp. 175-98.

[30] The quotations are again taken from the edition by D. Wuttke, no. 7.

drinking. In this play he is not the type who provides a short exposition but, instead, one of the principal characters, the father of the bridegroom: knowing that the young couple have already had sexual relations, the parents want them to be married. But the quarrel arises very quickly as to the morals of the bride, called Geut, a contention which breaks up the party and leads to a thrashing. Somebody mentions an illegitimate child of hers, somebody else tries to recommend her as a 'versuchte diern' ('an experienced girl'), and another peasant gives more details of the favours she granted to the servants at harvest time. The anti-feminism here develops into blame of the bride's immoral behaviour, some of the peasants themselves pretending to know her intimately, and providing a kind of burlesque image of her, decorated with metaphors for genitals; even her own father indulges in a negative portrait which in his case ends up in scatology. At first interested in the dowry, the bridegroom finally asks to be delivered from Geut.

All the peasant bystanders, taking the side of one family or the other, are interchangeable characters. Even when they recount their personal experience, there is no trace at all in their speech of individualization. The same is true of the older generation, the fathers, whose interest is limited to the desire simply to conclude the match. The bridegroom himself, Heintz, at least shows a degree of evolution by gradually becoming afraid of Geut and by ultimately losing interest in her.

Let us now consider the bride Geut, certainly the most important character in the play, as two thirds of the lines prepare us for her appearance. Without taking part in the discussion (and probably entering later than the other characters), but in some way confirming her image of a young woman conscious of her powers and her desires, Geut puts forward her two conditions in a personal way:

Das wir das nöttigest nit vergessen,
Frag, ob er auch mug epffel essen.

[In order not to forget the most important thing, / ask him whether he likes to eat apples, (an allusion to sexual interest) (lines 115-16)], and:

Ir herrn, noch ains das ding ich auss:
Ich wil sein ungeschlagen gar.

[Gentlemen, one more condition, I require: / I do not wish to be beaten, (lines 128-29)]

She is a young woman with her own point of view, with clearly defined personal desires and the strength to live up to them and to defend them. To make sure she will be understood, she immediately exercises her strength on one of the peasants, who hypothetically promises her a good thrashing if she were his wife. Certainly her speech and actions confirm the general image of women marked by anti-feminism as being both sensual and quarrelsome, but Geut is one of the persons able consciously to take upon herself these characteristics. And finally, the same Geut, after being refused by the bridegroom Heintz, is capable of a disgusting self-portrait of ironic and insulting ugliness ending in the traditional scatological detail. This character is certainly not an image of beauty or charm, but we find expressed in her some personal ideas and desires.

At the time of Hans Sachs in the middle of the sixteenth century, the form of the Shrovetide play had changed because of developments in stagecraft at that time. The ritual beginning and ending with a specially informed person, a herald or proclaimer who remains outside the plot, was seen as no longer necessary, and there remains little contact with the audience in a given play, which is performed on a special stage in front of people who had come there for that purpose, and were thus prepared to see a performance. What remains of the 'supplementary text' is mainly expressed in the very last lines in the form of a moral, giving a lesson and also providing the signature of the author Hans Sachs.[31]

Taking as an example *Das Kälberbrüten* ('The Hatching of Calves')[32] of 1551, we become aware that Hans Sachs, also an experienced writer of regular comedies and tragedies in the Renaissance style, based his Shrovetide plays largely on monologues. The monologues in this play, however, in contrast to those of most earlier carnival plays, are no longer simply a narration of what had happened before or backstage, but are often performative, in the sense that they indicate a character's next movement in phrases such as: 'Ich will...' ('I am going to...'); or else they are often real monologues of decision as we know them from later developments in the theatre, as in Shakespeare, for example.

Das Kälberbrüten is a play about an unhappy marriage. The country woman, Gredt, is the main character, having both the opening

---

[31] Among so many critiques of Hans Sachs' work, a good introduction can be found in the collection of essays ed. by H. Brunner, G. Hirschmann, and F. Schnelbögl, *Hans Sachs und Nürnberg* (Nürnberg: M. Edelmann, 1976), in our context especially the articles by H. Brunner, D.R. Moser and B. Könneker.

[32] *Fastnachtspiele des 15. und 16. Jahrhunderts*, ed. by D. Wuttke, no. 12.

monologue and the closing speech. Gredt complains about her lazy and stupid husband, who oversleeps in the morning, whereas she has already milked the cow and is ready to go off to market. The marriage situation is somewhat different from most others featured in farces or Shrovetide plays. Here, the wife's dominant position is not contested by the husband. It is true that she has done most of the work, but he spontaneously promises to do the housework in her absence. Of course, she has further orders and instructions to give him before leaving. In terms of traditional values, their's is a topsy-turvy world, in which the wife decides and gives the orders, goes off to market, and stops off for a drink on the way back; whereas Hans, the husband, does the housework, from sweeping to cooking. Or rather that is what he is supposed to do according to the orders of his wife, but being phlegmatic and simple-minded, he oversleeps and forgets what she has bidden him to do. Hans is certainly not a person capable of rebellion, but he naïvely tries to find expedients, thinking that calves are hatched like chicken or geese. For this reason, he sits on a slab of mouldy cheese, hoping to get calves out of the worms. The wife gets the priest to exorcize her husband, but the priest is of the opinion that the husband should be the master. There is no need to relate the context in detail; the basic pattern clearly provides consecutive examples of Hans's foolish behaviour, but there is much more action than narration, and the plot is constructed so as to increase suspense. The priest is not an important character here and in contrast to many carnival clerics or monks he does not seem to be tempted by the woman. The only comic effect in relation to this character arises from the fact that he changes sides. First called upon by Gredt to help her in her problems with a husband who seems to be under some kind of spell, he expresses the conventional idea of the husband's dominant role; and when he is attacked by her, instead of exorcizing her demon as he would have wished, he cravenly runs away.

One might suppose that given their names and the traditional starting-point of a marital complaint, Hans and Gredt represent the traditional peasant and his wife. But there are quite a few changes and additions: the upside-down situation, more developed here than anywhere else, is well known from fools' literature, and intended in this play to make fun of both characters and to criticize their extravagant behaviour. But the action also provides an opportunity to develop the characters in a more individualized way. Hans, as we have seen, is lazy and simple-minded, and afraid of his wife, but he is also a good-natured person, willing to do the housework even before he is asked to do so:

So wil ich ein weil heußlich sein,
Die stuben kern und heitzen ein:
Das kan ich als so wol als du.

[Meanwhile I will stay at home,/ sweep the room and make a fire: / this I know as well as you, (lines 35-37)]

After his misbehaviour, he feels genuinely sorry, as well as afraid of his wife's reaction. In his most extended monologue we can see a person in some distress, a victim of self-doubt:

Das ist nun fehl! wie sols mir gehn?
Wie wirdt ich mit meim Weyb bestehen?

[This is now lost! What shall become of me? / How can I get on with my wife? (lines 109-10)]

He reflects on what the outcome might be, wondering about the hastily invented solution:

Was schatz, ob ich versuch die kunst?

[What harm is there, if I try the trick? (line 124)].

A simple-minded person, he is certainly conscious of the fact that his cowardly nature is the cause of all his strange behaviour, and thus admits the reasons for his actions:

Forcht, sorg und angst mich lehren thet,
Welche ich het zu meiner Frauen.

[Fear, sorrow and fright of my wife/ taught me a lesson (lines 248-49)]

In contrast to other fools of comic theatre, however, there is nothing malicious or cunning about him. He is quite unlike a Markolf or a Thibault Aignelet, even though his stock reply to the questions and speeches of Gredt and the priest is 'pff!, pff!, ch!, ch!', imitating a broody goose, and thus perhaps recalling the 'bee' of the foolish yet cunning shepherd of *Maître Pierre Pathelin*.[33] He only awakes from his sleepy mood when his wife and the priest try to get him out of his basket and fall down upon him.

---

[33] E. DuBruck sees an even more direct reminder of *Maître Pathelin* in Shrovetide play no. 107 of Keller's edition: *Der kluge Knecht* ('The Clever Servant'); the widespread popularity of *La Farce de Maître Pathelin* is well known.

THE NUREMBERG SHROVETIDE PLAYS

Let us conclude this brief review of the characters with a consideration of the characterization of the peasant's wife, Gredt. In contrast to the general image of womankind in Shrovetide plays, she completely lacks any sensuality. On the other hand, obstinacy and the desire to dominate are expressed to the extreme in her character. She is the one who organizes and issues orders – but she does most of the outside work, too. We have already mentioned that this attitude is part of the upside-down world and will be condemned by the authority of the priest. But Hans Sachs takes care to motivate his character's action. The initial monologue-prologue, a complaint by a mismatched wife, but without any allusion to their sexual life, serves to explain her behaviour to the audience. She is unhappy about the laziness of her husband, though she is readily inclined to exaggerate the situation of course, pretending that Hans would be condemned and hanged were it not for her. (What for? Even if sloth is considered one of the deadly sins, it is hardly a hanging offence.) But later on, returning home, she shows sympathy for Hans, or fear of a greater misfortune:

> Ich glaub, mein Narr hab sich erhenckt.
> Nit wunder wer, ich thet mich verfluchen.
>
> [I believe my fool has hanged himself. / This wouldn't be astonishing,
> [but] I would curse myself (lines 140-141)].

From experience she has no doubt that everything goes wrong at home, and finds a kind of revenge in drinking a glass of wine on her way home from market. Gredt, however, is not really inclined to complain quietly, for she is essentially a dominant person, threatening to beat her husband, as she often does (lines 150-51; 278-79), or to confine him to the house (line 299). She orders Hans to go out into the courtyard to chop wood, and if he refuses, she will not give him anything to eat:

> Haust du mir heind das holtz nit auff,
> So wil ich dir nit zfressen geben...
>
> [If you don't chop the wood today,/ I won't feed you (lines 316-17)].

When the priest sides with the husband, she threatens him as well and turns him out. After the quarrel is over, however, still grumbling at her husband, she realizes that there is no good complaining. Resigned to her situation, she sends Hans off to the tavern to fetch wine for them to drink and forget their anger:

Geh gleich inß Wirtzhauß, hol uns Wein,
Wöln das heutig marckgelt verzechen,
Zu samb sitzen, am Wein uns rechen
Und vergessen als ungemachs.
Glück bringt als wider, spricht H(ans) Sachs.

[Go quickly to the tavern and fetch wine for us; / we will drink the money from today's market, / stay together, take our revenge on the wine,/ and forget all mischief. / Fortune will bring back everything, so says Hans Sachs.]

Having outlined the social backdrop of fifteenth-century Nuremberg and having attempted a broad appreciation of Shrovetide plays, it has been my intention to focus on the characters in these plays. Most often it is clearly the peasant, the wife, the judge, the priest, who behave as representatives of their state and condition. However, I believe I have been able to show by means of a few examples taken from the fifteenth and the sixteenth centuries that there are indeed characters in Shrovetide plays who transcend the simple role of members of a social group or that of a mere voice in a chorus, to acquire a degree of individuality by virtue of their self-awareness. Knowing and admitting one's faults (*Der Bauer und der Bock*), living up to one's own ideas and desires (*Die Bauernhochzeit*), and being prone to self-doubt (*Das Kälberbrüten*) may be said to constitute so many indications of individual traits, even though the context may lend itself to allegorical interpretation, to anti-feminism, to ludicrous bodily functions, or to the image of a topsy-turvy world inhabited exclusively by fools.

Performing medieval Irish communities

ALAN J. FLETCHER

A READER WHO LOOKS for a stable meaning in this title will not find one. It is wilfully ambiguous. Yet while in that regard it may seem an unhelpful entrée to the topic of this chapter, it is the only just way of broaching it. The topic to be explored here – though for limitations of space perforce cursorily – is the dense question of performance in medieval Ireland.[1] In most scholarly histories of European drama and performance, Ireland remains a *terra incognita*, seldom even adverted to unless as a brief adjunct to discussion of her neighbour and, after 1169, colonizer, England.[2] And this virtual silence prevails despite the survival in Ireland of a unique body of textual evidence, rich and ancient, that bears stoutly on the matter. Which were the communities that did the performing, to read the ambiguous title one way, or to read it another, which were the communities that were performed? Both questions, mutually related, need asking in order to open up a largely neglected field of enquiry into performance history at the westernmost edge of Europe. Indeed, an effort to understand the landscape of early Irish performance may throw some comparative light on that of the Continental whole, and at a very early period. It may also help to divert some scholarly attention, hitherto largely Anglocentric, to greener pastures.

---

[1] A more sustained account will appear in A.J. Fletcher, *Drama, Performance and Polity in Pre-Cromwellian Ireland* (Toronto: Toronto University Press, 1999).

[2] E. Simon, ed. *The Theatre of Medieval Europe: New Research in Early Drama* (Cambridge: Cambridge University Press, 1991) is symptomatic. It mentions Ireland twice in 311 pages. The Dublin *Visitatio Sepulcri* play (see further on this below) is mentioned once (pp. 55-56) and that in a pan-European context, insensible of the play's immediate Irish circumstances. The other Irish reference (p. 83) is to an outdated, nineteenth-century view of the function and contents of the 1498 Dublin Corpus Christi pageant lists (see also further on these below).

It will become apparent as this discussion progresses that in it the word 'performance' has greater currency than the word 'drama', since hard evidence for some of the things that the word 'drama' today conjures up, like role impersonation, rehearsed dialogue, professional actors and so forth, is less clearly available in medieval Ireland than in other parts of medieval Europe. Of course, this does not mean that drama as now usually conceived never existed: firstly, absence of evidence should not be mistaken for evidence of absence; and secondly, there is in fact some sound evidence establishing the practice of drama of the more familiar sort, but it dates from the later Middle Ages, well after 1169, the year in which the Anglo-Norman invasion and settlement of Ireland began. So we must be clear about what moment of Irish history we are thinking of when we maintain that Ireland is less well supplied with evidence. A distinction must be entered: there is the Ireland before the 1169 watershed; and there is also the Ireland after it, a time of deepening ethnic complexity and cultural exchange. But before exploring the ambivalent senses of the chapter's title, a few scene-setting preliminaries may be helpful by way of introduction to a period, and I may even dare say to a country, not widely familiar.

At the beginning of the period in which Irish literary records substantially begin (that is, in about the seventh century), the indigenous Celts throughout Ireland were organized into numerous small tribal units or *túatha*, each *túath* ruled over by a local king or chieftain. Struggles for supremacy between them were common. Some *túatha* had also been coerced into larger lordships presided over by more powerful overkings: those in the north west, for example, were dominated by the Uí Néill dynasty, and those in the south west by the O'Briens. The evangelization of the island, though a slow and complicated business, had also by the seventh century been progressing for some two hundred years, and with the arrival of the clerical classes and their apparatus of Latin learning had also arrived the means for codifying Gaelic culture. The secular native legal texts are a case in point. Though invariably extant in later manuscripts, many were probably first committed to parchment in the seventh and eighth centuries. Monastic centres were established around which auxiliary settlements sprang up. Workshops at these centres were capable of turning out craftsmanship of extraordinary sophistication, as surviving examples of Celtic manuscript illumination and metalwork eloquently testify. By the late eighth century, this rich culture was attracting the Vikings' attention. Though initially landing as raiders, in time they settled, founding coastal towns well sited to serve their mercantile interests. Dublin on the east coast, already home to a native Gaelic monastic community before their arrival, was settled by them in the ninth century. It became their Irish headquarters, and in the Viking world a settlement of premier importance. Other places too were settled, with Cork, Limerick, Waterford, Wexford and Youghal ranking amongst the most significant.

When invaders and settlers from Scandinavia might effect such significant changes to Irish demography, it is a safe prediction that the impact of changes caused by invaders and settlers from Ireland's nearest geographical neighbour, Great Britain, might be even more profound. From 1169, the Anglo-Norman conquest and settlement, led by Richard FitzGilbert de Clare and his baronial associates, began securing Ireland in the name of the English Crown. By 1171, Dublin had been taken from the Hiberno-Norse and occupied by de Clare, though Henry II, aware of his barons' inclination towards maverick enterprise in this new land of theirs, came across in person in the same year to stamp their activities with his royal licence. The twelfth century in Ireland saw not only the beginnings of English colonial expansion, but also wide-reaching ecclesiastical reform. The Church's administration was restructured, its personnel and their moral conduct overhauled. During this period the diocesan system was introduced, first for the provinces of Armagh and Cashel (respectively in the north and south of the island), next for Dublin and Tuam (respectively in the east and west), and such native learned literary professions as poetry, history and law, which hitherto had gravitated around the monastic centres, now began to split away and become secularized. The Anglo-Normans respected these newly established diocesan divisions, but superimposed upon them their own administrative system. They began the shiring of Ireland (a process not completed until after the end of the period under review here).

While the Anglo-Normans were able to establish a few footholds in the north and west, it was principally in the east and south east of the country that they governed and, as was their wont, they consolidated their position by erecting castles and defences. Around these strongholds towns sprang up. Throughout the thirteenth century, the project of Anglo-Norman settlement pushed steadily further afield until, by about 1300, it had achieved its territorial height. Large areas continued to be ruled by native Gaelic chieftains with whom accommodations were reached so that, for the price of tribute and service, they might be left free to enjoy their old autonomy and privileges. Thus by this date Irish society saw Dublin and its environs administered by the Crown, parts of the provinces administered by the Anglo-Norman barons and other parts, territorially still the most extensive, by Gaelic chieftains. Consequently in many areas Gaelic traditions continued to flourish, and large parts of the country retained their cultural character much as in the ancient past.

But political tensions and internal conflicts, exacerbated by absenteeism and upheavals of invasion (notably, the Bruce campaigns from 1315 on), destabilized the Anglo-Norman colony in the fourteenth century. Native Irish chieftains grew restive in this unsettled political climate, and seized the opportunity to pursue their territorial interests more vigorously. Anglo-Norman parliaments complained of a Gaelic resurgence and pointed with alarm at the absorption of Englishmen of the colony into a Gaelic way of life. A mid-century plague dealt a further blow to colonial morale. With Irish revenues to the English treasury now dropping into unprofitability, the Crown looked for an appropriate moment to take the Irish situation in hand. The first major intervention came in 1361 when Edward III dispatched to Ireland his son Lionel, duke of Clarence. Clarence was active in Ireland until 1366, one of his last administrative acts being the summoning of the 1366 Kilkenny parliament whose statutes, amongst other things, aimed to turn the waxing tide of Gaelicization. The next major interventions before the century expired were led by Richard II himself, first in 1394-95 and again in 1399, though on the latter occasion his force was much smaller and he came dogged by a domestic danger that would result in his deposition shortly after returning to England.

By the fifteenth century, the century with which this chapter ends, the English had learnt the lesson that interventions in their Irish colony were costly, and past experience suggested that future ones would be equally unpromising: settlements achieved by direct intervention, like King Richard's, had begun unravelling soon after being made. During this century the colony was largely left to shift for itself. A fortified earthwork, the Pale, was built around the area on the east of the country administered by the Crown and with Dublin at its centre. Beyond the Pale, the country was either controlled by lords of Anglo-Norman stock, like the Butler earls of Ormond or the FitzGerald earls of Desmond, or by Gaelic chieftains. Already in the fourteenth century, some of these resurgent chieftains had started acquiring Anglo-Norman castles, either by leave or by force. As their fortunes continued to revive in the fifteenth and early-sixteenth century, many had stone tower houses built. Their lifestyle in this and many other respects caused them to resemble the Anglo-Irish descendants of the Anglo-Normans, most of whom had become acculturated to greater or lesser extents to a Gaelic way of life. The late medieval revival of Gaelic Ireland was accompanied by renewed patronage of those traditional members of Gaelic aristocratic entourages, the harpers, bards and storytellers, and this not only among the Gaelic Irish. Some Anglo-Irish lords were patronizing them too, to the dismay of purists like those who in drafting the Kilkenny Statutes had sought to keep the ethnic cleanliness of the colony unsullied. In Ireland by the end of the Middle Ages, then, three broad ethnic communities are to be discerned, of various blends at their borders where one community overlapped another: there were the ancient Gaelic communities; the hybrid Anglo-Irish ones; and those centred on the walled towns where a cognizance of things English loomed largest.

Fortified with this potted history and ethnographical overview, we can now turn more meaningfully to the interrelated questions raised at the outset of this chapter. On the one hand, each of Ireland's three chief ethnic communities was celebrated and *performed by* the performing artists whom it hosted. Amongst other things, performance was a public acclamation of the more or less implicit value systems holding society together. And on the other hand, the performers themselves often banded together into microsocieties of their own within the community at large. On occasions these bands toured in search of patronage and a livelihood further afield, and this led to them overstepping the bounds of their host community and coming into contact with the other great ethnic traditions on the island.[3] Let us begin our review with Irish society before 1169.

The evidence that survives from pre-Anglo-Norman Ireland amounts to a wealth of information on *performance*, some of which *may* have been dramatic in the narrow modern sense, yet if it was, this 'drama' seems to have existed only as a phase or aspect within a much broader spectrum of performance activity.[4] So if drama once existed in Ireland before 1169, it either eluded - something quite conceivable - the writings of literate society, the medium through which we are mainly obliged to study the entirety of early Irish culture, or it hides within texts which, though they may refer extensively to performance practices, were unconcerned to record for academic posterity the precise detail of what they referred to. As a result, they may have obscured phenomena that, had they been more fully described, we would have had no hesitation in labelling as dramatic. Gaelic Ireland, from the earliest period to which records give access, was inhabited by

---

[3] This is not to imply, of course, that individual performers did not tour too.

[4] In saying this I am thinking here principally of professional performance, not of a possible folk drama (evidence for which is reviewed in Fletcher, *Drama, Performance and Polity* forthcoming).

a multitude of performing artists and entertainers. Early sources witness to a taxonomy of Gaelic performance the like of which is unequalled anywhere in the British Isles. Since this is so, these sources afford a rare opportunity to reflect not only on Irish performance practices but also on ones that may once have been common throughout the British Isles, if not indeed throughout Europe generally, but which outside Ireland are far less substantially documented until much later in the medieval period. A preoccupation threading several early Irish texts concerns the arrangement of a king's hall: which household members are to sit where and, in some sources, what cuts of meat should they expect to receive from the banquet pig? For example, the Old Irish *Críth Gablach* ('Branched Purchase'?), a law text codified *c*. 700, poses the question directly, 'co sernar tech righ?' ('how is a king's hall arranged?'), and proceeds to answer itself, prescribing where everyone must sit.[5] Next to poets in the hall sit harpers, but in a place apart from these and sitting in the hall's south-west corner on their own are *cuisle* players (the *cuisle* was a variety of pipe), horn players and jugglers/tricksters/acrobats. The king himself is to sit at the east end of the hall, which means that these performers are placed in the far hall corner to his left (see Fig. 1). How far this prescription of seating etiquette was more than a literary scheme and actually replicated in reality must be uncertain, especially when other related texts had equally firm but very different ideas about where performing artists should sit. On the two ground plans of the *Tech Midchúarda* (the 'Hall of the Central Court'), for example, where seating takes pictorial form rather in the manner of some modern-day seating plan for a formal dinner, the *cuisle* players and horn players are remote from each other, not grouped together as in *Críth Gablach*, and a variegated assortment of low-class entertainers, corresponding perhaps most closely to *Críth Gablach*'s jugglers/acrobats, is distributed in various places towards the west end of the hall and near the door (see Plates 1 and 2).[6]

---

[5] D.A. Binchy, ed. *Críth Gablach*, Mediæval and Modern Irish Series Volume 11 (Dublin: Stationery Office, 1941), p. 23, lines 577-90. Note in the present discussion that Old Irish designates texts written between the seventh and ninth century, and Middle Irish texts written between the tenth and twelfth century.

[6] A selection of them from Plate 1 are as follows: *Clessanaig* ('jugglers', 'tricksters', 'acrobats') in the near-left rank, fourth from bottom; *Braigetori* ('farters') in the near-right rank, fourth from bottom; *Druth ríg* ('royal' or 'king's jester') in the near-right rank, third from bottom; and compare their counterparts from Plate 2 as follows: *Clessamnaigh* in the near-left rank, third from bottom; *Braigitoire* in the near-right rank, second from bottom; and *Druith rig* in the near-right rank, bottom. The ground plan in Plate 1 was copied in the late twelfth or early thirteenth century; that in Plate 2 in the late fourteenth century.

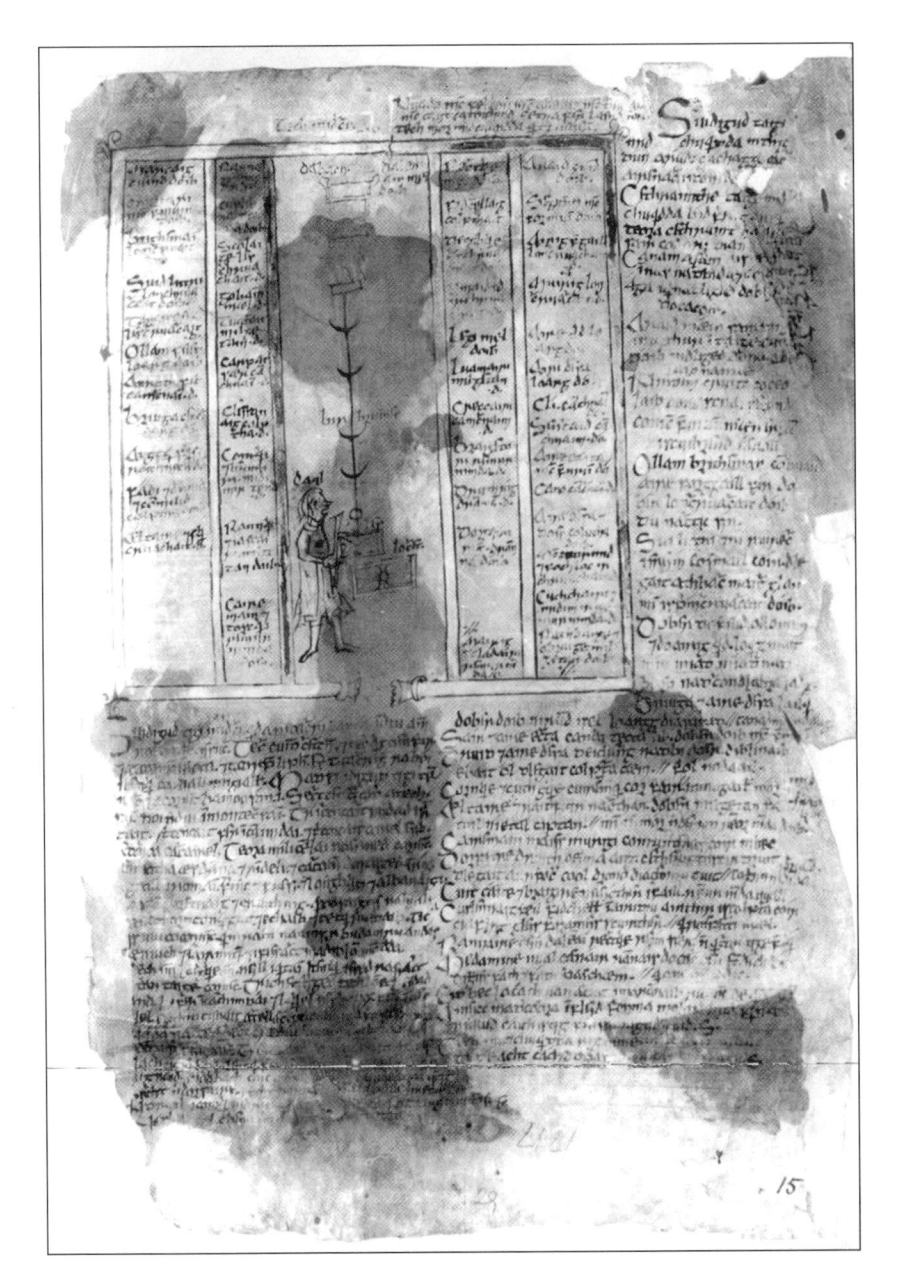

Plate 1
(Reproduced by courtesy of the Board of Trinity College, Dublin.)

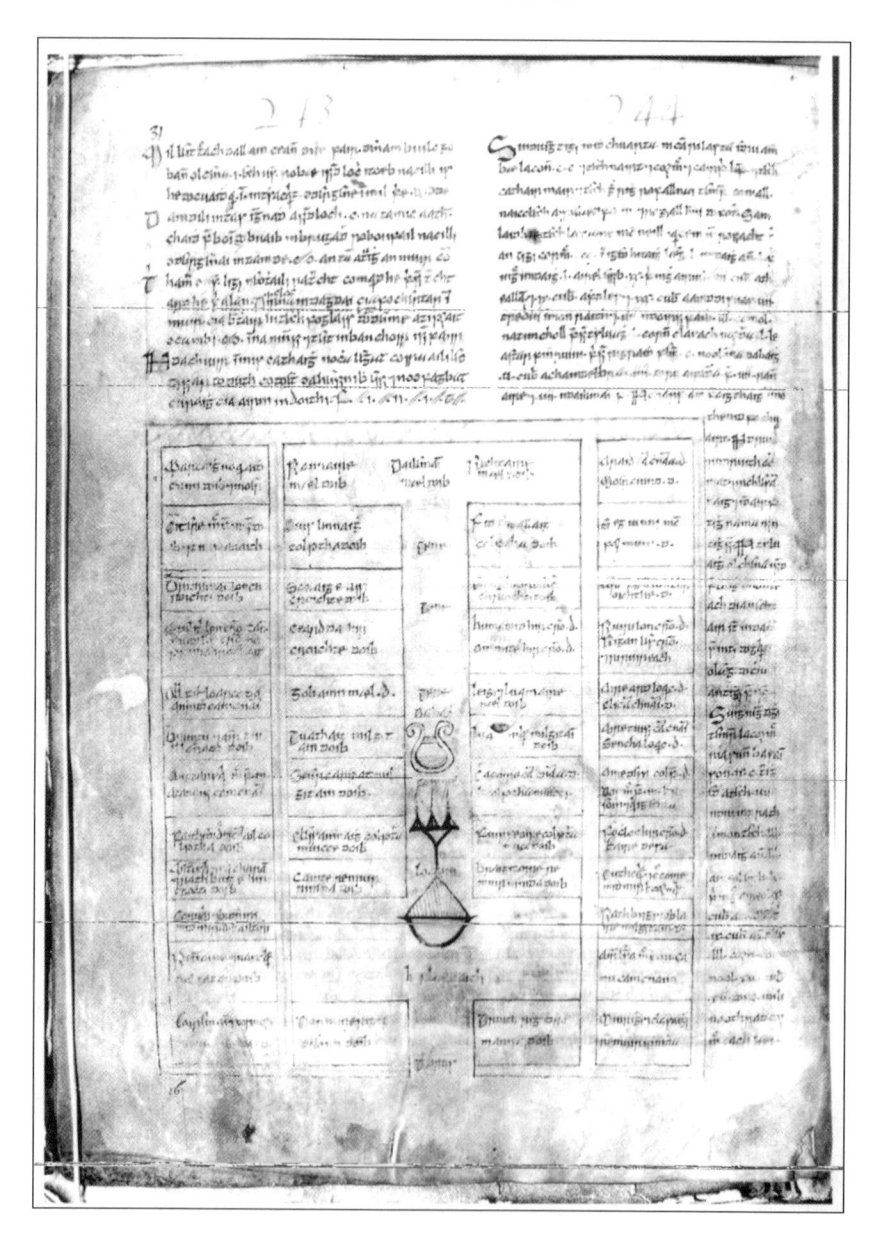

Plate 2
(Reproduced by courtesy of the Board of Trinity College, Dublin.)

In this respect the ground plans tend to agree with the Old Irish *Lánellach Tigi Rích 7 Ruirech* (the 'Full Complement of the Hall of a King and an Overking'), another text preoccupied with hall placings, where practitioners of buffoonery and satire were stationed by the doorposts.[7] But whatever about their points of detail, what all the sources agree on, and what was doubtless a historical reality, is that entertainers were an indispensable part of a royal household or entourage, and that they were capable of a wide range of performance skills.

The *Tech Midchúarda* diagrams provide an especially useful point of departure for exploring the diversity of Gaelic performance practice. In early Irish records, one of the commonest words for a performer is *drúth* (plural, *drúith*), a professional fool or buffoon, and it is clear from the company that a *drúth* might keep, and from the medley of skills at his disposal, that he sometimes encroached upon the performance specialisms of others whose names denoted very particular skills, people like the *réim*, the *clesamnach* or the *braigetóir* (what these performers did will be explained shortly). The word *drúth*, then, was semantically rich, a hold-all word capable of suggesting a person able to move from one end of the spectrum of Gaelic performance art to the other. As in modern English, the word for 'fool' in early Irish could also be used to signify a congenital idiot, probably because aspects of the behaviour of both types of person might strike onlookers as comparably bizarre. Occasionally this makes deciding which sense an early source intended, professional or congenital, a difficult matter, but on the *Tech Midchúarda* diagrams there is no ambiguity. Here the professional *drúth* is in question, and he appears into the bargain in one of his specialized incarnations as a *rígdrúth* (a 'royal' or a 'king buffoon'), though despite whatever grandeur this compound might seem to attribute to him, the term *rígdrúth* in fact reveals far more about the institutional centrality of the *drúth*'s office in early Gaelic society than about his actual social prestige. This, as the law texts make quite clear, was in fact very low. A suggestive account of some of the things that a *rígdrúth* might do is available in the saga narrative *Cath Almaine* (the 'Battle of Allen'), composed in about the tenth century about events which occurred in 722.[8] In this year, Fergal mac Maíle-dúin fought a fateful battle against Murchad mac Brain, overlord of north Leinster. On the eve of battle, the *rígdrúth* Úa Magleine was summoned to entertain Fergal's

---

[7] M.O Daly, 'Laµnellach Tigi Riµch 7 Ruirech', *Ériu* 19 (1962), 81-86.

[8] P. Ó Riain, ed. *Cath Almaine*, Mediæval and Modern Irish Series 25 (Dublin: Dublin Institute for Advanced Studies, 1978); see pp. xxvii-iii and 60-62.

army, and told the soldiers tales of battles fought in times past. The very real advantages of using such tale-telling to address the human needs and anxieties inevitably generated by the prospect of an impending battle are self-evident, and perhaps one actual historical function of the *rígdrúth* was indeed the telling of heroic tales to stiffen military resolve at times of crisis. In appropriating the role of storyteller, the *drúth*'s profession is seen here to border on that of the *scélaige* ('storyteller') or *senchaid* ('reciter of lore'), two other functionaries of early Irish society who in discharging their occupation might practice an art of public performance. This appropriation would not be surprising, and would simply provide a further instance of the performance mobility that the word *drúth* already implies.

Another skill in Úa Magleine's repertoire was the extraordinary *géim* ('shout', 'roar') that he was capable of emitting. Moreover, says *Cath Almaine*, ever since that day his shout has remained among the *drúith* of Ireland.[9] Here it looks as if the narrator of *Cath Almaine* was seeking to explain the origin of something else that *drúith* in his own time were famous for, their shout, probably some sort of practised and distinctive vocal art. *Drúith* are often presented as disruptively noisy in other contexts; they were never to be tolerated in a sick man's house, for example. At least two Old Irish legal texts forbade the *drúth*'s presence there, implying in their strictures that noise was the last thing that a sick man should have to put up with.[10] Vocal noise often accompanies capering and boisterous physical activity in general and, running true to expected form, the *drúth* seems characteristically to have indulged in both. Evidence suggestive of this is found in *Saltair na Rann* (the 'Verse Psalter'), composed *c.* 988-90, when its author, to whet appreciation of what King David actually did when he danced with all his might before the Ark of the Lord (2 Kings 6:14), applied a specifically Irish simile to him: David behaved *amal druth ic furseoracht*, 'like a *drúth* clowning'. His kingly capers thus literalized the concept of *rígdrúth* in an unusual way.[11] In some cases, the energetic mobility of the *drúth* might be narrowly focused upon his face, as when he trespassed into the province of the *réim* ('contortionist', 'girner') and postured with the mops and mows of

---

[9] Ó Riain, *Cath Almaine*, p. 9, lines 106-12.

[10] D.A. Binchy, 'Bretha Crólige', *Ériu* 12 (1938), 1-77; see p. 48; and D.A. Binchy, ed. *Corpus Iuris Hibernici*, 6 vols (Dublin: Dublin Institute for Advanced Studies, 1978), II, 369, line 30.

[11] W. Stokes, ed. *The Saltair na Rann* (Oxford: Clarendon Press, 1883), p. 98, line 6684.

comic facial distortion. The *drúth*'s physical antics of sundry sorts also extended to feats of legerdemain and juggling. Another *rígdrúth*, Tulchinne, in the eighth-century tale *Togail Bruidne Da Derga* (the 'Destruction of Da Derga's Hostel'), was also King Conaire's *clesamnach* ('juggler', 'trickster', 'acrobat'). Although the account of his juggling feats is fabulous, as one might expect from a saga narrative, there is still good reason to believe that behind its idealized evocation lay a real historical performance practice;[12] for example, the Old Irish *Bretha Étgid* ('Judgements of Inadvertence'), which as a law text might be thought *prima facie* to have had a greater purchase on historical reality than a literary one, lays down the penalties to be paid for any injuries sustained while watching a juggling act, and some of the implements juggled in the act sound very much like those manipulated by Tulchinne.[13]

Early Irish texts have also much to reveal about the physical appearance of *drúith*, their professional dress and the way in which they might band together in touring troupes. The description of another royal fool (though this time it is not *rígdrúth* but a related word, *rígóinmit*, that is used of him) features in the twelfth-century tale *Mesca Ulad* (the 'Intoxication of the Ulstermen'). The tale gives a strong impression of how outlandish a *drúth*'s appearance could be. The face of the royal fool Róimid was said to have been 'black like an Ethiopian's'.[14] Perhaps this is an early instance of face blackening, the traditional disguise of the fool of the morris side even to this day. Tulchinne also carried a bell to attract attention, and in this respect he stands as one of the earliest belled fools in any text surviving from the medieval British Isles.

While royal fools were the responsibility of their patron and may not have strayed far from his entourage on their own initiative, it is clear that some *drúith* were entirely free to roam, either singly or in groups. These went hunting for patronage wherever they could find it, even if only in the most modest form of once-off payments in kind. Most usually these payments were of food. *Drúith* evolved potent methods for getting what they wanted. The Church in particular found their attentions unwelcome, and tried to curb their wanderings with prohibitive legislation. Itinerant *drúith* are often spoken of in association with another important class of Gaelic performing artist,

---

[12] R. I. Best and O. Bergin, eds. *Lebor na hUidre* (Dublin and London: Royal Irish Academy, 1929), p. 231, lines 7556-59.

[13] Binchy, *Corpus Iuris Hibernici*, I, 288, lines 11-12.

[14] 'Aged ethiopacda slemangorm aci' ('His face was black like an Ethiopian's'). J. Carmichael Watson, ed. *Mesca Ulad* (Dublin: Stationery Office, 1941), pp. 30-31.

one similarly excoriated by clerics, the *cáinte* (plural, *cáinti*) or satirist, a low-grade poet whose satirical routine might be conducted in a highly performative and theatrical fashion.[15] Even the most élite members of the Gaelic poetic hierarchy could turn their hand to satire if they were driven to it, but *cáinti* were satire's habitual and professional practitioners: as the Old Irish law text *Míadślechta* ('Rank Sections') put it, a *cáinte* was a man who earned his food through threatening the blemish of satire.[16] The power of the *cáinti* – and of the *drúith*, who in some of the early Irish saints' lives were set on a par with *cáinti* and who were perfectly capable of behaving similarly – derived from the fact that early Gaelic society was a shame culture: public satirical destruction of a person's reputation was an institutionalized practice and something greatly to be feared. Indeed, satire was credited in some sources with quasi-magical potency. It had the power of being able to raise blemishes on the victim's face or, in extreme cases, even cause death. In the Old Irish *Epistle of Jesus*, *drúith* and *cáinti* consort in a list of itinerants whose Sunday peregrinations the *Epistle* sought to proscribe.[17] Similarly, the early Irish saints' lives are full of stories about rapacious *drúith* and *cáinti* harrassing saints with petulant demands for food or other gifts, and threatening satire if their demands were not satisfied.[18] Satire is also the domain, alongside that of music, in which evidence is thickest for female participation in the Gaelic performing arts.[19] Extant specimens of verse satire demonstrate the extent to which satirists declared open season on a whole range of perceived human imperfections,

---

[15] W. Stokes, 'The Second Battle of Moytura', *Revue Celtique* 12 (1891), 52-130; see pp. 119-21. A representative of each of the seven grades into which the Irish poetic hierarchy was traditionally divided was to go before sunrise to a hilltop at the boundary of seven lands. The back of each poet was to be turned to a hawthorn which should also be on the hilltop. The wind had to be blowing from the north. Each poet was to have a slingstone in one hand and in the other a thorn from the hawthorn. Each was to sing his peculiar verse to the slingstone and thorn, then deposit them at the foot of the hawthorn. If the poets were in the wrong, they might expect the earth to swallow them. Alternatively, the same fate would be visited upon the chieftain and members of his household, including his dog. A version of this text in Binchy, *Corpus Iuris Hibernici*, V, 1564, line 27; 1565, line 19 offers each poet the option of carrying a clay image of the man satirized; their thorns are to be stuck into the image.

[16] Binchy, *Corpus Iuris Hibernici*, II, 587, line 20.

[17] J.G. O'Keeffe, 'Cáin Domnaig', *Ériu* 2 (1905), 189-214; see p. 208.

[18] For example, W. W. Heist, ed. *Vitae sanctorum Hiberniae e codice olim Salmanticensi nunc Bruxellensi*, Subsidia Hagiographica 28 (Brussels: Société des Bollandistes, 1965), p. 296, § 29 (from the twelfth-century *vita* of St Flannán).

[19] For a tale in which a female satirist goes vividly into action, see S. O'Grady, ed. *Silva Gadelica*, 2 vols (London and Edinburgh: Williams and Norgate, 1892) I, 82-83.

imperfections presented with crippling scurrility. One Middle Irish lampoon offers a robust case in point. It targeted an anonymous woman for farting: *Atá ben istír, ní abraim a hainm, / maidid essi a deilm amal chloich a tailm* ['There's a woman in the land, I don't mention her name. Her fart flies from her like a stone from a sling'].[20] Indeed farting, doubtless precisely because of its social solecism,[21] lent itself in Ireland to refinement into a comically affronting performance art. It was the forte of a specialist group of performing artists known as the *braigetóiri* ('farters'). These also found their place reserved on the *Tech Midchúarda* seating plans and in other sources kept company with *drúith* and *cáinti*. Needless to say, their skills were equally abhorred by the Church, as a clerical aside in the twelfth-century tale *Aislinge Meic Con Glinne* (the 'Dream of Mac Con Glinne') makes plain.[22] Again, *drúith* may have encroached too upon the territory of the *braigetóiri*, if one possible interpretation of their behaviour in the Middle Irish *Suidigud Taigi Midchúarda* (the 'Settling of the House of the Central Court') is to be believed.[23]

So what the records amply illustrate is a Gaelic society which well before 1169 played host to a diverse range of performing artists, of whom the *drúth* may be conveniently regarded as the generic representative. For the most part these performing artists, while low-class, were tenaciously rooted in society. They catered not only to the noble households, but also to whoever might be prepared to offer them patronage. The occasions on which they performed were similarly various, and ranged from private or semi-private household functions such as feasts and banquets to public gatherings such as fairs and assemblies, the *oenaige* (singular, *oenach*), which chieftains were obliged to convene at regular intervals and at which social, political and, perhaps, commercial business was transacted. A prime example

---

[20] K. Meyer, ed. *Bruchstüke der älteren Lyrik Irlands* (Berlin: Academie der Wissenschaften, 1919), p. 34, no. 77.

[21] There is some evidence, though admittedly it is later (late sixteenth and early seventeenth century) and reported by Englishmen, that the Irish traditionally held farting in extreme abhorrence (J.O. Bartley, *Teague, Shenkin and Sawney, being an Historical Study of the Earliest Irish, Welsh and Scottish Characters in English Plays* (Cork: Cork University Press, 1954), p. 31).

[22] K.H. Jackson, ed. *Aislinge Meic Con Glinne* (Dublin: Dublin Institute for Advanced Studies, 1990), p. 18, lines 546-50.

[23] R.I. Best, O. Bergin, M.A. O'Brien and A. O'Sullivan, eds. *The Book of Leinster formerly Lebar na Núachongbála*, 6 vols (Dublin: Dublin Institute for Advanced Studies, 1954-83) I, 119, line 3758. Here the *druith delma aitt* ('fool strange of sound') is listed among other menials and entertainers. Possibly the strange sound, in the context here of the *drúth*, may have been interpreted as farting, one of the specialized meanings, in fact, of the noun *deilm* ('din', 'rumbling').

of the crowd of entertainers jostling at an eleventh-century *oenach* is found in one of the poems of the tradition known as *dindshenchas* ('history of notable places'). This *oenach* bustled with performance activity:

> Is iat a áda olla. stuic. cruitti. cuirn chroes tolla.ͻ
> cúisig timpaig. cen tríamna. filid 7 fęnchlíara.[24]

('These are [the *oenach*'s] great prerequisites: trumpets, harps,
hollow-throated horns, pipers, tireless players on the *timpán*, poets
and prawling bands of musicians.')
...
Pipai. fidli. fir cengail. cnamfhir 7 cuslennaig.ͻ
sluág etig engach egair. béccaig 7 buridaig.[25]

('Pipes, rebecs, gleemen, bones-players and *cuisle*-players,
an ugly, noisy, profane crowd, roarers and bellowers.')

The activity of the professional Gaelic musician, anticipated already and again here in this *oenach* description, adds an important dimension to the picture that is also worthy of notice. Although early Irish sources singled out the harp as the instrument most deserving respect and dignified it with the preeminent place in the Gaelic musical hierarchy,[26] it seems clear that some harpers also toured to wherever they might find an appreciative audience, and in this regard their profession was indistinguishable from that of the low-class entertainers described earlier. A good illustration of the association in

---

[24] Dublin, Trinity College, MS 1339 (H. 2. 18; Book of Leinster), fol. 165v, col. a (E. Gwynn, ed. *The Metrical Dindsenchas Part III*, Todd Lecture Series Volume 10 (Dublin: Royal Irish Academy, 1913), p. 18, lines 233-6). The possibility that the poem was composed to commemorate the *oenach* held by Conchobar úa Conchobair in 1079 is explored by Gwynn, *ibid.*, p. 471.

[25] Dublin, Trinity College, MS 1339 (H. 2. 18; Book of Leinster), fol. 165v, col. a (Gwynn, *ibid.*, p. 20, lines 257-60). In translating *égair* as 'prophane' I have followed Gwynn. The words *fir cengail* are also difficult; they might alternatively be rendered 'men without weapons'. It is not clear how these groups would have performed, whether collectively, individually, or both.

[26] Note, for example, the Old Irish law tract *Uraicecht Becc* which declared that harping was the one profession of minstrelsy worthy of honour-price. (The honour-price was a monetary valuation of a person's status calculated according to his circumstances at any given time; see F. Kelly, *A Guide to Early Irish Law*, Early Irish Law Series 3 (Dublin: Dublin Institute for Advanced Studies, 1988), pp. 8-9.) Compare the way in which harpers (*Cruittiri*) are set apart from most other entertainers on the *Tech Midchúarda* diagrams (see Plates 1 and 2, second from the top in the far-left rank).

practice between the high-class, theoretically aloof profession of harper and that of the low-class entertainers already surveyed occurs in the *Cath Almaine*. In 721, one year before his defeat by Murchad mac Brain, Fergal mac Maíle-dúin, wishing to discover his sons' true moral disposition, is said to have secretly visited their houses by night. Both houses sounded with harp playing, but while in the house of the second son it was *cruitireacht ciúin bínd* ['quiet, sweet harp playing'], in the house of the first it merely added one more strain to a riotous and giddy assembly of harpers, *timpán* players (the *timpán* seems to have been a variety of lyre),[27] clowns, satirists, whores and jugglers.[28] Therefore in practice, far from being hermetically sealed in some notionally élite world of musical preeminence, it is clear that certain harpers stooped to consorting with low-class performers. Moreover, they might combine their harping with other types of performance art: the mid-twelfth-century poet Gilla Mo Dutu Úa Casaide, for example, had no difficulty in presenting the legendary character Feidlimid as both a *scelaigi is chruttiri* ('a storyteller and a harper').[29] Whatever the theory, in practice it paid to be versatile, and narrow specialism was a luxury that relatively few performing artists would have been able to afford. So wherever professional musicians, including harpers, foregathered, the likelihood was that other performance skills were not far to seek.

After the Norman invasion of 1169, one of the earliest foreign reactions to Gaelic culture and its performing arts is distilled in the *Topographia Hiberniae* of Giraldus Cambrensis. His seminal work went through various Latin recensions and, after 1387, became more widely accessible again via John Trevisa's English translation of Ranulf Higden's *Polychronicon*.[30] In one redaction or another the *Topographia* conditioned English perceptions of Ireland throughout the Middle Ages and well into the sixteenth century. Giraldus had little that was positive to say about things Irish, but Irish harping, a notable exception, he praised for its musicality and wide cultivation throughout the island. Subsequent writers, by contrast, were far more hostile. This was not because they contested the harp's musical

---

[27] On its organology, see A. Buckley, 'What was the Tiompán? A Problem in Ethnohistorical Organology: Evidence in Irish Literature', *Jahrbuch für Musikalische Volks- und Völkerkunde* 9 (1978), 53-88.

[28] J.N. Radner, ed. *Fragmentary Annals of Ireland* (Dublin: Dublin Institute for Advanced Studies, 1978), p. 60.

[29] Best, Bergin, O'Brien and O'Sullivan, *Book of Leinster*, III, 542, line 16741.

[30] The *Topographia Hiberniae* was one of Ranulf Higden's prime sources (and see R. Waldron, 'The Manuscripts of Trevisa's Translation of the *Polychronicon*: Towards a New Edition', *Modern Language Quarterly* 51 (1990), 281-317).

qualities as celebrated by Giraldus – no one disagreed about them – but because they considered harpers to be agents of sedition whose activity undermined English strategies for the effective colonization of the island. A clear example of this from the century of Gaelic resurgence is to be seen in one of the articles of the Statutes of Kilkenny of 1366 which forbade 'Tympanors fferdanes, Skelaghes, Bablers, Rymors, Clercz ne nullez autres minstrells Irrois' ['*timpán* players, poets, storytellers, babblers, rhymers, clerics or any other Irish minstrels'] from coming among the English and thereby muddying the ethnic purity of the colony.[31] That the infiltration of the colony by Gaelic performing artists was not just the figment of an embattled imagination is suggested from a Crown plea from Co. Cork in the early years of the century. In 1315, one Muriartagh O Coyqnan (*sic*), harper and actor ('actor' possibly translating *histrio* in the lost original document), was prosecuted for various misdemeanours, including his 'habit of coming to the houses of the liege men of the country as a minstrel to ask for alms, and if they were refused him, of endeavouring to rob them'.[32] At the other end of the century and of the country, Archbishop John Colton of Armagh sought to legislate in his synodal statutes, drafted after the Kilkenny Statutes, sometime between 1381 and 1404, 'contra minos {*read* mimos} ioculatores poetas timpanistas siue citharedas & precipue contra kernarios ac importunas & improbos donorum petitores quin uerius extortores' ['against *mimi*, jesters, poets, *timpán* players or harpers, and especially against kerns and importunate [women] and dishonest seekers, or rather extorters, of gifts'].[33] And Kilkenny Statutes nothwithstanding, special cases and exemptions could be made for allowing Gaelic performing artists to continue entering the Pale with impunity subject to their good behaviour.[34]

What is clear, then, is that, hostile though the official English reaction almost invariably was to Irish harpers and their confederate performing artists, an accurate reflection can nevertheless be seen in it

---

[31] Lambeth Palace Library, MS 603 (Carew Papers), fol. 168 (H.F. Berry, ed. *Statutes and Ordinances, and Acts of the Parliament of Ireland. King John to Henry V* (Dublin: Alexander Thom & Co., 1907), p. 446).

[32] Dublin, National Archives, 2/448/1, KB 2/7, p. 36. The record is a transcript of a lost Justiciary Roll for 12 June 1315.

[33] Belfast, Public Record Office of Northern Ireland, DIO 4/2/3 fol. [151v] (the manuscript is imperfectly foliated; this attributed foliation begins counting from the first leaf containing text).

[34] E. Tresham, ed. *Rotulorum patentum et clausorum cancellariae Hiberniae calendarium* (Dublin: Irish Record Commission, 1828), p. 94 col. b, item 164 (abbreviations silently expanded).

of the continuity of central aspects of the ethos and conduct of the community of the Gaelic performing classes, aspects already in evidence before the Normans invaded in 1169. Moreover, these classes were actively seeking patronage from the English settlers in Ireland. A new market had opened up. One candid Gaelic poet of the fourteenth century, confessing the social amphibiousness of his class, makes it clear that he and some of the performing artists he knew inhabited their own microsocieties, loyalty to which might easily supersede the claims of any prior ethnic affiliation. They could easily doff that for the price of a meal:

> I ndán na nGall gealltar linn
> Gaoidhil d'ionnarba a hÉirinn;
> Goill do shraoineadh tar sáil sair
> i ndán na nGaoidheal gealltair.[35]

> ['In poetry for the foreigners [i.e., for anyone not of
> native Gaelic stock] we promise that the Gaels shall be
> expelled from Ireland; in poetry for the Gaels we promise
> that the foreigners shall be driven eastwards over the sea.']

So much is implicit in these arch lines: while this poet's *confrères* extolled the values of their patrons in the poems that they recited, they were not personally bound by those values, but treated them, as they did the rest of their art, like a rhetoric. These performers were a like-minded confederation, a microsociety with allegiances principally to themselves and finally beyond the provincial claims of any particular ethnic, political or regional faction; and they were peripatetic, active seekers of sponsorship from communities elsewhere.

I have dealt predominantly in this chapter with performing artists of the native Gaelic tradition because these are least likely to be familiar to the readers of this volume. In the space remaining, I must show, though unavoidably it will be a token demonstration, that when the English started arriving in Ireland, they also brought with them entertainers and performing artists of their own, and this from the earliest years of the colony's existence. Dublin's Guild Merchant roll, Ireland's oldest surviving civic muniment, mentions between the late-twelfth and the mid-thirteenth century several individuals bearing the

---

[35] E. Knott, *Irish Classical Poetry*, 2nd rev. edn (Cork: Mercier Press, 1966), p. 67. The poet, Gofraidh Fionn Ó Dálaigh (†1387), wrote this poem for Gerald FitzGerald, son of Maurice, first earl of Desmond. The Janus-like nature of the late-medieval Irish poet is also noted by J.E. Caerwyn Williams, 'The Court Poet in Medieval Ireland', *Proceedings of the British Acad*emy 57 (1971), 85-135; see p. 131 and note 1.

surname Le Harpur or Le Pipere; one Le Harpur even benefited from having a small harp sketched in the margin of the roll next to his name.[36] A playful rebus, merely? There is less reason to think so when other, early Dublin sources reveal harpers and pipers abroad in the city who undisputedly earned a living by playing those instruments from which their surnames derived. By the early fifteenth century, the English minstrels of the colony had organized themselves into some sort of guild, for in 1436 one William Lawless of Dublin, who styled himself *marescallus* ('marshal') of the liege English *mimi* of Ireland, petitioned for special powers to apprehend Irish *mimi* like 'clarsaghours, tympanours, crowthores, kerraghers, rymours, skelaghes, bardes & alii' ('harpers, *timpán* players, players on the crowd, gamblers, rhymers, storytellers, bards and others').[37] Clearly the 1366 Kilkenny Statutes were not working adequately, and Gaelic minstrels were continuing to enter the Pale and depart again, taking with them intelligence useful for the king's Irish enemies. One suspects they were also taking the food out of the mouths of the likes of William Lawless: the granting of his petition would have conferred upon him and his fellows the advantage of a monopoly over the provision of entertainment, though mercenary self-interest was not something that the terms of his petition acknowledged in as many words.

Just as performance had provided a unique means of voicing the identity of the Gaelic community, so too did it provide English settlers with a powerful means of articulating theirs in their newly adopted land. The larger corporate resources of their towns and cities in Ireland allowed performance to become proportionally more ambitious, and at the same time profoundly expressive of the civic ideologies which sustained performance and which, in turn, performance helped to sustain. Medieval Dublin was no exception, and it is from here that the bulk of Ireland's early urban evidence for performance survives. Now for the first time we also discover unequivocal proof of interest in performance that was dramatic in the narrow modern sense. Though it is atelous, the earliest extant morality play from the British Isles comes from Dublin. It was possibly originally composed there to address specific cultural needs, and was not just one further consumable or commodity imported into the colony like so many others from across the Irish Sea.[38] This is the play

---

[36] Dublin, Corporation Archives, G1/1, mb. 11 d col. a (*c.* 1200).

[37] Tresham, *Rotulorum patentum et clausorum*, p. 258 cols a-b.

[38] J. Mills, ed. *Account Roll of the Priory of Holy Trinity, Dublin, 1337-1346*, reprinted with a new introduction by J.F. Lydon and A.J. Fletcher (Dublin: Four

known as *The Pride of Life*.[39] From Dublin also survive the words and music for another rarity, a Latin liturgical *Visitatio Sepulcri* play.[40] This species of drama, once widely performed in the British Isles, is now only known from a tiny handful of examples, Dublin's being one. Apart from primary evidence like this for an interest in drama and performance, other sorts of evidence establish the central role of drama and performance in the life of the late medieval city. The pageants of Corpus Christi day, for example, which were fixed by a corporation edict of 1498, were but one link, if an outstanding one, in a yearly chain of dramatic, ceremonial events supervised by the corporation to celebrate the city's selfhood and to proclaim it in the face of whoever might be tempted to encroach upon civic jurisdictions and prerogatives.[41] The evidence is not entirely clear, but it is possible that the Corpus Christi pageants were associated with some sort of fully fledged dramatic presentation and were not just a procession of *tableaux vivants*.[42]

A need for civic ceremonial was the driving force behind much of the public dramatic display mounted in Dublin, just as it was in the interests of civic ceremonial that many of Dublin's musicians were employed. The Dublin waits, first on record from 1465 (though a band of pipers was already in existence by 1456), existed primarily to serve the civic weal, and were allowed to stray further afield in search of patronage only with the mayor's prior approval and then only for brief periods.[43] Like their Gaelic counterparts, musicians from the Pale too were inclined to wander.

Courts Press, 1996).

[39] N. Davis, ed. *Non-Cycle Plays and Fragments*, EETS, SS1 (Oxford: Oxford University Press, 1970), pp. 90-105.

[40] M. Egan-Buffet and A.J. Fletcher, 'The Dublin *Visitatio Sepulcri* Play', *Proceedings of the Royal Irish Academy* 90 (1990), 159-241.

[41] See A.J. Fletcher, 'Playing and Staying Together: Projecting the Corporate Image in Sixteenth-Century Dublin', in A.F. Johnston and W. Hüsken, ed. *Civic Ritual and Drama* (Amsterdam and Atlanta: Rodopi, 1996), pp. 15-37 and 'The Civic Pageantry of Corpus Christi in Fifteenth- and Sixteenth-Century Dublin', *Irish Economic and Social History* 23 (1996), pp. 73-96.

[42] Whether or not the pageants participated in some fully fledged drama, civic dramas were certainly performed from very early in the sixteenth century on fixed stages erected on the Hoggen Green, a public space just outside the city walls to the east. See Mills, *Account Roll*, p. xxxiii, n. 97.

[43] This is clear from the sixteenth century (Dublin, Corporation Archives, MR/5/10, mb. 32, an edict of 12 October 1599), but their inclination to wander is already implied in the fifteenth (Dublin, Corporation Archives, MR/5/2, mb. 6 dorse, an edict of 24 October 1466).

The evidence from medieval Dublin suggests that the colony was engaged in a network of drama and performance at once as essential to its corporate morale as to its recreational health. As in Gaelic Ireland so too in colonized Ireland, communities of performers were underwriting the community interests of their patrons. Whatever the détente, or lack of it, between the major ethnic groups on the island in the post-colonial period following 1169, the performing artists who legitimated and were legitimated by those groups had remarkably similar roles to play.

In sum and in brief, Ireland was a site of extraordinarily diverse activity when it came to the practices that today we are pleased to label drama and performance. Yet it was an activity with considerable mutuality of function. Theatre history and social history have once more been seen to be indivisible provinces, though this time in an Irish context: communities of performers performed the cultural interests of their sponsoring communities. It is to be hoped that this short excursus will at least have drawn attention to one thing, the prospect of how fruitful further enquiry promises to be into the relatively neglected domain of early Irish socio-theatrical history.

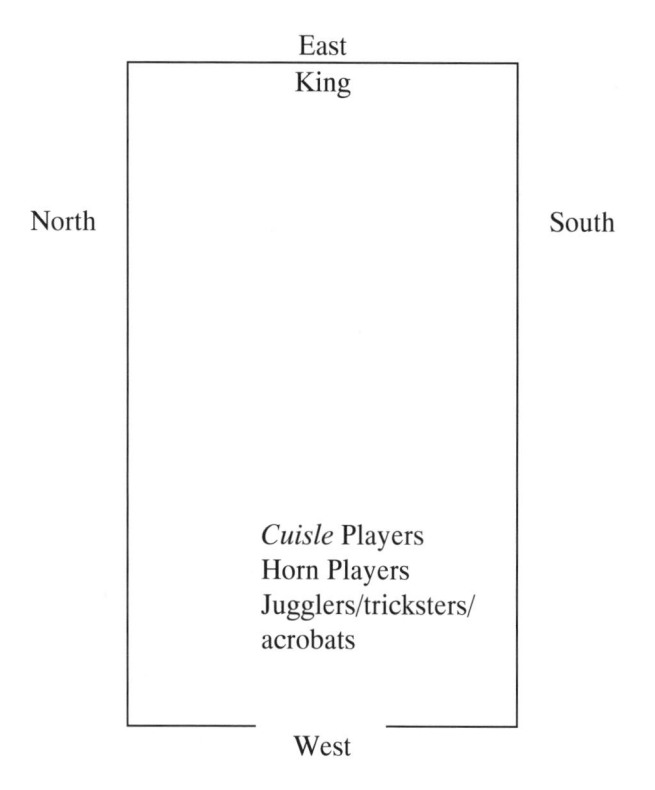

```
                    East
                    King
        ┌─────────────────────────┐
        │                         │
        │                         │
        │                         │
 North  │                         │  South
        │                         │
        │                         │
        │                         │
        │                         │
        │      Cuisle Players     │
        │      Horn Players       │
        │      Jugglers/tricksters/│
        │      acrobats           │
        │                         │
        └─────────────────────────┘
                    West
```

Fig. 1: Performers at the south-west end of the royal hall according to *Crith Gablach.*

Contemporary cultural models for the trial plays in the York Cycle

PAMELA M. KING

AT THE BEGINNING OF 1985, the heyday of Thatcherism in Britain, a civil servant called Clive Ponting was prosecuted for revealing restricted information to the press because, he believed, it was in the 'national interest'.[1] One of the judges in the case argued that the national interest and the interests of the government of the day were the same thing. Ponting convinced the jury that the national interest concerned a higher principle and was acquitted. The concept of the 'national interest' thereby took on a special political, ethical and juridical significance.

Jesus Christ was not so successful, although the higher principle which he was asserting in defiance of the laws of various governments of his day, from Middle Eastern petty despots to the might of the Roman Empire, was the law of God. At least that is how interpretations of the gospel narrative, and particularly dramatized interpretations, have popularly chosen to present the causality of events leading to Calvary. In our own time, *Jesus Christ Super Star* memorably exploited this reading to allude to the anti-Vietnam movement in the USA, by presenting a Judas intimidated by a lot of military hardware into betraying the happy hippy followers of a Christ who has 'gone too far'. And in Monty Python's *The Life of Brian* the by now familiar reading of Christ's persecution as an establishment plot is memorably parodied in that film's presentation of a number of splinter-group protest movements with confusingly similar names. Such portrayals of Jesus Christ as a freedom fighter martyred by an oppressive political establishment are not, however, restricted to secular late twentieth-century Anglo-Americans. This essay explores

---

[1] *Financial Times*, 12 February 1985.

how the narrative of Christ's Passion in the trial plays in the York Cycle sustains a number of subtexts which interweave the contemporary political with the paranormal, the satirical, as well as with the frankly devotional, for the urban mercantile community within which they were performed.

The author of the plays which deal with the trials before Annas and Caiaphas, before Pilate, Herod, then Pilate again, is the problematically designated 'York Realist'.[2] His technique is arguably not 'realism' so much as a mobilization of selected contemporary social forms and practices extrapolated from the biblical narrative material to locate it in the specific cultural community for which he wrote. The theatrical transaction between author and audience appears to assume not only a consensual understanding of certain contemporary practices relating to the operation of the law, but also a consensual and ambivalent attitude to those practices. The plays offer witness to a specific contemporary mentality that has not only aesthetic, but also social and topical political meaning. In common with commentaries on the Ponting case these are accounts of trials which propose an ethical hierarchy fundamentally threatening to an established hierarchy of social and political authority.

The processes of litigation have a number of rhetorical properties which lend themselves to dramatization, as films such as *The Dreyfus Case, The Winslow Boy, The Caine Mutiny, Kramer v. Kramer* illustrate. The ritual of the courtroom polarizes the issues under debate offering a stylized verbal rehearsal of oppositions in the form of pleading. Foregoing events can be summarized and, because trial presupposes verdict, the audience can be implicated as surrogate judge and jury. In the trials in the York Cycle preceding events are given the status of evidence to be judged. Some of those events, in particular Christ's miracles, can be more economically reported than performed. Those spoken accounts, because they are the testimonies of sworn witnesses, then also take on their own ritualized ethical meaning. The burden of legal pleading is to arrive at proof through reasoned argument. Legal procedures are, therefore, notoriously inadequate for dealing with anything paranormal, as another dramatist, Arthur Miller, demonstrated in *The Crucible*. In that play courtroom scenes are used to dramatize a famous miscarriage of justice in the Salem witch trials whilst setting up a strong topical subtext in critique of the repressive politics of McCarthyism. Whether it is Abigail Williams asserting that Mary Warren has conjured up a yellow bird to attack her, or Annas

---

[2] J.W. Robinson, 'The Art of the York Realist', *Modern Philology*, 60 (1962-63), 241-51.

and Caiaphas accusing Christ of the witchcraft of the miracles, the exposure of the limitations of the empirical methods of contemporary legal procedures, and their capacity for corruption when they are applied to inappropriate evidence and for factional advantage, is similar.

Scholastic habits of thought supply an intellectual environment for plays which treat the relationship between God and man as bound by a system of rights and duties. Much late medieval literature, devotional and satirical, explores relationships between human and divine society in quasi-feudal and legal terms. The problem of authority within a fixed hierarchy trickling down from God to man via established social structures is one of the major preoccupations in *Piers Plowman* and *The Canterbury Tales*, written in post-Black Death England. The events of 1381 showed how much those stabilities could be threatened by labour shortage, social mobility and the growth of an urban middle class whose wealth was not held as land. The flourishing community responsible for the production of the York Cycle was a product of these very social changes. In the cycle there is an over-arching logic in which the different dramatists of the plays of the Fall, the Temptation in the Wilderness, the Dream of Pilate's Wife, the Harrowing of Hell and the Last Judgment, all rely on the proposition that man's relationship with God is controlled according to juridical principles which enact the etymological link between 'ransom' (*rançon*) and 'redemption'. In this general context the trials in the Passion sequence present an interesting and potentially subversive test of official order, as feudal overlords overreach themselves by attempting to put God on trial. The consequent inversion of the hierarchy of authority must lead to a perversion of absolute justice, even if procedures were to be pursued in good faith. At points throughout the cycle God or Christ is involved in administering divine justice while demonstrating its inscrutability. The broad contrast between the mores of the Old and the New Laws is focused in Christ's continuing opposition to the Jewish scribes and Pharisees, as a boy before the doctors in the Temple, and in the episode of the Woman taken in Adultery, when he rebukes the Jewish judges (John VIII: 15), 'Ye judge after the flesh; I judge no man'. St Thomas Aquinas[3] warns that man can pass judgement on external actions only; God alone can judge the inner movements of the will.

In the trial plays in the York Cycle, Annas and Caiaphas are advocates of the Old Law which they attempt to impose

---

[3] St Thomas Aquinas, *Summa Theologiae*, ed. and transl. by Thomas Gilby (Cambridge, 1966), Vol. 28: *Law and Political Theory,* quaestiones 90-100.

inappropriately upon a Christ who is its fulfilment. The theological point is enacted as a demonstration of the inadequacies of human legal procedures in dealing with higher paranormal events. Annas and Caiaphas are characterized as inquisitors prosecuting Christ for witchcraft. They, like Satan in the Smiths' play of the Temptation (XXII), have failed to identify the accused as lying outside their jurisdiction, a fact underlined in one ironical exchange:

> Pilate: Yhis, his fadir with some farlis gan fare
>   And has lered þis ladde of his laie.
> Annas: Nay, nay sir, we wiste þat he was but a write...
>   (XXX, 502-04)[4]

> [Pilate: Yes, his father meddled with some tricks
>   And has taught this lad his lore.
> Annas: No, no sir, we understand that he was only a carpenter...]

There is later visible supernatural intervention in the last court-room play, when court officials twice involuntarily reverence Christ. Effective stage business is used to show, as Aquinas says,[5] that men are not subject to human law if they are under higher authority: in particular spiritual men are not subject to laws that are inconsistent with the guidance of the Holy Ghost.

The dramatist thus exploits Christ's special relationship with the law as transformer of the contract between God and humankind, for many local ironies, characteristic of his use of incidental concrete detail to illuminate broader doctrinal patterns. The intellectual logic of the sequence is in turn supported by dramatic oppositions. Most obviously, speech and silence are opposed as markers of power. Probably drawing on Luke's account (XXIII: 8-11) that Christ refused to speak to Herod, the traditionally bombastic tyrants of these plays are set against an almost completely silent Christ. The boasting speeches of the rival temporal powers are also used to assert differing power bases. Caiaphas is a bishop learned in the law:

> ...a lorde lerned lelly in youre lay.
> By connyng of clergy and casting of witte
>   Full wisely my wordis I welde at my will...   (XXIX, 4-6)

> [...a lord learned loyally in your law.

---

[4] Richard Beadle, (ed.), *The York Plays* (London: Arnold, 1983). All references to the text – Roman the play, Arabic the line numbers – are taken from this edition.
[5] *Summa Theologiae*, q. 96, 5a.

> Through the knowledge of clergy and calculation of intelligence
> I employ my words very wisely at will...]

Pilate is concerned to establish his earthly aristocratic lineage as his power base:

> For sir Sesar was my sier and I sothely his sonne...
>   And my modir hight Pila þat proude was o plight;
> O Pila þat prowde, Atus hir fadir he hight.
>   This 'Pila' was hadde into 'Atus' —   (XXX, 10, 13-15)

> [For Sir Caesar was my father and I truly his son...
>   And my mother was called Pila, proud in her bearing;
> Oh that proud Pila, her father was called Atus.
>   This 'Pila' was joined to 'Atus' –]

Herod is then presented as a despotic monster outside any system, however provisional. His is the anarchic will of the absolute tyrant, maintained by force – *'we schall choppe þam in cheynes'* (XXXI, 17) [clap them in irons]. Diction in the play of the trial before Herod is a particularly potent moral barometer, as Herod progresses through imitation French and Latin, to nonsense, having complained that Christ's silence is deafening (XXXXI, 189). There are also visual oppositions. The earthly judges indulge in conspicuous material display, contrasting again with Christ, who is stripped, whipped and dressed up as a fool then as a fool-king. Throughout the sequence earthly power is physically asserted, marked by material auspices, and protected by physical sanction, as the buffeting scenes which punctuate the action demonstrate in their violence.

The tension and immediacy of events depend above all on suggested analogies to different types of legal proceedings which we must assume held resonances for the original audiences. All the trials take place in secret circumstances: the dramatist has each judge in turn disturbed from sleep to emphasize this. That the arrest and trial take place at night is presented as a political move to staunch public opinion. Despite attempts to establish their juridical presence by the agents of judgment, Christ consistently refuses to bow to acknowledge the jurisdiction of the hearings or to confirm his own identity and commence pleading. There are two reasons to explain why Christ does not recognize the jurisdiction of the hearings: firstly his is the superior authority, and secondly each judge is in fundamental violation of basic legal principle. As law-givers, Annas and Caiaphas, Pilate and Herod all demonstrate intentions not connected with the common good, but with immediate political expediency, for example to heal the political rift between Pilate and Herod. Injustices perpetrated for the self-seeking ends of tyranny are, according to Aquinas, the chief violation of Natural Law.

These plays do not, however, simply illustrate details of post-scholastic juridical readings of heavenly and earthly society; they offer the possibility of more specific equations between events in sacral history and contemporary legal practices, which expose and subvert those practices. Throughout the group of plays under consideration, so that the politically required death penalty may legally be returned, a continuing project is to identify the crime for which Christ is being tried. Different crimes are tested against their counterparts in legal procedure. Annas and Caiaphas, bishops learned in the law, appear to apply the canon law. Unfortunately none of the textbooks on canon law give information on what actually happened in a court room.[6] Probably procedures varied from court to court, and the archbishop's court would operate very differently from the local courts of dean and chapter (the Peculiars) in the type of business, composition of the bench and officials involved. In the play, Miles III and IV seem to behave as the apparitors, the 'summoners', so famously maligned by Chaucer. They have taken Christ at night and red-handed in the company of his apostles, he has been identified by Judas, so they do not have to prove his identity but merely to make accusations. From this basis, Caiaphas in particular attempts to extract a confession. Once Christ has admitted that he is God's son, Annas considers that a confession to defamation has been achieved and that *'Nowe nedis nowdir wittnesse ne counsaille to call'* (XXIX, 300) [Now it is not necessary to call for witnesses nor advisers]. Christ proceeds to accuse the soldiers of wrongful arrest, as they have taken him secretly by night instead of in public as he preached. He also accuses them of bearing false witness. The bishops retreat at this point, dismissing the case and the possibility of a summary execution as a blemish upon their status, but they resolve to refer their assorted grievances against Christ to Pilate, who is *'domysman nere and nexte to þe king'* [judge nearest and closest to the king].

Annas and Caiaphas can accuse Christ only of witchcraft and of breaking the Ten Commandments, which Pilate points out are unsubstantiated offenses that cannot secure a conviction. When Christ is brought before Pilate on the first occasion, however, he is being brought before a representative of the civil law and the circumstances

---

[6] See Brian L. Woodcock, *Medieval Ecclesiastical Courts in the Diocese of Canterbury* (London: Oxford University Press, 1952); W. Lyndwood, *Provinciale* (Oxford, 1679).

of the hearing are interesting. In the eyes of the civil authorities, Christ could be accused of 'group intransigence directed at a social superior',[7] for this is effectively what he was engaged in when arrested. Failing to impress Pilate with their generalized accusations of witchcraft, this appears to be the area on which the accusers concentrate. Annas says before they approach Pilate,

> Sir Cayphas, ye kenne wele this caytiffe we haue cached
> That ofte-tymes in oure tempill hase teched vntrewly.
> Oure meyne with myght at mydnyght hym mached
> And hase drevyn hym till his demyng for his dedis vndewly...
> (XXX, 196-99)

[Sir Caiaphas, you know well that we have caught this scoundrel
Who has often taught falsely in our temple.
Our company set upon him at midnight with force
And have driven him to judgment for his unlawful actions.]

Riot was an offence against the King's peace, so was a plea of the Crown, but it did not carry the death penalty as it fell into the category of trespass or misdemeanour. It was punishable by being placed in the stocks or in prison, perhaps equivalents to the kind of summary physical abuse to which Christ is subjected after this first hearing before Pilate, as well as the imposition of draconian fines. He could be condemned to death, however, only if convicted of a felony. Riot, or illegal assembly, did not become part of the law of treason until the reign of Henry VII, after 1485, well after the likely range of dates for the play. So Annas and Caiaphas's manipulation of their accusations until they hit upon treason becomes increasingly critical.

There were a series of adjustments to the law governing illegal assembly in the early fifteenth century, building upon the legislation of Richard II's reign which attempted to deal with the abuses of maintenance and which were enhanced in the wake of the events of the 1380s.[8] The statute of 13 Henry IV states:[9]

---

[7] J.G. Bellamy, *Criminal Law and Society in Late Medieval and Tudor England* (Gloucester & New York: Sutton, 1984).

[8] See Paul Strohm, *Hochon's Arrow: the Social Imagination of Fourteenth-Century Texts* (Princeton NJ: Princeton University Press, 1992), esp. pp. 179-85.

[9] *The Statutes at Large 1413-1482, 1 Hen.V to 22 Edw. IV*, Vol. 3 (London, 1762), 2 Hen. 5, c.8 (1414), pp. 25-33. I am grateful to Olga Horner for bringing these to my attention and for her advice on the technical legal aspects of this chapter in general.

that if any riot, assembly or rout of people against the law be made in any part of the realm, then the justices of the peace, three or two of them at the least, and the sheriff or under-sheriff of the county where such riot assembly, or rout shall be made hereafter, should come with the power of the said county, if need were, to arrest them, and them should arrest; and the same justices, sheriff, or under-sheriff should have power to record that which they found so done in their presence against the law; and that by record of the same justices, sheriff or under-sheriff, such trespassers or offenders should be convict in manner and form as is contained in the stature of forcible entries...

It goes on to make provision that if the crowd disperses before arrests can be made, the same prosecutors have one month to establish the truth before they have to appear with twelve men to testify. The justices, sheriffs and under-sheriffs are then bound to enact the statute in the King's name. A further statute of 2 Henry V (1414) then made provision that if the justices and sheriff fail in this duty, the King's commission shall go out under the Great Seal by the direction of the Chancellor:

and that the chancellor of England for the time being, as soon as he may have knowledge of such riot, assembly or rout, shall cause to be sent the King's writ to the justices of the peace, and to the sheriff or under-sheriff of the county where they be so made, that they shall put the statute in execution upon the pain contained in the same...[10]

The first hearing before Pilate is conducted at dead of night. He has to be awakened from his bed, giving the performing guild, the Tapiters and Couchers, an excellent opportunity to display their wares. He then conducts the hearing in secret and alone, apparently according to procedures of summary justice. Statute law did not approve procedure by summary justice, which perhaps explains the secretive nature of the hearing, and calls to question the status of proceedings, for the play seems to make clear that justices could and did proceed in this manner despite its dubious legality. Pilate is, however, frustrated by his inability to extract a confession from Christ who refuses to acknowledge his authority.

The most important clue to the type of hearing, however, probably lies in that line in the previous play, when Annas calls Pilate, '*domysman nere and nexte to þe king*' (XXIX, 341). This designation could only properly be applied to the Chancellor, or his delegated Keeper of the Great Seal, one of the Chief Justices of the King's

---

[10] *Ibid.*, p. 29.

Bench.[11] If we understand that the dramatist is imagining a Chancery hearing in the first trial before Pilate, its apparently unconstitutional and summary nature can be more easily explained. In the second half of the fourteenth century, specific remedies came to be sought from the Chancellor, irrespective of whether a case were pending at common law. Redress tended to be sought *ad hoc*, and in the fifteenth century, the Chancellor issued decrees in his own name. Medieval chancellors 'were reinforcing the law by making sure that justice was done in cases where shortcomings in the regular procedure, or human failings, were hindering its attainment by due process'.[12] The Chancellor offered a way of short-circuiting usual procedures and possible injustices by operating a court of conscience:

> No original writ was necessary, and all actions were commenced by informal complaint, either by bill or by word of mouth... Pleading was in English and relatively informal. Evidence was taken by interrogation or written deposition. There was no jury; the court assembled a dossier of information until it saw fit to take action. The Chancery was always open... It could sit anywhere, even in the Chancellor's private house; and causes could be tried out of court by commission of *dedimus potestatem* to country gentlemen.[13]

Chancery procedure operated by teasing out the facts of the case rather than by attending to the application of law, the Chancellor acting as both judge and jury. Pilate begins by inviting Annas and Caiaphas to join him on the bench, an offer which they decline on the grounds that they are not of sufficient status. He is then strongly protective of Christ, asserting that his failure to show fitting reverence is because he is simple or confused: '*his witte is in warre*' (XXX, 401). It was the Chancellor's job to see that the poor and oppressed received proper justice. Pilate later rebukes Annas in particular for presenting prejudicial material.

Lurking in the background of the earlier hearings is the accusation which eventually does cause Pilate to change his consideration that Annas and Caiaphas are time-wasters. One of the random accusations which Annas and Caiaphas make in the first hearing is that Christ refuses to pay tribute to the emperor. Pilate says that such an offence

---

[11] Here I am following closely the description of Chancery proceedings given in J.H. Baker, *An Introduction to English Legal History*, 3rd edition (London: Butterworths, 1990), pp. 112-29. See also Alan Harding, *The Law Courts of Medieval England*, (London: Allen & Unwin, 1973), pp. 92-123.

[12] Baker, *Introduction*, pp. 118-19.

[13] *Ibid.*, p. 119.

would be a treason punishable by death (XXX, 468-70), but it appears to go unproven or be incorrectly formulated. When Christ is returned from Herod, Pilate remains reluctant to try him further, claiming that Herod has found nothing wrong with him either, so there can be no charges to answer. Caiaphas, however, asks for him to be brought to the bar for another hearing, eventually adding the clinching accusation:

>   To be kyng he claymeth, with croune,
>   And whoso stoutely wille steppe to þat state
>   3e suld deme ser, to be dong doune
>   And dede. (XXXIII, 329-32

[He claims to be a crowned king
  And whosoever will boldly advance himself to that state
    You should judge, sir, to be brought down
      And killed.]

to which Pilate replies:

>   Sir, trulye þat touched to treasoune...
>   (XXXIII, 33)
>   [Sir, truly that approaches treason...]

Treason is a felony, an unmendable wrong, 'a violation of the duty of allegiance which is owed to the sovereign'[14] in which the wrongdoer suffered the consequent penalty of losing all he had, including his life. Felonies were generally prosecuted by appeal, where the appellants lodged an oral accusation of the crime. Until the late fourteenth century, appeals of felony were usually instigated by hue and cry then brought before the county courts, the justices in eyre, but by the fifteenth century almost all appeals were heard before the King's Bench. Baker has noted that records of criminal proceedings show victims' appeals increasingly serving only to bring the accused to court, where they were then dropped and prosecution taken over in the King's name.[15] Christ's refusal to accept the jurisdiction of this final hearing in open court presents further difficulties under contemporary law. Everyone who pleaded 'not guilty' on a capital charge of felony was asked how he wished to be tried. The only answer was 'by God and the country', which meant by a local jury. Anyone refusing this was commonly killed without trial, often by

---

[14] David M. Walker, *Oxford Companion to Law* (Oxford: Clarendon Press, 1980), p. 1232.

[15] Baker, *Introduction*, p. 575.

pressing under heavy weights. If the jury was likely to convict anyway, this grisly death was preferable because, although the defendant died, with no guilty verdict his inheritance was not forfeit but was saved for his heirs.

There is little record of how a jury trial proceeded before the sixteenth century, as there was no systematic reporting, but Baker assumes that things had changed very little in the preceding century.[16]

> When the commissions had been read and the justices were seated, the grand jury was sworn and charged, and started to examine the bills of indictment produced by the clerk.

Once Pilate has accepted that another hearing should go ahead, Caiaphas leads the way in reiterating the accusations and offers to call a number of witnesses:

> I can reken a rable of renkes full right
> Of perte men in prese fro this place ar I pas,
> þat will witnesse, I warande, þe wordis of þis wight
>   (XXXIII, 108-110)

> [I can summon up a crowd of people very well
> Of sharp men from the crowd in this place before I go,
> Who will bear witness, I guarantee, to the words of this man...]

Pilate dismisses these as men likely to bare 'hatred in ther hartis' against Jesus, only to be reassured by Caiaphas that they are *'trist men and true'*. Pilate then agrees to have Jesus brought to the bar.

> The prisoners were then brought into court, chained together at the ankles, to await arraignment. When the indictments were produced, the prisoners named in them were brought to the bar of the court, with their shackles struck off, and asked to plead to the indictments.

Jesus is brought in by the soldiers, apparently shackled, at this point, but this is also the point when there is an involuntary departure from normal procedure, as the individuals in the court find themselves rising to reverence him, leaving Miles III to have to plead with Pilate and *'tho senioures beside 3ou'* [those elders beside you](180) not to punish them, for *'þis werke þat we haue wrought it was not oure will'*. [we did not intend to do this thing we have done](183).

---

[16] *Ibid.*, p. 581, quoted from in the following analysis; see also Thomas A. Green, *Verdict According to Conscience: Perspectives on the English Criminal Trial Jury 1200-1800* (Chicago: University of Chicago Press, 1985), pp. 90-96.

THE TRIAL PLAYS IN THE YORK CYCLE

> If a prisoner pleaded Not guilty, as most did, and put himself on the country, twelve jurors were sworn in from the panel provided by the sheriff. The clerk then called for anyone to give evidence against the prisoner.

In the play, because of what has just occurred, the clerk is sent out to find bigger men to hold the standards steady which Pilate's own soldiers were unable to do. Thus the judgment of the jury becomes an involuntary trial by will, rather than a rational assessment of evidence. Caiaphas is called upon to swear them in, then Annas again summons Jesus to the bar (264-67). This time both judge (Pilate) and 'jury' find themselves reverencing Christ, testifying physically to his innocence. Pilate is then eager to discharge the prisoner: *'wightly his wayes late hym wende...'* [let him go his ways quickly] (281).

> The witnesses who came forward for the Crown were sworn to tell the truth, and in telling their story might fall into altercation with the prisoner.

Caiaphas and Annas persist in pressing charges, and Pilate then asks Jesus to defend himself. Instead of doing so directly, he invokes the threat of another judgment, at Doomsday. It is at this point that Caiaphas finally hits upon the accusation which causes Pilate to take the charges more seriously: *'to be kyng he claymeth, with croune'*. Still no sentence is passed, however, but Christ, not having pled, is taken off for the buffeting and crowning with thorns. Unfortunately, after the flogging, there is a hiatus of fifty lines in the manuscript. What is supposed to happen next is that:

> the jury then gave its verdict, and according to its terms the prisoner was either discharged or remanded for sentence. At the end of the session, if any prisoners remained against whom no indictments had been found, a proclamation was made for evidence against them; if no one came forward, they were discharged.

Presumably the jury selected Barabbas to be released during the hiatus, for we rejoin the action as Pilate calls for water to wash his hands saying,

> For propirly by þis processe will I preve
> I had no force fro þis felawshippe þis freke for to fende.
> (XXXIII, 440-41)

[For personally by these proceedings I will prove
That I had no power to defend this man from this
                        company.]

He then pronounces the verdict. The circumstances are biblical, but the public nature of the final trial suggested to the dramatist that what began as a series of trumped-up charges for offences against the canon law has moved into the area of dubious but topical summary procedure for illegal assembly, and finally into a full arraignment for treason by Annas and Caiaphas. The jury returns a guilty verdict impelling the death penalty at last.

The plays in question cannot be dated precisely. The 1415 *Ordo Paginarum*[17] lists the characters in the Bowers and Fletchers play in a way that suggests it might already have taken a form similar to that which appears in the Register of the 1460s. The Tapiters and Couchers' play does seem to have been enhanced some time between 1415 and the 1460s copy, however, as the memorandum documents only Jesus, Pilate, Annas, Caiaphas, two counsellors and four accusing Jews, making no mention of the whole episode involving the dream of Pilate's wife. Consequently 'mid-fifteenth-century' is the closest we can come to dating the sequence on present evidence. York did have one celebrated brush with the establishment and its legal system in 1405, when the city supported its own archbishop, Richard Scrope, in his rebellion against Henry IV, which cast a long shadow throughout the years of Lancastrian rule. Although details of the sequence of events which led to Scrope's execution are inadequate to establish precise intentional parallels in the construction of the trial plays, there is enough to suggest the tantalizing possibilities of a contemporary subversive subtext.

Scrope failed to secure the protection of benefit of clergy which caused general scandal, particularly among York's merchant elite whose support he had won by attacking Henry IV's record of excessive government. John Capgrave's near-contemporary partisan account demonstrates just how closely Scrope's rebellion was connected politically to the interests of the mercantile community centrally concerned with the production of the mystery cycle.[18]

---

[17] Alexandra Johnson and Margaret Rogerson, *York: Records of Early English Drama* (Toronto: University of Toronto Press, 1979), p. 21.

[18] *John Capgrave's Abbreuiacion of Chronicles*, ed. by Peter Lucas, EETS 285 (Oxford: Oxford University Press, 1983), p. 227. I am grateful to Meg Twycross for her help in assembling details of the Scrope case.

THE TRIAL PLAYS IN THE YORK CYCLE

Thei [Scrope, the Earl of Mowbray and the Duke of Northumberland] cleped onto hem þe cite of ȝork and mech of þe cuntre, and set up certeyn articles on cherch-dores, expressing what was her entent:

> First þei desired þat þe puple of þe reme schuld haue fre eleccion of knytes of þe parlement aftir þe eld forme; the secunde, þat þer schuld be a remedie ageyns fals sugges|tiones, be which many men were disherid of her londis' the þirde, þat þere schuld be ordeyned a remedye ageyn þese greuous taskes, and ageyne þe grete extorciones, and eke oppressing of marchauntis.

[They called unto them the city of York and much of the country, and set up certain articles on church doors, expressing their intentions:

> First they desired that the people of the realm should have free election of the knights in Parliament following custom; secondly that there should be a remedy against false accusations by which men were disinherited of their lands, and thirdly that there should be ordained a redress against these grievous taxes and against the great extortions and also the oppressing of merchants.]

Capgrave further recounts how Scrope was defeated by deceit, being persuaded by the Earl of Westmorland to dismiss the rebels and come to parley, during which time he was violently seized. The Latin chronicles of York assembled by James Raine for the Rolls Series give the best detail of the difficulties the royal party then suffered in trying to secure a capital judgment on the archbishop.[19]

> *Henricus enim Quartus, rex Angliae, in camera manerii dicti archiepiscaopi, quod vocatur Bishopsthorp juxta Eboracum, mandavit Willelmo Gascoyne armigero, adtunc justitiario principali Angliae, ut sententiam mortis de praefato archiepiscopo proferret tamquam de proditore regis; qui hoc recusavit, et sic respondit: 'Nec vos, domine mi rex, nec aliquis nomine vestro vester ligeus, potestis licite secundum jura regni aliquem episcopum ad mortem judicare.' Unde praefatum archiepiscopum judicare omnino renuit. Quare idem rex ira vehementi exarsit versus eundem judicem, cujus memoria sit in benedictionem in saecula saeculi. Et statim mandavit domino Willelmo Fulthorp, militi et non judici, ut eodem die, scilicet feria secunda hebdomadis Pentecostes, qui fuit dies octavus mensis Junii, sententiam mortis in aula praefati manerii in archiepiscopum, quem vocavit proditorem, proferret. Et cum praedictus Willelmus Gascoyne, judex principalis Angliae, omnino renuit, praedictus dominus Willelmus Fulthorp in loco judicis sedit, et archiepiscopum adduci praeceperat.*

---

[19] James Raine, ed., *Historians of the Church of York and its Archbishops*, Vol. II, Rolls Series 71B (London: Longman, 1886), p. 306.

Quo archiepiscopo coram ipso nudo capite stante, hanc sententiam, ipso audiente et omnibus circumstantibus, protulit: 'Te, Ricardum, proditorem regis, ad mortem judicamus, et ex praecepto regis decollari mandamus...'

[Henry IV, King of England, in a chamber of the said archbishop's manor, called Bishopthorp near York, gave instructions to Sir William Gascoigne, then Chief Justice of England, so that a death sentence could be pronounced on the said archbishop as traitor to the king. Gascoigne was reluctant to do this, replying:

> Neither you, your Royal Highness, nor any of your liege in your name, have the lawful power according to the justice of royal authority to judge any bishop to death.

Accordingly he emphatically refused to judge the archbishop. Whereupon the king completely lost his temper with the judge, whose memory be blessed forever more, and immediately he ordered Sir William Fulthorp, a knight but no judge, in order that that very day, namely the Tuesday in the week following Pentecost, the eighth of June, he might pronounce a sentence of death on the archbishop as a traitor, in the hall of the aforesaid manor. And since the same William Gascoigne, Chief Justice of England, completely refused, the said Sir William Fulthorp sat in place of the judge and ordered the archbishop to be brought. He pronounced the following sentence on the archbishop, the same standing bareheaded in his presence, listening, and for all standing around:

> You, Richard, traitor to the king, we judge to death and order to be beheaded according to the king's command.]

After Scrope's death, his remains brought back to York Minster became the focus of a civic campaign to have him canonized. Chronicle accounts of his trial and execution accordingly lay heavy emphasis on his Christ-like last words, and the miracles which attended his death, as well as upon the local magnate Gascoigne's Pilate-like dilemma. Both the major chroniclers add that after the archbishop's defeat, the citizens of York came out to meet the king, barefoot and with halters around their necks.[20] Similar details are contained in Raine's compilation.[21] The field where the archbishop's blood was shed remained a place of miraculous crops and pilgrimage

---

[20] *Ibid.*, p. 32; Capgrave, p. 229.

[21] Raine, ed., *Historians of the Church of York and its Archbishops*, Vol. II, Rolls Series 71B (1886), 304-11; 431-33; Vol. III, Rolls Series 71C (1894), 288-94.

until, as Capgrave puts it, 'the tyme þat þe kyng forbade it, up peyne of deth', and all imply with some relish that Henry IV's later reputedly leprous and shrivelled condition may be directly attributed to the crime of permitting the condemnation of the saintly archbishop.[22]

The local sensitivity of the political context of these events is clear.[23] Scrope's rebellion was potentially explosive coming at a point when the Lancastrian succession's bid for legitimacy was so fragile, but it was also to prove a tenacious *cause célèbre* in York. Scrope had been condemned despite the pleadings of Archbishop Arundel, and the refusal of Gascoigne, Chief Justice of the King's Bench, to try the case. The royal pardon of August 1405 to the city of York for its part in the rebellion was extended to members of the crafts and trades of the city.[24] As Barrie Dobson puts it:[25]

> Most dramatically of all, it was popular enthusiasm for the 'glory of York' and 'loyal martyr of Christ' which came near to securing Richard Scrope's canonization in the face of Lancastrian opposition.

Those whose sympathies Scrope courted in the city were precisely those who would have been intimately involved in the production of the mystery plays and who, through membership of the big religious confraternities of St George and St Christopher, would have had lay association with the Minster. Henry IV was reconciled with the pope in 1408, but there are sundry testimonies to a continuing Scrope cult in York which remained strong enough to cause Henry V to appoint a keeper of the tomb. By the mid-century, Scrope had become firmly fixed in Yorkist martyrology, reinforcing the dynastic claims of Edward IV. He is featured complete with halo, in a clerestory window of the period in the Minster, opposite York's more securely sanctified St William, as well as in York's most famous fifteenth-century book of hours.[26]

---

[22] *Ibid.*, p. 229

[23] *Ibid.*, pp. 291-92.

[24] E.F. Jacob, *The Fifteenth Century, 1399-1485* (Oxford: Clarendon Press, 1978), pp. 58-62.

[25] Barrie Dobson, 'The late Middle Ages, 1215-1500', in *A History of York Minster* ed. by G.E. Aylmer and Reginald Cant (Oxford: Clarendon Press, 1977), pp. 44-109, 108.

[26] David O'Connor and Jeremy Haselock, 'The Stained and Painted Glass', in *A History of York Minster* ed. by G.E. Aylmer and Reginald Cant, pp. 317-93, 377-78; York Minster Add. MS 2, the so-called 'Bolton Hours', a manuscript of lay mercantile ownership; cf. Pamela M. King, 'Corpus Christi Plays and the "Bolton

I cannot demonstrate conclusively that the dramatist in the York plays of the trials of Christ presents a sustained allusion to contemporary legal procedures let alone the circumstances surrounding York's perception of the miscarriage of justice which had been inflicted upon its own man of God. He does, however, use procedural details as illuminating referents to expand on and render concrete his biblical narrative. This has the effect of enriching the potential meaning of these episodes as historical events with issues both metaphysical and immediate. The plays exploit the court-room context theatrically, by verbal and visual allusion to contemporary legal procedure, to expose and subvert contemporary practice. Christ as the delegate of all men is presented as victim because he has no chain of office, no crown, no recognized voice within the estates system. Arrayed against him, and systematically discredited, is the whole panoply of royal (Lancastrian) authority as it would have been perceived in early fifteenth-century York. Scrope was York's man of God who had the courage and audacity to join a rebellion against the ruling secular power in order to promote, amongst other things, the interests of the urban mercantile class. He was seized by treachery in the very act of convening an illegal assembly with treasonable intent, and subjected to a secretive trial in which the 'domysman nere and nexte to þe king' at first refused to preside then became a reluctant participant. And the trial took place in the week before Corpus Christi. Annas and Caiaphas exhibit for the urban mercantile class all the cabalistic exclusivity of the Church, the closed discourse of learning, criticized by the Lollards. Herod is a foreign tyrant, another repository of inaccessible discourses, constructed unconstitutionally. Pilate, for all his reluctance, is still the agent of secular authority, based upon aristocratic power, which comes of established birth and earthly lineage, of bearing arms. And the plays are constructed such that all authority is equated with unbelief, such that the law of man does not derive from the eternal law of God, but is opposed to it, setting itself above it in a manner conducive to universal disorder except amongst the community in York who recognize where true and false justice lie.

Hours": Tastes in Lay Piety and Patronage in Fifteenth-century York', *Medieval English Theatre*, 18 (1996), 46-62.

Festive drama and community politics in late medieval Coventry

CHRIS HUMPHREY

OVER THE LAST TWENTY-FIVE years there has been considerable discussion of the role which ceremony played in the late medieval urban community. As regards the English evidence, scholars such as Charles Phythian-Adams and Mervyn James have proposed that it was through ceremony that the urban community was able to maintain its social structure and diffuse the inevitable tensions which arose within it.[1] This model has gone on to enjoy considerable popularity as a way of thinking about and explaining the relationship between the events of the urban festival calendar and the social structure of towns.[2] More recently though, a number of scholars have drawn attention to the potentially divisive role of civic ceremony; Miri Rubin for example has noted the disputes that arose over the matter of which guild should take precedence in the York Corpus Christi procession in the fifteenth century.[3] What is noticeable is that whilst there has been a great deal of discussion of the occasions which are held to encourage a sense of community through its idealized depiction, such as the Corpus Christi procession, in my view there has not been sufficient critical thought given to the view of the observances which are held to constitute the

---

[1] C. Phythian-Adams, 'Ceremony and the Citizen: The Communal Year at Coventry 1450-1550', in *Crisis and Order in English Towns, 1500-1700: Essays in Urban History*, ed. by P. Clark and P. Slack (London: Routledge & Kegan Paul, 1972), pp. 57-85; M. James, 'Ritual, Drama and Social Body in the Late Medieval English Town', *Past and Present* 98 (1983), 3-29.

[2] See for example D.H. Sacks, *The Widening Gate: Bristol and the Atlantic Economy, 1450-1700*, The New Historicism: Studies in Cultural Poetics 15 (Berkeley, Los Angeles and London: University of California Press, 1991), pp. 140 and 391 n. 31.

[3] M. Rubin, *Corpus Christi: The Eucharist in Late Medieval Culture* (Cambridge: Cambridge University Press, 1991), pp. 265-67.

complement of these formal ceremonies. These are the customs that are thought to encourage community through an inversion rather than an idealization of norms, such as carnival, hocking and the boy-bishop's feast. These customs, which may be usefully labelled 'misrule', continue to be attributed with the function of relieving social tensions and helping to confirm the existing social structure through the temporary reversal of social norms.[4]

My contention has been that although this view of misrule addresses some very important themes regarding the role of festal culture in the medieval town, namely, how such customs were implicated in its local politics and in the reproduction of its social structure, what we may call the 'safety-valve' model is nonetheless inappropriate both as a metaphor and as a tool for the analysis of these themes.[5] Problems with this model include a lack of evidence showing how misrule worked to dissipate such tensions in practice, an insufficient appreciation of the diversity of the possible functions that misrule was able to have, and an inadequate model of the social dynamics of late medieval society.[6] A consideration of these problems has led me to propose a new approach to the study of medieval misrule. I have suggested that in order to appreciate the full range of meanings and functions that such customs were able to have, it is necessary to undertake a closer examination of those examples where sufficient contextual evidence survives. A series of such case-studies will I believe offer a more satisfactory means of establishing how misrule was involved in negotiating politics and social status in the late medieval urban community.[7] In this essay I explore how one particular form of misrule, the practice of gathering vegetation from private land during the summer, was bound up with the wider affairs of the community in Coventry in the fifteenth century.[8] My interest is

---

[4] See for example P. Burke, *Popular Culture in Early Modern Europe* (London: Temple Smith, 1978), pp. 201-04; M. Camille, *Image on the Edge: The Margins of Medieval Art* (London: Reaktion, 1992), p. 143; S. Shahar, 'The Boy-Bishop's Feast: a Case-Study in Church Attitudes towards Children in the High and Late Middle Ages', *Studies in Church History* 31 (1994), 243-60, (p. 249); S.-B. MacLean, 'Hocktide: A Reassessment of a Popular Pre-Reformation Festival', in *Festive Drama*, ed. by M. Twycross (Cambridge Mass; Woodbridge: D.S. Brewer, 1996), pp. 233-41 (pp. 238-39); P. H. Greenfield, 'Festive Drama at Christmas in Aristocratic Households', in *Festive Drama*, ed. by Twycross, pp. 34-40 (pp. 34 and 37).

[5] C. Humphrey, 'The Dynamics of Urban Festal Culture in Later Medieval England', (unpublished doctoral thesis, University of York, 1997), p. 8.

[6] Humphrey, 'Dynamics of Urban Festal Culture', p. 47.

[7] Humphrey, 'Dynamics of Urban Festal Culture', p. 8.

[8] This essay draws upon the study of vegetation-gathering at Coventry which constitutes the fourth chapter of my doctoral thesis (Humphrey, 'Dynamics of Urban

in the dynamic relationship between this custom and the social conditions in which it was performed; as well as examining how the meaning and significance of the custom changed in response to local circumstances, I also consider the role which the custom itself played in modifying the balance of power within the community at this time. I begin by giving a short introduction to the practice of vegetation-gathering, and I discuss briefly the background to this case.

Vegetation-gathering

Ronald Hutton's account of the ritual year in England c.1490 to c.1540, which forms the first chapter of *The Rise and Fall of Merry England*, supplies an overview of the ways in which vegetation was used in festival occasions in late medieval England. These uses include holly and ivy for decoration at Christmas, branches for Palm Sunday, rushes and flowers on Easter Day, maypoles at May Day, and branches for bonfires and decoration at Midsummer.[9] As regards holly and ivy, Hutton notes that '[t]he urban churchwardens' accounts for the period virtually all show payments for these evergreens, and their absence from the accounts of country churches is almost certainly due to the fact that they were freely available in the parish'.[10] This would suggest the existence of a market for seasonal vegetation in towns, with demand coming from churches, guilds and householders. Individuals wanting vegetation did not necessarily have to pay for it though, since there is also evidence for customary rights to vegetation from private land at festival periods. Although it comes from fourteenth-century France, a well-documented case of vegetation-gathering provides a clear example of the sorts of issues that were at stake when such a practice encroached upon private land.[11] In 1311, a dispute arose between the Hôtel-Dieu of Pontoise and the commune of Chambly, over the use of the wood of the Tour du Lay:

> The wood of the Tour du Lay had been given to the Hôtel-Dieu of Pontoise by Saint Louis in 1261. The religious claimed that they had enjoyed uncontested possession of it since then, but it emerges from the dispute that the inhabitants of Chambly had by custom exercised

---

Festal Culture', pp. 84-108).

[9] R. Hutton, *The Rise and Fall of Merry England: The Ritual Year 1400-1700* (Oxford: Clarendon Press, 1994), pp. 5-48 (pp. 5-6, 20-21, 25-26, 27-30, 37-39).

[10] Hutton, *The Rise and Fall of Merry England*, p. 5.

[11] A.W. Lewis, 'Forest Rights and the Celebration of May: Two Documents from the French Vexin, 1311-1318', *Mediaeval Studies* 53 (1991), 259-77. I am grateful to John Arnold for this reference.

some rights to gather wood and other materials from it [...] According to the spokesmen for the religious, in the past the *ministres* of the Hôtel-Dieu, in their goodness and innocence, had allowed the townsfolk to gather flowers and leafy boughs from the wood on feast days during the month of May; but the spokesmen claimed that only twenty persons at a time had gone there for that purpose. On two occasions in early May 1311, however, large crowds from the town - five hundred persons on the first day, more than one thousand on the second - went to the wood at the direction of the communal officials, collecting great quantities of timber and doing extensive damage to the forest.[12]

It is sufficient to note that in the accord of 1318 that was concluded between the officers of Chambly and the Hôtel-Dieu, the townspeople were limited to collecting just one bundle or handful of greenery each from the wood on 1 May until noon.[13]

Where vegetation-gathering did encroach upon private land in this way, the practice fits the criteria of misrule, where laws or norms were temporarily transgressed as part of a festival occasion. Misrule itself may be considered as one category in a wider class of activities that are grouped under the heading of 'festive drama', those practices which are associated with a festival occasion such as processions, folk customs and drama itself.[14] The practice of vegetation-gathering has not received anything like the degree of attention in the secondary sources that other examples of misrule such as hocking have had, probably because the evidence for it is fairly scarce; cases are only likely to have been recorded when the custom became disputed locally or where it was involved in a more substantial incident. In the latter class we may consider 'Evil May-Day' in London in 1517, where an alleged plot to murder foreigners in the city took place on the day that the city's apprentices went into the fields to gather decorative flowers and branches.[15] There is also evidence to suggest that the practice of

---

[12] Lewis, 'Forest Rights and the Celebration of May', 259-60 (p. 260).

[13] Lewis, 'Forest Rights and the Celebration of May', 266.

[14] M. Twycross, 'Some Approaches to Dramatic Festivity, especially Processions', in *Festive Drama*, ed. by M. Twycross, pp. 1-33 (pp. 1-2).

[15] For discussions of this incident see for example J.J. Scarisbrick, *Henry VIII* (London: Eyre Methuen, 1976), pp. 98-99, and T. Pettitt, '"Here Comes I, Jack Straw:" English Folk Drama and Social Revolt', *Folklore* 95 (1984), 3-20 (pp. 3, 5). See also Steven Justice's arguments regarding the association between the gathering of vegetation for Midsummer bonfires and the public burning of documents during the English Rising of 1381; S. Justice, *Writing and Rebellion: England in 1381*, The New Historicism: Studies in Cultural Poetics 27 (Berkeley: University of California Press, 1994), pp. 150-56.

vegetation-gathering became bound up with larger issues of the rights and access to the common lands of Coventry in the later fifteenth century. A brief background to these events will be given before I move on to consider the main details of this case.

Medieval Coventry

The historic association of Lady Godiva with Coventry is well known: Leofric, Earl of Mercia, had married Godiva by 1035 and the couple founded a Benedictine abbey at Coventry in 1043. This abbey was taken over by the Bishop of Chester when he transferred his seat to Coventry in the late eleventh century, and it henceforth became a cathedral priory. Using forged charters the bishop established the priory's right to Holy Trinity Church and its parish, giving the prior jurisdiction over the northern part of the town, whilst the southern part was under the lordship of the earls of Chester.[16] Although there has been considerable discussion of the extent to which this situation created a distinct 'Earl's Half' and 'Prior's Half' in the town, this division may have mattered less in practice than in theory.[17] In 1330 the manor of Cheylesmore devolved on Isabella, queen of Edward II, and following a judgement against the priory during this decade she became the sole lord of the town.[18] Coventry subsequently gained the right to elect its own council, mayor and bailiffs, these privileges being granted in 1345.[19] The priory continued to contest these settlements, and whilst a tripartite indenture between Isabella, the mayor and bailiffs and the priory in 1355 sought to resolve the situation, there were further disputes over rights to land in the fifteenth century, and it is these matters which form the basis of this essay.[20] Most of the evidence that I will be drawing on is taken from the town's first 'Leet Book', the record of the legislation and correspondence pertaining to the Easter and Michaelmas 'Leets' or courts of justice at which minor offences were heard and civic ordinances passed.[21]

---

[16] *The Atlas of Historic Towns*, ed. by M.D. Lobel, 3 vols (London: Lovell, 1969-91), 2 'Coventry' p. 3.

[17] See C. Phythian-Adams, *Desolation of a City: Coventry and the Urban Crisis of the Late Middle Ages* (Cambridge: Cambridge University Press, 1979), p. 118 n. 1, and A. and E. Gooder, 'Coventry before 1355: Unity or Division?', *Midland History* 6 (1981), 1-38.

[18] *Atlas of Historic Towns*, ed. by Lobel, 2 'Coventry' p. 6.

[19] *Calendar of Charter Rolls, 1341-1417*, p. 36.

[20] *Atlas of Historic Towns*, ed. by Lobel, 2 'Coventry' p. 6.

[21] *The Coventry Leet Book*, ed. by M.D. Harris, EETS O.S. 134, 135, 138, 146 (1907-

A major dispute occurred in the town in 1469, after a number of measures had been introduced to regulate the use of the River Sherbourne and the common lands of the town in the mayoralty of William Saunders.[22] The Michaelmas Leet of 1469 forbade any encroachment on or pollution of the river and decreed that the bounds of the city were to be ridden every three years. Furthermore, no uncommonable beasts were to be grazed on the common lands, and all common lands that were unlawfully enclosed were to be reopened before 1 November that year.[23] These measures were designed to protect the rights of the citizens of the town to use the common lands for grazing their animals and for recreational purposes. An immediate consequence of these measures was that they brought the town into renewed conflict both with the Bristow family, who were owners of land at Whitley, to the south of the city, and with the cathedral priory. On 4 December the citizens threw open land which they claimed had been unlawfully enclosed by Bristow at Whitley, and on 6 December some of the priory's lands outside of the city walls at New Gate and at Whitmore Park were similarly targeted.[24] These actions brought about some rather complicated litigation, and some hard and shrewd bargaining; in return for firm guarantees protecting their lands in the future, the priory appear to have agreed to drop their case against the city, who were left with only Bristow's suit to contend with.[25] However, by 1480 the city, the priory and Bristow were again embroiled in disputes about the status of the common lands, and it is to these events that I now turn.

Disputes with Bristow and the Priory, 1480

The main focus of my enquiry is to look at a bill of complaints that was submitted by Prior Deram to the mayor of Coventry in November 1480. This bill contained details of a large number of grievances,

---

13), p. xix.

[22] William Saunders is named as mayor on 25 January 1469 in the *Coventry Leet Book*, ed. by Harris, p. 339. The spelling of names from the *Leet Book* has been left in the original where that person is cited only once or twice here; the names of individuals who are cited more often have been standardized in line with modern usage.

[23] *Coventry Leet Book*, ed. by Harris, pp. 347-48.

[24] *Coventry Leet Book*, ed. by Harris, pp. 349-52.

[25] In 1481 the prior alleged that the deal with the New Gate land and other fields in 1469 had been made so that the priory should not be troubled in the future, in return for not pursuing their suit when Bristow was pursuing his; see below (*Coventry Leet Book*, ed. by Harris, p. 471).

which ranged from the rather serious allegation that the terms of the 1355 tripartite indenture had been broken, through to the charge that the townspeople had blocked the gate of the Prior's Orchard with dung, and so prevented him from taking his carriage through it as he was accustomed to do.[26] Several of the complaints are of particular interest in that they provide evidence to suggest that certain activities were being employed in a confrontational way at Coventry in this period, probably as part of a wider tactical campaign. These activities included vegetation-gathering and the sport of roving, which Mary Dormer Harris has suggested was the practice of shooting at movable targets.[27] The prior's bill of complaints was delivered after a turbulent few months in city politics, and it will be helpful to summarize in brief the details of these events.

Laurence Saunders and William Hede, both dyers, were elected as chamberlains of Coventry in January 1480. It was their insistence on fulfilling their duties to the letter rather than according to the customary practices which suited other members of the city government that led to a protracted conflict which ran from the April to the October of that year.[28] Laurence was the son of William Saunders, the mayor who, as we saw above, introduced the measures to safeguard the common lands in 1469. After taking up the position of chamberlain in 1480 Laurence spent the next decade and a half campaigning to protect the common lands from encroachment and enclosure, before disappearing into the Fleet in November 1495.[29] William Hede was on the common council of the town by 1477, and whilst he held with Saunders during the events of 1480, he eventually broke with his fellow officer and submitted to the then mayor, William Shore, in the October of that year.[30] There were two disputes

---

[26] *Coventry Leet Book*, ed. by Harris, pp. 443-53 (pp. 444, 447).

[27] *Coventry Leet Book*, ed. by Harris, pp. 445-46 and 446 n. 1.

[28] Laurence Saunders and William Hede are named as chamberlains on 25 January 1480 in the *Coventry Leet Book*, ed. by Harris, p. 424. Laurence is named as a dyer on p. 510 and William on p. 403. This episode is recorded on pp. 430-43.

[29] Other incidents involving Laurence Saunders can be found in the *Coventry Leet Book*, ed. by Harris, on pp. 510-13, 556-57, 564, 574-80. The bill set up on the door of St Michael's Church after Lammas in 1495 also comments upon his situation (pp. 566-67). Laurence was committed to the Fleet in November 1495 (pp. 579-80). For an account of Saunders' campaign see M.D. Harris, 'Laurence Saunders, Citizen of Coventry', *English Historical Review* 9 (1894), 633-51 and *Life in an Old English Town: A History of Coventry from the Earliest Times, Compiled from Official Records* (London; New York: Sonnenschein; Macmillan, 1898), pp. 219-28, 236-52.

[30] Named as a member of the forty-eight in 1477 in the *Coventry Leet Book*, ed. by Harris, p. 421; he submitted to the mayor on 14 October 1469 (pp. 435-36). William Shore is named as mayor on 25 January 1480 (p. 424).

which arose during their term of office, both of which appear to have resulted from differences of opinion over the responsibilities of the position of chamberlain. One dispute arose with the mayor, William Shore, probably in May 1480. The chamberlains had refused to pay the wages of labourers who had been digging stone for the city wall, with Laurence telling the mayor that whoever had set the labourers to work should pay for them. Hede and Saunders were committed to ward and bound under a recognizance of £40 to obey the mayor and council in future, and a fine of £4 was also levied.[31] The second dispute arose over rights to pasture on the town's common land, and lasted from April to October 1480. The events of these months are recorded in a petition which the chamberlains submitted to Edward, Prince of Wales, on 20 September; Laurence had requested permission to ride to Southampton, but instead rode to Ludlow to deliver the petition, a copy of which is entered into the Leet Book.[32] The first incident that is described in the petition took place on 8 April of that year, when the chamberlains distrained two hundred sheep belonging to William Deister which were found grazing on common land. However, the chamberlains were committed to prison by the mayor for doing so, and the sheep were freed without the fee of pinlock being levied, the charge usually made by the chamberlains for penning animals which were grazing illegally. Mary Dormer Harris suggests that the animals were distrained either because they exceeded the number that each individual was allowed, or because sheep were non-commonable animals.[33] On 18 April, having been prevented from speaking at the Easter Leet, the chamberlains were bound £40 each by the recorder, the town's legal officer, and were told that pinlock was to be taken as he saw fit.[34] Later in the year, when sheep belonging to William Bristow and the prior were grazed on common land, the chamberlains were again prevented from levying a charge.[35]

After correspondence between the mayor and brethren and the Prince about the chamberlains' petition at the end of September and the beginning of October, a meeting was arranged, and William Hede was one of those who rode to Ludlow, after having submitted himself to the mayor's rule.[36] The verdict of the Prince and his advisors,

---

[31] *Coventry Leet Book*, ed. by Harris, pp. 430-32.

[32] *Coventry Leet Book*, ed. by Harris, p. 432; the chamberlains' petition is on pp. 436-40.

[33] *Coventry Leet Book*, ed. by Harris, p. 437 and n. 2.

[34] *Coventry Leet Book*, ed. by Harris, pp. 437-38.

[35] *Coventry Leet Book*, ed. by Harris, pp. 438, 439.

[36] *Coventry Leet Book*, ed. by Harris, pp. 432-36.

contained in a letter dated 22 October, was that Laurence Saunders was to be punished, and that the citizens of the town should obey the mayor's rule. Some time after the receipt of the Prince's reply, Saunders was summoned to appear at St Mary's Hall, where the Prince's letter was read to him. Saunders knelt before the mayor, acknowledged his offences and sought forgiveness; he was committed to prison until a recognisance of £500 was taken from his friends, obliging him to appear at subsequent general sessions until his behaviour was considered to be satisfactory.[37]

The prior's bill of complaint was delivered to the mayor and brethren on 16 November, and so it began another dispute just as the episode with the chamberlains was drawing to a close.[38] A number of the grievances contained in this bill relate to incidents that have already been discussed. For example, the prior complained that he had never received satisfaction for the incident at Whitmore in 1469, having not been able to sue those responsible; he was later to suggest that he had agreed not to take any action at this time because William Bristow was pursuing his suit, in return for sureties regarding a croft outside New Gate and other lands.[39] Another complaint was that he suffered slander from Laurence Saunders and other persons who said that he kept pastures enclosed which ought to have been common; these claims were amongst those that were made in Saunders' petition to the Prince.[40] Other grievances appear to have been of a more personal nature, perhaps as part of a campaign of harassment. The prior complained that the people of the city were depositing dung, refuse and house-sweepings against the wall and gate of the Prior's Orchard, so that he was not able to take his carriage through the orchard as he had previously been accustomed to do. The inclusion of refuse in the deposits meant that people from the country did not now come and take them away, as they had done previously.[41]

The complaints that are most interesting in respect of the present enquiry are those which allege that people of the city trespassed on and caused damage to priory lands through their sports and festival customs. In the fifth article of his bill, the prior complained that the people of the city yearly in summer took away the prior's undergrowth, and birch, holly, oak, hawthorn and other trees at

---

[37] *Coventry Leet Book*, ed. by Harris, pp. 441-43.

[38] *Coventry Leet Book*, ed. by Harris, pp. 443-53.

[39] *Coventry Leet Book*, ed. by Harris, pp. 444, 471; on the grants made following the events of 6 December 1469, see pp. 350-52.

[40] *Coventry Leet Book*, ed. by Harris, pp. 447-8, 439-40.

[41] *Coventry Leet Book*, ed. by Harris, p. 447.

Whitmore Park and other places, causing a hundred shillings of damage annually.[42] As the different types of vegetation named in this article were all used for decorative purposes at summer festivals, the prior's complaint is clear evidence that the vegetation required for summer festivals was being procured from lands outside of the town and without the consent of the landowner at Coventry. For example, the churchwardens' accounts of St Mary at Hill, London, record a payment of 3d. for birch-boughs at Midsummer in 1488, as well as in other years, whilst John Stow includes green birch as one of the types of vegetation that was used to decorate the doorways of houses in London at the feasts of St John the Baptist and Sts Peter and Paul.[43] In addition, the mention of oak and hawthorn corresponds well with the details of an ordinance from Leicester, where in November 1551 it was decreed that any man, woman or child taking oak or hawthorn boughs to set at their doors or windows in summer was to forfeit 12d. and be sent to prison.[44] Other complaints that are also worth noting are the ninth article of the bill, which alleges that the people of the city have broken the hedges and dikes of the prior in diverse places in their sport of roving, again causing a hundred shillings of damage annually and sometimes more. Finally, the eleventh article claims that people of the city have damaged the prior's orchard with shooting and other games, and that when they have been challenged by the prior's servants, the townsfolk have told them in no uncertain terms that they will have it as their sporting-place.[45]

There are two sorts of explanation which we can consider here. It may be that although vegetation-gathering was tolerated whilst relations between the town and the priory were amicable, by late 1480 the climate had deteriorated to the extent that the prior was no longer willing to sustain it. This view is borne out in some measure by the town's reply, which appeals to the goodwill of lords and gentlefolk, as we shall see below. Another possibility is that a proportion of the townspeople, dissatisfied with the priory's use of common land, chose to take advantage of this activity in order to cause damage to priory lands in a situation where more legitimate means may not have been

---

[42] *Coventry Leet Book*, ed. by Harris, p. 445.

[43] *The Medieval Records of a London City Church (St Mary at Hill) A.D. 1420-1559*, ed. by H. Littlehales, EETS O.S. 128 (London: Kegan Paul, Trench, Trubner & Co., 1905), p. 131; J. Stow, *A Survey of London*, ed. by C. L. Kingsford, 2 vols (Oxford: Clarendon Press, 1908), I p. 101.

[44] *Records of the Borough of Leicester*, ed. by M. Bateson, 3 vols (London: Clay, 1899-1905), III p. 68.

[45] *Coventry Leet Book*, ed. by Harris, pp. 445-46.

possible or to their advantage. Evidence to support this view comes from the fact that the townspeople appear to have been exploiting other activities, such as roving and rubbish disposal, in order to harass the prior; indeed, the prior complained that the obstruction of his orchard was caused by a recent change in the sort of refuse that the townspeople chose to deposit at its gateway. These are both plausible explanations, and there is little point in trying to argue for one over the other, as both factors may have been in play simultaneously. What we can say is that the customarily tolerated encroachment in question was a negotiated compromise which had been arrived at locally and at a particular historical moment; as such, it was open to change, whether through a shift in attitude on the prior's part or because it was exploited by some of Coventry's inhabitants.

The mayor and brethren took their time in responding to the prior's bill; their answers were recorded on 26 December and delivered to the prior on 2 January 1481.[46] The answers to the complaints about roving and vegetation-gathering are interesting, in that they recognize their transgressive nature but appeal to a customary tolerance of them. In response to the prior's complaints about roving on his land, the mayor and brethren claim that this is a matter concerning individuals rather than the generality, and so by implication it is not something that they should have to deal with. However, whilst noting that roving is a punishable offence, they go on to appeal to a customary tolerance of the activity, claiming that the damage caused by roving is something which is endured in London and all other great cities. They also refer to town ordinances forbidding the practice, and suggest that if the names of offenders are given to the mayor, he will seek to reform them.[47]

In response to the prior's complaints about the loss of vegetation from his lands, the mayor and brethren make a similar appeal to the principle of customary tolerance. They say that the mayor commands the masters of every craft to warn their people against such deeds, as they are breaching both spiritual and temporal laws. However, they go on to say that those who do commit such offences should not suffer blame, since the people of every great city, including London, damage the woods and groves near to cities by taking boughs and trees from them in summer, and yet lords often endure such activities out of their goodwill.[48] Initially then, the mayor and brethren claim that the practice of procuring vegetation is an offence which they annually

---

[46] *Coventry Leet Book*, ed. by Harris, pp. 454-68 (pp. 454, 473).

[47] *Coventry Leet Book*, ed. by Harris, pp. 457-58.

[48] *Coventry Leet Book*, ed. by Harris, p. 455.

denounce. It is the sort of answer that we might expect to be given by one set of governors to another, invoking the spiritual and temporal laws for which they each had responsibility. However, they then go on to excuse such actions by an expansive appeal to custom. This disjunction in the statement is striking; it is as if we have two quite different ways of perceiving the custom of vegetation-gathering, one in terms of 'the law', where responsibility is taken and delegated, and the other a much more sober outlook on the realities of urban life. It is interesting to note how closely some of the language of this passage resembles the defence of Gladman's riding which was put forward by the citizens of Norwich c.1448; the 1443 riding was said to be a custom that was practised in any city or borough throughout the realm on Shrove Tuesday.[49]

There is further evidence to support the claim that the custom of vegetation-gathering was practised in other cities and indeed in Coventry itself. An order issued at the Easter Leet in 1448 indicates that wood was being procured for use at St John's and St Peter's Eves, 23 and 28 June respectively, in this period:

> No one to do damage in pastures, closes, or other places in cutting branches, under the penalty of 12s. And that no one break the pavement to place branches on it on St John's and St Peter's eves, but every one to have coal and large fuel [grossum ffocale] on the same penalty.[50]

The fact that this order was issued at all suggests that some damage was being done to private land, and although there are examples of where people were punished for taking vegetation from private land in Coventry in the late fourteenth century, these incidents took place outside of the summer months. In addition there is also evidence of vegetation-gathering from private land in a number of other English towns into the mid-sixteenth century.[51] Whilst the mayor and brethren's claim that vegetation-gathering was a widespread activity is thus a fair one, what is also clear from the Coventry case is that the significance of the practice was something which varied depending upon the local circumstances at a particular point in time; it was not something which was always necessarily tolerated. Hence the mayor and brethren's appeal to a yearly harm that is suffered in every great

---

[49] C. Humphrey, '"To Make a New King": Seasonal Drama and Local Politics in Norwich, 1443', *Medieval English Theatre* 17 (1995), 29-41 (p. 32).

[50] *Coventry Leet Book*, ed. by Harris, p. 233 (Harris's translation).

[51] Humphrey, 'Dynamics of Urban Festal Culture', pp. 105-7.

city is not a literal description of the treatment of the custom in England in this period, but rather it is a rhetorical statement which seeks to legitimize to some extent the local practice under a certain set of circumstances.

In his reply to the mayor and brethren, made 4 January 1481, Prior Deram did not pursue the issue of vegetation-gathering on his land any further.[52] The following Lent, John Boteler, Coventry's steward, went to London to meet the prior and establish a date on which the two parties could meet in Passion Week, but the prior died whilst in London and the matter was postponed. Richard Coventre was elected as the new prior on 4 June 1481, and appears to have been less combative than his predecessor, as no more is heard of the matter.[53]

* * *

In this essay I have examined a body of evidence from medieval Coventry, in which both the details of a festive custom and the circumstances surrounding its performance are reasonably well-documented. I have suggested that an exploration of these kinds of conjunctions of evidence is critical to a larger project which seeks to determine how misrule was bound up with politics and social structure in the late medieval urban community. In conclusion, it is clear that the custom of vegetation-gathering became a matter of contention between the priory and the citizens of Coventry in the later fifteenth century, and that this matter formed only one part of a wider dispute about land use in and around the town in this period. It is not possible to establish with any certainty whether there was a deliberate exploitation of the custom by disaffected citizens to cause excessive damage, or whether a particular prior merely chose to clamp down on this activity at this time. However, the fact that the custom continued to be practised at a time of strained relations at least had the *effect* of producing a sense of harassment, as is evident from the prior's complaint, and this is the more significant conclusion to draw. Clearly, the meaning of the activity changed in response to developing events in the town, and these meanings were also contested at the legal level through particular discourses of financial loss (the priory) and of customary tolerance (the mayor and brethren). As regards the outcome of the dispute, it may be inferred that the clandestine activities against the priory had somewhat more success than

---

[52] *Coventry Leet Book*, ed. by Harris, pp. 468-73 (p. 470).

[53] *Coventry Leet Book*, ed. by Harris, p. 474; *Calendar of Patent Rolls, 1476-85*, p. 257.

Laurence Saunders' attempts to pursue his complaints through the proper channels, although the stance of the mayor and brethren in each case appears to have been crucial. By paying close attention to the social context in which this particular example of misrule took place, I have been able to show that contrary to the predictions of the safety-valve model, misrule could and did play a part in bringing about actual social change in the late medieval urban community.

Prompting in full view of the audience: a medieval staging convention

PHILIP BUTTERWORTH

THE REMARKABLE CONVENTION OF prompting in full view of the audience sits uneasily alongside modern understanding of present and some earlier forms of European theatre. A number of modern scholars and commentators are suspicious of this practice because they can not envisage it working, or if they can, it is considered to be an exceptional and primitive device used to promote, excuse or disguise naïve performance. The sparseness of available evidence also makes it vulnerable to disparagement.

Some examples of this convention constitute the evidence to be examined. The principal English account of this practice is well known and provided by the Cornish antiquarian Richard Carew in his *Svrvey of Cornwall* published in 1602.[1] As part of a description of the 'Guary miracle, in English, a miracle-play', Carew describes the convention as follows: 'the players conne not their parts without booke, but are prompted by one called the Ordinary, who followeth at their back with the booke in his hand, and telleth them softly what they must pronounce aloud'.[2] By way of humorous amplification of this convention Carew relates an anecdote in which a performer unquestioningly follows every word and action uttered by the 'Ordinary' which brings about a comic situation when the 'Ordinary' becomes angry with the performer. According to Carew this process takes place in 'an earthen Amphitheatre, in some open field, hauing the Diameter of his enclosed playne some 40. or 50. foot.'[3]

---

[1] Richard Carew, *The Svrvey of Cornwall* (London: Printed by S. Stafford for John Jaggard, 1602), pp. 71-72.

[2] Carew, *The Svrvey*, p. 71.

[3] Carew, *The Svrvey*, p. 71.

Fig. 1. 'The Martyrdom of St Apollonia', from *Les Heures d'Etienne Chevalier*. (Reproduced courtesy of the Musée Condé, Chantilly)

Fig. 2. 'The Rape of the Sabine Women', B.N. Fr. 20071, fol.9ʳ (Reproduced courtesy of the Bibliothèque Nationale de France)

An additional source to be considered in relation to this convention is that provided by the even better known miniature by Jean Fouquet of *The Martyrdom of Saint Apollonia*[4] [Fig.1].The figure with book and baton in hand is the putative prompter. Further corroborative evidence of this figure is supplied by the little known Fouquet miniature, *The Rape of the Sabine Women*, which is used to illustrate this incident in a French translation of Roman history by Livy[5] [Fig.2].

Another source to be examined is that provided by the present-day *Representación de Moros y Cristianos* in the village of Trevelez in the Sierra Nevada in Spain.[6] In this case the process of prompting is not simply confined to supplying actors with forgotten lines. Here the 'maestro' stands behind the performers, in full view of the audience, and provides them with all their lines. Thus the 'maestro' is seen to cue, prompt and organize delivery of the performance [Figs.3-5].

Fig.3 The Trevelez 'Maestro' in action.

---

[4] *The Hours of Etienne Chevalier: Jean Fouquet*, Introduction by Claude Schaefer (London: Thames and Hudson, 1972), pl. 45.

[5] Paris, Bibliothèque Nationale, MS Fr. 20071, fol. 9^r.

[6] The Trevelez *Representación de Moros y Cristianos* is one a number of such examples of the form in Spain. Trevelez lies south-east of Granada. In 1997 the four-day fiesta took place between 13-16 June and the *Representación* was held in the late afternoon of Saturday 14 June. See Max Harris, 'Muhammed and the Virgin: Folk Dramatizations of Battles Between Moors and Christians in Modern Spain', *The Drama Review* 38, 1 (Spring, 1994), 45-61.

PROMPTING IN FULL VIEW OF THE AUDIENCE

Fig.4 The Trevelez 'Maestro' signals to the band leader "wait".

Fig.5 The Trevelez 'Maestro' signals to the band leader "Be ready".

Although Carew's description of the 'Ordinary' and Fouquet's miniature of *The Martyrdom of Saint Apollonia* have been referred to many times, there has been little examination of the role of the 'Ordinary' or the baton-carrying (blue-coated) figure in respect of the effect they have upon performance conditions. Similarly, only limited investigation has taken place in relation to the same figure in the relatively unknown miniature of *The Rape of the Sabine Women*. Examination of the role and impact of the Trevelez 'maestro' upon theatrical representation, performance style and its communication has not taken place in previous studies. Nor has the evidence been used to illuminate the Fouquet or Carew material.

A range of responses to the Carew and Fouquet evidence has occurred from those who accept the provenance of the material to those who express doubts and advise caution as to the reliability of the presented information. Another series of responses and interpretations is based upon unacknowledged assumptions that are sometimes presented as fact. Such conjecture often occurs in attempts to suggest wider yet related roles to the ones determined by the evidence. For example, J.W. Robinson reasons that 'the evidence from France, Germany and Cornwall makes it likely that in England, too, the prompter was a formally recognised personage. The circumstances of the performance probably forced the prompter out into the open...'[7] This statement occurs in a discussion by Robinson of *The Castle of Perseverance* where he asks: 'What happened when an actor forgot his lines?' His response is to suggest that 'A prompter concealed in God's *locus* would have been of little use if the lapse of memory occurred far north in the Devil's *locus*. It is possible that, as in some modern open-air productions, there were several prompters concealed in various different places, or the "stytleres" may have served as prompters'.[8] The main assumption here is that the prompter 'was a formally recognised personage' who was also involved in performance of *The Castle of Perseverance*. A second assumption is that this functionary was 'forced [...] out into the open, [...]' by virtue of having 'been concealed in various different places'. Why should it be assumed that the prompter, when and if used, was ever concealed? Is there any evidence to state or imply concealment?[9]

R. Morton Nance regards the method of prompting as described by Carew as a 'slovenly method' and in contrast to Robinson's view asserts that it 'was not relied on by 15th-century players we know, because of Mr. Jenner's lucky discovery at the British Museum of one

---

[7] J.W. Robinson, 'Three Notes On The Medieval Theatre', *Theatre Notebook*, 16, No.2 (Winter, 1961/62), 61.

[8] Robinson, 'Three Notes', p. 61.

[9] *OED*, 'Prompter' 2.b. spec.Theat. 'A person stationed out of sight of the audience, to prompt or assist any actor at a loss in remembering his part.' Interestingly, none of the examples offered here refer to such a person being 'out of sight of the audience'. See also 'Prompt' II, 2.b. 'spec in Theat.'. All examples noted here are later than 1784.

actor's part in a play ...'[10] 'Mr. Jenner' is more circumspect about his discovery when he writes: 'This fragment, which seems by the writing to be about 1400, may be part of a drama, and I am inclined to think that it is, but there is not enough to be quite certain.'[11] The existence of a possible part of a Middle Cornish text from an unspecified play is used by Nance to downgrade the application of the Cornish practice described by Carew. Although Nance appropriately questions wider use of the convention of prompting, he does so upon the assumption that players elsewhere used a text to 'conne' their parts.

The specific role ascribed to the 'Ordinary' by Carew has been extended to encompass related roles by some writers and assumed or argued as fact. For instance, Nance refers to 'the "Ordinary", who was stage-manager, producer and prompter in one...'[12]. F.E. Halliday considers the role of the 'Ordinary' to have embraced a stage management function: 'his eye always ahead to see that his properties are ready...'[13] Halliday also assumes that the 'Ordinary' is 'responsible for the production of the play'.[14] George E. Wellwarth regards the 'Ordinary' as the '"chief-manager"; everything was done as he prescribed and spoken as he prompted'.[15] Glynne Wickham considers the function of the prompter to have been 'extended beyond that of the modern prompter to that of the repetiteur in opera who cues in all the singers by repeating the entire text loudly enough to be audible to them, but not to the audience.'[16] Wickham further ascribes this role to that of the 'pageant master'.[17] Richard Southern refers to the 'Ordinary' as the 'nebulous figure the medieval prompter-stage manager.'[18] A.M. Nagler also couples an extended function to that of the prompter, as demonstrated by Carew and Fouquet, when he describes the figure as the 'medieval régisseur-prompter'.[19]

---

[10] R. Morton Nance, 'The Plen An Gwary Or Cornish Playing-Place', *Journal of the Royal Institution of Cornwall*, 24 (1935 for 1933-34), 209.

[11] Henry Jenner, 'The Cornish Drama', *The Celtic Review*, 3 (1906-1907), 360.

[12] Nance, 'The Plen An Gwary', p. 209.

[13] F.E. Halliday, *The Legend of the Rood* (London: Duckworth, 1955), p. 30.

[14] Halliday, *The Legend of the Rood*, p. 29.

[15] George E. Wellwarth, 'Methods of Production in the Mediaeval Cornish Drama', *Speech Monographs*, 24 (1957), 213.

[16] Glynne Wickham, *The Medieval Theatre* (London: Weidenfeld and Nicolson, 1974), p. 83.

[17] Wickham, *The Medieval Theatre*, p. 83.

[18] Richard Southern, *The Medieval Theatre in the Round* (London: Faber, 1957; rpt. 1975), p. 87.

[19] A.M. Nagler, *A Source Book in Theatrical History*, (New York: Dover

In addition to the assumed and extended functions of the 'Ordinary', there are a number of scholars who doubt the accuracy of Carew's account. Even so, it is sometimes difficult to identify the specific reasons for these misgivings. Although the historical accuracy of Carew's *Survey of Cornwall* is not generally doubted, considerable selective scepticism and disparagement is applied to his description of the 'Ordinary'. Why is this? One of the reasons for this treatment of the account is that the function of the 'Ordinary' is illuminated by the humorous anecdote which is seen to belittle the worth of the convention and thus weaken its historical accuracy. Brian Murdoch dismisses the account through criticism of the anecdote: 'The joke is old, and need not even be taken at face value; certainly it need not be used as general evidence'.[20] Is it Murdoch's intention to suggest that the joke is older than the account offered by Carew? If so, is there any evidence of this? If not, what is the significance of the age of the joke to the reliability of Carew's account? Murdoch further suggests that 'Carew's comments have frequently been taken as reliable, but the wisdom of doing so can be questioned...'[21] Elsewhere, Murdoch reinforces this view by pointing out that 'Carew's comments must be treated with caution and their specific relevance is questionable'.[22] Apart from the fact that Murdoch considers others have taken Carew's account at face value, and that the evidence is questionable, he presents no actual reasons for doubting the accuracy of Carew's description. William L.Tribby does not doubt 'That the prompter was used in England and on the Continent in the medieval period...', although he has serious doubts about 'the nature of this figure's activities' for he 'has been allowed to run comparatively rampant through the halls of conjecture. As a result, we are too often led to the comfortable, but, I believe, erroneous, assumption that the medieval prompter operated, with book in hand and with a portable and sure-footed position behind and/or beside the actors, in full view of the audience.'[23] This statement seemingly ignores Carew's evidence but then creates the impression that the convention of

---

Publications, 1959), p. 51.

[20] Brian Murdoch, *Cornish Literature* (Cambridge; Rochester, N-Y: D.S. Brewer, 1993), p. 43.

[21] Murdoch, *Cornish Literature*, p. 6.

[22] Brian Murdoch, 'The Cornish medieval drama', in *The Cambridge Companion to Medieval English Theatre*, ed. by Richard Beadle (Cambridge: Cambridge University Press, 1994), p. 216.

[23] William L. Tribby, 'The Medieval Prompter: A Reinterpretation', *Theatre Survey*, 5 (1964), 71-72.

prompting in this fashion was widespread. Jane A. Bakere's doubts concerning Carew's account arise out of information that she presents about his family background when she writes: 'This background may be partially responsible for the generally disdainful tone of the passage, the accusations of grossness and tediousness'.[24] Bakere also considers Carew to be 'inevitably out of sympathy with drama so closely associated with the old ways.'[25] She further asserts that: 'It is by no means certain from the *Survey* that Carew had himself witnessed a guary-miracle', and that: 'Even if Carew were himself a spectator, his limited knowledge of Cornish as revealed in the *Survey* makes it doubtful how much he would have understood of what was happening'.[26] However, it does appear that Carew understood languages other than English. On Carew's death, his son, Richard, caused to have placed a 'plain grey marble slab set in the north wall' of Antony church upon which is written the following inscription : 'RELIGIOSO INGENIOSO VIRO DOCTO ELOQVENTI LIBERALI MAGNANIMO INTEGERIMO GRECE ITALICE GERMANICE GALLICE HISPANICE'[27] [A religious and talented man, learned, eloquent, liberal, magnanimous, and honourable; self-taught in Greek, Italian, German, French, and Spanish]. It must be noted that the above conjectural comments by Bakere are intended to express caution and raise doubts concerning the accuracy of Carew's account. Why might this be so? Why might Tribby, Murdoch, Bakere and others make such strenuous efforts to demote the accuracy and value of Carew's description when based on such conjecture?

Possible reasons for such implicit and explicit resistance to the accuracy of Carew's account may be complicated, but the following concerns might be applicable. Firstly, there is an inevitable temptation (and possibly inescapable need) to view events of the past through experience of the present. Although there are other historical English examples of prompting in full view of the audience,[28] the principal

---

[24] Jane A. Bakere, *The Cornish Ordinalia: A Critical Study*, (Cardiff: University of Wales Press, 1980), p. 13.

[25] Bakere, *The Cornish Ordinalia*, p. 13.

[26] Bakere, *The Cornish Ordinalia*, p. 13.

[27] F.E. Halliday, *Richard Carew of Antony* (London, 1953), pp. 69-70.

[28] 'This daie, after supper, about ix^{ne} of the clock at night, was plaid before her Grace, in the aforenamed Chapel, by the Students of Kinge's Colledge onely, a Tragedie named "Dido" in hexametre verse, without anie chorus. Whyle this was a handling, the Lord Robert, Steward to the Universitie, and Master Secretarie Cecil, Chancellor, to signifye their good wille, and that things might be orderlye done, vouchsafed to hold both books on the scaffold themselves, and to provide also that sylence might be kept with quietness.' Alan H. Nelson, ed. *Records of Early English*

convention of indoor European theatre for the last 300-400 years has required the prompter to be out of sight of the audience. Secondly, Carew's description of the function of the 'Ordinary' and Fouquet's depiction of the blue-coated figures relate to examples of outdoor theatre. Modern understanding and experience of the conventions of theatre is frequently informed by indoor varieties. Thirdly, contemporary insights into the nature of theatre still tend to be dominated by two-dimensional considerations despite twentieth-century re-discovery of three-dimensional forms. Such forms require three-dimensional solutions to their expression and communication. If two-dimensional conventions are applied to three-dimensional forms then the result is inevitably weak or incomplete by comparison. Fourthly, despite the influence of Brecht, expectations and understanding of the relationship between theatrical reality and illusion, as conditioned by modern indoor European theatre conventions, is relatively fixed and frequently unquestioned. The existence of other conventions which promote the theatrical reality/illusion relationship is often ignored.

Clearly, Carew's evidence is specific and describes precisely a working convention and the principal agent of its operation. However, the iconographic evidence presented by the blue-coated figures in the miniatures by Fouquet do not permit definitive assessments of their roles. By their very nature these depictions invite speculation. It is therefore not too surprising that these figures have attracted additional designated roles that are different from, yet related to, that of prompting.

I have written elsewhere of Carew's 'Ordinary', Fouquet's blue-coated figures and the Trevelez 'maestro'.[29] However, the Trevelez

---

Drama: Cambridge, 2 vols (Toronto; London: University of Toronto Press, 1989), p.231; 'The stage was erected on two waggons outside some building, usually in connection with a public-house, and was so arranged that the players as they made their exits passed into a sort of Green Room within the building itself, where they were regaled with cakes and ale whilst awaiting their next call. As a rule, no more than two players were on the boards at the same time, except in the final scene. On the stage in full view of the audience sat the chairman with his book, who acted as Prompter and Call Boy in one. The actors received no pay, but were entertained by the innkeeper free of expense. The country folk seem to have come from miles round to the representations, as many as 1000 people being present on some occasions; the performance itself usually lasted about three hours, and was followed by "fiddling and dancing," in which the spectators joined.' Charlotte Sophia Burne, ed. *Shropshire Folk-Lore: A Sheaf of Gleanings*, Part II (London: Trübner & Co., 1883; rpt. Wakefield: EP Publishing, 1974), p.494.

[29] Philip Butterworth, 'Book-Carriers: Medieval and Tudor Staging Conventions', *Theatre Notebook*, 46, 1 (1992), 15-30; Philip Butterworth, Jean Fouquet's "The

PROMPTING IN FULL VIEW OF THE AUDIENCE

'maestro' requires further investigation if he is to be considered as a means of illuminating or explaining the convention of prompting in full view of the audience.

The Trevelez *Representación de Moros y Cristianos* is performed as part of the annual four-day fiesta known as the *Fiestas Populares* and is held on or around 14 June. Men of the village enact a mock battle between Moors and Christians in honour of the patron saint of the village, St Antony of Padua. The performance takes place outside the town hall on a wooden platform of some three square metres which is constructed across the width of the sloping street [Fig.6]

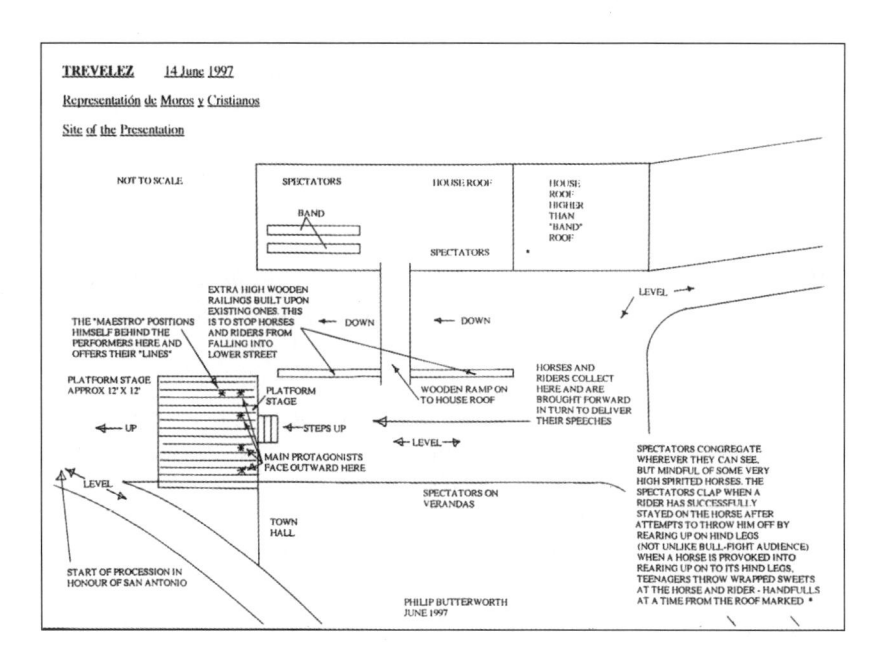

Fig. 6 Ground Plan of the Trevelez *representación*

Steps at the front of the platform provide access. Consequently, the platform is traversed before, during and after the performance by villagers going about their normal business or in order to change their viewing points during the event. Although the speeches delivered from the platform provide the principal focus of the performance, some lines issue from protagonists who arrive on horseback in front of the platform.

Proceedings begin with the arrival of the band which has processed through the village up to the performance area. When the band stops

---

Martyrdom of St.Apollonia" and "The Rape of the Sabine Women" as iconographical evidence of medieval theatre practice, *Leeds Studies in English*, 29 (1998), pp.55-67.

playing, its members walk across narrow planks that bridge the playing area in front of the platform to the flat-topped roof of a house in a street below. The band is thus on roughly the same level as the main action of the performance. Then the 'personajes' or 'characters' arrive on horseback. There are four 'mores' and four 'cristianos'. They all dismount and line up with the 'maestro' on the platform in order to pose for photographs. The 'maestro' has arrived inconspicuously on foot and unlike the main protagonists is not costumed; he is dressed in grey flannels and a white shirt. The 'personajes' on the side of the Moors are *Rey* (Moorish King); *General*; *Embajador* (Ambassador); *Espia o diablillo* (spy or little devil), and the Christians are represented by equivalent 'personajes'. Costumes of these figures are based on traditional elements although the Christian *Espia o diablillo* is dressed in a more modern military uniform.

The action, in brief, is thus: the Christian King begins by haranguing his troops. Then, the Moors dismount from their horses. The Christian General speaks after a triumphant campaign against the Moors who have been invading La Alpujarra and La Contraviesa. The Moorish Embassy, through the Ambassador, offers a challenge which results in a sword battle. The Moors win this battle and the Christian King is taken prisoner. Another battle takes place and this time the Christians are victorious. The Christian King extends mercy to the Moors who are converted. The work concludes with a final masquerade and a mimed dance of the 'little devils'. The band accompanies this mime.

With the exception of the mock battles and the mimed dances, the 'maestro' prompts throughout the performance. He changes his position behind different 'personajes' who line up at the front of the platform. The 'maestro' does not prompt from a book or text of the event, but stands with his arms folded or his hands in his pockets. He memorizes the entire proceedings and speaks the lines at a volume that can be heard by the performer but not the spectators. The audience does not hear these words because of the background noise created by itself. The 'maestro' provides the 'personajes' with all their lines, so his function is not concerned with correcting an omission created by the performer. Within this convention, the actors do not need to know their lines in the first place. The 'maestro' gives emphasis and expression to the line in order to create sense and meaning. Attempts are made by each of the 'personajes' to repeat this intention. A short interval of time occurs during which the actor may be seen to listen for his next line and cue. The performer often looks towards the ground as he waits for his new line. On receiving the line from the 'maestro, the 'character' lifts up his eyes and bodily attitude to repeat it to the audience. The style of performance is declamatory. 'Personajes' certainly 'project' their lines although the distinction between the 'projecting' and 'shouting' of these harangues is not always clear.

Not all prompting is done by the 'maestro'; in total there are four prompters. Perhaps the busiest of these is the Moorish *Espia o diablillo* who 'doubles up' his role by taking on the function of prompter to those 'characters' on horseback in front of the platform. He moves around the area with some agility in order to position himself so that he can be heard by the performer on horseback. At the same time he tries to avoid being kicked by the spirited horse. Other prompters give the impression that they are 'learning their trade' for they prompt from texts on sheets of paper. These prompters operate the humorous sections at the beginning and end of the event.

The mimed dances involving each *Espia o diablillo* are not dances in a conventional sense, but stylized sequences where the two figures walk around each other aiming mimed 'blows'. The Christian *Espia o diablillo* is armed with a wooden sword and his Moorish counterpart carries a pole of some 1½ metres in length that is topped by a sphere covered in lambswool. This stick with a ball on the end is used by the Moorish *diablillo* to hit horses and members of the audience. In this respect his behaviour is not unlike the fool figure in the English Mummers' play.[30]

There is, however, a danced quality to the battles fought by the eight 'personajes'. They face each other in two lines of four with the lines alternately advancing and retreating. The stylized battles that take place are simply choreographed by a rhythmical shuffling forwards or backwards whilst engaging in mock sword fight. The band accompanies the sequences which are cued by the 'maestro'.

'Cueing' is an important function of the 'maestro'. The process occurs in a straightforward manner when the 'maestro' reaches the end of his line. However, it needs to be acknowledged that cueing also works as a returned impulse to the 'maestro' from the 'personaje' when the repeated line has been completed. On other occasions he cues the band as well as horses and riders to come forward before the

---

[30] R.J.E. Tiddy, *The Mummers' Play* (Oxford: The Clarendon Press, 1923), pp. 208, 216; Sir Edmund Chambers, *The English Folk-Play* (Oxford: The Clarendon Press, 1923), p. 90; Alan Brody, *The English Mummers and Their Plays* (London: Routledge and Kegan Paul, 1970), pp. 36, 39; Alex Helm, *Eight Mummers' Plays* (Aylesbury: Ginn and Company Ltd., 1971), pp. 29, 33. See also Herbert Halpert and G.M. Story, *Christmas Mumming in Newfoundland* (Toronto: University of Toronto Press, 1969), pp. 171, 175, 176, 177, 221.

platform. Cues to the band are signalled by the shout of 'Musica'. Enthusiastic individuals in the audience eagerly anticipate such cues and attempt to shout out at the same time as the 'maestro'. Frequently, the timing of such cries from the audience is poor and often precedes that of the 'maestro'. In turn, he has to correct the cue by signalling to the band leader. Conventionally, the 'cue' requires an instantaneous reaction, however, responses from horses and riders are inevitably slower than ones concerning the text. Responses to cues by the band are not often immediate.

The 'maestro' fulfils a further function in performance. During the mimed dances, he retrieves the swords that are used during the stylized battles. Again, this simple stage management function of ensuring that properties are in place is conducted quite openly.

These, then, are the principal functions of the Trevelez 'maestro'. His role is both normal and essential within the context and purpose of the Trevelez *Representación de Moros y Cristianos*. How might the conditions that surround his role inform understanding of Carew's 'Ordinary' and Fouquet's blue-coated figures?

Of all the functions so far considered, it is that of cueing which may be considered to be common to Fouquet's blue-coated figures, Carew's 'Ordinary' and the Trevelez 'maestro'. Possession of the baton by the blue-coated figures in the Fouquet miniatures indicates the need to point and thus cue action. Just as cueing is governed by initiatives concerning timing, so too is the task of prompting. This process cannot be divorced from the same sort of impulses of timing that determine cueing. Since the function of Carew's 'Ordinary' is to prompt, it may be presupposed that he is also required to cue. The Trevelez 'maestro' also fulfils both functions. If the role of the Fouquet blue-coated figures is to be considered for extension, then reference needs to be made to the purpose and function of the book and its supposed contents. If the book is a text or annotation of it, then these figures possess both the capacity to anticipate and follow the action of the event. If this is the case, what use is made of the information contained in the book? One possibility arises out of available information concerning the role of the town clerk, or his representative, in the Corpus Christi play at York.[31] Here the purpose of holding the book during performance seems to have been to enable this person to check adherence of the performance to the text

---

[31] Peter Meredith, 'Scribes, texts and performance', in *Aspects of Early English Drama*, ed. by Paula Neuss (Cambridge: D.S. Brewer; Totawa, NJ: Barnes and Noble, 1983), pp. 15-18; Alexandra F. Johnston and Margaret Rogerson, eds. *Records of Early English Drama: York*, 2 vols (Toronto: University of Toronto Press, 1979), pp. 244, 280, 313, 330, 351, 352.

contained in the book. This function may be considered to have operated independently of the progress of the performance. It is possible that the blue-coated figures fulfil a civic function, as at Yorık, which lies outside that of aiding the performance. However, possession of the baton by these figures in the Fouquet miniatures suggests a direct involvement in the development of the action. If the function of Fouquet's blue-coated figures is concerned with promotion of the performance, then the simplest of available functions, over and above that of cueing, is prompting. Further extension of this conjectured role assumes the task of affecting conduct of the performance through a stage management function. Such a role in performance would amount to communication of instructions as to 'what', 'where' and 'when' action, or provision for it, needed to be completed. If greater participation of such an assumed role is to be considered then it may be that the blue-coated figures deal out instructions as to 'how' to accomplish necessary action. This sort of role might be defined as the 'director in performance' and/or the 'director of performance'.[32]

Although a book is not used in performance by the Trevelez 'maestro', the text of the *Representación* is first recorded in a volume dating from *c*.1870.[33] It is unclear whether the presentation occurred before this date, although a similar text to this one exists for a *Representación de Moros y Cristianos* in the neighbouring village of Valor. Here the text is recorded as early as 1872 and was published locally in 1972.[34] The text of the Trevelez *Representación* is almost the same as that of another neighbouring village, Juviles. A text of this event was published in 1946.[35] However, the presentations at

---

[32] In his 'Postcard from Mexico City', Clive James describes a similar convention used in the making of a daily soap opera in Mexico City. Here the actors are fed their lines by a prompter via ear-pieces. In this case the prompter is not seen by the audience but he feeds all the lines to be spoken and offers stage directions as to where to move, how to say the lines and how to respond. One of the principal performers sums up the function of the prompter as follows:

> It's easy, because it's one person who speak, who tells you everything. O.K. Then they say 'Go, go to the door. Go to the door. Come back, come back, come back. O Maria I love you. Yeah, me too. Me too. Cry, cry, cry.' O.K. It's like that and it's very crazy, but it's easy.

'Postcard from Mexico City', written and presented by Clive James, directed by Robert Payton, executive producer, Richard Drewett, Carlton UK Television, 1996.

[33] Demetrio Brisset, *Fiestas de moros y cristianos en Granada* (Granada: Diputacion de Grenada, 1988), p. 47.

[34] Brisset, *Fiestas de moros y cristianos*, pp. 49-50.

[35] Brisset, *Fiestas de moros y cristianos*, p. 42

Valor and Juviles do not make use of the same prompting convention used at Trevelez.

If it may be considered that the Trevelez *Representación* is old enough to be thought of as a traditional custom, the annual re-enactment of it may carry with it a means of regenerating its power and significance to the local community. Also, the distinctiveness of the event and its conventions may encourage a sense of identification and ownership among the audience. Such affinity with the *Representación* may be promoted further by religious and social purpose.

Motivation of the annual *Fiestas Populares* at Trevelez is concerned with honouring the patron saint of the village, St Antony of Padua. The *Representación de Mores y Cristianos* is one event among a number that is dedicated to the saint. Distinctive characteristics of these events define their nature and purpose. Villagers are proud of their customs and are convinced that their ways of celebrating and honouring their saint exist as a model for other communities. Here, common faith serves as the glue between performers and audience. Although respective roles of performers and audience members are different, the development of a collective empathy provides a bond that unites audience and performers in communal experience. Form and content of the *Representación* serve to reinforce purpose and expression of the event and to remind the audience of what it is to be a member of the Trevelez community; the creation is that of its inhabitants. This is why the convention of prompting in full view of the audience is not a strange or alien one. The gap in action created by the time taken for the 'maestro' to proffer the next line must be accepted by the audience as normal conduct. The extent to which the convention is accepted, tolerated or understood may vary, although the preponderant response is likely to be one of acceptance.

Because the Trevelez 'maestro' prompts all the spoken lines, he may be considered to exist at one end of a scale which is occupied at its other end by a hypothetical prompter who says nothing because all the performers have remembered their lines. Other prompters, however, might be expected to operate within the extremities of this range. The position of Carew's 'Ordinary' on such a presumed scale is unclear, although the evidence would not preclude an interpretation that likened the extent of his intervention to that of the Trevelez 'maestro'. Indeed, it may be considered that the Trevelez 'maestro' does not intervene at all, for his contribution is integral to the pre-determined structure of the *Representación*. This 'seen' yet 'unseen' figure is indispensable and would render the 'personajes' ineffective without his support and direction. Might it be presumed that the

PROMPTING IN FULL VIEW OF THE AUDIENCE

Cornish 'Ordinary' was this important within the context of the 'Guary miracle'? Why did Carew think it worth reporting the function of such a figure? Was it to poke fun at the convention? Or was it to point to the importance of this figure in the composition of the 'Guary miracle' and its presentation?

Given that the mechanics of prompting in full view of the audience at Trevelez may be seen to demonstrate ways in which Carew's 'Ordinary' or the blue-coated figures in Fouquet's miniatures might have operated, it is the active involvement of respective audiences that must be the means by which acceptance and approbation confirmed the process.

English community drama in crisis: 1535-80

ALEXANDRA F. JOHNSTON

THE SURVIVING EVIDENCE FOR performance of all kinds from the late medieval and early modern period is documenting the ways in which a wide variety of mimetic activities were central to the expression of community across England. Since 1976, the Records of Early English Drama project, based at the University of Toronto but with editors in many countries, has been systematically locating, transcribing and editing this evidence in uniform volumes. Like every project that seeks to recover the historic record, REED has been hampered by such factors as the uneven survival of the evidence and the laconic nature of much of what has come down to us. Nevertheless, with half the evidence now in print and close to 80 per cent gathered, it is beginning to be possible to analyze the information and draw conclusions which, though they cannot be definitive, are closer to being so than those drawn by that great Edwardian compiler of evidence, Sir Edmund Chambers.[1]

Communities of every size celebrated their sense of themselves through mimetic, musical or ceremonial traditions. These traditions – whether parish, town or civic – were inextricably bound into the liturgical year and when the old patterns of liturgical practice were challenged, then upheld, and eventually destroyed by the advance of the English Reformation, the communities themselves suffered severe fragmentation. What into the early sixteenth century had been a pattern of community celebration gave way, as the century progressed, to partisan religious polemic. This essay will trace the patterns of community drama from before Henry VIII's break with Rome in

---

[1] E.K. Chambers, *The Medieval Stage*, 2 vols. (Oxford: Oxford University Press, 1903) and *The Elizabethan Stage*, 4 vols. (Oxford: Oxford University Press, 1923).

ENGLISH COMMUNITY DRAMA IN CRISIS

1534-35 until the Elizabethan Settlement was finally established by 1580[2] with a look beyond that date to the community customs that would not be suppressed.

Before 1535

The surviving parish evidence from across the kingdom illustrates how mimetic activities were entwined in the life of the communities in sometimes widely different ways. One of the accepted imperatives for such activity at the parish level was the necessity to raise money. Churchwardens of England were faced with the upkeep of church buildings that were often over five hundred years old in 1500. The part of the fabric of the church east of the rood screen was the responsibility of the clergy, but the parishioners were charged with the upkeep of the fabric west of the rood screen: the nave, the roof, the tower, the bells, the porch and the churchyard. To secure sufficient income for the purpose, churchwardens used various techniques. The general name for the fundraising event was the church ale, most often held at the time of the spring or summer festivals: Whitsun, May Day or Midsummer. Such an ale could last as long as a week as it did at Kingston-upon-Thames and include a lord, a lady, or a lord and lady of the festival (and so be called a 'king game') as well as minstrels, morris dancers, and Robin Hood and his followers.[3] Another opportunity for fundraising was provided in the Thames Valley through Hocktide gatherings[4] and in the north and east through the custom of Rushbearing.[5] In the South-East, a play was a major feature of fundraising activity in many parishes such as New Romney where

---

[2] Eamon Duffy, *The Stripping of the Altars* (New Haven: Yale University Press, 1992), p. 2.

[3] This evidence is discussed in detail in Alexandra F. Johnston, 'Summer Festivals in the Thames Valley Counties', in *Custom, Culture and Community*, the Proceedings of the 17th International Symposium of the Centre for the Study of Vernacular Languages, Odense University (Odense: Odense University Press, 1994), pp. 37-56; and Sally-Beth MacLean, 'King games and Robin Hood: play and profit at Kingston-upon-Thames', *Research Opportunities in Renaissance Drama*, 29 (1986-87), 85-93.

[4] For a discussion of the hocking customs see Alexandra F. Johnston and Sally-Beth Maclean, 'Reformation and Resistance in Thames/Severn Parishes: the Dramatic Witness,' in *The Parish in English Life*, ed. by Kumin, Gibbs and French (Manchester: Manchester University Press, 1997), pp. 178-200.

[5] See David George, 'Rushbearing: A Forgotten British Custom' in *English Parish Drama* ed. by Alexandra F. Johnston (Amsterdam and Atlanta: Rodopi, 1996), pp. 17-30; and Elizabeth Baldwin, 'Rushbearings and Maygames in the Diocese of Chester before 1642', *ibid*, pp. 31-40.

they mounted a Passion Play[6] and the plays in the Essex towns of Heybridge and Great Dunmow that gathered support from many neighbouring villages.[7] The single most impressive parish profit recorded in East Anglia by a play was the £18 19s 5d earned by the village of Boxford in 1535 to repair the steeple of the church.[8] By contrast, the parish religious plays in the Thames Valley netted very little profit. Four parishes (Kingston-upon-Thames, Thame, St Laurence Reading and Henley) record the production of single-episode biblical plays that included Old Testament themes and Easter plays in all four parishes.[9] These plays seem to have been mounted for religious reasons rather than for profit, largely because the assured parish money maker in the Thames Valley was the Robin Hood gatherings in their several forms including Robin Hood plays, some of which toured from parish to parish. Robin Hood was equally popular as a parish fundraiser in the west and south but he is not at all common in East Anglia.[10]

Three large Midland and Northern cities – York, Chester and Coventry – performed biblical plays annually in complex partnerships between the city councils and the craft guilds.[11] York also had two other important plays on the Creed and the Pater Noster performed by the city and the religious guilds.[12] Other cathedral towns such as Canterbury and Lincoln performed large saints' plays in co-operation with the ecclesiastical authorities[13] while still others had processions

---

[6] See James Gibson, '"Interludum Passionis Domini": Parish Drama in Medieval New Romney' *ibid*, pp. 137-48.

[7] John Coldewey, 'Early Essex Drama' (unpublished doctoral dissertation, University of Colorado, 1972), pp. 228-60.

[8] John Wasson and David Galloway, *Records of Plays and Players in Norfolk and Suffolk, 1330-1642* (London: Malone Society *Collections XI*, 1980), pp. 137-38; and Ian Lancashire, *Dramatic Texts and Records of Britain to 1558* (Toronto: University of Toronto Press, 1984), p. 87.

[9] 'Reformation and Resistance', p. 181.

[10] For a full discussion of the Robin Hood phenomenon see Alexandra F. Johnston, 'The Robin Hood of the Records' in *Robin Hood: The Legend as Performance, 1500-1993*, ed. by Lois Potter (Cranbury, NJ: University of Delaware Press, 1998).

[11] See Alexandra F. Johnston and Margaret Rogerson, eds., *York*, Records of Early English Drama (Toronto: University of Toronto Press, 1979), L.M. Clopper, ed., *Chester*, Records of Early English Drama (Toronto: University of Toronto Press, 1979) and R.W. Ingram, ed., *Coventry*, Records of Early English Drama (Toronto: University of Toronto Press, 1981).

[12] Alexandra F. Johnston, 'The Plays of the Religious Guilds of York – the Creed Play and the Pater Noster Play,' *Speculum*, 50 (1975), 55-90.

[13] Giles Dawson, *Records of Plays and Players in Kent 1450-1642* (London: Malone Society *Collections VII*, 1965), Appendix B, pp. 192-98. Stanley J. Kahrl, *Records of*

with pageants on Corpus Christi Day or Whitsun.[14] In both Norwich and Newcastle the figures of St George and the dragon figure prominently.[15] The larger centres also spent lavishly on ceremonial royal entries where the monarch was greeted with historic and didactic pageantry.[16] These larger centres (and some of the smaller ones) also were host to travelling players from the late fourteenth century on. Some of these players were patronized by great magnates of the realm but many, especially in more rural areas, were players from neighbouring towns and villages.[17] Although the pattern of types of activities vary across the country, mimetic activity was clearly a part of every community, whatever its size, before the Reformation.

1535-1553

Evidence for much activity begins to disappear soon after 1535. St Laurence, Reading, records the last occurrence of their two-part Easter play in 1538, the year the great Benedictine abbey that had dominated the town was dissolved. The last recorded Easter play in the Thames Valley counties was in Thame, Oxfordshire, in 1539.[18] The story of the suppression of the St Thomas Play at Canterbury remains to be told in all its detail[19] but the outline is fairly clear. The shrine of the

---

Plays and Players in Lincolnshire 1300-1585 (London: Malone Society *Collections VIII*, 1974), p. 24 ss.

[14] For Boston and Louth see Kahrl, pp. 3-5, 76-84; for Bridgenorth and Shrewsbury see J. Alan B. Somerset, ed. *Shropshire*, 2 vols., Records of Early English Drama (Toronto: University of Toronto Press, 1994), pp. 14-18 and 151-204; for Bristol see Mark Pilkinton, ed., *Bristol* Records of Early English Drama (Toronto: University of Toronto Press, 1997), pp. 19-64; for Worcester see David N. Klausner, ed., *Herefordshire/Worcestershire*, Records of Early English Drama (Toronto: University of Toronto Press, 1990), pp. 308-423.

[15] For Norwich see David Galloway, ed., *Norwich 1540-1642*, Records of Early English Drama (Toronto: University of Toronto Press, 1984), pp. 4-47; for Newcastle see John Anderson, ed., *Newcastle Upon Tyne*, Records of Early English Drama (Toronto: University of Toronto Press, 1982), pp. 13-16.

[16] For York see Johnston and Rogerson, pp. 9, 73-74, 121, 130-33, 137-52, 193-98; for Hereford see Klausner, pp. 113-15; for Bristol see Pilkinton, pp. 7-14, 84-110.

[17] Since the publication of *Norwich 1540-1642* each REED collection has included an appendix listing the travelling companies and their patrons. 'Patrons' lists' for the earlier volumes *York, Chester* and *Coventry* have subsequently been published in the *Reed Newsletter*.

[18] 'Reformation and Resistance,' p. 187.

[19] This will be discussed by James Gibson in his forthcoming edition of the records of Kent, Diocese of Canterbury for Records of Early English Drama. I am grateful to Dr Gibson for allowing me access to his work before publication.

martyr who upheld the rights of the Pope against the will of Henry II was an obvious target for Thomas Cromwell and his animosity. But the priory at Canterbury also sponsored an annual play depicting the martyrdom performed on a pageant wagon. Until 1537-38 this play is referred to as the 'St Thomas play' but that year the records refer to 'Bishop Beckett's pageant'[20] and in that same year Cromwell's stridently Protestant players were in town. The next year the same troupe now called 'Bale & his ffellowes', after the central figure in the group, the ex-monk and polemical playwright John Bale, were paid by the city.[21] In 1539-40 the 'Cart of Byshop Bekettes' pageant was sold.[22]

The presence of Cromwell's players in Canterbury at this crucial moment when Henry VIII's supremacy over the English church was being enforced introduces a new element of the story of drama in sixteenth-century England. The ancient role of mimetic activity was to express community. But here we see a counter thrust. Drama seems to have been used here polemically. As Paul Whitfield White has argued, the use of drama to argue one side or the other of the religious/political debate is an important thread in the history of Tudor theatre.[23]

The events that followed hard on the heels of Henry's break with Rome in 1534 pre-date the first official injunction against plays and playmaking to survive issued by Edmund Bonner, Bishop of London, in 1542. Bonner forbade 'common plays, games or interludes to be played' in the sanctuary.[24] This injunction must have had companions elsewhere in the country that touched on other issues than the use of Church property because after 1542 other customary practices began to disappear. The last evidence for a procession and pageants in Ipswich in Suffolk is in 1542.[25] Boston's Corpus Christi Procession that included the carrying of Noah's ark is last recorded in 1545.[26] In

---

[20] Canterbury Cathedral Archives: Chamberlains' Accounts CCA:CA/FA 12 (1530-38) fol. 369v.

[21] For a discussion of Bale's players see Paul Whitfield White, *Theatre and Reformation* (Cambridge: Cambridge University Press, 1993), pp. 12-41.

[22] Canterbury Cathedral Archives: Chamberlains' Accounts CCA:CA/FA13 (1539-45) fol. 62v.

[23] White, *passim*.

[24] *Visitation Articles and Injunctions of the Period of the Reformation*, ed. by W.H. Frere and W.M. Kennedy, II, Alcuin Club Collections XV (London: Longmans, Green & Co., 1910), p. 88.

[25] Wasson and Galloway, p. 183.

[26] Kahrl, p. 4.

the same year the Corpus Christi Procession in Bridgnorth in Shropshire ended.[27] In 1546-47 the Bristol Corpus Christi Procession with its carried pageants was suspended[28] and the last event featuring a mimetic representation of St George (the patron saint of the parish)ı in the parish of Morebath, Devon is recorded.[29] In 1547-48, the great St George procession in Norwich with its splendid dragon was reduced to divine service followed by a guild dinner[30] and the town of Louth records its last Corpus Christi Procession.[31] The effect of these suspensions of ancient community custom can be inferred from the bare accounts of the city of Lincoln. On 13 June 1547 the St Anne's play was ready to go as usual. On 5 November of the same year all the gear for that play was sold off.[32]

With the accession of Edward VI and his Protestant advisors, the situation did not improve. The immediate effect on the biblical cycle in York was the suspension of the plays devoted to the Virgin.[33] The Shrewsbury Corpus Christi Procession was cancelled.[34] All records concerning the Christmas play and the Robin Hood activity of Ashburton, Devon were suspended in 1547-48.[35] The play at Wymondham in Norfolk had its last performance in 1549.[36] The effect on parish activity was equally sweeping. The Edwardian injunctions (with the Bonner prohibitions still in place) turned their attention to church porches and churchyards during service time. Hooper's articles for the diocese of Gloucestershire and Worcestershire repeated this injunction and added the further stricture that the minister should not be disturbed 'whiles he is at Divine Service within the Church or churchyard, with any noise, brute cries, clamours, plays, games, sports, dancing and such like'.[37] These do not seem to touch directly on such activities as the summer festivals but a letter from the King's commissioners to the bishop of Wells dated 1 November 1547 was

---

[27] Somerset, p. 18.

[28] Pilkinton, p. 57.

[29] John Wasson, ed., *Devon*, Records of Early English Drama (Toronto: University of Toronto Press, 1986), p. 211.

[30] Galloway, p. 23.

[31] Kahrl, p. 83.

[32] Kahrl, p. 64.

[33] Johnston and Rogerson, pp. 291-92.

[34] Somerset, p. 200.

[35] Wasson, p. 27.

[36] Wasson and Galloway, p. 129; see also Lancashire, pp. 291-92.

[37] Frere and Kennedy, pp. 277-78.

more direct. All archdeacons were urged to instruct the parishes in their care to give up holding church ales 'because it hath byn declared unto us that many inconveniences hath come by them'. The commissioners recognized the financial importance of the ales in the next sentence, 'Nevertheless requiring the said churche wardeans to make yerely collection for the reparacion of their churchies, and for the sustentacion of other commune charges of the parish accordinglie'.[38] This letter exacerbated an important parish tension of the English reformation – the insistence that the parish maintain its own fabric and other 'commune charges' while prohibiting the age-old method of fundraising.

1553-1558

Many of the annual community celebrations that had been laid aside during Edward's reign were revived with enthusiasm under Mary. In York, the plays on the Virgin were reinstated along with the Corpus Christi Procession and the St George Riding.[39] Lincoln,[40] Louth[41] and Bristol[42] revived their communal customs. An order of the town council of Worcester in 1555-56 states 'that all companeis shale prepayre there shewes vpon corpus chrysti daye as hath bine of ould time accustomyd etc'.[43] There is, also, an excited sense of renewed customary activity at the parish level. Ashburton in Devon revived its old customs and went so far as to mount a new play in this period as we can deduce from the evidence of gloves bought for 'hym that played god almyghty a Corpus Christi daye'.[44] In Thame, Oxfordshire, where Edwardian entries (perhaps concealing more extensive festive activity) had given evidence only of a continuing ale, the churchwardens responded to the new regime with exuberance, paying their summer lord 6s 6d for his expenses on Whitsun, 1554, and hiring a taborer from London for the event. Many more Thames Valley parishes revived the customs discreetly suppressed during Edward's reign. Hock gatherings resumed at Lambeth, all three Reading parishes and Wing, while new evidence for the custom

---

[38] W.H.B. Bird and W.P. Baildon (eds.), *Calendar of the Manuscripts of the Dean and Chapter of Wells,* ii (London, 1914), p. 265.

[39] Johnston and Rogerson, pp. 310-20.

[40] Kahrl, p. 65.

[41] Kahrl, p. 83.

[42] Pilkinton, pp. 60 ss.

[43] Klausner, pp. 422-23.

[44] Wasson, p. 28.

begins at St Botolph, Middlesex, however briefly (1554-55), and the parishes of the city of Oxford. Parishes also renewed their summer games, the other central celebratory and fundraising events. An undated Henley account that internal evidence suggests is from the mid-1550s, has a list of expenses for the refurbishing of the morris costumes, the repairing of the garters of bells, and rewards to one man for playing 'the fool' at Whitsuntide and another for playing his tabor. In Reading, the biggest event under Mary was also a revival of the Whitsun games mounted by the parish of St Mary. On Whitsun 1555 the wardens raised £6 9s 7d at their ale which also incurred expenses for the summer lord's costume, minstrels, liveries and three dozen bells for the dancers. The next year, St Mary's held events on both May Day and Whitsun. This time expenses included a hobby horse, the making of morris costumes, shoes for the dancers and four dozen more bells as well as payment to minstrels. These festivities continued until 1559. A number of other Thames Valley parishes record renewed summer games during this period, although in less detail. Guildford's summer lord reigned once more in the North Downs, while the parishes of Stanford-in-the-Vale, Berkshire, and Pyrton, Oxfordshire, raised summer poles for their ales.[45]

Two pieces of evidence from this period support the contention that plays were taking on a more polemical tone. The Visitation Articles of Cuthbert Scott, Bishop of Chester, dated 1556-58 included the question, 'Also whether you here tell of any assembles or conventicles wherein is redd privie lectures sermons or playes to thindrance or derysion of the Catholic faythe'.[46] In Poole, in Dorset, the sum of £5 3s 4d is recorded for 'prechars and players' for the year 1557-58[47] and for the next year £11 6s 5d was paid out 'to prechars & in the Lord*es* players'.[48] The players referred to are clearly travelling companies, part, as we shall see, of a limited number of troupes on the road in Mary's reign.

---

[45] For a more detailed discussion of the Marion revival in the Thames/Severn watershed see 'Reformation and Resistance', pp. 188-89.

[46] David George, ed., *Lancashire*, Records of Early English Drama (Toronto: University of Toronto Press, 1992), p. 213.

[47] Poole Borough Archives, 26(4), fol. 57; see Rosalyn Conklin Hays, C.E. McGee, Sally L. Joyce and Evelyn M. Newlyn (eds.), *Dorset / Cornwall. Records of Early English Drama* (Toronto: Toronto University Press, 1999), p. 242.

[48] *ibid.*

ALEXANDRA F. JOHNSTON

1558-1568

The accession of Elizabeth was not an occasion for general rejoicing. As Norman Jones has put it:

> The first Elizabethans did not know they were Elizabethans. When Queen Mary died just before dawn on 17 November 1558 her passing did not mean to contemporaries the beginning of the reign of Gloriana, the Virgin Queen Elizabeth whose reign would be synonymous with English greatness. It meant more political and religious confusion to overlay the difficulties and joys of life.[49]

The last surviving child of Henry VIII carried with her the taint of bastardy and her single state alarmed many of the most powerful men in government. As her reign opened there was uncertainty over religion, over her character, over the succession. The English people had lived through three previous reigns that had left them confused and wary of any new authority. One only needs to read the sustained runs of churchwardens' accounts from such parishes as St Laurence's, Reading, to grasp what the religious changes meant at the very basic level. Under Henry, the churchwardens stopped their biblical plays, under Edward, all mimetic activity stopped and they sold off the 'trappings of popery' – vestments and liturgical accoutrements such as processional crosses, chalices, reliquaries – only to buy them again when his sister became queen.[50] Now, with the new queen, the Protestant cause seemed once more in the ascendancy. In 1559 what has come to be known as the Elizabethan Settlement was proclaimed but it took almost twenty years to be generally accepted.

Historians have carefully examined the first decade of Elizabeth's reign, dominated as it was first by the marriage question, then the related problem of Mary, Queen of Scots, then the rising of the Northern Earls in 1569 and its suppression.[51] Finally, the declaration by the Pope of Elizabeth's excommunication in 1570 added a new element to what was essentially a struggle for the minds and souls of the English people.[52]

---

[49] Norman Jones, *The Birth of the Elizabethan Age* (Oxford: Blackwells, 1993), p. 4.

[50] Berkshire Record Office D/P 97 5/2, 1499-1626.

[51] See Wallace MacCaffrey, *The Shaping of the Elizabethan Regime* (Princeton: Princeton University Press, 1968); Conyers Read, *Mr Secretary Cecil and Queen Elizabeth* (London: Jonathan Cape, 1955); and Jones, *The Birth*.

[52] The excommunication of the queen negated her validity as a monarch in the eyes of the papacy. Her Catholic subjects were, therefore, free to rebel against their illegitimate ruler. To further civil and religious disobedience the first Jesuits sent to

Suppression of communal activities at the parish level in the early years of Elizabeth's reign depended on the zealousness of the diocesan officials especially the bishop and his archdeacons.[53] Pew rentals, parish levies and other taxes were preferred by the reforming bishops to more convivial ways of raising money, but these methods did not find favour with many of the parishes of the Thames Valley and the west. Although the churches in Protestant Bristol quickly conformed as did the parishes in the town of Reading that fell under the watchful eye of the local magnate, Sir Francis Knollys, the most puritan of Elizabeth's council, many parishes went back to their old ways of raising money during Mary's reign and continued them well into the reign of Elizabeth.[54] As we have seen, many of the injunctions turn on the use of Church property and some parishes such as Melton Mowbray in Leicestershire and Thame in Oxfordshire avoided the issue entirely by holding the celebrations elsewhere. The events were held in the town hall or other secular spaces with the profits still accruing to the Church.[55] In the west country, the Robin Hood customs continued to thrive. In 1567-68, the Dorset parish of Netherbury held an ale with 'Robin hoode and Littell John & the gentle men of the said parish the chief actors in it'.[56] The same resistance to the eradication of communal custom can also be seen in the rural parts of the Thames Valley. For example, the accounts of Wantage survive from 1565 and it is clear that this was a parish that celebrated the Whitsun festival with gusto. They called their event a revel and had morris dancing accompanied by minstrels hired from a sufficient distance to pay them board during revel time.[57] But not every community was united in its revival of old practices. In 1560-

---

reconvert England, Thomas Campion and Robert Parsons, arrived in England at Easter, 1580. See Claire Cross, *The Puritan Earl* (London: MacMillan, 1966), pp. 239-40.

[53] 'Reformation and Resistance', p. 195.

[54] *ibid*, pp. 189-93.

[55] Leicester, Leicestershire Record Office, Melton Mowbray Townwardens' Accounts DG 36/285-7; 284/4, 284/6-7, 284/10-11; the Leicestershire material was gathered and transcribed by the late Alice Hamilton. It is now deposited in the REED office in Toronto awaiting further editorial attention. The parish of Thame consisted of two separate villages and there were always two ales held in each village: see Oxfordshire Archives; DD Par Thame c.5; b.2. When the accounts of Newbury, Berkshire, begin in 1602 the ale is being held in the Guild Hall (Berkshire Record Office, D/P 89 5/1, fol. 2v).

[56] This information is in an antiquarian account (Dorset Record Office D1/7623, [fol.1 17v] from REED *Dorset/Cornwall* forthcoming).

[57] 'Reformation and Resistance,' pp. 191-92.

61, two years before his death, John Bale recounted an example in Canterbury of what will become an all-too familiar pattern as the turn of the century approaches: rioting between the supporters of May games and the supporters of the preachers inveighing against such practices.[58] Later evidence from the ecclesiastical courts documents ever bitter divisions at the parish level between those of increasingly puritan outlook and the supporters of the old customs.[59]

But other things were happening in the 1560s. In East Anglia several towns mounted elaborate plays. At New Romney in Kent (which was the only town to record a local performance during the Marion period),[60] the Passion Play was performed in 1560 and apparently again in 1563-64 but by 1567-68 the play parts are called in.[61] In 1562, the town authorities of Maldon in Essex hired a 'property player', produced a play but sold the gear by the end of the year.[62] Bungay in Suffolk mounted a large play between 1566 and 1568 but then all evidence stops.[63] The most famous of these East Anglian extravaganzas was the huge production at Chelmsford in 1562-63 which was a financial disaster.[64] John Coldewey has argued that the plays being mounted were those that have come down to us in the Digby manuscript.[65] At least one of these plays, the Conversion of Paul, shows some evidence of being rewritten to suit more Protestant tastes. Elsewhere in the kingdom parish and town drama is also recorded during the decade although sometimes, as with the plays at Ashburton, Devon, for only one last time in 1559-60.[66] Attempts do seem to have been made to make the texts of the traditional plays more palatable to the ecclesiastical authorities either by excising blatantly Catholic sections (such as the plays on the Virgin at York) or

---

[58] Lambeth Palace Library MS 2001, John Bale, 'A retourne of Iames Canceller's rylinge boke' ff ii-iiiv. This will be part of James Gibson's forthcoming REED collection, *Kent, Diocese of Canterbury*.

[59] See particularly James Stokes, ed. with Robert Alexander, *Somerset with Bath*, Records of Early English Drama (Toronto: University of Toronto Press, 1996), pp. 484-88 and Alexandra F. Johnston, 'English Puritanism and Festive Custom', *Renaissance and Reformation*, NS XV (1991), 289-97.

[60] James Gibson, 'Interludum Passionis Domini', p. 145.

[61] *ibid*, pp. 146-47.

[62] Coldewey, pp. 274-78.

[63] Wasson and Galloway, pp. 143-45.

[64] Coldewey, pp. 296-312.

[65] *ibid*, pp. 189-214.

[66] Wasson, p. 29.

by more intrusive tinkering with the texts.[67] Some towns, however, such as Boston in Lincolnshire[68] and Shrewsbury in Shropshire[69] mounted new plays written by local schoolmasters, and Lincoln mounted a play based on the story of Tobias from 1563 to 1567.[70] The author of the Shrewsbury plays, Thomas Ashton, the headmaster of Shrewsbury School, is later described as 'a good and godly Preacher'.[71] His plays undoubtedly had Protestant themes and it is probable that the others did as well.

In the larger centres where there had been town and guild plays and processions the evidence is mixed. In Norwich in 1558-59 'for pastyme' the famous dragon of the old St George play was allowed 'to come In and shew hym selff as in other yeares'.[72] On 15 April, 1565 the Norwich council agreed that 'souche pagentes as were wonte to go in tyme of whitson holydayes shall be Set forthe by occupacions as tymes past haue bene vsyd'.[73] Nothing more is heard of the procession. The last mention of the actual mounting of the procession of pageants in Newcastle is in 1561 although the pageants continue to be mentioned in guild ordinances.[74]

A major new development in the first decade of Elizabeth's reign is the explosion of evidence documenting the activities of troupes of players travelling under the patronage of prominent members of the aristocracy. Acting companies whose repertoires were clearly promoting the protestant cause had first appeared under the patronage of Thomas Cromwell in the 1530s. David Bevington and Paul White have shown how these plays were part of the strategy of the reformers.[75] What has been less carefully noticed is that the same policy seems to have been in place in the 1560s. Bevington notes that

---

[67] See, for example, the discussion of the 'parallel' texts in Chester: David Mills and R.M. Lumiansky, *The Chester Mystery Cycle: Essays and Documents* (Chapel Hill: University of North Carolina Press, 1983), pp. 39-40; 189-94, and for Coventry in R.W. Ingram, '"To find the players and all that longeth therto": Notes on the Production of Medieval Drama in Coventry', in *The Elizabethan Theatre V,* ed. by G.H. Hibbard (Toronto: MacMillan, 1975), pp. 17-44.

[68] Kahrl, p. 5.

[69] Somerset, pp. 204-20.

[70] Kahrl, pp. 67-68.

[71] Somerset, p. 243.

[72] Galloway, p. 47.

[73] *ibid*, p. 51.

[74] Anderson, pp. 28-29.

[75] David Bevington, *Tudor Drama and Politics* (Cambridge, Mass: Harvard University Press, 1968), and *Theatre and Reformation, passim.*

the 'Count of Feria [...] reported that Cecil was actually directing the efforts of certain playwrights as Cromwell had done'[76] but he finds little evidence that the government was using plays as part of its strategy. I think it is possible to argue that the government was aware of the power of drama as a tool of propaganda and used every means at hand in the early days of the new reign to establish, in the countryside, positive responses to the Settlement. Eamon Duffy's magisterial work, as well as the work of Reformation historians, has shown how deep the roots of traditional religion were in the countryside.[77] It was there rather than in Protestant London that the campaign was launched. As John Foxe, the author of *The Book of Martyrs,* wrote in 1562, 'Players, Printers and Preachers be set up of God as a triple bulwark against the triple crown of the Pope, to bring him down'.[78]

During the five years of Mary's reign, evidence for only seventeen performances by travelling companies survives.[79] Yet for the period from 1558 to 1569, the year of the Rising of the Northern Earls, three-hundred and fifteen performances are recorded by troupes of thirty-one patrons. There is activity in all regions of the country except the north but, from the evidence we noted earlier of Bishop Scott's Visitation question, this may be more the result of lack of surviving evidence than lack of performances.[80] Only three patrons were at this time openly Catholic – the duke of Norfolk, the earl of Arundel and Lord Chandos. Only eleven performances are recorded by the troupes patronized by these men. Other members of the nobility such as the Stanleys, earls of Derby, and the earl of Worcester who, from later actions were clearly sympathetic to the Catholic cause, chose to remain loyal to the crown in this difficult first decade of Elizabeth's reign. Despite the urging of the rebels, the Stanleys did not take part in

---

[76] Bevington, p. 127. He cites *The Calendar of State Papers, Spanish*, N.S. I (1558-67), p. 62.

[77] Duffy, *The Stripping of the Altars.*

[78] *ibid*, p. 2.

[79] The analyses of the patterns of visits by the travelling companies that follow are based on the published REED volumes, the Malone Society volumes for Kent, Norfolk and Suffolk and Lincoln, my own unpublished work on Berkshire, Buckinghamshire and Oxfordshire and the unpublished work of Diana Wyatt (Beverley), Evelyn Newlyn and Sally Joyce (Cornwall) and John Coldewey (Nottinghamshire). I am grateful to all these colleagues for allowing me access to their work. Until REED has collected all the evidence, there will inevitably be inaccuracies in the exact counts. Nevertheless, the emerging pattern is significant.

[80] Very little survives from this period in Lancashire; see George, *passim.*

the Rising of the Northern Earls in 1569 at all.[81] Although Worcester 'at heart [...] remained a Roman Catholic', he was nevertheless a staunch member of the court.[82] It is unlikely that either of them would sanction any polemical stand by their players. Worcester's troupe was the more active in this period. Twenty-three references to their performances appear between 1563 and 1569, while troupes patronized by the Stanleys are recorded nine times between 1564 and 1569. The earl of Sussex, though related to the duke of Norfolk and later suspected of Catholic sympathies, prided himself on being a loyal member of the court. After his long sojourn in Ireland, he took on the Presidency of the Council of the North in 1568 and was instrumental in suppressing the 1569 uprising.[83] Evidence for Sussex's men appears only three times in the last year of the decade. Fifteen recorded performances were done by players of patrons (mainly somewhat obscure local landowners) whose religious persuasion is unknown. However, all the other evidence of performances (over two-hundred and fifty or 80 per cent of the total) is of troupes patronized by the Protestant courtiers such as Robert Dudley, earl of Leicester, his brother the earl of Warwick, the duchess of Suffolk, the earls of Oxford and Northampton, Lord Hunsdon and Sir John Fortescue. Other troupes were patronized by staunch Protestants in the provinces such as William Alley, Bishop of Exeter and James Blount, Lord Montjoy. One of the most active troupes was patronized by the queen herself. It seems probable that these patrons, zealous as most of them were in the cause of the godly, were prepared to use their actors to carry the Protestant message throughout the kingdom promoting at the same time the government policy concerning religion. The 1559 royal injunction against the performance of plays that were 'heretical, seditious, or vnseemely for Christian eares'[84] should be read in light of the vigorous activity of the players of the privy councillors and their friends in the next decade. This may well be an injunction against the performance of plays sympathetic to the Catholic cause, not plays that treated religious subjects and so support rather than question the observation of the Spanish ambassador.

---

[81] MacCaffrey, *The Shaping*, p. 342.

[82] *The Compact Edition of the Dictionary of National Biography* (Oxford: Oxford University Press, 1975). MacCaffrey refers to Worcester as 'a senior surviving Catholic nobleman' in his discussion of the trial of Mary, Queen of Scots, *The Shaping*, p. 428.

[83] Jones, *The Birth*, pp. 81-83; MacCaffey, *The Shaping*, 334 ff.; Read, *Mr Secretary*, pp. 458-59.

[84] Chambers, IV, pp. 264-65.

Both Bevington and White have noted the number of Protestant plays that were registered and printed in this period. Indeed, a very crude count of the plays (as opposed to masks and pageants) listed by Harbage and Schoenbaum between 1558 and 1570 shows that thirty-nine of the eighty-six plays (45%) are characterized as moral or religious.[85] Paul White has struggled with the problem of associating particular plays with acting troupes. There is little direct evidence but many hints of associations within the tight-knit circle of Protestant writers, patrons, players and printers. Indirect evidence leads White to associate Leicester with the plays of William Wager.[86] James de Vere, sixteenth earl of Oxford, whose troupe was active in the early years of Elizabeth's reign was the brother-in-law of Arthur Golding, the translator of Theodore Beza's *Abraham's Sacrifice*.[87] William Alley, bishop of Exeter was himself the author of a play *Aegio* listed by Harbage and Schoenbaum for 1560. Among other plays 'offered for acting' in this decade were Ulpian Fulwell's *Like Will to Like* and Thomas Garter's *The Most Virtuous and Godly Susanna*. Identification of plays with specific troupes has often been made through other references such as court calendars. In this period, the countryside, not the court, was the object of the campaign and the plays 'offered for acting' could easily have been bought up by the companies preparing their repertoires.

The other side of this apparent propaganda programme was the suppression of the great civic drama in the north that had barely begun before the suppression of the Rising of the Northern Earls. It is important to remember that the Creed Play in York was suppressed and the last performance of the biblical cycle took place during the period leading up to the rising and that the city of York was the seat of the northern administration of the Lord President of the North, the earl of Sussex. The *eminence grise* in the suppression of the large civic religious plays in the diocese of York was Matthew Hutton, Dean of York and Secretary to the Council of the North and its Ecclesiastical Commission. Hutton had come up to Cambridge in 1546 and became a fellow of Trinity during Mary's reign in 1555.[88] Here he became a member of the circle of Edmund Grindal, Bishop of London (1559-70), becoming his chaplain in 1561. Amongst his other patrons at this time was Robert Dudley, earl of Leicester, one of Elizabeth's 'godly'

---

[85] Alfred Harbage and Samuel Schoenbaum, *Annals of English Drama 975-1700* (Philadelphia: University of Pennsylvania Press, 1940), pp. 34-41.

[86] White, pp. 64-65 and 91 ss.

[87] *DNB* 797 and 2152; White, p. 210.

[88] Peter Lake, 'Matthew Hutton – a Puritan Bishop?' *History*, 64 (1979), 183.

courtiers and patron of one of the most active touring companies. During his early years at Cambridge, Hutton experienced Mary's regime at first hand. It left a strong impression on his Calvinist soul and, as Peter Lake has written, 'It was the fragility of the protestant hold on the mass of the English people and the ever present threat of Rome that were to form the dominant concerns of Hutton's career'.[89]

The mid-1560s saw Hutton appointed to York as dean of the Minster. He rapidly attached himself to the Council of the North as secretary and became a key figure in the Ecclesiastical Commission. With a man of his conviction in such a powerful position in York, it should come as no surprise that the great Catholic drama of the city would come under attack. Although there is no evidence for the performance of the cycle for the years 1559 and 1560, it was played again without the Marian sequence in 1561, 1562 and 1563. The play was again suspended for the three years 1564-66 to be played again in 1567 with special attention paid to the text.[90] Hutton made his first move against York drama in 1568. On 13 February, the city council recorded a detailed discussion of the plans for the production of the Creed Play, once the property of the Corpus Christi Guild but by this time lodged with the 'bretherne of St Thomas hospitall'.[91] On 24 March, Hutton wrote to the council giving them his advice on the text:

> yf I were worthie to geue your lordshipp and your right worshipfull brethren consell: suerlie mine advise shuld be, that it shuld not be plaid. ffor thoghe it was plausible 40 yeares agoe, & wold now also of the ignorant sort be well liked: yet now in this happie time of the gospell, I knowe the learned will mislike it and how the state will beare with it I knowe not.[92]

He then proceeded to commit the Council to the 'tuition of gods spirit'. By specifying '40 yeares agoe' Hutton identified the play clearly as part of the Catholic past, acceptable in a time before the Henrician Reformation but no longer 'in this happie time of the gospell'. On 30 March, the Council, having received Hutton's letter and understood him to say that 'the Creyd play is not meet to be playd', agreed 'to haue no play this yere'. But the community was not giving up its drama easily. On 27 April, the Council considered a

---

[89] *ibid.*

[90] Johnston and Rogerson, pp. 329-51.

[91] *ibid*, p. 353; Johnston, 'The Plays of the Religious Guilds'.

[92] Johnston and Rogerson, p. 353.

request from 'dyverse commoners' that the Corpus Christi Play should be played that year. Having been rebuked already by the ecclesiastical authorities, the Council would 'not agree, but that the book thereof shuld be perused / and otherwise amendyd / before it were playd.'[93] Although not performed that year evidence from the Bakers' Guild makes it clear that the civic cycle was played for the last time the next year, 1569.[94]

1568-1580

Evidence for parish activity becomes more and more sporadic as the archdeacons, in some parts of the country at least, became more zealous in their visitations.[95] Nevertheless, ales with their attendant activities continued to be held, though not always every year. The Robin Hood activities in Woodbury, Devon, for example, survive until 1577[96] and in Yeovil, Somerset, until 1578.[97] More remote parishes, such as Wantage and Childrey in Berkshire also continued their ales regularly until after 1589[98] while tiny Aston Abbots in Buckinghamshire records an ale in 1569, 1570, 1572 and 1579.[99] Town drama in East Anglia gradually disappears in the 1570s. Braintree in Essex records income from play money in 1570, but that same year they begin to rent their costumes.[100] The next year they sell their playbook[101] and in 1579 they finally sell the costume stock. In Maldon, in 1573 one Richard Wells and others are fined for performing a play and an archdeacon who preached against the play was given dinner by the town.[102] The next year, however, in the last play evidence to survive from the town, three men were licensed to perform a play.[103] Chelmsford begins to sell off its large stock of

---

[93] *ibid*, p. 354.

[94] *ibid*, p. 358.

[95] 'Reformation and Resistance', pp. 195-96.

[96] Wasson, pp. 284-85.

[97] Stokes, p. 411.

[98] Wantage Churchwardens' Accounts 1565-1665 (Berkshire Record Office D/P 143 5/1); and Childrey Churchwardens' Accounts 1568-1688 (Berkshire Record Office D/P 35 5/1).

[99] Aston Abbots Churchwardens' Accounts 1562-1669 (Buckinghamshire Record Office; PR 7 5/1).

[100] Coldewey, p. 226.

[101] *ibid*, p. 227.

[102] *ibid*, p. 281.

[103] *ibid*.

costumes in 1576[104] and Bungay in Suffolk, whose play was last performed in 1568, sells off its costumes in 1577.[105]

It was this decade that saw the end of the civic drama. In 1570, Edmund Grindal became archbishop of York, joining his reforming friend Matthew Hutton in the north. The last actual performance of the old drama in York was the production of the Pater Noster Play in 1572 when two Protestant Council members, Beckwith and Herbert, refused to see the play with the rest of the Council as was the custom and took the dispute to the new Lord President of the North (the stoutly Protestant earl of Huntingdon) and the Council. The playbooks were called in.[106] In November that year Grindal and Hutton were both signators to a letter to the Council ordering the cancellation of the 'rude and barbarouse custome', the Riding of Yule and Yule's Wife.[107] In 1579, the Council agreed to produce the Corpus Christi Play but agreed 'that first the books shalbe caried to my Lord Archebisshop and Mr Deane to correcte, if that my Lord Archebisshop doo well like theron'.[108] Nothing is heard of the play that year but the next year, in the last mention of the civic religious drama in York 'the Commons did earnestly request of my Lord Mayour and others this worshipfull Assemblee that Corpus christi play might be played this yere'.[109] The Council agreed to consider it but the play is never mentioned again in the city records.

Hutton and Grindal also turned to other towns and cities in the diocese where playmaking had been part of the Catholic past. It was Hutton who signed the letter from the Council's Ecclesiastical Commission to stop the play at Wakefield in 1576 that included a portrayal of the godhead.[110] The story of the suppression at Chester is well known. An intriguing new twist to that story, however, has recently come to light in a Welsh archive. A Protestant divine named Goodman was the person who wrote to Grindal to stop the performance in 1572 citing lines from the Last Supper play stating the

---

[104] *ibid*, p. 321.

[105] Wasson and Galloway, p. 146.

[106] Johnston and Rogerson, pp. 365-68.

[107] *ibid*, p. 369.

[108] *ibid*, p. 390. Grindal had by this time become Archbishop of Canterbury. Edwin Sandys succeeded him in York in 1577 and is the archbishop referred to here.

[109] *ibid*, pp. 392-93.

[110] A.C. Cawley, ed., *The Wakefield Pageants in the Towneley Cycle* (Manchester: Manchester University Press, 1958), p. 125. The original document is in the York Diocesan papers in the Borthwick Insitute of Historical Research in Yorki.

doctrine of transubstantiation.[111] Clearly that year the Chester Plays had a Catholic tone. The last performance of the Chester Whitsun plays was in 1575 according to an antiquarian account 'in contempt of and Inhibition and ye primates letter from ye Earle of Huntington'.[112] The controversy stirred up by that performance found its way to the Privy Council in London.[113] The Corpus Christi Play at Coventry, under the jurisdiction of the Bishop of Lichfield and the Archbishop of Canterbury, was suspended for one year in 1575 and stopped abruptly in 1580. By this time Grindal had become Archbishop of Canterbury.[114]

The number of named acting companies on the road in this period rises by 50 per cent over the decade 1558-68. However, 18 per cent of these companies are recorded fewer than five times and 31 per cent fewer than ten times. Of the visits, 69 per cent, were made by the companies of the queen, four magnates (the earls of Leicester, Sussex and Worcester and Lord Berkeley) and the Stanleys of Derby (both the earl and his son Ferdinando, Lord Strange). However, the repertoire of the companies has changed radically from the previous decade. As Paul White has shown, by the 1570s 'the Word dramatized, as opposed to the Word preached' had come under attack from the more extreme wing of the Protestants.[115] Only 15 per cent of the plays listed in Harbage and Schoenbaum have any clear religious content. The critical moment for the security of the Settlement had passed with the suppression of the Rising of 1569. It was no longer as necessary to use drama as part of the propaganda war. The fashion in plays became less political. Leicester's company performed such romances as *Predor and Lucia* and *Panicia* and such comedies as *The Collier*.[116] The company of the earl of Sussex becomes very active in this decade. Sussex came south from his success in suppressing the Rising of 1569 and became a member of the Privy Council late in 1570. During the following decade when his players were second only

---

[111] David Mills, *Recycling the Cycle: The City of Chester and its Whitsun Plays* (Toronto: University of Toronto Press, 1998), pp. 181-82.

[112] Clopper, p. 109.

[113] Mills and Lumiansky, p. 193.

[114] This is the last performance of biblical drama recorded in city accounts. However, in 1644, a witness reported that he had heard about a Corpus Christi play at Kendall in Lancashire from a man who reported seeing 'a man on a tree and the blood ran down' in his youth. This was probably the performance witnessed to in 1603. Douglas and Greenfield, p. 219.

[115] White, p. 168.

[116] Harbage and Schoenbaum, pp. 42-44.

to those of Leicester in their provincial visits, the two men were also keen rivals within the Council itself. Sussex's players added such variants as histories, tragedies and classical themes to their staple of romances.[117] The professional companies were establishing permanent houses in London by the mid-1570s and the history of English drama was about to take a radical new direction away from community and towards a market driven entertainment industry.

Afterword

During the last decades of Elizabeth's reign battles continued to be fought in the countryside over church ales and other parish customary practices especially in regions remote from centres of authority. Parishes can be seen to be responding to reprimands from visitations but then, as the need for ready cash for repairs became imperative again, parishes such as Wantage, for example, recorded a sudden influx of cash from a church ale.[118] James I became involved in the continuing controversy with the publication of the King's Book of Sports in 1617.[119] At Whitsuntide 1628, in perhaps a consciously antiquarian gesture, the deeply conservative parish of Woodstock in Oxfordshire held a summer festival. The lord of the summer festival turned over £9 3d to the support of the parish while Robin Hood and Little John turned over £7 7s 1d.[120]

In general it can be said that little purely parish biblical drama survived the reign of Edward. In the Thames Valley, at least, there was no attempt to revive that tradition. The biblical drama sponsored by the secular authority or a combination of parish and town was largely gone by 1580. But here again there are locations that do not conform to the pattern. The town of Tewkesbury in Gloucestershire had taken over the old monastic church at dissolution and made it the parish church. This was a deeply conservative community who had been very late to divest themselves of their altars and images.[121] Also, very soon after the surviving churchwarden's book begins in 1563 we find a steady stream, as in many East Anglian churches in this decade, of receipts for play gear rented and repaired. There are also payments

---

[117] *ibid*, pp. 44-49.

[118] Wantage Churchwardens' Accounts 1565-1665 (Berkshire Record Office D/P 143 5/1).

[119] For the controversy caused by the issuance of the *Book* and its re-issuance by Charles in 1633, see Stokes, pp. 484-85, and Douglas and Greenfield, pp. 365-86.

[120] Oxfordshire Archives: MS DD Par. Woodstock c.12, p.17.

[121] 'Reformation and Resistance', pp. 193-95.

for the repair of damage done in the church itself during the performance of plays. From an inventory of costumes taken in 1585, it is clear that the play (or plays) was on a New Testament theme featuring Christ, the apostles and the devil. The last unequivocal evidence of a performance of this play in the church is in 1575, a date that fits well with the general suppression of such drama. However, they are still renting their gear in 1585 and in 1600 the parish undertook the production of three plays that netted them over £12 to repair the crumbling battlements on the tower of the church.

Whether this 1600 production in Tewkesbury was of the parish's New Testament text we will never know. Similarly we cannot know the content of other performances recorded in other parish records – such as the 'godly interlude' played in the parish church in Winslow in Buckinghamshire in 1580 or another play that took place there in 1595.[122] We do know from the evidence given in the archdeacon's court of Oxfordshire in 1584 that the play performed in the Duns Tew parish church was performed by a travelling company since the wardens insisted they 'did not know whose men they weare'.[123] The reference to a play in the church loft of Great Marlow in Buckinghamshire in 1593 was also to a travelling company.[124] From evidence from the interregnum, it seems clear that parishes continued to consider a parish play a potential source of income and that the content did not need to be religious. On 3 February, 1652, a troupe of parish players from Stanton Harcourt in Oxfordshire arrived in the larger town of Witney, anxious to perform the play that they had been rehearsing since Michaelmas.[125] The play was *Mucedorus*,[126] a long-forgotten relic from the 1590s probably bought by a member of the parish a half century before and discovered in a forgotten cupboard. They had already performed at home and in the neighbouring villages of Moore, Stanlake, South Leigh and Cumner. Now they were looking for a much larger audience that would make the whole venture an economic success. They approached the bailiff burgesses for permission to play in the town hall but were refused and so they set up

---

[122] Hertfordshire Record Office: Archdeacon of St Alban's Court Book ASA 7/10, fol. 34v and ASA 7/17.

[123] Oxfordshire Archives: Ms Oxf. Archd. papers Oxon. c.7, fol. 121.

[124] Buckinghamshire Record Office Great Marlowe Churchwardens' Accounts 1593-1674, PR/140/5/1, fol. 4.

[125] John Rowe, *Tragi-Comedia* (Oxford, 1653). This is a Puritan tract that describes the events of the performance in considerable detail.

[126] *Mucedorus* is an anonymous play of the early 1590s. Harbage and Schoenbaum, p. 54.

in the local pub. At seven p.m., at the sound of the drum and the trumpet, the crowd began to gather and the entertainment started with dancing and general conviviality. Finally the play got under way but, before the end, the floor of the pub that, as it turned out, was a badly secured second floor put into an old brew house, collapsed under the weight of the crowd and half the people were shot into the lower room where at least six children were smothered and many others injured. We know about this event because it was used by a Puritan pamphleteer as an example of the just retribution of God:

> The Lord from heaven, having given a check to such wanton sports, teaching men what they must look for, and that he will not bear with such grosse open profanenesse in such an age of light as this is. That he will so farre take notice of the Atheisme, and profanenesse of men in this world, as shall keep the world in order, though he hath reserved the great and full recompense for another day, and place.[127]

As the details of each individual location within the regions of the country begin to emerge as the work of the REED project moves forward, the picture that is growing is a complex and multifaceted one. However, one general trend is clear. The English Reformation, theologically and politically tangled as it was, irrevocably changed the character of English communities. Before Henry VIII's break with Rome, communities of neighbours in parishes, towns and cities marked the passing of the year with traditional ceremonies and pastimes that potentially involved each member of the community, crossing barriers of age and class. Whether it was a church ale in a tiny parish in the Chilterns or the great biblical cycle at York, the mounting of the event demanded co-operative energy from many people for it to be successful. After 1535 such traditional practices came to be associated with the Catholic past and although the moderate Protestants tried, in the early years of Elizabeth's reign, to reform rather than abolish the community events, their efforts found lasting favour with neither the traditionalists nor the increasingly strident puritan preachers. Other factors (such as economic conditions and the threat of attack from abroad) also forced change upon the people of England. But none affected them as profoundly as those we have been tracing since these affected their relationships with God and their neighbours.

---

[127] This is the last paragraph of the section of the pamphlet called 'The Narrative'. The pamphlet is unpaginated.

York Guilds' Mystery Plays 1998: the rebuilding of dramatic community

JANE OAKSHOTT

'This July [1998] the Mystery Plays were reclaimed by the people of York.'

Philip Bowman, September 1998 [1]

ON THE FACE OF it this is an extraordinary statement. Since 1951 the community productions in the grounds of St Mary's Abbey have been famous the world over, linking 'Mystery Plays' inextricably with York in the public consciousness. But in those impressive fixed-stage productions the hundreds of local people were always told what to do by a professional director brought in from outside; and because the primary funding was received from the City Council, the productions were at the mercy of politics and economics. Community drama it was, but the community was a closed one of participants rather than one encompassing the city as a whole.

Processional staging by its nature is more broadly based in the community at large. The street setting makes the performance accessible to a wide audience; and each play in the Cycle demands individual leadership and responsibility. By 1998 this type of performance was no longer an alien concept in York: the quadrennial York Festival had always featured a single pageant on a wagon in the street; in 1988 and 1992 impressive productions of sections of the York Cycle were played at stations along part of the original route, the first to do so for over 400 years;[2] and in 1994 nine plays representing the complete Cycle were produced by local York groups, also for the

---

[1] Master of the Gild of Freemen, concluding the formal part of the 'Post Plays Do' (de-briefing and party), Merchant Adventurers' Hall, 15 September 1998.

[2] Performed by different University groups, under the overall direction of Meg Twycross.

first time since the sixteenth century.[3] These processional productions were immensely successful dramatically. They also set up an expectation for more of the same.

But the continuation of a dramatic event demands a robust infrastructure and the conjunction of many converging elements. The productions of 1988 and 1992 had experimental purpose but no local input; and Mystery Plays '94, performed by local drama groups with the motives of enjoyment and discovery, lacked a solid structural base. These research and social purposes were present in Mystery Plays '98, but in addition there was a third element with the potential to fuse with the other two to form the basis for a long-term future. This was the participation of the York Guilds. Their active involvement in the plays for the first time in 400 years underpinned community enthusiasm with deep-set foundations in the life of the city.

Given this background Philip Bowman's statement, above, falls into perspective: it refers back to the broad-based community nature of Mystery Plays '98; and, more importantly, forward to the possibility of a future tradition of performance based in the everyday concerns of York citizens. Philip Bowman continued:[4]

> The second thing which has emerged this evening [...] is the long-term commitment to the Mystery Plays by the Early Music Foundation. I think I speak for all the Guilds, and indeed anyone who was involved in the July production, when I express our appreciation to you, sir, for that undertaking. On the foundation of that commitment we can build our own.

Like the earlier processional productions Mystery Plays '98 reproduced important characteristics of the original: the wagons, the streets, the close actor/audience relationship, the variety, the sheer entertainment value.[5] The production was the result of several converging motivations. Participants from Mystery Plays '94 were keen to reinforce their experience of wagon staging; and by this stage, in terms of research, the city context was clearly the most fruitful area for future experiment in the processional mode. At the same time the York Guilds were looking for a way to raise their profile in the city. The conjunction of these elements—in particular, the participation of

---

[3] Directed by Jane Oakshott for the Friends of York Festival as an associated event in the York Early Music Festival.

[4] In response to the speech earlier in the evening by Robin Guthrie, Chairman of the York Early Music Foundation, expressing the Foundation's interest in supporting further processional productions.

[5] For the programme of plays, see Table 1.

the Guilds for the first time in over 400 years – made Mystery Plays '98 different from any production that had gone before.

We know from the medieval records that it was the Guilds who were responsible for the production of the mystery plays during their 250-year history, though the performances were set in motion each year by the City Council.[6] The Council provided the physical framework (the streets) and an element of control (regulations on public order, and on standards of performance):

- by ordering that the Plays be done each year (or not, for example in times of plague);
- by deciding which route the plays should take, and on the positions of the playing stations;
- by organising controls on the standards of performance by sending round experienced actors to check on rehearsals;
- by setting the Common Clerk to check each play in performance at Station One. If the previously licensed script was altered too radically1, or the performance deficient in any way, the offending group was fined.

Within this framework of control provided by the city, each Guild was entirely responsible for the production of a single play. Once a Guild had been ordered to perform in any particular year the usual sequence of events seems to have been:

- The Guild Searchers were sent out to collect the 'pageant silver' from Guild members. In many cases this production fund was swelled by fines for transgressions by members throughout the year.
- Actors were alerted, each probably cast in the same role every year, where possible.
- The wagon, set and properties were fetched out of store and refurbished as necessary; occasionally new items were bought.
- Rehearsals were held, with attention given to refreshments, paid for by the Guild.
- On the day of performance, wagon crews were paid for their heavy work, and selected Guild members were required to accompany their wagon on pain of heavy fines for non-attendance.
- After the performance a further meeting, with dinner, was held, for the Guild officials to agree the pageant accounts for that year.

Though performed for only one day each year, it is clear that the mystery plays were an integral part of the Guilds' financial and social life in the medieval city.

---

[6] REED, York *passim.*

YORK GUILDS' MYSTERY PLAYS 1998

Today seven Guilds exist in York, all inspired by a Christian ethic, and having the same basic administrative structure. The full Guild Courts, which meet at most four times a year, have the final say in all matters; these courts are not usually concerned in day to day management but rather in decisions on major financial issues or changes in policy. Management issues are decided in principle by the Courts of Assistants, much smaller courts made up of all current Officers. In all the Guilds this means a Master (Governor in the Company of Merchant Adventurers), a Deputy or Junior Master, a number of Wardens and a Clerk. Several Guilds also have a Beadle or Mace-Bearer, Senior and Junior Searchers, and one, the Cordwainers, still keeps the office of Pageant Master.[7] In addition the Courts of Assistants are attended by a number of Past Masters. The Courts of Assistants, and of course any sub-committees for particular events, meet much more frequently than the full Guild Court but must wait for that Court's decision on important issues.

Certain fixed events occur annually. All the Guilds hold at least two major feasts in the year, to the more formal of which the Master and certain officers of the other Guilds are invited. Many of these feasts have highly evocative names: the Merchant Adventurers' Company celebrates its Goose Feast and the Venison Feast in November; the Butchers' Company holds the Shrove Tuesday Court and Feast; the Cordwainers organize a Martinmas Feast and a Livery Dinner in May.

Many other social events are held: dinners in the Merchant Taylors' Company; lectures and industrial visits in the Guild of Building; in the Gild of Freemen, visits to Freemen of other cities. Charity is a fundamental part of all the Guilds. Each new Master nominates an outside charity for his year in office; and in the Cordwainers' Company, for example, one of the Past Masters acts as almoner, with responsibility for the welfare of Guild members.

The Clerks of the Guilds meet together four times a year to discuss common policy, and items such as the Lord Mayor's Parade, which the Guilds are jointly invited to support. The one event in the year in which the Guilds all take part officially is the United Guilds' Service, held in the Guild Church of All Saints, Pavement.[8] Before the service, members of all the Courts of Assistants process in their robes to the

---

[7] In all the Guilds a new Master is sworn in every year, at which point the other officers move up a rank. In most Guilds the vital post of Clerk may be kept by the same person for many years.

[8] Angelo Raine, Rector of All Saints', Pavement, from 1937 to 1957, did much to encourage the revival of the Guild movement and was instrumental in founding the Gild of Freemen in 1953. Canon Jack Armstrong, rector of the church and Guild Chaplain from 1971-91, is also a strong supporter of the Guilds.

church from the Merchant Adventurers' Hall.[9] Other links between the Guilds are personal and social rather than formal.

Though having many administrative and ceremonial features in common, the individual Guilds are different both in history and in present character, and this goes some way towards explaining the very different ways in which they participated in Mystery Plays '98.[10] The Guilds may be divided into three groups by their history.

Three survive since the Middle Ages:

i) The Company of Merchant Adventurers

This is the oldest, the most influential and, by common consent, the leading Guild. Its origins can be traced back to 1357, when a group of the wealthier shopkeepers formed themselves into a social and religious fraternity which founded an almshouse licensed in 1373. The Guild was incorporated by charter in 1430 as the Guild of Mercers and only changed its name to Company of Merchant Adventurers in 1581, these names reflecting the Guild's changing membership. Entry to the present-day Company is still by birthright or by invitation and, though no longer encompassing a single trade or profession, the Company retains the principles on which it was first founded – enhancement of trade, of the fraternity, and of alms-giving. The majority of the Company's social occasions have a charitable or educational purpose, and in dealing with the Company one has a strong sense of public responsibility in the Company as a body.

The medieval Mercers' play, *Doomsday*, was the most lavish in the Cycle, and provided an awe-inspiring finale to an impressive day.

ii) The Company of Merchant Taylors

The origin of the Company is one of gradual evolution. Tailors are

---

[9] Only the Merchant Adventurers and the Merchant Taylors have retained their ancient Halls. The Butchers' Hall in Gell Garth Yard fell into disrepair and was sold to the Corporation in 1929: the Company's present Hall is in Trinity Lane, Micklegate. Three Guilds – Building, Cordwainers and Freemen – share the refurbished Bedern Hall.

[10] See Table 2. For information I am most grateful to the Clerks of the Guilds: Ivison S. Wheatley MA (retired since August 1998) and James G. Finlay OBE, Company of Merchant Adventurers; Dr J.L. Baily, Company of Merchant Taylors; John Yeomans, Company of Butchers; Roger Taylor, Guild of Scriveners; Roger Lee, Gild of Freemen; and Edward Howland, Guild of Building. Also to Past Masters Mrs P.L. Crossley, Company of Cordwainers; Noel Shouksmith, Guild of Building; and Nigel Wright, Company of Butchers.

recorded among the earliest names in the York Freemens' Register of 1272-3, and the *Ordinances de Taillours* of 1386 list 128 tailors in and around the city.[11] One of the earliest references to the Corpus Christi plays (1336-7) refers to Searchers of the Company;[12] and the first Royal licence was given in 1453. The present Taylors' Hall, built some time between 1380 and 1413, first housed the social and religious Society of St John the Baptist. The Company later amalgamated with the Drapers (in 1551) and the Hosiers (in 1585). Today the number of craft members in the Guild is very small as the York area has few people in the tailoring and allied crafts. Membership, still by birthright or by invitation, is offered predominantly to local people who are felt by the members to be willing to support the continuation of the Guild and of its Guild Hall. The Company is mostly concerned with the maintenance of the Hall, which is used for many local functions, as well as in charitable work.

Ascension was the Taylors' own play but because of their connection with the Hosiers' and Drapers' Guilds since the sixteenth century, the Company could reasonably claim association with the *Pharaoh* and *Death of Mary* plays for the 1998 production.

iii) The Company of Butchers

The York Register of Freemen includes the names of two butchers, Robert Witheskirtes and Nicholas de Nunnewk, as early as the year 1272-3.[13] In addition to the usual work of controlling their trade in York, the Butchers' Guild was responsible for public executions in the city; this provides the connection with the subject of their play, *The Death of Christ*. The Company flourished until the eighteenth century. Membership then began a decline which ended in 1940 when the single surviving member was persuaded to swear in new members, so that the present Guild is able to claim continuity from its medieval roots. All the Guild's members are either Master Butchers or are concerned with allied trades or businesses, which makes it one of the few genuine craft guilds to survive.

Two Guilds have been re-formed:

---

[11] *Register of the Freemen of the City of York*, ed. by Francis Collins, Vol. I, 1272-1558. (London: Surtees Society, 1897).

[12] The A/Y Memorandum Book: REED, York, p. 4.

[13] Surtees Society. See note 11.

JANE OAKSHOTT

i) The Company of Cordwainers

The earliest entry in the York Freemen's Roll for 1272-3 is of one 'Thomas de Fulford, Cordwainer', that is, a worker in fine Cordova leather. References to the 'York Artefice des Cordwainers' appear in the A/Y Memorandum Book in 1395, and by the early fifteenth century the Cordwainers are also referred to as an Occupation, Craft, or Mysterie. References to an incorporated company appear only at the end of the sixteenth century. The Company was dissolved in 1808. In 1977 the Cordwainers' Company was re-formed. Membership is still restricted to those working in, or having an ancestor involved in, the leather and allied trades: shoe makers or repairers, or those in the leather dyeing and associated chemical industries. As in many of the other Guilds the Christian ethic is strong: Court meetings begin and end with prayers, and it is normal for children born to Guild members to be christened in the Guild church, in the presence of the Master. Decisions are made through unanimity rather than vote-taking.

From the first reference in the 1415 list of pageants for Corpus Christi the Company was always associated with the *Agony in the Garden and Betrayal*.[14]

ii) The Guild of Scriveners

The Guild first appears in the 1415 pageant list, where it is named in conjunction with the Illuminers, Pardoners, Questors and Dubbers.[15] Their play, *The Incredulity of Thomas*, survives in the only 'originall' (that is, working copy of a single play) from the York Cycle. The modern Guild was re-formed in 1991. Members are qualified accountants, licensed insolvency practitioners, barristers, patent agents, actuaries or solicitors. Solicitors, accountants and other financial people are well represented. The Guild has become well-known throughout the city for reviving the medieval Sheriff's Assize of Ale, now a popular fundraising event for charity.

Two Guilds are recent creations:

i) The Gild of Freemen

Though in medieval times it was essential to be a freeman before one could become a member of a Guild, the Gild of Freemen was a

---

[14] REED York, p. 20.

[15] *ibid.*, p. 23.

completely new foundation in 1953. It was the idea of a small group of descendents of Freemen who wished to encourage a sense of civic pride and social responsibility to offset the post-war depression. Formerly the city's freemen, among other things, owned the city strays and regulated rights of pasture. The strays were lands exempt from enclosure, set aside for the specific use of the freemen of the four York wards. In addition to its charitable work amongst its members and the York community, the Gild's main concern is still with the strays, in particular their continued use by the public. Membership of the Gild is granted on application to any freeman of the City of York, an honour held by birthright. There are some thousands of freemen of the city worldwide and the Gild has just over 500 members from across the social and occupational spectrum.

Because all the medieval Guilds were made up of freemen the Gild had, appropriately, a completely free choice of play for the 1998 production. The *Temptation of Christ* was chosen on the grounds of excellence and suitability to the Gild; but as an episode from Christ's Ministry, the play also fitted well into the programme shaped by the 'fixed' Guild plays.

ii)   The Guild of Building

In the Middle Ages there were many different Guilds each representing small sections of the building trade. In the pageant lists we find different plays assigned to the Plasterers, the Tilers, the Masons, the Tilemakers, the Pinners and the Carpenters. These Guilds could cover a variety of trades within the blanket title for example, the Carpenters included all workers in wood—the carpenters, carvers, joiners and sawyers. The modern Guild was founded in 1954 to provide a meeting point for all the many different branches of the construction industry. It includes the design professions of architect and surveyor as well as the original construction trades and building managers. The programme of lectures and industrial visits regularly brings members together for ceremonials and socializing based on common professional interests.

Through the links with all branches of the building trade, the Guild had a very free choice in their play for Mystery Plays '98. *Creation to the Fifth Day* was chosen because it offered the scope for construction skills as much as dramatic ones. The play also gave a Guild presence right at the beginning of the performance, balancing the Merchant Adventurers' *Doomsday* at the end.

The modern Guilds had clearly defined reasons for deciding to become involved in a production of the Mystery Plays: the identification with Guild traditions; a concern for education and heritage; a wish for the Guild to contribute to the life of the city; fun; and the opportunity to raise the Guilds' profile in York and beyond.

It was concern for their heritage that led all the Guilds to perform or sponsor their own play wherever possible. Roger Lee, Clerk to the Gild of Freemen, commented after the production:[16]

> The specific links of the Plays to the Guilds were very important; a general arts project or similar would not have been supported.

The plays owned or chosen by the Guilds gave Mystery Plays '98 the framework of a representative, albeit abbreviated, Cycle. The participation of local drama groups enabled us to make a more complete picture.[17]

Joint Guild participation in Mystery Plays '98 took just over two years to establish. The Guilds are safeguarded against hasty decisions by the double court system, but even so two years is proportionately a rather longer time than is usual with standard productions. This was partly because the decision to back the proposal had to be taken by each of the seven Guilds, separately and together; but there were two further reasons for careful deliberation. One was that the Guilds had to be sure that the proposed experimental and public production would enhance their historic status rather than otherwise. The other was the understanding that Guild commitment should be considered as a long-term affair. The *Discussion Paper for the Guilds of York* formally proposing the production ends:[18]

> The Guilds are the natural guardians of the Plays: it would be well for them to consolidate that position at the beginning of York's emergence as an international centre of performing excellence.

---

[16] In answer to the questionnaire which I sent to all the Guilds in February 1999. (See also Table 2). The object was to relate information on the modern Guilds to that surviving in the medieval records; and to gain feedback on the modern Guilds' reactions to their participation in Mystery Plays '98.

[17] See Table 1.

[18] For *Discussion Paper:* see below, note 21. The 'excellence' referred to is that of the York Early Music Foundation which at that time was in the process of setting up a centre for the study, performance and recording of early music. The centre is situated in the deconsecrated St Margaret's Church, Walmgate, and is due to open at Easter, 2000.

After the production the Guild of Building echoed this long-term thinking as one of their reasons for taking part:[19]

> A desire to be actively involved in the rebirth of the Guilds' involvement in the Plays.

Because of the court system, the decision-making process proceeded at roughly six-monthly intervals. It started indirectly with the informal suggestion in Autumn 1994 that the Guilds should once more take the leading role in their own plays.[20] Further to that suggestion I was invited to attend the next quarterly meeting of Guild Clerks, for preliminary discussion; and after that, in Autumn 1995, to submit a proposal and budget for consideration by the Guild Courts.[21] The Guilds' decision to go ahead with the project was made in April 1996.

The next stage, setting up an administrative structure, was nearly the end of the project. The immediate problem of 'Whose logo on the notepaper?' merely crystallised the fact that there was no central, officially constituted organizing body. The modern Guilds, like their medieval counterparts, have no corporate legal entity: so although a Steering Committee of Guild representatives had been set up, it had no legal authority.[22] This meant that the project, as it stood, was unable to receive funding.[23]

The legal *impasse* was resolved in September 1996 when the York Early Music Festival offered to act as legal 'umbrella' for the plays, providing a collection point for money, and a base for insurance

---

[19] Noel Shouksmith (Immediate Past Master) and Edward Howland (Clerk). Questionnaire; see note 16, above.

[20] This was in conversation with Ivison Wheatley, then Clerk to the Merchant Adventurers; he had contacted me on behalf of the Company to offer help with rehearsal or performance space should a wagon performance, similar to Mystery Plays '94, be arranged again.

[21] Jane Oakshott, *Discussion Paper for the Guilds of York,* September 1995.

[22] Chaired by John Yeomans, Clerk to the Butchers' Company, whose positive support moved the project forward at this difficult stage.

[23] In the Middle Ages this problem of corporate legal identity did not of course arise. The overall governing body was quite simply the Council on whose orders the plays were produced, and who controlled the land on which they were performed. Furthermore, neither central responsibility nor funding was in question since each Guild simply provided for its own play. In 1998, however, the Guilds had no tradition of performance and therefore no stock of costumes or sets. Instead even basic necessities such as wagons were supplied through a central administrative team; hence the need for central funding and a legally constituted body to receive and administer it.

cover, council indemnity and other technicalities. Since the Festival was set up to encourage authentic performance of early music, the link was practical though strictly speaking against the Festival's music-based constitution. As well as solving the immediate problem, this collaboration very helpfully brought the production under the wing of the Festival's stage management and box-office systems.

The Guilds had already agreed to contribute a pump-priming sum. Delma Tomlin, the Early Music Festival's Administrative Director, suggested that the Festival match a rather larger contribution from the Guilds.[24] This larger sum was set for all at the level which the least wealthy Guild could manage. It was only after Christmas 1996 that the last of the seven Guilds decided to agree to those terms; and our formal press launch was held in Merchant Adventurers' Hall three weeks later, in January 1997.

Although total Guild responsibility for each play, as in the Middle Ages, would have been a historian's dream, it was not remotely a practical proposition for a production in 1998. We therefore set up Central Production, a team of professionals which acted on two levels.[25] On one level, Central Production took the place of the medieval City Council in providing the overall framework of performance: for example, the route and public safety, in collaboration with the police and the City Centre Authority.[26] On the smaller scale, the central production team replaced the tradition of performance common to the medieval Guilds, by providing intellectual help (information, interpretation, style) and materials (wagons, sets, props) as needed. Central Production was also responsible for finance, sharing the central fund among the performing groups as appropriate; for example on the grounds of cast numbers and complication of set.

Given this practical and stylistic support the Guilds were able to choose from a wide range of ways in which to participate, which fall into two main categories:

1) complete delegation of the play to a drama group; or

---

[24] I am not at liberty to give any specific detail of the financial arrangements.

[25] Jane Oakshott (Director), Richard Rastall (Musical Director), Pauline Chambers (Costume Supervisor), Griff Rowlands (Set Supervisor), Jude Brereton (Administrator from December 1997). We were also most grateful to Chris Jowett, Technical Director of Leeds University Workshop Theatre, for his advice and practical help.

[26] All negotiations with outside bodies were conducted in conjunction with the York Early Music Festival whose help and support were invaluable.

2) taking direct responsibility for the production of their play but co-opting outside help, in addition to that from Central Production, as needed. Most of the Guilds contributed in some extra way which mirrors the medieval practice – by putting in expertise, goods, services or money. Some had a strong influence on the production as a whole; others imparted a distinctive character to their own play without otherwise affecting the overall production.

The three Guilds surviving since the Middle Ages all took the first approach. The Merchant Adventurers immediately delegated their play *Doomsday* to Settlement Players, a drama group having a high reputation in York for over eighty years and known to the Guild through a family connection. No Guild members took an active part, though two Guild representatives were elected to act as liaison where needed. Through them the Company gave generous extra finance to *Doomsday*, and a great deal of help in kind to the mystery plays' production as a whole. For example, the Company arranged for the provision of an excellent professional director for *Doomsday*;[27] and when needed, workshop space was found for that play's set constructor. The use of Merchant Adventurers' Hall was generously offered on many occasions both business and social – for example, for the press launch, the fundraising revel, and the 'Post Plays Do'. The Guild's leadership and sense of responsibility was apparent throughout, to the great benefit of the production as a whole.

The Companies of Merchant Taylors and of Butchers also chose to delegate, though in different ways. Again because of family connections, the Merchant Taylors' Company invited the University of York postgraduate drama group, The Lords of Misrule, to act for them, with a representative of the Guild to act as liaison between the two. The Guild had associations with three plays: its own *Ascension* play; *Pharaoh;* and *The Death of Mary*.[28] Eventually the strongest historic connection was the deciding factor, even though *Ascension* is not superficially as exciting as, for example, the *Pharaoh* play. However, there was excitement enough as it was the only play to be performed in Middle English, and the only one with a practicable Heaven.[29] The Guild was not actively involved in the production, but one of its members was one of our most generous individual sponsors.

---

[27] Richard Digby Day, a former Director of York Theatre Royal and until 1998, Director of the National Theater Institute, Connecticut.

[28] See above.

[29] Due to the informed collaboration of David Crouch (Director) and Phillip Harris (set design and construction).

Although the Butchers' Company decided to delegate their play *The Death of Christ* to a drama group, they nevertheless hoped to involve some of their York members in the production. However, the most suitable group to perform this play was Howdenshire Live Arts, based some thirty miles out of York;[30] any attempt at involving Guild members was therefore reluctantly, but realistically, considered to be impractical. On the other hand, the Guild representative for the plays retained contact throughout the production from 200 miles away. On the day of performance the wagon crew was composed of members of the Guild; and the Guild formally showed its pride in its play as the Master and chief members of the Court of Assistants, all in livery, led their pageant wagon along the whole procession route. This gesture of support added a ceremonial dimension to *The Death of Christ*.

All four of the revived and new-created Guilds preferred to take direct responsibility for their own play. The Cordwainers' Company has always been associated with *The Agony and Betrayal of Christ*, but the modern Guild had not the numbers nor the experience to produce it alone. (The play is a difficult one and has a cast of sixteen men). They solved the dilemma by inviting the Director of the York Academy of Drama to direct the *Agony*.[31] They were also obliged to look outside the Guild for all but four of the actors.

The Cordwainers' Mystery Plays on Wagons Sub-Committee was set up immediately after the mystery plays' launch in spring 1997, and quickly organised two fundraising events in St Crux Church, in the following May and September. (The catering for these events was run by the Company's Pageant-Master). The money was used, not directly for their own production, but to cover the agreed pump-priming sum to be paid into the central Mystery Plays fund.

The Company's influence and involvement went beyond their play. For example, two of the *Betrayal* guards volunteered (on request) to escort the Lord Mayor at the Proclamation of the Banns; the interest of the Guild led to our running a very popular Shoe Making Workshop for which the leather was generously donated from one of the Company's members;[32] and the Master of the Cordwainers, Kit Bird, kindly agreed to speak at the Leeds International Medieval Congress the following week on his experience of playing Christ in his Guild's Play.[33]

---

[30] A large group with an imaginative director, Mike Carter.

[31] Kathleen Foster, who is a Cordwainer.

[32] The workshop was held in collaboration with the Yorkshire Museum of Farming at Murton Park.

[33] See also below, note 41.

YORK GUILDS' MYSTERY PLAYS 1998

It was interesting to discover that some of the Cordwainers' leather was exchanged for wood from the Guild of Building, who wanted to make authentic leather hinges. The Builders' wood went to support the skyline in the Cordwainers' Garden of Gethsemane. Though the exchange was made through Central Production, probably without either Guild being aware of it, it is a pleasing example of the sort of transaction that undoubtedly took place in the medieval productions, without going through any account books.

The Gild of Freemen, formed in 1953, had, appropriately, the widest choice of play, since they could claim connection with any of the medieval plays. The court's first decision was to choose an inspired director.[34] Ossie Heppell had very definite ideas on the type of play he was willing to direct; but he was prepared to make his choice to fit in with those plays which were fixed to a Guild by historical association. After careful deliberation he chose *The Temptation of Christ* because, apart from its outstanding dramatic quality, it represents the ultimate freedom – that of the spirit.

Working well in advance under very difficult conditions Ossie designed and constructed a towering set – Satan's final fall to ground level was from fifteen feet up. The Gild made this impressive construction possible by adding generously to the money from Central Production funds. The last stages of construction and decoration were done by other Gild members; and a co-director was also chosen from the Gild.[35] On the day, the wagon crew were all Gild members, though the cast of four was chosen from outside the Gild in open auditions. Out of 500 Gild members (some 250 in the Greater York area) only fourteen were eventually involved in the production, but the fact that leadership, artistic drive and financial support came from within meant that the Gild certainly did take responsibility for its own production.

Only one Guild, the Scriveners, was willing or able to produce and cast its play entirely from within its own ranks, starting with the choice of a strong director.[36] Philip Bowman kept close control of the design of both set and costumes. Because very few of the large stock of borrowed costumes fitted Philip's design for the play, the costumes for Christ and the angels were made specially, at the Guild's expense.[37] The Scriveners' play, *The Incredulity of Thomas*, is

---

[34] Ossie Heppell, founder of York Art Centre.

[35] David Wilde, local councillor and internationally known puppeteer,

[36] Philip Bowman, from a long-established York family. See also footnote 1.

[37] Costumes were on loan from the University of Hull Drama Department; from the Chester Cycle Wardrobe, designed by Meg Twycross and now owned by the

deceptively simple and has considerable emotional power. It also poses a very interesting dramatic problem when Christ makes three appearances and disappearances in quick succession. The Scriveners' set created the effect by a device which could well have been used by the Guild in medieval times. Christ stood behind a black gauze cut into a door at the back of the set, becoming visible only when lit from above by the opening of a small trapdoor above him. When the trap shut, Christ disappeared again. The wooden trap was silvered on the underneath to cast maximum but cold light downwards. It was worked from ground level by a simple lever.

The Scriveners went into the mystery plays project because 'they are indeed the Guilds' Plays, and the Guild wished to support a Guilds' performance.'[38] After the performance they found that the benefits had been greater than that, in terms of 'building team spirit within the Guild and a camaraderie amongst those who were involved'.[39]

The Guild of Building played a striking part in the production, not least through sponsoring a lecture on Medieval Technology.[40] The raising of technology's profile had an effect throughout the production, for example, in the Scriveners' device just described and in the magnificent opening hell-mouth designed for the *Harrowing of Hell*.[41] The Guild also contributed space for an open workshop on banner-making; and took part in the first Delivery of the Billetts since the sixteenth century.[42]

This Guild started the production process very quickly, setting up meetings as early as spring 1997 with me and all the relevant departments – Construction, Drama, Art and Design – of the York College with which the Guild has a close relationship through apprenticeship schemes and student awards.[43] The meetings were to understand the play; to assimilate information on authentic staging; and to work out how best to proceed.

The play *Creation* was chosen because of the opportunity it offered for the use of medieval machinery as part of the set. The play was

---

University of Leeds Workshop Theatre; and from the York Mystery Plays Wardrobe administered by the Friends of York Festival.

[38] Roger Taylor (Clerk). Questionnaire; see above, note 16.

[39] *ibid*.

[40] Delivered on 21 October 1997 in the Guild's headquarters, Bedern Hall, York, by Dr Alex Keller of Leicester University.

[41] Designer: Mark Comer, St Luke's Church.

[42] The record of the Delivery of the Billetts is translated in REED, York, p. 703.

[43] Formerly York College of Further and Higher Education.

therefore at once central to, and an extension of, the working concerns and regular activities of the Guild: and they seemed to come very close to the experience of a medieval craft Guild whose social and pro-fessional life coincided in their play. Regular set-building sessions increased the sense of unity and pride in their craft. The first of the benefits noted by this Guild in the Questionnaire is 'the feeling of camaraderie within the team involved'.[44]

With seven machinery operators and only one actor, they retained the emphasis on the set rather than on the acting commitment. The set, complete with speaking tubes, was worked by simple machinery which would have been available in the Middle Ages: levers, turning screws, pulleys. Reclaimed timber from demolition sites was used for the more solid and less visible parts of the framework. Thanks to the College, the Guild had the advantage of adequate workshop space, and a safe storage facility, appropriately in the Antique Restoration Department. The idea of period style was taken very seriously, but as time went on this concern modified, and became less important as group dynamics took over. So, for example, the image of God which dominated the set until the live God made his appearance, had a very modern face, in Tolkien cartoon style. The Guild took great and justifiable pride in their moving set, and also as builders enjoyed the fact that 'we came in on time and under budget'.[45]

The Guilds were the essential part of York Mystery Plays '98, but they were not alone. Both by necessity and by design many areas of the community were involved in the production. The local Drama Groups were essential.[46] Six of those from Mystery Plays '94 were still in existence – all of them keen to take part – plus a newcomer, Wheldrake Village. Three of the groups were asked to perform for an existing Guild, while the other four chose from plays to match their resources and fill in essential parts of the story round the fixed Guild plays.

Central organizations, whose cooperation was vital, were actively helpful and positive about the importance of this first Guilds' production. North Yorkshire Police and the City Centre Authority dealt with the route, traffic and public safety. Commercial organisations provided help in kind – for example, the Yorkshire

---

[44] Questionnaire; see above, notes 16 and 19.

[45] Noel Shouksmith, Immediate Past Master of the Guild of Building, and Head of the Department of Construction at York College, while chairing *Medieval Technology from a Different Angle,* Session 1317, Leeds International Medieval Congress, 15 July 1998.

[46] I regret that limited space prevents discussion here of the contribution from the drama groups, which was invaluable.

Farming Museum provided properties and soldiers for the Delivery of the Billetts, and a Midland Bank messenger flagged a signal to the Minster change ringers at the end of the performance. York Minster held a Service of Blessing on the plays: a formal civic event, attended by the Lord Mayor and beginning with a procession of liveried Guild representatives and the Guild banners. Smaller local groups were also involved wherever possible. For example, when we needed extra large tights for the wagon crews, rather than simply buy them, we sent out a local media appeal for knitters: several individuals and a group from the New Earswick Machine Knitting Club made over 90 pairs between them.

A sense of community was deliberately fostered through the publicity campaign. The main vehicles for local publicity were practical workshops, and the re-enactment of medieval ceremonies, intended to bring the participants closer together. They were, however, deliberately not exclusive. The teaching workshops, for example, were publicized as Mystery Play events that were open to all. Most of these, such as shoemaking, hat-making, or banner-painting, sprang directly from professional interest among the Guilds and were sponsored by them. Each brought new people into the production, often people who had never thought of becoming involved in theatre before.

In all the publicity our main target was a core audience who would give a ballast of understanding to the floating crowds always present in the York streets. We therefore aimed at: international theatre/history specialists; Early Music Festival audiences; and local Guild/drama group members and supporters. Such people would all be reasonably sure to turn out whatever the weather, and should appreciate what they were watching. This is exactly what happened, and it is clear that the publicity strategy was partly responsible for the feeling of 'playing to a large number of friends and relatives at each station'.[47]

Above all it was the Guild involvement that made Mystery Plays '98 into a more deeply-rooted community event than plays performed simply for entertainment. Members of drama groups meet to perform plays: plays are what they do. Guilds meet for other reasons, of which a play is an extra. With members from the commercial, financial and legal areas of the city, the Guilds have a rich infrastructure of social and professional life to which the play is an extension. In the business

---

[47] Kit Bird, Master of the Company of Cordwainers, about his experience of playing Christ in the Guild's Play *The Agony and Betrayal*, in *The York Guilds' Mystery Plays: Then and Now,* Session 1417, Leeds International Medieval Congress, 16 July 1998.

life of York, Guild members are continually meeting, and the Guild plays thus again become a common topic of conversation in board room and canteen. In 1998, reunited with the Guilds' infrastructure, the plays came truly back to their roots – social, professional, historic and spiritual.

Will the Guilds take part again? The support is certainly there for the beginning of a new tradition inspired by Guild involvement. Discussions are in the offing for a performance in 2002, but as ever finance will be a big consideration. It is clear, however, that the Guilds felt they had benefited greatly from Mystery Plays '98, in three main areas: camaraderie, sense of achievement, and raising of public profile. A sense of civic pride and duty started the modern Guilds' involvement, but, if anything, it is the positive nature of the experience that will keep them repeating it:

> It is easy to forget that the Company has existed with unbroken history as a Craft Guild since medieval times. To participate in a production which the Company did annually for hundreds of years really brings home the historic significance of the Company and the imperative of maintaining these activities for future generations to enjoy. To be able to participate in the live production within the City streets was a quite extraordinary personal experience. Everybody involved wants to do it again.[48]

John Yeomans, February 1999.

---

[48] Questionnaire; see above, note 16. The statement was made on behalf of the Butchers' Company.

JANE OAKSHOTT

Table 1

Running order

York Mystery Plays

12 July 1998

1	Creation to Day 5	Guild of Building + York College
2	Creation of Adam and Eve	Parish of Wheldrake
3	Fall of Adam and Eve	Poppleton Players
4	The Flight into Egypt	Foxwood Players
5	The Temptation of Christ	Gild of Freemen
6	Agony in Garden	Company of Cordwainers + Academy of Performing Arts
7	Death of Christ	Howdenshire Live Arts for Company of Butchers
8	Harrowing of Hell	St Luke's Church
9	The Incredulity of Thomas	Guild of Scriveners
10	Ascension	Lords of Misrule for Company of Merchant Taylors
11	Judgement	Settlement Players for Company of Merchant Adventurers

YORK GUILDS' MYSTERY PLAYS 1998

Table 2

		Mt. Adventurers	Mt. Taylors	Butchers	Cordwainers	Scriveners	Freemen	Building
1	No. of members in 1998	150	89	c. 65	52	c. 56	500	160
2	Criteria for membership	By invitation or patrimony	By invitation, to craft and suitable others	Master Butchers or allied trades	Business or ancestral connection with leather trade	Legal and financial professions	By birthright. Wide social and occupational mix.	Construction industry and allied professions and trades
3	No. of members in York City and 50 mile radius	The majority, but fewer each year	50% city, 50% 30 mile radius	50/50	46 within 50 mile radius	99%	c. 50%	100%
4	Numbers attending Guild events	Depends on event: average over 50%	Formal dinners attended at capacity of Hall (135)	75%	30%	c. 30%	Varies. Can be quite small	20-25%
5	Numbers actively involved in Mystery Plays	Two members acted as liaison with Settlement Players	One member acted as liaison with Lords of Misrule	One member as liaison with HLA. 10-15 on the day	8 in production team and cast, +8 on day	c. 24 (no outsiders involved)	14	30-35

Contributors

Philip Butterworth

Philip Butterworth is Deputy Head of the Faculty of Arts with responsibility for research at Bretton Hall, University of Leeds. His most recent publication is *Theatre of Fire*, published by the Society for Theatre Research, London, 1998. His current research preoccupations are with stage-directions, special effects and staging conventions.

Robert L.A. Clark

Robert L.A. Clark is Associate Professor of French at Kansas State University. In addition to his work on the *Miracles de Nostre Dame par personnages*, he has published articles on the *Jeu d'Adam*, *Yde et Olive*, and medieval confraternities, as well as two collaborative articles with Claire Sponsler on cross-dressing in medieval and early modern drama. His translation of the *Chanson de Sainte Foy* appeared in Pamela Sheingorn's *Book of Sainte Foy's Miracles*. Current editorial projects include the collected papers of C. Clifford Flanigan, a volume of essays (co-edited with Kathleen Ashley) on issues of medieval conduct, and a critical edition of the *Mistere de la sainte Hostie*. He is also working on a book on ideology and gender in medieval theatre.

Alan J. Fletcher

A graduate of the Universities of Leeds and Oxford, Alan J. Fletcher is a lecturer in English at University College, Dublin. Apart from various articles on medieval English literature and drama, he has currently been working on early performance in Ireland. The results of this research were published in 1998 by Toronto University Press under the title of *Drama, Performance and Polity in Pre-Cromwellian Ireland*. He has also recently published with Four Courts Press, Dublin, a book entitled *Preaching Politics and Poetry in Late Medieval England*.

Alan Hindley

Formerly Head of the Department of French at the University of Hull, Alan Hindley has published editions of medieval French texts, co-authored a book on the Old French Epic, and has just completed an *Old French-English Dictionary* with Frederick Langley and Brian Levy. His interest in the performance of medieval French plays has led to video-productions of *La Farce du Cuvier* and *Maistre Pierre Pathelin* in the *Hull French Tapes* Series. Recent publications in medieval drama have been on the old French morality plays, on which he is currently writing a monograph.

Chris Humphrey

Chris Humphrey is currently a British Academy Research Fellow in the Centre for Medieval Studies at the University of York. He completed his doctoral thesis on 'The Dynamics of Urban Festal Culture in Later Medieval England' at the University of York in 1997, and his current project is an exploration of time and temporality in the medieval English town, 1300-1550.

Wim Hüsken

Wim Hüsken is lecturer in Dutch at the University of Auckland, New Zealand. He has published extensively on various aspects of historical Low Countries literature and is editor of 'Ludus', a series in late medieval and early Renaissance drama. He has recently completed an eight-volume edition of the play-collection of the Haarlem Chamber of Rhetoric, 'Trou Moet Blycken'.

Alexandra F. Johnston

Department of English, Victoria College, University of Toronto; Principal, Victoria College 1981-91. President of *SITM* and Medieval and Renaissance Drama; Director of *REED* and chair of the board of the 'Poculi Ludique Societas' since the mid-1970s. Major publications include *York*, with Margaret Rogerson, the first collection in the *REED* Series, 1979. Most recent publications include *English Parish Drama*, Rodopi, 1996, and *Civic Ritual and Drama*, Rodopi, 1997, both collections of essays. Most recent production by PLS – ALL of the York cycle in one day: 20th June, 1998.

Pamela M. King

Pamela King is Head of the English Department at the University College of St Martin in Lancaster where she holds a Personal Chair in English. Before coming to Lancaster, she taught at Westfield College in the University of London for a number of years and helped to found the Centre for Medieval Studies there. She has published on medieval English theatre, literature and the arts, as well as on contemporary Spanish religious theatre. She is currently co-director of York Domesday Project, which is engaged in assembling a multi-media archive of primary sources relating to the York Cycle and publishing related materials in digital form.

Alan E. Knight

Alan E. Knight is Professor Emeritus of French at the Pennsylvania State University. He is the author of *Aspects of Genre in Late Medieval French Drama* and the editor of *The Stage as Mirror: Civic Theatre in Late Medieval Europe*. He has also written numerous articles on the history and social function of theatre in medieval and early modern France. He is currently editing a collection of fifteenth-century mystery plays from the city of Lille.

Frederick W. Langley

Frederick Langley is a lecturer in the French Department at the University of Hull. His research interests are predominantly in the areas of medieval French drama, courtly literature, and literary and linguistic computing. He is has just completed an *Old French-English Dictionary* with Alan Hindley and Brian Levy.

Lynette Muir

Formerly Reader in French and Director of the Centre for Medieval Studies in the University of Leeds. Since taking early retirement, she has worked on the association between medieval literature and society (*Literature and Society in Medieval France*, 1986) and European religious drama in the Middle Ages, especially the treatment of the biblical stories (*The Biblical Drama of Medieval Europe*, 1995).

Jane Oakshott

A practical theatre historian, specializing in large-scale community theatre, Jane Oakshott has been responsible for a series of Mystery Play 'firsts': Leeds '75, the first processional production since the sixteenth century; Wakefield '80, the first city-centre processional production; Chester '83; York '94; and York '98, the first Guilds' production since 1568. Former Head of Drama at the University of Otago, New Zealand, Jane has also lectured in Universities in America, Canada and Great Britain and has published articles on the staging of medieval plays. She now lives in Leeds and runs *Presentation Plus, Communication Consultants.*

Graham A. Runnalls

Graham Runnalls holds a Personal Chair in French Medieval Drama at the University of Edingurgh, where he has taught since 1966. He has published widely on the medieval French theatre, and is the author of twelve critical editions of miracle and mystery plays. His book, *Etudes sur les Mystères* (Paris: Champion, 1998), is a retrospective collection of twenty-two articles on the late medieval French religious theatre. He is a founder-member and former president of the *Société internationale pour l'étude du théâtre médiéval,* and is a member of the editorial committee of *Le Moyen Age* and *Théâtre Opéra Ballet.* His latest book, *Les Mystères français imprimés*, has just been published by Champion.

Konrad Schoell

Konrad Schoell has been Professor of Romance Literatures at the University of Erfurt since 1992. His main research interests are in the field of drama and theatre studies from the Middle Ages to the present day, in the short story and fantastic tales, in meta-theatre and meta-novel, and in the relationship between the evolution of society and that of literary genres. His publications include: *Das Theater Samuel Becketts* (1967), *Das französische Drama seit dem Zweiten Weltkrieg* (1970), *Das komische Theater des französischen Mittelalters* (1975), *Die französische Komödie* (1983), *La Farce du quinzième siècle* (1992).

Elsa Strietman

Elsa Strietman is the University Lecturer in Dutch and a Fellow and Tutor of New Hall, Cambridge. She is responsible for the Dutch Section of the Department of Other Languages in the Faculty of Modern and Medieval Languages at the University of Cambridge. Her research is now focused on fifteenth- and sixteenth-century drama in the Low Countries, in particular that produced by the Chambers of Rhetoric. Most of her work in this respect studies the historical, political, social and religious aspects of the plays and the importance of the Chambers within their communities.

John Tailby

John Tailby has just taken early retirement from his post as Senior Lecturer in the Department of German at the University of Leeds. His publications have dealt with both late medieval religious drama, especially the staging of the Lucerne Passion play, and secular drama, notably Shrovetide Plays, *Fastnachtspiele*, in the transition from late medieval to early modern forms and ideas. His publications in English include *The Staging of Religious Drama in Europe in the Later Middle Ages: Texts and Documents in English Translation*, with Peter Meredith (Kalamazoo: Michigan, 1983; reprint 1990).